Lecture Notes in Computer Science 7799

Commenced Publication in 1973
Founding and Former Series Editors:
Gerhard Goos, Juris Hartmanis, and Jan van Leeuwen

T0172201

Matthew Roughan   Rocky Chang (Eds.)

Passive and Active Measurement

14th International Conference, PAM 2013
Hong Kong, China, March 18-19, 2013
Proceedings

 Springer

Volume Editors

Matthew Roughan
University of Adelaide
School of Mathematical Sciences
Innova21 Building, Adelaide, SA 5005, Australia
E-mail: matthew.roughan@adelaide.edu.au

Rocky Chang
The Hong Kong Polytechnic University
Department of Computing
Hunghom, Kowloon, Hong Kong SAR, China
E-mail: csrchang@comp.polyu.edu.hk

ISSN 0302-9743   e-ISSN 1611-3349
ISBN 978-3-642-36515-7   e-ISBN 978-3-642-36516-4
DOI 10.1007/978-3-642-36516-4
Springer Heidelberg Dordrecht London New York

Library of Congress Control Number: 2013931228

CR Subject Classification (1998): C.4, C.2.0-6, C.5.3, D.4.6, D.4.8, K.6.5

LNCS Sublibrary: SL 5 – Computer Communication Networks
and Telecommunications

Typesetting: Camera-ready by author, data conversion by Scientific Publishing Services, Chennai, India

Printed on acid-free paper

Springer is part of Springer Science+Business Media (www.springer.com)

Preface

Welcome to the Proceedings of the 2013 Passive and Active Measurement (PAM) Conference. The event, which was held in Hong Kong this year, focusses on research in and the practice of Internet measurements. This was the 14th PAM, and the first to be held in China. Following its genesis in 2000, the conference has maintained a strong workshop feel, providing an opportunity for the presentation of innovative and early work, with lively discussion and active participation from attendees.

In 2012 the conference broadened its scope, reflecting the widening uses of network measurement and analysis methods. The aim was to facilitate the under-standing of the expanding role that measurement techniques play as they become building blocks for a variety of networking environments, application profiling, and for cross-layer analysis. In 2013 we continued with this wider scope, although we did not neglect PAM's core topics.

PAM 2013 attracted 74 submissions. The papers came from academia and industry from around the world. It was especially pleasing to see the strength of the submissions from the Asia-Pacific region, adding to the historic strength from Europe and the Americas.

The Technical Program Committee was chosen from a group of experts in Internet measurement, drawing on past contributors to PAM including distin-guished academic and industrial researchers, but also with a group of first-time members. Additionally, we aimed to have a strong global representation on the committee, and achieved this with eight members from Europe, the USA and the Asia-Pacific region, and two from Latin America.

The final program of 24 papers was selected after each submission was care-fully reviewed by at least three members of the Program Committee (PC), at least one of whom rated themselves as "knowledgeable" with regard to the con-tent of the paper. We were delighted with the quality of reviews – they were careful, insightful, and paid attention to detail. The reviews were followed by an extensive discussion phase. PAM has traditionally avoided a large PC meeting and the difficulties it creates for a global PC and instead uses on-line discus-sions. This year, these were impressively robust: reviewers provided more than 300 comments on papers, some almost as detailed as the reviews themselves. All of the final papers were then shepherded by PC members.

This year's conference also included new selection criteria related to repro-ducible research. It is our belief that one of the most pressing issues in the field of Internet measurement research is the fact that many papers report on datasets that are never disclosed, and in the interest of promoting publication of data the submission instructions contained the following:

> We hold the view that an inherent principle of scientific research is the ability to replicate and build upon existing published works. This

requires data and tools used in publications to be public, but as that is sometimes in conflict with the requirement to preserve privacy, PAM will adopt the following policy to encourage reproducible research:

1. Authors must state in the paper (both for review, and in the final version) whether data and/or tools will be available to other researchers, and under what conditions they will be available: e.g., general public access, access under license, or only via NDA. Authors should also describe the steps used to ensure that the data will remain available, say after graduate students finish, or the current project ends.

2. If data or tools won't be made available, authors are required to explicitly justify this decision. Papers based on datasets and/or tools that are made available to the research community will be given higher priority.

Ethics and reproducibility compliance was then rated as part of the review process. We are very interested to get feedback on these reproducibility criteria.

In addition, the PC selected nine papers to appear as posters at the conference, and these are included in this volume as extended abstracts.

The final program included papers on a wide range of measurement topics, and included authors from 16 countries and five continents. Our most sincere thanks go to the PC members for their diligence and care in reviewing, discussing, and shepherding the papers that appear here, and to Weichao Li and Waiting Fok for organizing and maintaining the HotCRP site for us.

We are also most grateful to the Steering Committee, and to The Hong Kong Polytechnic University for providing the meeting venue and WIFI access.

We hope that you enjoy the papers in these proceedings.

March 2013

Matthew Roughan
Rocky K.C. Chang

Organization

Organizing Committee

Conference Chair

Rocky K. C. Chang   The Hong Kong Polytechnic University,
Hong Kong SAR, China

Program Chair

Matthew Roughan   The University of Adelaide, Australia

Local Arrangement Chair

Waiting Fok   The Hong Kong Polytechnic University,
Hong Kong SAR, China

Webmaster

Weichao Li   The Hong Kong Polytechnic University,
Hong Kong SAR, China

Steering Committee

Nevil Brownlee	The University of Auckland, New Zealand
Ian Graham	Endace
Arvind Krishnamurthy	University of Washington, US
Bernhard Plattner	ETH Zurich, Switzerland
Fabio Ricciato	University of Salento/FTW, Italy
George Riley	Georgia Institute of Technology, US
Neil Spring	University of Maryland, US
Nina Taft	Technicolor Palo Alto Research Center, US

Program Committee

Bernhard Ager	ETH Zurich, Switzerland
Mark Allman	International Computer Science Institute (ICSI), US
Chadi Barakat	INRIA, France
Nevil Brownlee	The University of Auckland, New Zealand
Edmond W.W. Chan	Huawei Noah's Ark Lab, Hong Kong SAR, China
Kenjiro Cho	IIJ Research Laboratory, Japan
Italo Cunha	Universidade Federal de Minas Gerais (UFMG), Brazil

Amogh Dhamdhere	CAIDA, US
Elias P. Duarte Jr.	Federal University of Paraná, Brazil
Marios Iliofotou	NARUS, US
Changhyun Lee	Korea Advanced Institute of Science and Technology (KAIST), KR
Simon Leinen	SWITCH, Switzerland
Xiapu Luo	The Hong Kong Polytechnic University, Hong Kong SAR, China
Olaf Maennel	Loughborough University, UK
Bruce Maggs	Carnegie Mellon University (CMU), US
Anirban Mahanti	NICTA, Australia
Michael Rabinovich	Case Western Reserve University, US
Fabian Schneider	NEC Laboratories Europe, DE
Aaditeshwar Seth	Indian Institute of Technology (IIT) Delhi, India
Yuval Shavitt	Tel Aviv University, Israel
Oliver Spatschek	AT&T Labs, US
Rade Stanojevic	Telefonica Research, ES
Paul Tune	The University of Adelaide, Australia
Steve Uhlig	Queen Mary, University of London, UK
Udi Weinsberg	Technicolor Palo Alto Research Center, US
Zhi-Li Zhang	University of Minnesota, US

Sponsoring Institutions

The Hong Kong Polytechnic University, Hong Kong SAR, China

Table of Contents

Protocol and Application Behaviour

Characterization of Network Usage

Network Security and Privacy

Poster Abstracts

Measurement Artifacts in NetFlow Data

Rick Hofstede, Idilio Drago, Anna Sperotto, Ramin Sadre, and Aiko Pras

University of Twente
Centre for Telematics and Information Technology
Design and Analysis of Communications Systems (DACS)
Enschede, The Netherlands
{r.j.hofstede,i.drago,a.sperotto,r.sadre,a.pras}@utwente.nl

Abstract. Flows provide an aggregated view of network traffic by group-
ing streams of packets. The resulting scalability gain usually excuses the
coarser data granularity, as long as the flow data reflects the actual network traffic faithfully. However, it is known that the flow export process
may introduce artifacts in the exported data. This paper extends the
set of known artifacts by explaining which implementation decisions are
causing them. In addition, we verify the artifacts' presence in data from
a set of widely-used devices. Our results show that the revealed artifacts
are widely spread among different devices from various vendors. We believe that these results provide researchers and operators with important
insights for developing robust analysis applications.[1]

Keywords: Network management, measurements, NetFlow, artifacts.

1 Introduction

Cisco's NetFlow [2] and the recent standardization effort IPFIX [11] have made
flow export technologies widely popular for network monitoring. They owe this
success to their applicability to high-speed networks and widespread integration
into network devices. The pervasiveness of these technologies has resulted in a
variety of new application areas that go far beyond simple network monitoring,
such as flow-based intrusion detection [13] and traffic engineering [4]. Regardless
of the application, flow data is expected to reflect the network traffic faithfully.

Flow export is a complex process that includes both real-time aggregation
of packets into flows and periodic export of flow information to collectors. This
aggregation naturally results in a coarser view on the network traffic. Several
works have already compared the precision of flow-based applications to their
packet-based counterparts [4, 12]. The scalability gain of using flow data normally excuses the loss of precision. Any flow-based application will, however, be
impaired by flow data of poor quality, which can be caused by implementation
decisions. For example, the imprecision in flow timestamps has already been
discussed in [9, 14]. Similarly, artifacts found in flow data from Juniper devices

---

[1] All measurement scripts used for our analysis are made public at
http://www.simpleweb.org/wiki/NetFlow_Data_Artifacts

M. Roughan and R. Chang (Eds.) PAM 2013, LNCS 7799, pp. 1–10, 2013.
© Springer-Verlag Berlin Heidelberg 2013

are extensively analyzed in [3]. However, these works do not investigate how widespread these artifacts are in flow data from different flow export devices.

The goal of the paper is twofold. Firstly, we report on our experience acquired while operating a Cisco Catalyst 6500, which is one of the most widely deployed switching platforms [7]. We provide an analysis of artifacts identified in flow data exported by this device, along with a detailed description of their causes. Secondly, inspired by [3], we analyze whether these artifacts are also present in flow data from other devices. Active experiments and flow data analysis are combined to evaluate the quality of six different flow exporters.

This paper is organized as follows. In Sect. 2 we analyze and explain the artifacts observed on a Cisco Catalyst 6500. After that, we investigate whether the revealed artifacts are also present in flow data from other devices. The experiment setup is presented in Sect. 3. The results of our analyses are discussed in Sect. 4. Finally, our conclusions are presented in Sect. 5.

2   Case Study: Cisco Catalyst 6500 (SUP720-3B)

The Cisco Catalyst 6500 is a widely deployed series of switches that can be found in many service provider, enterprise and campus networks. In this section, we discuss five artifacts that are present in flow data from a specific device of this series[2], located in our production network. This knowledge is, therefore, gained from our operational experience. It is important to note that this list is by no means comprehensive, since artifacts are load- and configuration-dependent. Moreover, artifacts related to clock imprecisions discussed by previous works, which we have observed as well, are not covered.

Imprecise Flow Record Expiration – Expiration is the process of removing flow records from the *NetFlow table* (*i.e.*, flow cache). This can be done for a variety of reasons, such as timeouts and exporter overload. However, according to the documentation, flow records can be expired as much as 4 seconds earlier or later than the configured timeout [1] when the device is not overloaded. Moreover, the *average* expiration deviation should be within 2 seconds of the configured value. This is because of the way in which the expiration process is implemented: A software process scans the *NetFlow table* for expired flow records. Due to the time needed for scanning all flow records, expiration is often pre- or postponed.

TCP Flows Without Flag Information – TCP flags are accounted for few TCP flows, since they are solely exported for software-switched flows [1]. These flows are processed by a generic CPU, while hardware-switched flows are processed using Application Specific Integrated Circuits (ASICs). Whether a flow has been switched in hardware or software can be concluded from the *engineID* field in the flow records. Since most packets are hardware-switched, only few TCP flows with flags can be found in the exported data. Another observation can be made regarding the handling of flags of hardware-switched TCP flows:

---

[2] The exact configuration can be found in Table 1 (Exporter 1).

In contrast to what is specified in [1], TCP FIN and RST flags trigger the expiration of flow records. As such, TCP flags are considered in the expiration process, even though they are not exported.

Invalid Byte Counters – It has been observed before that byte counters in flow records are not always correct [9]. The counters represent the number of bytes associated with an IP flow [2], which is the sum of IP packet header and payload sizes. IP packets are usually transported as Ethernet payload, which should have a minimum size of 46 bytes according to IEEE 802.3-2008. If the payload of an Ethernet frame is less than 46 bytes, *padding bytes* must be added to fill up the frame. However, stripping these *padding bytes* is not done for hardware-switched flows, resulting in too many reported bytes.

Non-TCP Flow Records With TCP ACK Flag Set – The first packet of a new flow is subject to Access Control List (ACL) checks, while subsequent packets bypass them for the sake of speed. Bypassing ACL checks could also be done by fragmenting packets, since packet fragments are not evaluated. To overcome this security problem, Cisco has implemented a poorly documented solution that has two implications on software-switched flows. Firstly, flag information in flow records is set to zero for all packet fragments, which are always software-switched. Secondly, flag information in flow records of all other software-switched traffic is set to a non-zero value, and TCP ACK was chosen for that purpose.

Gaps – Similarly to the devices analyzed in [3], this exporter often measures no flows during short time intervals. This is caused mostly by hardware limitations, combined with a configuration that is not well adjusted to the load of the network. When a packet has to be matched to a flow record, its key fields are hashed and a lookup is done in a lookup table (*NetFlow TCAM*). In our setup, both the lookup table and the table storing the flow records (*NetFlow table*) consist of 128k entries with a hash efficiency of 90%, resulting in a net utilization of roughly 115k entries. A table (named *alias CAM* or *ICAM*) with only 128 entries is available to handle hash collisions, so that up to two flows with different keys but identical hashes can be stored. The event in which a packet belonging to a new flow cannot be accommodated because of hash collisions is called *flow learn failure*. The evolution of *flow learn failures* in this device can be monitored using the CISCO-SWITCH-ENGINE-MIB (SNMP).

3 Experiment Setup

To understand whether the artifacts presented in the previous section can also be identified in flow data from other flow exporters, several devices from three vendors, installed in campus and backbone networks throughout Europe, have been analyzed. Table 1 lists these devices, together with their hardware configuration and software versions. Given the variety of hardware configurations, we cover a wide range of hardware revisions of widely used devices.

Table 1. Assessed flow exporters and their configurations

No.	Model	Modules	Software version
1.	Cisco Catalyst 6500	WS-SUP720-3B (PFC3B, MSFC3)	IOS 12.2(33)SXI5
2.	Cisco Catalyst 6500	WS-SUP720-3B (PFC3B, MSFC3)	IOS 12.2(33)SXI2a
3.	Cisco Catalyst 6500	VS-SUP2T-10G-XL (PFC4XL, MSFC5) + WS-X6904-40G	IOS 15.0(1)SY1
4.	Cisco Catalyst 7600	RSP720-3C-GE (PFC3C, MSFC4)	IOS 15.2(1)S
5.	Juniper T1600	MultiServices PIC 500	JUNOS 10.4R8.5
6.	INVEA-TECH FlowMon	-	3.01.02

The first two devices, both from the Cisco Catalyst 6500 series, have identical hardware configurations and similar software versions, but are exposed to different traffic loads. We can therefore analyze whether the load of these devices affects the presence of artifacts. The third Cisco Catalyst 6500 has a significantly different hardware configuration and software version. The Cisco Catalyst 7600 series, represented by our fourth device, is generally similar to the Cisco Catalyst 6500 series, but uses different hardware modules. Device 1, 2 and 4 use the same hardware implementation of NetFlow (EARL7), while Device 3 is significantly newer (released in 2012) and uses Cisco's EARL8 ASIC. The fifth analyzed device is a Juniper T1600, which has also been analyzed in [3]. The inclusion of this device allows us to extend the results in [3]. Finally, we have included a dedicated flow exporter (probe) from INVEA-TECH. In the remainder of this paper, we denote each of the devices by its number in the table.

4 Artifact Analysis

Sect. 2 described a set of artifacts present in flow data from a Cisco Catalyst 6500 (Exporter 1). This section evaluates whether these artifacts are also present in flow data from the other exporters listed in Sect. 3. For each artifact, we define the experiment methodology, followed by a description of our observations in both flow and SNMP data. After that, we show some examples in which the artifacts have impact on specific analysis applications. Also, we discuss whether the artifacts are repairable or non-repairable.

Imprecise Flow Record Expiration – Flow exporters are expected to expire flow records at the configured active timeout T_{active} and idle timeout T_{idle}, and possibly after a packet with TCP FIN or RST flag set has been observed. We perform the following experiments to evaluate the behavior of the flow exporters:

– **Active Timeout:** We send a series of packets with identical flow key to the flow exporter for a period of $T_{active} + d$. The inter-arrival time of the packets is chosen to be less than T_{idle}. The experiment is performed for $d = -2, -1, \ldots, 16$ seconds. For each value of d, we repeat the experiment 100 times and count how often the flow exporter generates two flow records from the received packets. Ideally, one should see only one flow record per experiment for $d < 0$ and always two flow records per experiment for $d \geq 0$.

- **Inactive Timeout:** We send two packets with identical flow key to the exporter, separated by a time difference of $T_{idle} + d$. The rest of the experiment is performed as for the active timeout. Again, one ideally sees only one flow record per experiment for $d < 0$ and always two flow records for $d \geq 0$.
- **TCP FIN/RST Flag:** We send one packet with the FIN or RST flag set, followed by another packet after d time units. The rest of the experiment is performed as for the active timeout (only for $d = 0, 1, \ldots, 16$). Ideally, the exporter always generates two flow records.

For all experiments, the packets are generated such that they are processed in hardware by the exporter, if applicable[3]. In addition, several initial packets are generated where necessary, to avoid that special mechanisms for the early expiration of records of small and short flows (such as Cisco's *fast aging* [1]) are applied. All exporters use an active timeout between 120 and 128 seconds, and an idle timeout between 30 and 32 seconds. Note that we do not rely on the timestamps in flow records, which means that we are not susceptible to the errors described in [14]. Instead, we use the time from the machines running the measurement scripts, which are placed close to the analyzed exporters.

The experiment results are shown in Fig. 1a–1c for the three expiration mechanisms, respectively. For each value of d (in seconds, on the x-axis) we give the fraction of experiment runs (on the y-axis) for which the flow exporter has generated two flow records. With regard to the active timeout (Fig. 1a), Exporter 1–3 behave similarly: The number of experiments with two flow records increases linearly for $d \in [0, 8]$. Although this timespan of 8 seconds is in line with Cisco's documentation, the center of the timespan is incorrect: Instead of being at $d = 0$, our experiments show that it is at $d = 4$. Exporter 4 behaves similarly to the previous exporters, although the linear increase takes place for $d \in [-2, 6]$. Exporter 5 shows unexpected behavior: Even for $d = 16$, only 20% of the experiments result in two flow records. Additional experiments have shown that the expiration does not stabilize at all. Moreover, incorrect start times are reported for flow records expired by the active timeout (which confirms the findings in [3]). Finally, only Exporter 6 works as expected and always generates two flow records for $d \geq 0$.

The results obtained from the idle timeout experiments are shown in Fig. 1b. Exporter 1–4 show identical behavior and the linear increase of the curve for $d \in [0, 4]$ confirms that the flow record expiration works according to its specification [1]. Exporter 5 performs better compared to the active timeout experiments: For $d \geq 11$ always two flow records are generated, which is in line with the findings in [3]. Flow records from Exporter 6 are expired up to 15s after the idle timeout, approximately linearly with $d \in [0, 15]$. We have observed that the behavior of this exporter also depends on the absolute value of the inactive timeout. In Fig. 1d, we show for different inactive timeouts the value of d (on the y-axis)

---

[3] http://www.cisco.com/en/US/products/hw/switches/ps708/
products_tech_note09186a00804916e0.shtml

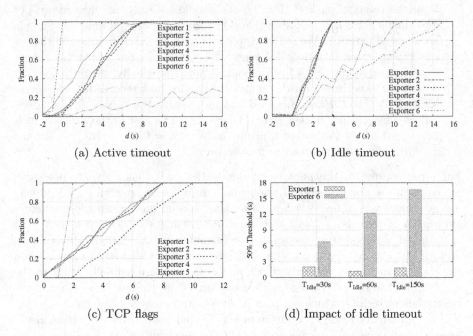

(a) Active timeout   (b) Idle timeout

(c) TCP flags   (d) Impact of idle timeout

Fig. 1. Results of the flow record expiration experiments

where 50% of the experiments yield two flow records, comparing the behavior of Exporter 1 and Exporter 6. While these values are always close to $2s$ for Exporter 1, they increase with the timeout for Exporter 6.

Fig. 1c shows the results for the expiration based on TCP flags. The expiration behavior of Exporter 3 differs from the other Cisco devices, due to a different implementation of NetFlow (see Sect. 3). Overall, the number of correctly exported flow records increases linearly with d. The deviation d for which Exporter 5 wrongly exports only one flow record, is small: Three seconds after the FIN/RST flag was sent, always two records are exported. Exporter 6 does not expire flow records based on TCP flags by specification.

The flow record expiration behavior of Exporter 1-4 shows a clear linear slope in Fig. 1a–1c, which suggests the presence of a cyclic process to expire and export the (hardware) flow tables. The fact that flow records are not expired exactly on the defined timeouts may not be a problem if flows are aggregated afterward. This is especially the case for flow records expired by the active timeout. However, when the idle timeout or TCP flags are used to signal the end of a flow, this artifact may result in non-repairable data damage. For example, in [12] it is shown that some applications (*e.g.*, peer-to-peer clients) often reuse sockets shortly after a TCP connection attempt failure. When timeouts and TCP flags are not observed strictly, packets from different connections may be merged into a single flow record.

Table 2. Artifact analysis results

Exporter	TCP Flows Without Flag Information	Invalid Byte Counters
1 + 2	No flags exported for hardware-switched flows	Invalid byte counters for hardware-switched flows
3	Flags exported	
4	No flags exported for hardware-switched flows	
5 + 6	Flags exported	Byte counters OK

TCP Flows Without Flag Information – Our analysis results for this artifact are summarized in Table 2. The oldest assessed devices, Exporter 1, 2 and 4, do not export flags for hardware-switched TCP flows. Since the vast majority of flows is hardware-switched, TCP flags are rarely exported. We have observed that approximately 99.6% of all TCP flow records exported by Exporter 1 and 2 have no flag information set during a measurement period of one week. However, flags are respected for flow record expiration, even in the case of hardware-switched TCP flows. In the case of Exporter 3, 5 and 6, TCP flags are exported.

The lack of TCP flag information in flow records can be problematic for several types of data analysis. From a network operation perspective, TCP connection summaries can help to identify connectivity or health problems of services and devices. From a research perspective, many works rely on TCP connection state information. For example, [5,6,8] use it for inferring statistics from sampled flow data and [10] for optimizing sampling strategies. None of these approaches works on flow data without TCP flags.

Invalid Byte Counters – The results for this artifact are also summarized in Table 2. None of the Cisco devices strips the padding bytes from Ethernet frames of hardware-switched flows. Exporter 5 and 6 strip these bytes properly. The impact of this artifact depends on the fraction of Ethernet frames that carry less than 46 bytes of payload. To understand the distribution of packet sizes in current networks, we analyzed a packet trace from the University of Twente (UT) campus (1 day in 2011), and a trace from the CAIDA 'equinix-sanjose' backbone link[4] (1 day in 2012). In both traces, around 20% of the frames contains less than 46 bytes of payload, which would be reported incorrectly. The number of incorrectly counted bytes lies around 0.2% of the total number of bytes in both cases. The impact of this artifact on accounting applications is, therefore, very small.

Non-TCP Flow Records With TCP ACK Flag Set – Our analysis has shown that only flow data from older Cisco devices (*i.e.*, Exporter 1, 2 and 4) contains this artifact. On average, the number of non-TCP flow records with TCP ACK flag set accounts for approximately 1% of the total number of flow records on Exporter 1 and 2.

When analysis applications do not use properly-defined filters on flow data containing this artifact, this can lead to unexpected results and misconceptions.

---

[4] The CAIDA UCSD Anonymized Internet Traces 2012 - 16 February 2012
http://www.caida.org/data/passive/passive_2012_dataset.xml

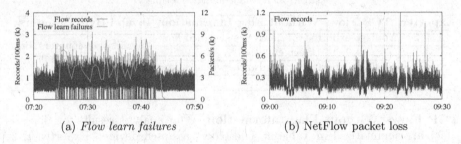

(a) *Flow learn failures*   (b) NetFlow packet loss

Fig. 2. Impact of *flow learn failures* and NetFlow packet loss on flow time-series

For example, a filter for flow records with the TCP ACK-flag set includes also UDP flows in the case of Exporter 1, 2 and 4. Popular analysis applications, such as *nfdump*, accept these filters without showing any warning to the user. As long as the transport-layer protocol is specified in the filter together with the flags, this artifact will not have any semantic impact on data analysis.

Gaps – In this section we characterize the effects of *flow learn failures* on flow data. This helps to understand whether this artifact is also present in data from other exporters, without having access to any flow cache statistics. Our experiments have shown that the first packets of flows are more likely to be subject to *flow learn failures*, because subsequent packets of accounted flows are matched until the records are expired. Smaller flows are therefore more likely not to be accounted at all, while larger flows may have only their first packets lost. Fig. 2a shows a time-series of the number of flow records in intervals of 100ms. This data has been collected early in the morning, when Exporter 1 normally starts to run out of capacity. A constant stream of flow records without gaps can be observed until around 7:25, when the number of records increases. Simultaneously, *flow learn failures* (in packets/s) start to be reported by SNMP agents, and several short gaps appear in the time-series. Note that the series are slightly out of phase, because of the higher aggregation of the SNMP measurements.

Interestingly, the gaps caused by *flow learn failures* are periodic, especially when the network load is constantly above the exporter's capacity. When analyzing data from Exporter 1 for two weeks, we have observed that the distribution of the time between gaps is concentrated around multiples of 4s. Furthermore, gaps are not larger than 2s in 95% of the cases. This confirms our assumption about the presence of a cyclic process for expiring records from the flow cache.

Gaps can also be caused by other factors, such as the loss of NetFlow packets during their transport from exporters to collectors, or packet loss on the monitored link. Both are typically random events that tend to result either in a homogenous reduction in the number of flow records, or in non-periodic gaps. Fig. 2b illustrates the example NetFlow packet loss by showing the time-series of flow records observed at a highly overloaded collector. NetFlow packet sequence number analysis confirms that more than 5% of the NetFlow packets have been lost by the collector during this interval. Several short periods with a reduced number of flow records can be observed, but the series never reaches zero in this example. This demonstrates that gaps in flow data cannot be irrefutably traced back to *flow learn failures*.

We can confirm the existence of gaps in flow data from Exporter 1 and 2. Exporter 3-5 could not be tested, either because they are in production networks or because we were not able to exhaust their flow capacity. Exporter 6 handles collisions in software using linked lists and is, therefore, not subject to *flow learn failures*. Under extreme load, it exports flow records earlier, ignoring timeout parameters completely.

Although this artifact has a severe impact on any analysis because of the resulting incomplete data set, we discuss only two examples: anomaly detection and bandwidth estimation. The detection of anomalies (especially flooding attacks) is often based on large sets of small flows. Since the first packets of a flow are especially susceptible to *flow learn failures*, they are more likely to be lost during the flow export process. Anomalies can therefore stay undetected. Besides dropped flow records, peaks in the network traffic may be smoothed due to the load-dependency of the artifact. Since the identification of peaks is essential for bandwidth estimation, traffic analysis may provide invalid estimates.

5   Conclusions

In this paper we have identified, analyzed and quantified several artifacts occurring in flow data exported by six different devices. These artifacts are related to the way such devices handle the flow expiration, TCP flags and byte counters, and to imprecisions in the number of exported flow records.

Our analysis shows that the impact of the identified artifacts on the quality of flow data varies, and that in some cases mitigation and recovery procedures can be considered. For example, *non-TCP flow records with TCP ACK flag set* can be repaired easily. The *imprecise flow record expiration* artifact can in many cases be ignored if the flow collector aggregates records belonging to the same flow before analysis. However, the remaining artifacts cannot easily be mitigated and they adversely impact the quality of the exported flow data.

The severity of the identified artifacts ultimately depends on their impact on the applications that are using the data. Analysis applications are usually built to be generic and applicable to any flow data. However, the experience gained during this study convinced us that a better way for designing flow-based applications would be to take data artifacts into account. Since the types of artifacts differ from exporter to exporter, we believe that researchers and operators need to be aware of these artifacts to build more robust analysis applications.

One of the areas that remained untouched in this work is the influence of packet sampling on the flow data artifacts, which we plan to address in future work. Also, we plan to work on a data cleanup tool that aims at detecting and repairing artifacts in flow data.

Acknowledgements. This work has been supported by the EU FP7-257513 UniverSelf Collaborative Project and SURFnet's GigaPort3 project for Next-Generation Networks. Special thanks to Jeroen van Ingen Schenau and Roel Hoek (University of Twente, NL), Jan Vykopal and Tomas Plesnik (Masaryk University, CZ), and Luuk Oostenbrink (SURFnet, NL), for their valuable contribution to the research.

References

1. Cisco Systems, Inc.: Catalyst 6500 Series Switch Cisco IOS Software Configuration Guide (2009), http://www.cisco.com/en/US/docs/switches/lan/catalyst6500/ios/12.2SXF/native/configuration/guide/122sxscg.pdf (accessed on December 14, 2012)
2. Claise, B.: Cisco Systems NetFlow Services Export Version 9. RFC 3954 (Informational) (2004)
3. Cunha, Í., Silveira, F., Oliveira, R., Teixeira, R., Diot, C.: Uncovering Artifacts of Flow Measurement Tools. In: Moon, S.B., Teixeira, R., Uhlig, S. (eds.) PAM 2009. LNCS, vol. 5448, pp. 187–196. Springer, Heidelberg (2009)
4. de Oliveira Schmidt, R., Sperotto, A., Sadre, R., Pras, A.: Towards Bandwidth Estimation Using Flow-Level Measurements. In: Sadre, R., Novotný, J., Čeleda, P., Waldburger, M., Stiller, B. (eds.) AIMS 2012. LNCS, vol. 7279, pp. 127–138. Springer, Heidelberg (2012)
5. Duffield, N., Lund, C., Thorup, M.: Properties and Prediction of Flow Statistics from Sampled Packet Streams. In: Proceedings of the 2nd ACM SIGCOMM Workshop on Internet Measurement, pp. 159–171 (2002)
6. Duffield, N., Lund, C., Thorup, M.: Estimating Flow Distributions from Sampled Flow Statistics. IEEE/ACM Transactions on Networking 13(5), 933–946 (2005)
7. Follett, J.H.: Cisco: Catalyst 6500 The Most Successful Switch Ever (2006), http://www.crn.com/news/networking/189500982/cisco-catalyst-6500-the-most-successful-switch-ever.htm (accessed on December 14, 2012)
8. Gu, Y., Breslau, L., Duffield, N.G., Sen, S.: On Passive One-Way Loss Measurements Using Sampled Flow Statistics. In: INFOCOM 2009, pp. 2946–2950 (2009)
9. Kögel, J.: One-way Delay Measurement based on Flow Data: Quantification and Compensation of Errors by Exporter Profiling. In: Proceedings of the 25th International Conference on Information Networking (ICOIN 2011), pp. 25–30 (2011)
10. Kompella, R.R., Estan, C.: The Power of Slicing in Internet Flow Measurement. In: Proceedings of the 5th ACM SIGCOMM Conference on Internet Measurement (IMC 2005), pp. 105–118 (2005)
11. Sadasivan, G., Brownlee, N., Claise, B., Quittek, J.: Architecture for IP Flow Information Export. RFC 5470 (Informational) (2009)
12. Sommer, R., Feldmann, A.: NetFlow: Information loss or win? In: Proceedings of the 2nd ACM SIGCOMM Workshop on Internet Measurement, pp. 173–174 (2002)
13. Sperotto, A., Schaffrath, G., Sadre, R., Morariu, C., Pras, A., Stiller, B.: An Overview of IP Flow-Based Intrusion Detection. IEEE Communications Surveys & Tutorials 12(3), 343–356 (2010)
14. Trammell, B., Tellenbach, B., Schatzmann, D., Burkhart, M.: Peeling Away Timing Error in NetFlow Data. In: Spring, N., Riley, G.F. (eds.) PAM 2011. LNCS, vol. 6579, pp. 194–203. Springer, Heidelberg (2011)

Efficient IP-Level Network Topology Capture

Thomas Bourgeau and Timur Friedman

LIP6-CNRS and LINCS Laboratories, UPMC Sorbonne Universités

Abstract. Large-scale distributed network route tracing systems obtain the IP-level internet topology and can be used to monitor and understand network behavior. However, existing approaches require one or more days to obtain a full graph of the public IPv4 internet, which is too slow to capture important network dynamics. This paper presents a new approach to topology capture that aims at obtaining the graph rather than full routes, and that employs partial rather than full route tracing to achieve this aim. Our NTC (Network Topology Capture) heuristics use information from previous tracing rounds to guide probing in future rounds. Through simulations based upon two months of traces that we obtained, we find that the heuristics improve significantly on the state of the art for reducing probing overhead while maintaining good graph coverage. We also conduct the first study of how such a distributed tracing system performs in its ability to capture network dynamics.

1 Introduction

A few large-scale distributed route tracing systems, Ark [1], DIMES [2], and iPlane [3], are in continuous operation, each mapping a significant portion of the public IPv4 internet. Each takes at least a day to complete a single probing round. The data that they produce are widely used for understanding the structure of the internet. However, as Bourgeau (co-author on the present paper) has described [4], looking at this timescale leaves out important aspects of network dynamism. Those who wish to study network dynamics either turn towards systems that conduct a narrower range of measurements at a higher frequency, such as RIPE's TTM [5] or our own TopHat TDMI [6], or they create their own system, such as Latapy et al.'s (non-distributed) Radar for the Internet [7].

The three big distributed route tracing systems consist of tens (Ark) to thousands (DIMES) of agents, continuously probing towards destinations in each of the 9.1 million /24 IPv4 address prefixes. Implicit in these numbers is a network discovery probe packet budget that is hard to compress. Lakhina et al. demonstrated that measuring from too few sources can introduce biases in the discovered graph [8] and Shavitt et al. have shown how a broad distribution of sources and destinations yields good estimates of graph properties [9].

There is a small body of prior work on how to increase the efficiency of distributed route tracing systems while maintaining all sources and destinations. The Doubletree algorithm, by Donnet et al. [10] (including a present co-author), introduces cooperation between agents so that one can avoid probing where the

M. Roughan and R. Chang (Eds.) PAM 2013, LNCS 7799, pp. 11–20, 2013.
© Springer-Verlag Berlin Heidelberg 2013

others have already probed. Gonen and Shavitt [11] examine what the minimum set of source-destination pairs for route traces might be in order to fully cover the network graph.

Our essential insight is that, the graph of the internet being an object of considerable interest in its own right, a system can aim to obtain the network graph rather than full end-to-end route traces. By conducting partial route traces, chosen, on the basis of knowledge from the system's own prior probing rounds, to reduce redundancy, significant savings can potentially be realized in the probing budget.

The Network Topology Capture (NTC) heuristics presented in this paper are the first realization of such an approach. Emulating NTC on a measurement dataset that we collected using TDMI on the PlanetLab [12], NTC consumes as little as 6% of the probing budget of a classic system conducting end-to-end traceroutes. In so doing, it still covers 95% of the network topology. This outperforms the state of the art Doubletree approach, which (on another, similar, dataset) required 25% of a classic probing budget and discovered 93% of the network topology.

With such a reduced probing budget, it should be possible to speed up tracing systems by an order of magnitude. This might make them more useful for such tasks as network monitoring (e.g., [13]). It might also open the way for development of accurate IP-level network dynamics emulators, to complement the topology generators (e.g., [14]) that researchers use today. The present paper is the first to evaluate the ability of a distributed route tracing system to capture network dynamics.

2   A Generic Distributed Tracing (GDT) Framework

Distributed network tracing systems tend to be similar to each other. Each has a number of lightweight agents and a heavier weight central server. Probing is conducted in rounds, with each agent working from a fixed set of instructions for a round. Results from the agents are sent back from time to time to the central server. We formalize these notions into a Generic Distributed Tracing (GDT) framework. The framework leaves room for many different specific probing heuristics to be applied. The following section describes related work in the context of this framework, and the section after that describes our own NTC (Network Topology Capture) heuristics.

The actors in the generic framework are a **server** and a set of **agents**. Tracing is conducted in a series of **rounds**, with three **phases** to each round: **dispatch**, in which instructions are sent from the server to the agents; **probing** by the agents; and **update**, in which the probing results are sent back to the server, which uses them to prepare the next round. Let us further detail each phase.

Dispatch Phase: The information classically provided to agents in a distributed tracing system is simply a list of destinations that each one should probe, using full route traces. Once this information has been provided to the agents for a first round, it tends not to change much in subsequent rounds. However, the two changes that we introduce to tracing methodology – conducting partial route traces and using previously detected features to guide probing – require agents to receive fuller information and round-by-round updates. For the partial traces, the server must communicate not only the destination, but also the hop counts for a trace. And for the previously detected features, the server must inform an agent about what to expect to see in each partial trace.

We formalize a partial trace instruction as a **query**, in the sense that the agent will 'query' the network regarding the existence of a single edge of the network graph. We must clarify what we mean by an edge because of the well-known phenomenon of unresponsive interfaces, commonly called 'stars', that often appear in route traces, as well as the less frequently seen non-public or otherwise illegal IP addresses. For our purposes, an **edge** consists of two legal IP addresses: v_1, seen at a hop count h in a route trace from source s (the agent) to destination d; and v_2, seen at hop count $h + \ell$, where ℓ is a positive integer. If $\ell > 1$, this means that there are intermediate hops consisting of stars and/or illegal IP addresses, which we exclude from our graph of the network topology. In order to try to revisit the edge $e = (v_1, v_2)$, the query $q = (s, d, h, \ell)$ instructs agent s to probe towards d, starting at h and ending at $h + \ell$.

We formalize the notion that the agent is launching query q explicitly to visit edge e as an **expected view** $c = (q, e)$. By knowing the expected view, the agent can autonomously undertake additional probing if e should not be present. Not all probing can be based on prior experience, however. Typically, an agent's first probing round will consist of full route traces towards a set of destinations. There might be a reason to introduce full traces in other rounds as well, for instance to promote additional exploration. So the full instructions that a server provides to an agent consist in a set C of expected views complemented with a set D of destinations for full traces.

Probing Phase: Agents carry out their instructions in the probing phase, recording the results to send back to the server. Agents might take autonomous action beyond their direct instructions, conducting more or less probing in response to what they, and possibly other agents, are seeing in the current round. A result might simply be that an expected edge has been seen. If it has not been seen, or if additional probing was conducted, then the trace information (destination, hop count, interface seen, for each hop) must be communicated. If probing is less than instructed, then a reason might be communicated.

Update Phase: In the update phase, the server collects the results from each agent and updates its database of expected views. If history extends back only one round, all new information overwrites the old. A more sophisticated approach stores information from all rounds, allowing the next dispatch phase to be based on the fullest record possible.

3   Related Work

This paper situates itself in the context of the small body of work on improving the efficiency of distributed route tracing systems. The distributed work builds on earlier work on the efficiency of single-agent systems. The essential distinguishing feature of the distributed problem is that the work can be divided among agents. (See Donnet et al. [10] for single-agent references.) There are two prior approaches to the distributed problem: Donnet et al.'s Doubletree [10] and Gonen and Shavitt's work [11].

Seen within the GDT framework described above, **Doubletree** innovates in the probing phase. It divides the destination set into as many subsets as there are agents, and it divides the probing phase of each round into that many sub-rounds. During each sub-round, an agent works on its own unique subset of the destination set. When it passes that subset on to the next agent for the next sub-round, it also passes along information about the IP addresses that it has seen when probing towards each destination in the subset. Those address-destination pairs form a tracing "stop set", allowing the next agent to avoid redundant probing. With each sub-round, each agent adds its own information to the stop set. The stop sets are not kept beyond the end of the probing phase, and each round begins anew.

Again, as seen within the GDT framework, **Gonen and Shavitt** have innovated in the dispatch phase. Their server designates destination sets for each agent that are subsets of the full destination set. Based upon knowledge of the route traces from a prior round, these instructions are aimed at reducing probing redundancy as much as possible while still maintaining 100% coverage in the current round.

Both approaches function within the paradigm of the production route tracing systems, in which route traces are full end-to-end traces from each agent to every destination in a specified set. Doubletree allows partial traces to be conducted, but only on the condition that other information is available from which all full traces can be reconstituted (subject to some, hopefully small, error). Gonen and Shavitt dispense with the aim of being able to reconstitute traces from each agent to every destination in the set, focusing instead on obtaining the network graph topology that results from the complete set of traces. They allow a subset of the complete set of traces to be conducted.

Our NTC (Network Topology Capture) approach is the first to fully embrace the graph-based perspective. As with Gonen and Shavitt, we aim at obtaining the fullest possible graph, and are ready to dispense with some routing path knowledge in order to do so efficiently. We are also ready, however, to dispense with full route traces as the means to obtaining the graph, thereby opening up the possibilities for much greater efficiency.

Previous work has looked, as we also do, at the effect of more efficient distributed tracing on network graph coverage. However, ours is the first work to look at the impact on the ability of such systems to effectively capture network topology dynamics.

4   Network Topology Capture (NTC) Heuristics

Within the GDT framework described above, we employ two heuristics (see Fig. 1 and below) that, together, we call our Network Topology Capture (NTC) approach to distributed tracing.

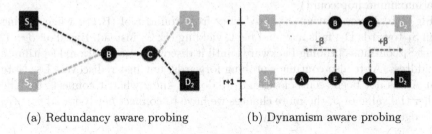

(a) Redundancy aware probing   (b) Dynamism aware probing

Fig. 1. Network Topology Capture (NTC) heuristics

Redundancy Aware Probing: We know from the Doubletree work [10] that a considerable amount of probing redundancy is due to a small proportion of discovered edges (80% of the probes sent discover just 10% of the edges in their case). Our redundancy aware probing heuristic looks at prior rounds' probing results and counts the number of different queries capable of seeing each edge. These include both multiple queries from a single agent to various destinations ("intra-monitor redundancy" in Doubletree terms) and queries from multiple agents (which goes beyond Doubletree's "inter-monitor redundancy" because there is no constraint that the traces must be towards the same destination). The heuristic intervenes at the dispatch phase by globally capping the number of queries per edge, across all agents, in a round at a value α. These expected views are chosen at random.

The dispatch phase of the first round is an exception. Since there is no prior history, full traces are conducted from all agents towards all destinations. The full results are collected in the update phase, which provides the basis for subsequent dispatch phases. Since not all expected views are queried in each probing round, the question arises as to how to age these views. NTC keeps them, replacing them only when measurement indicates that they are no longer valid.

In Fig. 1(a), prior probing has show that four queries, two from S_1 and S_2 towards D_1 and D_2, yield the edge (B, C). With $\alpha = 1$, redundancy aware probing dispatches only a single expected view for (B, C), tracing from S_1 towards D_2 at the appropriate hop counts. In practice, because network dynamics might cause queries to fail, we might explicitly allow introduce edge redundancy by using an α value greater than 1.

Dynamism aware probing: When a query fails to yield the expected edge, this is a sign that routing has changed. An agent could content itself with reporting back just the interfaces that it has seen, but to do so would be to forgo the possibility of discovering more information surrounding the change. Our dynamism aware probing heuristic intervenes at the probing phase, in which the agent continues probing forwards and backwards from the expected view until it has discovered a number β of legitimate IP addresses in both directions (or until tracing terminates for the normal reasons of reaching source or destination or a maximum hop count).

Fig. 1(b) shows that an expected view from round r of (B, C), when tracing from S_1 towards D_2, fails in round $r+1$, yielding (E, C) instead. Based on $\beta = 1$, agent S_1 continues probing backwards until it discovers one additional legitimate IP address, A. It also continues probing forwards, but just rediscovers D_2. Note that A has not been seen before, and we do not know what it connects to. The higher the value of β, the more chances we have to connect newly-found vertices and edges to the known topology.

5   Performance Evaluation

This section evaluates how well the NTC heuristics just described do at covering the graph of the network in each probing round and how well they do at capturing the graph dynamics between probing rounds. There is a trade-off between the discovery budget, on the one hand, and the degrees of coverage and captured dynamics on the other. We explore this trade-off through the two tunable parameters that we have introduced: α, governing how many different ways we try to reprobe each edge, and β, governing how far we search for previously-seen IP addresses when we encounter unexpected IP addresses in our reprobing. Higher α and higher β both mean a greater discovery budget, and, as we see below, both bring gains of different sorts for coverage and capture. The maximum values that we have used ($\alpha = 10$ and $\beta = 30$) correspond to a probing budget of roughly 25% of a full trace probing budget, which is the budget reported for the state of the art Doubletree algorithm [10].

Our evaluation is based upon a real dataset that we have captured, with full traces from every source to every destination, on which we simulate how discovery would have proceeded if we had been conducting selected partial traces based on the NTC heuristics. Existing datasets [1,2,3] were not suitable to our purposes for a couple of reasons. First, their time granularity is coarser than we would wish for a study of network dynamics. An individual probing round taking on the order of days for Ark [1] and DIMES [2], and one day for iPlane [3]. Second, we were concerned that traces that did not employ Paris Traceroute [15] would introduce false dynamics due to the interaction between per-flow load-balancing routers and the way in which classic Traceroute modifies the flow identifier for each probe packet that it sends. Among the big three distributed probing systems, only Ark has deployed Paris Traceroute. We collected our measurements[1] over the course of two months, from 25 May to 25 July 2010, using the TDMI measurement

---

[1] Our dataset and algorithm description are available at http://ntc.top-hat.info

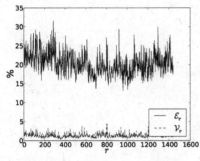
(a) Portion of dynamic events observed

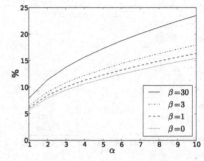
(b) Proportion of discovery budget used

Fig. 2. Network topology analysis and NTC discovery budget reduction

infrastructure that is associated with the TopHat system [6]. We employed TDMI agents at over 230 PlanetLab nodes worldwide (accessed through PlanetLab Europe, http://planet-lab.eu) that we chose for their relative stability. Each agent performed one measurement round per hour, for a total of $R = 1480$ rounds. A round consisted of Paris Traceroutes towards 800 destinations, which are themselves PlanetLab nodes. With Paris Traceroute, we traced a single path per source-destination pair, taking care to use the same flow identifier each time.

For each round r, we aggregate the discovered paths to build a directed graph $\mathcal{G}_r = (\mathcal{E}_r, \mathcal{V}_r)$ that we refer to as the **network topology**. Since there are typically unresponsive interfaces, or 'stars', in a route trace, and since non-public or otherwise illegal IP addresses can also appear, we define an edge $e \in \mathcal{E}_r$ to consist of two consecutive **legitimate interfaces** (public IP addresses), $v_1, v_2 \in \mathcal{V}_r$, separated by a number $\ell - 1$, possibly zero, of **unknown interfaces**: $e = (v_1, v_2, \ell)$. We term **network topology dynamism** to be the symmetric difference between two consecutive discovered graphs: $\mathcal{G}_r \, \Delta \, \mathcal{G}_{r-1}$. The appearance or disappearance of a vertex or an edge between rounds is a **dynamic event**.

The graphs on average contained 13,950 vertices and 61,881 edges. Fig. 2(a) plots the rate of dynamic events per round. We see that **vertex dynamism**, $|\mathcal{V}_r \, \Delta \, \mathcal{V}_{r-1}|/|\mathcal{V}_r|$, represents a small portion of approximately 2% of all vertices, whereas **edge dynamism**, $|\mathcal{E}_r \, \Delta \, \mathcal{E}_{r-1}|/|\mathcal{E}_r|$, represents on average 20% of the edges. We attribute the relatively high proportion of edge dynamism to the appearance and disappearance of unknown interfaces, a phenomenon already noted by Gunes and Sarac [16].

Discovery Budget: The discovery budget is the number of probes that are sent per round. Fig. 2(b) shows the budget when using NTC as a proportion of the budget consumed by conducting full traces, plotting the averages over all rounds. Depending upon the particular values of α and β that we choose, the budget is anywhere from 6% to 24% of the full trace budget. Since we still obtain excellent

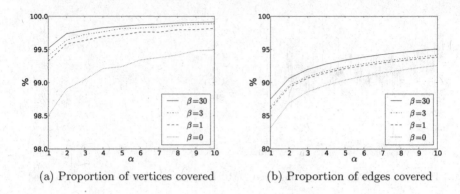

(a) Proportion of vertices covered   (b) Proportion of edges covered

Fig. 3. Proportion of vertices and edges covered when using NTC heuristics

coverage (see below), this means that our NTC heuristics outperform the state of the art Doubletree, which in a similar scenario uses a probing budget of at best 25% of the full trace budget [10].

Network Topology Coverage: The network topology coverage is the proportion of the graph that is discovered in an NTC round, in comparison to the graph that is obtained from full traces. If $\mathcal{V}(\alpha, \beta)_r \subseteq \mathcal{V}_r$ is the set of vertices discovered under NTC, with parameters α and β, in round r, the vertex coverage for that round is $|\mathcal{V}(\alpha, \beta)_r|/|\mathcal{V}_r|$, edge coverage being calculated similarly. We plot the mean coverage over all rounds. We see in Fig. 3(a) that vertex coverage is between 98% and 99%, and in Fig. 3(b) that edge coverage varies between 82% and 95%, depending upon the parameter choices. For comparison, Doubletree, in similar circumstances, covers at most 93% of the edges that are seen in a full trace (and, as just noted, for a higher discovery budget).

Dynamic Event Capture: As for budget and coverage metrics, we calculate dynamic event capture as a proportion, comparing the results when applying the NTC heuristics to those of full traces. If d_r is the vertex dynamism, as defined above, for full traces, and $d(\alpha, \beta)_r$ is the vertex dynamism between the vertices $\mathcal{V}(\alpha, \beta)_r \subseteq \mathcal{V}_r$ found in round r, and the vertices $\mathcal{V}(\alpha, \beta)_{r-1} \subseteq \mathcal{V}_{r-1}$ found in round $r - 1$, under NTC, then the vertex capture rate is $d(\alpha, \beta)_r/d_r$. Similarly for the edge capture rate.

Fig. 4(a) shows that the NTC heuristics capture over 80% of the vertex dynamics, and as much as 96% for the parameters that we studied. In Fig. 4(b), we see that the corresponding figures for edge dynamics are 44% and 75%. As we have already noted, we believe that a large part of edge dynamism results from changes in unknown interfaces, such as a 'star' appearing or disappearing in a route trace, and these dynamic events prove comparatively hard to capture.

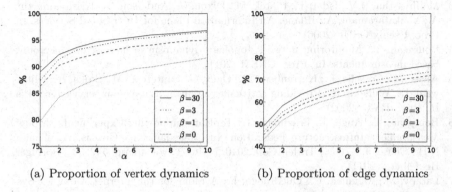

(a) Proportion of vertex dynamics   (b) Proportion of edge dynamics

Fig. 4. Proportion of dynamic events captured when using NTC heuristics

6   Summary and Future Work

This paper has opened a new approach to distributed network route tracing: one that uses partial traces, guided by knowledge from prior probing, in order to more efficiently obtain the network graph. Simulations of our NTC (Network Topology Capture) heuristics on actual route traces show the potential for considerable savings (in this case, of 94% in the discovery budget while still covering 95% of the edges in the graph that is revealed by full traces). This should make it possible to conduct significantly more probing rounds within the same time on a fixed budget.

Approaches such as this should make it possible for large-scale tracing systems to better capture network dynamics. This paper looked, for the first time, at the impact of lowering the probing budget on the quality of dynamics capture.

We have only started to examine possible heuristics, and future work will look for yet more efficient ones than we describe here. We will strive to have such heuristics incorporated into production systems. These systems would provide the basis for a range of interesting studies of the network dynamics that they reveal.

Acknowledgements. We thank Jordan Augé and Marc-Olivier Buob for their assistance in providing measurement data through the TopHat measurement system (`http://top-hat.info`). The research leading to these results has received funding from the European Union's Seventh Framework Programme (FP7/2007-2013) under grant agreement n° 287581 – OpenLab.

References

1. Claffy, K., Hyun, Y., Keys, K., Fomenkov, M., Krioukov, D.: Internet mapping: from art to science. In: Proc. CATCH (2009)
2. Shavitt, Y., Shir, E.: DIMES: Let the internet measure itself. ACM SIGCOMM Computer Communication Review 35(5), 71–74 (2005)

3. Madhyastha, H.V., Isdal, T., Piatek, M., Dixon, C., Anderson, T., Krishnamurthy, A., Venkataramani, A.: iPlane: An Information Plane for Distributed Services. In: Proc. Usenix OSDI (2006)

4. Bourgeau, T.: Monitoring network topology dynamism of large-scale traceroute-based measurements. In: Proc. CNSM (2011)

5. Alves, M., Corsello, L., Karrenberg, D., Ogut, C., Santcroos, M., Sojka, R., Uijterwaal, H., Wilhelm, R.: Providing active measurement as a regular service for ISP's. In: Proc. PAM (2002)

6. Bourgeau, T., Augé, J., Friedman, T.: TopHat: Supporting Experiments through Measurement Infrastructure Federation. In: Magedanz, T., Gavras, A., Thanh, N.H., Chase, J.S. (eds.) TridentCom 2010. LNICST, vol. 46, pp. 542–557. Springer, Heidelberg (2011)

7. Latapy, M., Magnien, C., Ouédraogo, F.: A radar for the internet. Complex Systems 20, 23–30 (2011)

8. Lakhina, A., Byers, J.W., Crovella, M., Xie, P.: Sampling biases in IP topology measurements. In: Proc. IEEE INFOCOM (2003)

9. Shavitt, Y., Weinsberg, U.: Quantifying the importance of vantage points distribution in internet topology measurements. In: Proc. IEEE INFOCOM (2009)

10. Donnet, B., Raoult, P., Friedman, T., Crovella, M.: Deployment of an algorithm for large-scale topology discovery. IEEE Journal on Selected Areas in Communications (JSAC) 24, 2210–2220 (2006)

11. Gonen, M., Shavitt, Y.: A $\Theta(\log n)$-approximation for the set cover problem with set ownership. Information Processing Letters 109(3), 183–186 (2009)

12. Chun, B., Culler, D., Roscoe, T., Bavier, A., Peterson, L., Wawrzoniak, M., Bowman, M.: PlanetLab: an overlay testbed for broad-coverage services. ACM SIGCOMM Computer Communication Review 33(3), 3–12 (2003)

13. Katz-Bassett, E., Scott, C., Choffnes, D.R., Cunha, I., Valancius, V., Feamster, N., Madhyastha, H.V., Anderson, T., Krishnamurthy, A.: LIFEGUARD: practical repair of persistent route failures. In: Proc. ACM SIGCOMM (2012)

14. Quoitin, B., Van den Schrieck, V., Francois, P., Bonaventure, O.: IGen: Generation of router-level internet topologies through network design heuristics. In: Proc. ITC (2009)

15. Augustin, B., Friedman, T., Teixeira, R.: Measuring multipath routing in the internet. IEEE/ACM Transactions on Networking (TON) 19(3), 830–840 (2011)

16. Gunes, M.H., Sarac, K.: Analyzing Router Responsiveness to Active Measurement Probes. In: Moon, S.B., Teixeira, R., Uhlig, S. (eds.) PAM 2009. LNCS, vol. 5448, pp. 23–32. Springer, Heidelberg (2009)

Detecting Third-Party Addresses
in Traceroute Traces with IP Timestamp Option

Pietro Marchetta, Walter de Donato, and Antonio Pescapé

University of Napoli Federico II Italy
{pietro.marchetta,walter.dedonato,pescape}@unina.it

Abstract. Traceroute is one of the most famous and widely adopted diagnostic tool for computer networks. Although traceroute is often used to infer links between Autonomous Systems (ASes), the presence of the so-called *third-party* (TP) addresses may induce the inference of false AS-level links. In this paper, we propose a novel active probing technique based on the IP timestamp option able to identify TP addresses. For evaluating both the applicability and the utility of the proposed technique, we perform a large-scale measurement campaign targeting – from multiple vantage points – more than $327K$ destinations belonging to about $14K$ ASes. The results show how TP addresses are very common and affect about 17% of AS-level links extracted from traceroute traces. Compared to a previously proposed heuristic method, our technique allows to identify many more TP addresses and to re-interpret part of its results.

1   Introduction

An accurate knowledge of the Internet topology is essential for a deep understanding of such a complex and ever-evolving system [7, 11, 19, 20]. In the last decade many attempts have been done to overcome the incompleteness of BGP-derived AS-level topologies [12] using traceroute [4, 8, 13]. However, traceroute is known to be inaccurate and to induce errors when its results are used to infer the Internet topology [15, 17, 27].

One source of inaccuracy is represented by the so called *third-party* (TP) addresses [14, 18], i.e. addresses associated to interfaces which are not actually traversed by the IP packets sent toward the traceroute destination. While several other causes may impact the accuracy of AS links derived from traceroute – such as divergence between data and control paths, anonymous hops, unmapped hops, Internet exchange points (IXPs), multi-origin AS prefixes, and siblings – TP addresses (when shared between peering AS neighbors) were recently defined by Zhang et al. [27] as "the last and the most difficult cause to be inferred" and as "a huge obstruction towards the accuracy of traceroute measurements". Several works, by using heuristic methods, tried to deal with such issues with different objectives: to explain the mismatches between BGP- and traceroute-derived AS paths [8, 27], or to complement the AS-level topology inferred from BGP repositories [4, 8, 13]. However, to the best of our knowledge, only two

M. Roughan and R. Chang (Eds.) PAM 2013, LNCS 7799, pp. 21–30, 2013.

works tried to isolate and study the phenomenon of TP addresses in order to quantify their impact, achieving different conclusions. By adopting a heuristic method based on IP-to-AS mapped traceroute traces, Hyun et al. [14] conclude that TP addresses mostly appear at the border of multi-homed ASes and cannot be a significant source of AS map distortion. On the other hand, by using pre-computed AS-level graphs and pre-acquired knowledge about routers interfaces, Zhang et al. [27] conclude that TP addresses cause 60% of mismatches between BGP- and traceroute-derived AS paths, where mismatches affect from 12% to 37% of the paths depending on the vantage point.

In this paper, for shedding light on this controversial topic, we propose the first active probing technique able to directly detect the presence of TP addresses in traceroute IP paths. Our technique is based on the IP prespecified timestamp option [5] and requires no previous knowledge about routers interfaces, nor AS paths provided by BGP or IP-to-AS mapping. Performing a large scale measurement campaign, we evaluate the technique showing that: (i) the same IP address may be a TP or not depending on both the source and the destination of the IP path; (ii) TP addresses affect 17% of the AS links extracted from our dataset and (iii) they appear in a significant portion of the detected AS-level loops. We further compare our technique with the method proposed by Hyun et al. [14], which is the only other method not using AS paths extracted from BGP. The comparison reveals that only 1.5% of IP addresses detected as TP by our technique are recognized as such by their heuristic, explaining the underestimation of the phenomenon.

The paper is organized as follows. Sec. 2 introduces TP addresses and explain their effect when traceroute is used to infer topological information; Sec. 3 presents our active probing technique to identify TP addresses in traceroute traces; Sec. 4 describes the methodology adopted to evaluate the proposed technique as well as the main findings; Sec. 5 concludes the paper.

2   Understanding TP Addresses and Their Impact

The RFC1812 [5] states that the source address of an ICMP error packet should correspond to the outgoing interface of the ICMP reply, rather than the interface on which the packet triggering the error was received [14]. This behavior can cause a traceroute IP path to include addresses associated to interfaces not included in the path actually traversed. For instance, the trace from S to D in Fig. 1 contains the sequence (a, b, c) of IP addresses (hereafter IPs), where a and b are associated to the incoming interfaces of routers A and B respectively, and c is the interface used by router C to send ICMP replies to the traceroute originator. The IP c is a TP address since it is associated – in this specific trace – to an interface not effectively traversed by the packets sent from S to D.

The occurrence of TP addresses can have a significant impact on some traceroute applications. The major impact is related to the inference of AS-level links from traceroute traces: as shown in previous works [14, 27], TP addresses may cause the inference of false AS links. Consider again Fig. 1: if the IP address b

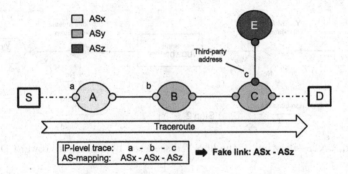

Fig. 1. TP addresses inducing the inference of false AS links

belongs to *ASx*, and *c* belongs to the *ASz* addressing space, then the IP-to-AS mapping of the trace will induce the inference of a false AS link, i.e. $ASx - ASz$. Note also how the TP address hides the *ASy* which, tough traversed, does not appear in the mapped AS-level trace.

While TP addresses may also impact subnet positioning [26] and alias resolution [25], forcing the adoption of several complex heuristics, in this paper we focus on their impact on the AS-level links inferred from traceroute traces.

3   Detecting TP Addresses

Our technique only requires two probes to understand if an IP address discovered by traceroute lies on the path (OP) or not (TP).

Basic Principles. Our technique is based on the IP prespecified timestamp (TS) option [23]. It allows to prespecify in a single packet up to four IP addresses from which a timestamp is requested. Hereafter, we adopt the notation PROBE X|ABCD introduced in [24], where PROBE is the probe type, X is the targeted destination and ABCD is the ordered list of prespecified IPs from which a timestamp is requested[1].

Thanks to a large-scale measurement campaign targeting more than 1.7M IP addresses [10], we detected that most routers (including Cisco devices), when processing such option, insert one timestamp every time the probe passes through the interface associated to the prespecified address. Such behavior can be easily detected by targeting Y with an $ICMP^{echo}_{request}$ Y|YYYY probe. According to [10], if the $ICMP^{echo}_{reply}$ message contains 1 timestamp, it means that the interface Y was only traversed by the probe when entering the router. If it contains 2 timestamps, Y was traversed by the probe providing either one timestamp when both entering and leaving the router or two timestamps just when entering. Finally, 3 timestamps occur if the probe was stamped twice when entering the router, but only once when leaving it. In such three cases the targeted router exposes a per network interface stamping behavior, which can be exploited to understand if a traceroute hop is part or not of the forward IP path.

---

[1] The order implies that B cannot insert its own timestamp before A, and so on.

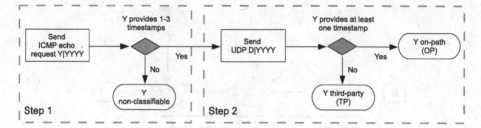

Fig. 2. Classification of the hop Y discovered by traceroute toward D

TP Address Detection Technique. In order to understand if the hop Y discovered by traceroute toward D is a TP address, the proposed technique works according to the following steps (see Fig. 2): (1.) it targets Y with an $ICMP^{echo}_{request}$ Y|YYYY probe to verify if it is classifiable or not (see below); (2.) if Y is classifiable, it targets D with UDP D|YYYY[2]: if the TS option brought back into the payload of the $ICMP^{port}_{unreach}$ message contains at least one timestamp, Y is classified as OP, otherwise it is a TP address.

The first step is necessary because there are other less common router behaviors that may lead the technique to misleading results. Indeed, adopting a conservative approach, a traceroute hop Y is considered *non−classifiable* every time there is no clear evidence that its router has a per network interface stamping behavior, as in the following circumstances:

- **Private Address (PVT):** Y is part of a private addressing block and it may be unreachable by the $ICMP^{echo}_{request}$ message or it may be employed in different networks along the path toward the destination. In the latter case, a timestamp in the $ICMP^{port}_{unreach}$ message may be inserted by a different router.
- **Lack of Reply (NO−REP):** No reply is received to $ICMP^{echo}_{request}$ Y|YYYY, thus either the targeted device dropped the probe or the reply was filtered along the path[3].
- **The TS Option is Removed (NO−OPT):** The $ICMP^{echo}_{reply}$ message received from Y contains no TS option, thus either the targeted hop did not replicate the option in the reply or the option was removed along the path.
- **Zero Timestamps (NO−TS):** The targeted device simply ignores the TS option, without inserting any timestamp in the $ICMP^{echo}_{reply}$ message.
- **Four Timestamps (JUN):** The targeted device provides 4 timestamps. Such behavior has been already observed in the case of Juniper routers, which insert their timestamp also when the prespecified address is associated to *any* owned interface [10]. Hence, the presence of a timestamp in the $ICMP^{port}_{unreach}$ message obtained during the second step would not allow to classify Y.

In other words, a traceroute hop Y is considered *classifiable* only if it provides from 1 to 3 timestamps when directly probed with $ICMP^{echo}_{request}$ Y|YYYY.

---

[2] UDP probes allow to avoid ambiguities caused by the reverse path [10].

[3] In [10], we observed how equipping classic active probes with the TS option causes a strong reduction of the responsiveness.

We also implemented and made publicly available [4] an enhanced traceroute version, based on paris−traceroute [3], which applies our technique to classify the hops discovered along the path toward the destination.

4   Experimental Evaluation

In this section, we describe the large scale measurement campaign conducted to evaluate the proposed technique as well as the main findings.

4.1   Measurement Campaign

To evaluate our technique, we selected more than $327K$ destinations in $14K$ ASes among the ones showing stable responsiveness to both ping, according to the PREDICT project [2], and UDP probes carrying the TS option[5]. To perform a large scale measurement campaign, we used 53 PlanetLab nodes [6] located in different ASes as vantage points (hereafter VPs).

In particular, each node was instructed to (1.) send UDP probes toward the destinations and select those which reply and preserve the TS option; (2.) launch UDP paris-traceroute toward the selected destinations; (3.) launch an $ICMP^{echo}_{request}$ Y|YYYY toward each intermediate hop Y; (4.) select the classifiable hops as the ones providing $1-3$ timestamps; (5.) send an UDP probe toward the traceroute destination prespecifying each time a different classifiable hop collected on the path. In order to avoid ambiguities caused by load balancers, the UDP probes used to classify the hops and the ones generated by traceroute are crafted as part of the same flow according to [3].

After removing the traces affected by filtering, the final dataset − publicly available [4] − consisted of ~12M traces for a total number of $\sim 443K$ addresses.

4.2   Main Findings

Since every VP traced IP paths toward the same destinations, a specific IP address may be discovered by multiple VPs: this happens especially for those located close to the destinations. Fig. 3 shows how many distinct VPs discovered the same IP address: more than 96% of IPs were captured by at least two VPs, while about a half were captured by more than 35 VPs.

Hops Classifiability. When an IP address is captured by multiple VPs, each node independently states if it is classifiable or not. However, the TS option may trigger the filtering of the $ICMP^{echo}_{reply}$ message on some paths inducing a subset of VPs to consider the targeted device as non−classifiable (NO−REP). Fig. 4 reports the number of nodes not receiving replies from a device which successfully replied to at least one VP: only 15% of addresses did not experience such in-transit filtering, while on average 4 VPs were forced by filtering to consider a device as non−classifiable. We can conclude that the number of VPs is a key point for applications based on the TS option [16, 24].

---

[4] http://traffic.comics.unina.it/tpa/
[5] According to a campaign conducted from our laboratory at University of Napoli.

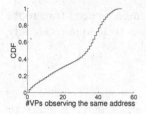
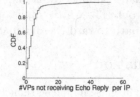
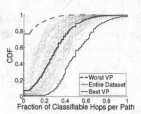

Fig. 3. VPs observing each IP of the dataset

Fig. 4. In−transit filtering

Fig. 5. Classifiable hops per traceroute trace

When some VPs labeled an IP address as non−classifiable and the other VPs judged the same address as classifiable, we did not consider it as a conflict. Our VPs unanimously agreed about more than 97% of IPs labeling 51% of addresses as classifiable and 47.6% as non−classifiable. Conflicting verdicts regarded a limited number of IPs (1.4%) and were mainly caused by the removal of the TS option on some reverse paths. Tab. 1 reports a breakdown of non−classifiable IPs per category (see Sec. 3): our technique was unable to classify such IPs mostly because of devices not replying (16.4%), ignoring the TS option (14.6%), or belonging to the JUN category (10.4%). We also found 9 IPs exposing multiple behaviors to distinct VPs, mainly caused by non−RFC compliant routers (a phenomenon deeply investigated in [10]).

Besides non−classifiable hops, more than a half of IPs in the dataset were classifiable by our technique. Adopting a per-trace point of view, Fig. 5 shows the fraction of classifiable hops per trace (*i*) for each VP and (*ii*) over the entire dataset: on average 4%, 52% and 30% hops are classifiable in each trace respectively by the most filtered node (Worst VP), the less filtered one (Best VP) and over the entire dataset. As reported in the following, although not all the hops in each trace are classifiable, our technique allows to investigate the TP addresses impact on traceroute applications.

Classification Results. Most classifiable hops appeared in several paths from multiple VPs toward multiple destinations. Fig. 6 shows the percentage of classifiable IPs always classified as TP or OP and those classified as both (Mix), on the paths in which they appeared. Such paths are aggregated in three different ways: paths originated (1.) by the same VP toward multiple destinations, (2.) by multiple VPs toward a single destination, (3.) by multiple VPs toward multiple destinations. The obtained results highlight an unexpected general trend: most traceroute traces contain many more TP than OP addresses. Hence, according to the router behavior described in Sec. 3, most of the intermediate routers encountered along the path reply to the traceroute originator using an interface different from the ones traversed by the packets sent to the targeted destination. For both the aggregations 1 and 2, most of addresses were always classified as TP or OP. However, some IPs were also variably classified and this phenomenon is much more important in the aggregation 3. Such an evidence allows to conclude that *the same address discovered with traceroute may lie or not on the IP path depending on the (i) originating node and (ii) the targeted destination, essentially due to both inter- and intra-domain routing.*

Table 1. Root cause analysis of non−classifiable IPs

Category (Sec. 3)	IPs	%IPs
PVT	9,428	2.2
NO−REP	72,775	16.4
NO−TS	64,641	14.6
JUN	45,963	10.4
NO−OPT	18,039	4
Multiple Behaviors	9	∼0
Non−classifiable IPs	**210,885**	**47.6**

Impact on Derived AS Links. While $224K$ IPs were classified at least once as TP address, not all the TP addresses impact the AS-level links derived from traceroute. Mapping each hop to the owner AS [9], we identified in our dataset $14,783$ different ASes. In order to avoid ambiguities caused by the presence of IXPs, we removed from our traces the hops associated to them according to the datasets provided by *peeringDB* [22] and *PCH* [21]. From the resulting $34,414$ AS-level links, we removed 38 links involving sibling ASes according to [1].

Taking into account that the same AS link may appear in several traces toward distinct destinations and depending on the involved IPs, a single AS link may be associated to multiple classifications according to how the two involved IPs were classified each time by our technique. In order to deal with this phenomenon, we applied the following methodology: (1.) if both the involved IPs were classified as OP at least once, we are confident that the corresponding AS link actually exists; else, by adopting a conservative approach, (2.) if both the involved IPs were non−classifiable by our technique at least once, we consider the link as possible; finally, (3.) the AS links which always involved at least one TP address are considered potentially false (see link ASx−ASz in Fig. 1). We counted $1,897$ existing links and $25,990$ possible links. On the other hand, we found $6,299$ potentially false AS links corresponding to about 17% of the links extracted from the dataset.

AS-Level Loops. False AS links caused by TP addresses may also generate bogus AS-level loops. In our dataset, we registered $587,126$ traces normally reaching

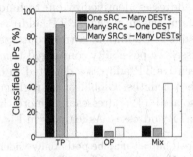

Fig. 6. Addresses classification

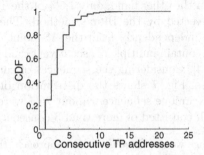

Fig. 7. TP address patterns

the destination, in which an AS-level loop appeared. Among these traces, about 4,144 loops involved sibling ASes. Thanks to our technique, we discovered that TP addresses are involved in at least 37% of such loops[6]: $105K$ and $149K$ loops respectively started or ended with a TP address, while 6,083 loops involved a sequence of consecutive TP addresses. For instance, considering the AS1 AS2 AS3 AS1 sequence, if AS2 and AS3 are associated to TP addresses, one possibility is that the corresponding path is entirely contained in AS1, thus generating a bogus loop.

4.3   Implications of the Results of Our Technique

The surprising high value of potentially false AS links suggests that TP addresses can be a significant source of AS maps distortion. Such conclusion confirms the one drawn by Zhang et al. [27] and is totally different from the one given by Hiun et al. [14]. Here, we investigated the basic reasons of such contradiction. According to the heuristic method proposed by Hiun et al., a *candidate* TP address is an intermediate hop that resolves to an AS that differs from the ASes of both adjacent IPs in the same path. The method takes into account also path stability, AS ownerships and hostnames.

On the one hand, applying the Hiun's method on our dataset, 7,457 IPs were classified as candidate TP addresses. Such addresses appeared in 56,595 different IP1 IP2 IP3 sequences where all the IPs were mapped to different ASes and IP2 represents the candidate TP address. Each sequence appeared in multiple traces and each time the involved IPs were classified by our technique[7]: (i) 166 sequences resulted as real AS1 AS2 AS3 transitions, since all the three IPs were classified at least once as OP; (ii) although the candidate TP address was non−classifiable by our technique in 39,824 sequences, in 15,850 of them we recognized as TP address the previous or the next hop, which could be the real responsible of a false AS link; (iii) in the remaining 16,605 sequences, our technique always classified the central address as TP in 85% of cases (the two techniques validate each other in such cases) and as OP in 14% of sequences (in contradiction to the response of the Hiun's method). In the last case, we also found 52 sequences classified as both TP and OP depending on the traceroute destination and the VP used.

On the other hand, only 1.5% of the TP addresses identified by our technique is detected by the Hiun's method. The main reason is that a TP address is such independently from the AS point of view. In addition, a traceroute path may contain multiple consecutive TP addresses – a possibility considered *remote* in [14]. Considering the sequences of consecutive TP addresses detected in our traces, Fig. 7 shows the distribution of their lengths. Globally, we registered $680K$ unique sequences: about 25% were isolated TP addresses, but more than a half consisted of more than 3 consecutive TP addresses. As for ASy in Fig. 1,

---

[6] Since we used a conservative approach, the real impact may be potentially wider.

[7] As described above, the address identified by Hyun as candidate TP address may effectively lie or not on the IP path depending on the source and the destination.

if a traceroute path only crosses border routers exposing TP addresses mapped to other ASes, consecutive TP addresses may entirely hide an AS from the path.

5 Conclusion

In this paper, we presented and evaluated – to the best of our knowledge, for the first time in literature – an active probing technique able to identify TP addresses in traceroute traces. Differently from most previous works, our technique does not rely on information provided by BGP monitors and it allows to conclude that TP addresses can be a significant source of AS map distortion. Thanks to a large scale measurement campaign, we draw the following general conclusions: (i) the same address may be a TP address or not depending on the originating host and the targeted destination; (ii) TP addresses may also be responsible for bogus AS-level loops. We further observed that our technique was able to classify more than half of the total discovered IPs and, surprisingly, about 17% of traceroute-derived AS-level links were affected by TP addresses, being thus potentially false. Finally, our results confirmed the conclusion drawn by Zhang et al. [27] on the severity of this phenomenon and allowed to explain why such conclusion conflicts with the one achieved by Hyun et al [14]: on our dataset, their heuristic method was able to discover only 1.5% of the TP addresses recognized by our technique.

In our ongoing work, we aim at quantifying the magnitude of the map distortion introduced when combining traceroute- and BGP-derived information to infer the AS-level topology of Internet. We also plan to investigate if and how TP addresses can explain known incongruities, such as *extra*, *missing*, and *substitute* hops arising when comparing the AS paths derived from traceroute with the ones extracted from BGP monitors [27].

Acknowledgements. The work of the authors is partially funded by the PLATINO (PON01_01007) and S^2-MOVE (PON04a3_00058) projects financed by MIUR.

References

1. The CAIDA AS Relationships Dataset (June 2012),
   http://www.caida.org/data/active/as-relationships/
2. IP Address Hitlist, PREDICT ID USC-LANDER internet- address- hitlist- it47w-20120427, 2010-03-29 to 2012-05-30, http://www.isi.edu/ant/lander.
3. Augustin, B., Cuvellier, X., Orgogozo, B., Viger, F., Friedman, T., Latapy, M., Magnien, C., Teixeira, R.: Avoiding traceroute anomalies with paris traceroute. In: Proc. ACM SIGCOMM IMC (2006)
4. Augustin, B., Krishnamurthy, B., Willinger, W.: IXPs: mapped? In: ACM SIGCOMM IMC (2009)
5. Baker, F.: IETF RFC1812: Requirements for IP version 4 routers
6. Bavier, A., Bowman, M., Chun, B., Culler, D., Karlin, S., Muir, S., Peterson, L., Roscoe, T., Spalink, T., Wawrzoniak, M.: Operating system support for planetary-scale network services. In: NSDI (2004)

7. Botta, A., de Donato, W., Pescapè, A., Ventre, G.: Discovering topologies at router level: Part ii. In: GLOBECOM, pp. 2696–2701 (2007)
8. Chen, K., Choffnes, D., Potharaju, R., Chen, Y., Bustamante, F., Pei, D., Zhao, Y.: Where the sidewalk ends. In: Proc. ACM CoNEXT (2009)
9. Cymru, T.: IP to ASN mapping (2012),
   http://www.team-cymru.org/Services/ip-to-asn.html
10. de Donato, W., Marchetta, P., Pescapé, A.: A Hands-on Look at Active Probing Using the IP Prespecified Timestamp Option. In: Taft, N., Ricciato, F. (eds.) PAM 2012. LNCS, vol. 7192, pp. 189–199. Springer, Heidelberg (2012)
11. Donnet, B., Friedman, T.: Internet topology discovery: a survey. IEEE Communications Surveys and Tutorials (2007)
12. Gregori, E., Improta, A., Lenzini, L., Rossi, L., Sani, L.: On the incompleteness of the AS-level graph: a novel methodology for BGP route collector placement. In: Proc. ACM SIGCOMM IMC (2012)
13. He, Y., Siganos, G., Faloutsos, M., Krishnamurthy, S.: Lord of the links: a framework for discovering missing links in the internet topology. IEEE/ACM Transactions on Networking (2009)
14. Hyun, Y., Broido, A., Claffy, K.C.: On third-party addresses in traceroute paths. In: Proc. PAM (2003)
15. Hyun, Y., Broido, A., Claffy, K.C.: Traceroute and BGP AS path incongruities. Technical report, CAIDA (2003)
16. Katz-Bassett, E., Madhyastha, H.V., Adhikari, V.K., Scott, C., Sherry, J., van Wesep, P., Anderson, T.E., Krishnamurthy, A.: Reverse traceroute. In: Proc. NSDI (2010)
17. Luckie, M., Dhamdhere, A., Murrell, D., et al.: Measured impact of crooked traceroute. ACM SIGCOMM Computer Communication Review (2011)
18. Marchetta, P., de Donato, W., Pescapé, A.: Detecting third-party addresses in traceroute ip paths. In: Proc. ACM SIGCOMM (2012)
19. Marchetta, P., Mérindol, P., Donnet, B., Pescapè, A., Pansiot, J.-J.: Topology discovery at the router level: A new hybrid tool targeting isp networks. IEEE JSAC (2011)
20. Marchetta, P., Mérindol, P., Donnet, B., Pescapé, A., Pansiot, J.J.: Quantifying and Mitigating IGMP Filtering in Topology Discovery. In: Proc. IEEE GLOBECOM (2012)
21. Packet Clearing House. IXP directory, https://prefix.pch.net/
22. PeeringDB. Exchange points list, https://www.peeringdb.com/
23. Postel, J.: Internet Protocol. RFC 791 (Standard) (September 1981)
24. Sherry, J., Katz-Bassett, E., Pimenova, M., Madhyastha, H.V., Anderson, T., Krishnamurthy, A.: Resolving ip aliases with prespecified timestamps. In: IMC 2010, pp. 172–178. ACM, New York (2010)
25. Tozal, M., Sarac, K.: Palmtree: An ip alias resolution algorithm with linear probing complexity. Computer Communications (2010)
26. Tozal, M., Sarac, K.: Tracenet: an internet topology data collector. In: Proc. ACM SIGCOMM IMC (2010)
27. Zhang, Y., Oliveira, R., Wang, Y., Su, S., Zhang, B., Bi, J., Zhang, H., Zhang, L.: A framework to quantify the pitfalls of using traceroute in as-level topology measurement. IEEE JSAC (2011)

FlowSense: Monitoring Network Utilization with Zero Measurement Cost

Curtis Yu[1], Cristian Lumezanu[2], Yueping Zhang[2], Vishal Singh[2],
Guofei Jiang[2], and Harsha V. Madhyastha[1]

[1] University of California, Riverside
[2] NEC Labs America

Abstract. Flow-based programmable networks must continuously monitor performance metrics, such as link utilization, in order to quickly adapt forwarding rules in response to changes in workload. However, existing monitoring solutions either require special instrumentation of the network or impose significant measurement overhead.

In this paper, we propose a push-based approach to performance monitoring in flow-based networks, where we let the network inform us of performance changes, rather than query it ourselves on demand. Our key insight is that control messages sent by switches to the controller carry information that allows us to estimate performance. In OpenFlow networks, PacketIn and FlowRemoved messages—sent by switches to the controller upon the arrival of a new flow or upon the expiration of a flow entry, respectively—enable us to compute the utilization of links between switches. We conduct a) experiments on a real testbed, and b) simulations with real enterprise traces, to show accuracy, and that it can refresh utilization information frequently (*e.g.*, at most every few seconds) given a constant stream of control messages. Since the number of control messages may be limited by the properties of traffic (*e.g.*, long flows trigger sparse FlowRemoved's) or by the choices made by operators (*e.g.*, proactive or wildcard rules eliminate or limit PacketIn's), we discuss how our proposed passive approach can be combined with active approaches with low overhead.

1 Introduction

Enterprises are deploying flow-based programmable networks to support diverse performance- or reliability-based application requirements such as deadline guarantees [8], quick failure recovery [4], or fast and reliable big data delivery [5,10]. In flow-based networks, a centralized controller locally computes the routes that satisfy a set of requirements and installs them remotely in the forwarding tables of switches. To ensure that traffic flows according to the pre-defined goals and to adapt rules quickly to workload or infrastructure changes, the network must continually monitor the utilization of every link.

Flow-based network utilization monitoring must be not only accurate and responsive in detecting variations, but it must also scale with minimal overhead on

M. Roughan and R. Chang (Eds.) PAM 2013, LNCS 7799, pp. 31–41, 2013.

the network [3]. Existing monitoring techniques do not satisfy all of these goals simultaneously. Active monitoring techniques (*e.g.* SNMP polling) inject measurement probes and require careful scheduling to scalably monitor the entire network. Passive "capture-and-analyze" tools (*e.g.*, SPAN, netflow, tcpdump) need expensive instrumentation and infrastructure to gather and process measurements. Recently, several tools take advantage of the functionality provided by software-defined networks (SDNs), which allow the controller to poll switches for utilization-based statistics [11,6]. Though this eliminates the need for additional instrumentation, control packets used for polling still impose overhead.

In this paper, we propose a new approach for high accuracy utilization monitoring with *zero* measurement cost. Rather than rely on on-demand active polling of switch counters, we infer performance *by passively capturing and analyzing control messages between the switches and the centralized controller*. This is made possible by the physical separation of the control and data planes in SDNs. In particular, we use the control messages that notify the controller of changes in network traffic (*e.g.*, flow arrival, flow expiration). Such changes in traffic may result in changes in performance; by detecting the time and magnitude of these changes, the controller can monitor network utilization locally, without additional instrumentation or overhead.

To explore the feasibility of our control traffic based monitoring, we design FlowSense to measure link utilization (the bandwidth consumed by flows traversing the link) in OpenFlow networks [7]. FlowSense relies on PacketIn and FlowRemoved messages, sent by switches to the controller when a new flow arrives or when a flow entry expires. FlowRemoved messages contain information about the size and duration of flows matched against the entry. To compute utilization over an interval, the controller analyzes all PacketIn and FlowRemoved messages corresponding to the arrival of flows and to the expiration of the flows that were active during the interval.

Relying on control traffic to compute network utilization fails when there is little or no control traffic. This may happen due to the properties of data traffic (*e.g.*, long flows that lead to few flow expiration events) or due to measures taken by network operators (*e.g.*, to limit the amount of control traffic and preserve scalability, they install flow rules proactively that potentially never expire). In this paper, we study the feasibility of our monitoring approach, both in terms of effectiveness (*how accurate is it?*) and compatibility with current networks (*how is it affected by traffic patterns and network deployment scenarios?*).

To summarize, our primary contributions are two-fold. First, we introduce a push-based approach to flow-based network performance monitoring with zero measurement cost, where we let the network inform us of performance changes, rather than query it ourselves. We describe FlowSense, a system to measure link utilization that is simultaneously fast, accurate, and imposes no overhead. Using preliminary experiments on a small OpenFlow deployment, we show that the utilization computed using control plane messages closely resembles that measured on the data plane.

Second, we explore the feasibility of FlowSense in today's networks. We use real world traffic measurements to estimate the impact that the properties of data traffic have on the performance of FlowSense. We find that we can refresh link utilization measurements at most as frequently as every few seconds. Although, to compute utilization at any point in time, FlowSense must wait for all the flows active at that time to finish and trigger FlowRemoved, the wait time is reasonable: we can accurately estimate link utilization in under 10 seconds of delay. Since the network deployment can limit the effectiveness of FlowSense, we discuss combining active and passive techniques. Ultimately, passively capturing control messages can serve as a building block towards more scalable, accurate, flexible, and general flow-based network monitoring.

2 OpenFlow Overview

In this section, we describe the general operation of an OpenFlow network and review research that uses OpenFlow to monitor network performance.

2.1 Operation

We consider a network of OpenFlow-enabled switches that are connected with a logically centralized controller using a secure, lossless TCP connection. The network operates in the following (simplified) way:

Flow Arrival. On the arrival of the first packet of a new flow, the switch looks for a matching rule in the flow table and performs the action associated with the rule (*e.g.*, forward, drop). If there is no matching entry, the switch buffers the packet and notifies the controller that a new flow has arrived by sending a PacketIn control message containing the headers of the packet. The controller responds with a FlowMod message that contains a new rule matching the flow that is to be installed in the switch's flow table. The switch installs the rule and forwards the buffered packet according to it. Subsequent packets in the flow are forwarded without triggering PacketIn's.

Flow Completion. Each flow table rule is associated with two timeout values that define when the entry should expire: a hard timeout counted from the time at which the entry was installed, and an soft timeout counted from the time of the last packet which matched the entry. When the flow entry expires, the switch notifies the controller by sending a FlowRemoved control message. The FlowRemoved contains, among others, the duration for which the entry was present in the switch, and the number of packets and number of bytes that matched the entry.

2.2 Monitoring with OpenFlow

The OpenFlow protocol provides functions to query switches for the number of packets or bytes in flows matching against a specific rule or traversing a specific port. Prior work relies on this capability to compute utilization in the network [11,6]. OpenTM [11] measures network-wide traffic matrix by periodically

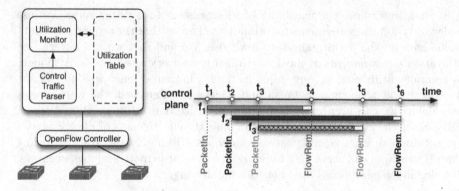

Fig. 1. (**left**) FlowSense design: Parser module captures control traffic and sends it the monitor. The monitor updates utilization values at every checkpoint according to Algorithm 1. (**right**) Visualization of how link utilization is estimated with the aid of PacketIn and FlowRemoved messages.

polling one switch on each flow's path and then combining the measurements. Polling a single switch does not impose significant load on the network but may affect accuracy if the switch is not carefully chosen. Jose *et al.* [6] detect heavy hitters by continually adapting polling rules to focus on the flows that are more likely to have high volume. Both approaches have to carefully schedule measurements to limit the polling overhead and maintain reasonable accuracy. FlowSense, on the other hand, incurs zero measurement cost because it relies on control traffic that the switches already send to the controller.

Ballard *et al.* use OpenFlow to enable flexible monitoring of network traffic for security problems [1]. Their tool, OpenSAFE, directs spanned network traffic towards pre-defined sinks (*e.g.*, IDS) according to pre-specified policies. While such an approach could be used to compute network utilization (by analyzing the redirected traffic), the overhead it creates by copying all network traffic is prohibitive.

3   FlowSense

In this section, we describe the design of FlowSense and how it uses control traffic to measure the utilization of every link in the network.

3.1   Design

FlowSense uses FlowRemoved and PacketIn messages to compute network utilization on inter-switch links. FlowRemoved's are triggered by switches when flow entries expire, and they inform the controller of several properties of the expired entry. Three of these properties are most important to us: (1) the duration of the entry in the flow table, (2) the amount of traffic matched against it, and (3) the input port of traffic that matches the entry (we do not consider wildcard rules

---

Algorithm 1. Pseudocode of FlowSense's utilization monitor.

```
1:  procedure UTILIZATIONMONITOR(Utilization Table UT, Packet p)
2:      Active_List ← set of p.in_port's active flows
3:      if p is a PacketIn packet then
4:          if p's flow ∉ Active_List then
5:              Flow active_flow
6:              active_flow.flow ← p.flow
7:              active_flow.time ← p.time
8:              Add active_flow to Active_List
9:          end if
10:     else if p is a FlowRemoved packet then
11:         flow ← matching flow from A
12:         Remove flow from Active_List
13:         Checkpoint chkpt
14:         chkpt.time ← p.time
15:         if p was from soft timeout then
16:             chkpt.time ← chkpt.time − p.soft_timeout
17:         end if
18:         chkpt.active ← |Active_List|
19:         chkpt.util ← p.byte_count/p.flow_length
20:         for active c in UT do
21:             if c.time is between flow.time and chkpt.time then
22:                 c.active ← c.active − 1
23:                 c.util ← c.util + chkpt.util
24:             end if
25:             if c.active = 0 then
26:                 Declare c final and inactive
27:             end if
28:         end for
29:         Insert chkpt into UT
30:     end if
31: end procedure
```

---

for now). This information helps us infer the number of bytes that the flows that matched this entry contributed to the utilization on the link that ends in the specified input port.

Whenever a flow entry expires and triggers a FlowRemoved message, we add a new checkpoint for the corresponding link. We set the timestamp for the checkpoint as the time at which traffic last matched the expired flow entry. If an entry's soft timeout expires, the checkpoint is the FlowRemoved timestamp minus the soft timeout. If the entry's hard timeout expires, we cannot tell how long the flow was actually active for, so we set the checkpoint as the FlowRemoved timestamp and assume it has been active for the entire flow duration.

At every checkpoint, FlowSense can estimate the contribution to the link's utilization made by flows that matched the expired entry as the ratio of the number of bytes matched against the expired entry to the duration of the flows that matched the entry. However, there may be other active flows on the same link that contribute to the total utilization. FlowSense uses information from PacketIn messages, which are triggered when a new flow arrives at a switch, to infer which flows are active at a given time. To compute the utilization contribution of these active flows, we must wait for them to expire and trigger FlowRemoved's. Thus, we incur a delay in estimating the instant total utilization on a link at a checkpoint. We evaluate the magnitude of this delay in Section 4.

Figure 1(right) illustrates an example scenario for our estimation of link utilization as above. In this example, f_1, f_2, and f_3 are flows that start at times t_1, t_2, and t_3, and t_4, t_6, t_5 are the times at which those flows end; FlowSense determines the start and end times based on PacketIn and FlowRemoved messages. If f_1, f_2 and f_3 had utilizations of 10, 20 and 40 MBps, then, when the first FlowRemoved message arrives at t_4, FlowSense will know the utilization for f_1 by dividing the byte count from the FlowRemoved message by the duration of the flow, and it also creates a checkpoint at t_4. When the FlowRemoved packet at t_5 arrives, flow f_3 ends and its utilization of 40 MBps is recorded and added to the checkpoint at t_4 leaving it with a current known utilization of 50 MBps (the sum of f_1 and f_3). Finally, at t_6, flow f_2 ends and its utilization is added to the checkpoints at both t_4 and t_5 giving the final checkpoint utilizations recorded to be: 70 MBps at t_4, 60 MBps at t_5, and 40 MBps at t_6.

FlowSense consists of two main modules: the control traffic parser and the utilization monitor. The parser captures control traffic and extracts information from FlowRemoved and PacketIn messages. The utilization monitor maintains a utilization table where it records the current utilization value and a list of active flows at all known checkpoints. The monitor updates the table on every new PacketIn or FlowRemoved data received from the parser. Figure 1(left) shows the design of FlowSense.

The algorithm that FlowSense uses for monitoring utilization on a network works as follows. When the controller receives a PacketIn message, FlowSense creates a new flow and adds it to a list of active flows ($Active\_List$) associated with the new flow's input port. On a FlowRemoved message, FlowSense removes the corresponding flow from $Active\_List$ and creates a checkpoint ($chkpt$) with a timestamp ($chkpt.time$) equal to the current time minus the soft timeout. It then makes note of the number of currently active flows ($chkpt.active$) and uses the utilization of the flow as the starting utilization of the checkpoint $chkpt.util$. Each previously known active checkpoint (c) for the same input port in the Utilization Table (UT) is then checked to see if its timestamp is between the start and end time of the newly ended flow. If it is, then c's number of active flows and utilization are updated. When a checkpoint's number of active flows hits 0, FlowSense declares that checkpoint final and inactive. Finally, FlowSense inserts $chkpt$ into UT for future lookup purposes. Algorithm 1 describes the steps involved in the utilization monitoring in a more detailed manner.

3.2   Limitations

Using control traffic to compute utilization has two limitations. First, we are able to compute utilization only at discrete points in time. These checkpoints are determined by FlowRemoved arrivals at the controller and by the values of the timeouts associated with the expired entry. In Section 4.2, we show that the average difference between consecutive checkpoints on a link is less than two seconds.

Second, how quickly we are able to estimate the utilization at a checkpoint depends on the type of traffic; long flows that last forever can delay indefinitely the computation of utilization. Our results in Section 4.3 show that, if FlowSense is willing to tradeoff 10% of accuracy, it can measure total utilization at a checkpoint in under 10 seconds. We also discuss ways to improve the estimation delay by combining active and passive measurements.

Finally, FlowSense is limited to reporting the average utilization over a flow entry's duration and cannot capture instant utilization at any point in time. Thus, it works best in environments with many short flows, such as data centers or enterprises [2], where the small duration of a flow and the small difference between consecutive checkpoints make the average utilization a good approximation of the instant utilization.

4   Evaluation

We evaluate FlowSense from three perspectives: (1) how accurate are its utilization estimates?, (2) how often can it refresh its estimate for a link's utilization?, and (3) how quickly can it estimate the utilization at a specific time? To answer these questions, we perform experiments using a small OpenFlow testbed and simulations on a real-world enterprise trace.

4.1   Accuracy

To estimate the accuracy of utilization monitoring, we set up a small testbed comprising two OpenFlow switches, A and B, that are connected to each other. hostA is connected to A, and hostB1 and hostB2 to B. Initially, the rule tables of the two switches are empty. When new flows arrive, we always add rules with no hard timeout and a soft timeout of 1s. We use *iperf* to simultaneously perform two data transfers from hostA to hostB1 and hostB2 for a period of three minutes. The transfer from hostA to hostB2 has a constant rate of 10MBps, while the transfer from hostA to hostB1 varies across three different rates over time: 20MBps, 45MBps, and 30MBps. Before changing the transfer rate, we briefly interrupt the transfer for a little more than a second to allow the soft timeout to expire and trigger FlowRemoved messages.

We compare the utilization obtained by FlowSense with that gathered from continually polling A and B at 1s intervals. Figure 2(left) presents the results obtained for the link connecting A and B. FlowSense reports utilization values that are similar to those inferred through polling. In comparison to the values obtained with polling, utilization measured with FlowSense shows a small shift to the right because flow entry timeouts have a precision at the granularity of seconds. Thus, it may take up to a second for FlowRemoved to trigger after a timeout expires. Since FlowSense is only working with a single PacketIn and FlowRemoved message per flow, it does not experience the same jittery behavior as the polling method because its readings are an average utilization over that flow's lifetime.

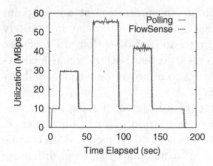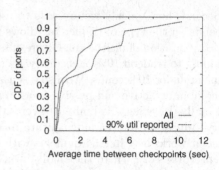

Fig. 2. (left) Accuracy of utilization monitoring. We compare FlowSense's estimates with the values obtained by continually polling the switch counters at 1s intervals; **(right) Granularity of utilization monitoring** for all flows and for flows that have 90% of their utilization reported after 10s. We assume flows are mapped to 24 distinct links.

4.2   Granularity

Many applications need to monitor utilization as often as possible to quickly react to traffic changes. How often FlowSense captures utilization depends on the distribution of flows, in particular on how frequently and how rapidly flow entries expire and trigger FlowRemoved's.

To evaluate the granularity of measurements, we simulate FlowSense on a real-world enterprise trace. We use the *EDU1* trace collected by Benson *et al.* [2], capturing all traffic traversing a switch in a campus network for a period of two hours. We identify all network flows (*i.e.*, pairs of IP addresses and application ports) in the trace, along with their start and finish times. The finish time of a flow is an approximation of when the flow entry associated with the flow would expire and trigger a FlowRemoved message in an OpenFlow network. We consider a flow as finished if there is no traffic between the associated endpoints for at least five seconds. We compute the average time between FlowRemoved events, under the assumption that all flows arrive on the same link, and find that a flow expires, and thus enables us to refresh the utilization measurements, every 16ms.

In reality, however, flows arrive at a switch on different input ports. Because the traffic trace does not contain input port information, we simulate a 24-port switch using the following heuristic. We first associate every distinct /p prefix (where p is, in turn, 32, 30, 28, 20, or 24) of source IP addresses in the trace with a port and then assign each individual flow to the link (or input port) associated with its source IP /p prefix. We group flows by prefix because routing in the Internet is typically prefix-based. Below, we present results for $p = 28$.

We compute the average time between two consecutive utilization checkpoints for each port and plot the cumulative distribution in Figure 2(right). Here, consider the line labeled "All". For half of the incoming links, the average time between two utilization measurements is at most one second and for almost

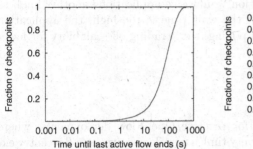
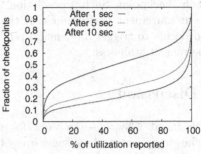

Fig. 3. (**left**) Distribution of waiting times to compute the total utilization value at every FlowRemoved event. (**right**) Utilization reported after 1s, 5s, and 10s following the expiry of a flow entry. Around 70% of links have 90% or more of total utilization reported after 10 seconds.

90% of the links under 3 seconds. We also performed the heuristic to simulate a 48-port switch with various prefix sizes and obtained similar results.

4.3 Staleness

To compute the total utilization at a checkpoint, FlowSense must wait for all the flows active at the checkpoint to finish and trigger FlowRemoved messages. For each checkpoint, we define the utilization wait time as the time until the last active flow expires. Figure 3(left) shows the cumulative distribution of the utilization wait times for each checkpoint in the trace described in Section 4.2, where flows are assigned to one of 24 incoming links. The median utilization wait time is 98s: for almost half of the checkpoints, FlowSense would have to wait more than 100s to capture the complete utilization.

The long delay in computing the total utilization may be caused by active flows that are very long but do not send a lot of traffic (e.g., ssh sessions). Next, we show that if an application is willing to tradeoff some accuracy for timeliness, it can have a reasonable estimate of a link's utilization at a particular checkpoint in under 10s, rather than having to wait for 100s. We compute how much of the total utilization at a checkpoint is reported by FlowSense 1s, 5s, and 10s after the checkpoint is created. Figure 3(right) shows that FlowSense reports around 60% of the total utilization for 50% of the checkpoints after 1s, and 90% of the total utilization for 70% of the checkpoints after 10s.

The granularity of measurements does not decrease by much when considering only the 70% of checkpoints that capture 90% after 10s. The line labeled "90% util reported" in Figure 2(right) shows the distribution of the average time between these checkpoints. The median time is only around 1.7s (increasing from 1.1s when considering all checkpoints).

To summarize, FlowSense is able to refresh utilization less than every 2s on average and obtain 90% of the total utilization at these refresh checkpoints in under 10s. We are investigating ways to predict the utilization wait time at each checkpoint. Such a prediction would give applications another knob to tune measurement performance: if the wait time is too high, the application could decide to trigger on-demand polling, thus trading off scalability for lower measurement staleness.

5   Discussion

We designed FlowSense to work for reactive OpenFlow deployments, where switches trigger control messages every time a new flow arrives or a flow entry expires. The presence of a large number of flows triggers many control packets and can overwhelm both the controller, which cannot process all control traffic in a timely fashion, and the switches, which cannot operate at line speed and quickly exhaust their flow tables [12]. Previous research shows that such deployments are feasible for medium-sized networks with a powerful controller or a collection of controllers. For example, controllers in networks of 100 switches, with new flows arriving every $10\mu s$, may have to process up to 10 million PacketIn messages per second [2].

In practice, the need for scalability pushes operators to increasingly adopt alternative OpenFlow deployments: distribute controller functionality across different machines, set up rules proactively to never expire (e.g., with infinite timeouts) so as to avoid triggering control traffic, and use wildcard rules to reduce the amount of control traffic. We discuss next the applicability of FlowSense in such scenarios.

Distributing the Controller. Distributing the controller does not affect the amount or frequency of control traffic. Using a mechanism similar to FlowVisor [9], FlowSense could still capture incoming control traffic and synchronize the information gathered across controllers.

Proactive Rules and Large Timeouts. When operators install rules proactively, new flows at a switch do not trigger PacketIn's because they find a matching rule in the flow table. Further, if rules have large timeouts, they take long to expire and trigger FlowRemoved's. Some entries may even be set up to never expire or to not trigger a FlowRemoved when they expire. In such scenarios, control traffic is scarce or missing completely and polling switch counters for utilization provides more frequent utilization estimates, albeit at the expense of network overhead. For reactive applications that rely on traffic changes, they will have to either rely on stale data or begin active polling as previously stated.

Wildcard Rules. Wildcard rules limit the number of FlowRemoved messages and forces us to resort to active solutions such as polling counters more often. More importantly, certain wildcard rules can make the utilization computation impossible. If a rule has a wildcard for the input port then the rule is not associated with a single link. Thus, we cannot infer how the traffic that matches against the rule is divided among the input ports to which the wildcard refers to and we cannot compute utilization on the links that end in these input ports.

6   Conclusions

We presented FlowSense, a tool to efficiently infer link utilization in flow-based networks by capturing and analyzing control messages between switches and the controller. Using experiments on a small OpenFlow testbed and simulations on a traffic trace from a campus network, we showed that our method is accurate and provides up-to-date information when control messages are abundant. Our work is the prelude to a larger research direction that we intend to explore in the future: how can we leverage information carried on the control channel of flow-based networks, that is unavailable in traditional networks, to build more robust and accurate monitoring systems and tools.

References

1. Ballard, J.R., Rae, I., Akella, A.: Extensible and scalable network monitoring using OpenSAFE. In: INM/WREN (2010)
2. Benson, T., Akella, A., Maltz, D.: Network traffic characteristics of data centers in the wild. In: ACM IMC (2010)
3. Cai, Z., Cox, A.L., Ng, T.E.: Maestro: A System for Scalable OpenFlow Control. Technical Report TR11-07, Rice University (2011)
4. Genesis Hosting Solutions, http://www.nec.com/en/case/genesis/index.html
5. IBM and NEC team up,
   http://www-03.ibm.com/press/us/en/pressrelease/36566.wss
6. Jose, L., Yu, M., Rexford, J.: Online measurement of large traffic aggregates on commodity switches. In: USENIX Hot-ICE (2011)
7. McKeown, N., Anderson, T., Balakrishnan, H., Parulkar, G., Peterson, L., Rexford, J., Shenker, S., Turner, J.: OpenFlow: enabling innovation in campus networks. ACM Sigcomm CCR 38, 69–74 (2008)
8. Selerity, http://seleritycorp.com/
9. Sherwood, R., Gibb, G., Yap, K.-K., Appenzeller, G., Casado, M., McKeown, N., Parulkar, G.: Can the production network be the test-bed. In: USENIX OSDI (2010)
10. Tervela, http://www.tervela.com/
11. Tootoonchian, A., Ghobadi, M., Ganjali, Y.: OpenTM: Traffic Matrix Estimator for OpenFlow Networks. In: Krishnamurthy, A., Plattner, B. (eds.) PAM 2010. LNCS, vol. 6032, pp. 201–210. Springer, Heidelberg (2010)
12. Yu, M., Rexford, J., Freedman, M.J., Wang, J.: Scalable flow-based networking with DIFANE. In: ACM Sigcomm (2010)

How to Reduce Smartphone Traffic Volume by 30%?

Feng Qian[1], Junxian Huang[2], Jeffrey Erman[1], Z. Morley Mao[2],
Subhabrata Sen[1], and Oliver Spatscheck[1]

[1] AT&T Labs – Research
[2] University of Michigan

Abstract. The unprecedented growth in smartphone usage has fueled a massive increase in cellular network traffic volumes. We investigate the feasibility of applying Redundancy Elimination (RE) for today's smartphone traffic, using packet traces collected from 20 real mobile users for five months. For various RE techniques including caching, file compression, delta encoding, and packet stream compression, we present the first characterization of their individual effectiveness, the interaction among multiple jointly applied RE techniques, and their performance on mobile handsets. By leveraging several off-the-shelf RE techniques operating at different layers, we can achieve an overall reduction of smartphone traffic by more than 30%.

1 Introduction

Mobile data traffic is experiencing unprecedented growth. Cisco predicted that from 2011 to 2016, global smartphone traffic will increase by 5000% [4]. Meanwhile, in 2011, the cellular infrastructure expenditure was expected to be only a 6.7% increase over 2010 [1]. From the customers' perspective, reducing the bandwidth consumption effectively lowers usage-based data charges, and decreases page download times.

Network Redundancy Elimination (RE) plays a crucial role in bandwidth reduction by preventing duplicate data transfers and making the transferred data more compact [8]. In our recent work [17], we investigated HTTP caching on smartphones. We found that for web caching, there exists a huge gap between the protocol specification and the implementation on today's mobile devices. A surprisingly high 17% reduction in the traffic volume can be achieved if just the HTTP caching protocol is fully supported and strictly followed by smartphone applications and mobile browsers. This begs the question: *What about other off-the-shelf RE techniques?* The potential savings from applying these techniques to smartphone traffic are not known quantitatively.

To answer this question, we investigate the feasibility of redundancy elimination for today's smartphone traffic, using packet traces collected from 20 real mobile users for five months. For various RE techniques including caching, file compression, delta encoding, and packet stream compression, we present the first characterization of:

- **Their effectiveness on smartphone traffic.** Previous studies [8][6][7][15] investigated RE techniques for wired traffic, whose content and protocol compositions significantly differ from those of smartphone traffic.

M. Roughan and R. Chang (Eds.) PAM 2013, LNCS 7799, pp. 42–52, 2013.

- **Their interaction when jointly applied.** Prior work [10][14][18] only studied RE techniques in isolation for mobile networks. Jointly employing multiple techniques can potentially save more bandwidth.
- **Their computation load on mobile handsets.** Such considerations are important given mobile handsets are more limited in computation capabilities compared to desktop counterparts.

Our key finding is that, a judicious composition of several off-the-shelf RE techniques operating at different protocol layers can achieve an overall reduction in smartphone traffic by more than 30% with acceptable runtime overheads. In comparison, HTTP caching by itself saves as much as 17% of the overall traffic (§5.2). Such high savings become more interesting and somewhat surprising given that a major fraction of the traffic is video, audio, or image which are already compactly encoded.

2   Related Work

We describe related work in three categories.

RE Algorithms. Data compression techniques, such as gzip, are the most well-known RE approach. An orthogonal approach is caching. Specifically, web caching can be extremely useful in reducing HTTP traffic [10]. Other methodologies include delta encoding [13] and packet stream compression [19][14]. We study the effectiveness and efficiency of these well-established techniques for smartphone traffic.

RE Measurements. A recently study [10] explored the potential benefits of in-network caching at the cellular gateway. Gember *et al.* [12] reported high intra-user redundancy of handheld traffic in campus Wi-Fi networks. The above studies motivated us to make a further step by examining different RE techniques and their interplay when applied jointly for mobile traffic. Anand *et al.* [8] conducted a trace-driven study of packet stream compression [19] for university and enterprise traffic. Earlier RE measurements also focused on delta encoding and file compression [15].

RE Systems. [6] proposed incorporating RE into an IP-layer service on routers. The SmartRE [7] architecture eliminates network-wide redundancy by coordinating multiple devices. EndRE [5] is an end-to-end service where packet-stream-based RE is put into the protocol stack. PACK [20] is an RE system designed for cloud computing customers. Our measurement provides useful insights for designing future RE systems for mobile networks, which none of the above systems specifically focuses on.

3   The Measurement Data

The dataset used in this study was collected from 20 users from May 12 to October 12 2011. They were given 11 Motorola Atrix and 9 Samsung Galaxy S smartphones, all running Android 2.2, with unlimited voice, text and data plans from a large 3G carrier in the U.S. This dataset was also used in our earlier study of smartphone HTTP caching [17][1]. We deployed custom data collection software on the 20 handsets. It runs

---

[1] The dataset will be available for verification purposes under NDA after relevant IRB approvals.

in the background and collects the full packet traces (with payload) for both cellular and Wi-Fi traffic. We collected 118 GB of packet traces during the five-month trial.

The participants were selected to be students from 8 departments at University of Michigan. Their individually contributed traffic volume ranges from 0.3 GB to 23.6 GB. Overall, 15,683 distinct values of **Host** fields appeared in HTTP requests. Across all user pairs (X, Y), the overlaps of **Host** sets $|H_X \cap H_Y|/|H_X \cup H_Y|$ range from 1% to 25% (H_X consists of all **Host** strings in the requests made by user X). We therefore believe the 20 participants are reasonably diverse smartphone users.

4　Explored RE Techniques

We explored four different RE approaches. These are extremely popular and representative techniques for reducing network traffic redundancy.

HTTP Caching. In [17], we found for web caching, there exists a huge gap between the protocol specification and the implementation on today's mobile devices. A 17% reduction in the overall traffic volume can be achieved if the HTTP caching protocol is fully supported and strictly followed by smartphone apps and mobile browsers.

Delta Encoding. In Delta encoding, instead of transferring a file in its entirety, only any difference from its previously transferred version (if exists) is sent. We used VCDIFF [13] (RFC 3284), known as the best overall delta encoding algorithm[16].

File Compression. We study three off-the-shelf file compression techniques selected due to their popularity: gzip, bzip2, and 7-zip[2]. gzip is based on the well-known DE-FLATE algorithm [9]. bzip2 employs diverse compression techniques such as Huffman coding, Burrows-Wheeler transform, and run-length encoding. 7-zip uses Lempel-Ziv-Markov chain algorithm (LZMA), which is also a dictionary-based approach similar to DEFLATE but features a higher compression ratio.

Packet Stream Compression. Compression can also be performed in an *application-agnostic* manner where the IP packet stream is compressed at one end of a network path (*e.g.,* the cellular gateway) and is decompressed at the other end (*e.g.,* a handset). We employ MODP [19], a representative packet stream compression algorithm. MODP was also used in existing RE systems such as [6].

We briefly explain how MODP works. Two *packet caches*, whose contents are synchronized, are deployed at both ends of a network path. To compress an incoming packet, the ingress end (*i*) fingerprints byte subsequences in the packet by sliding a running window over it, (*ii*) matches the fingerprints against a *signature table*, which contains mappings from fingerprints to pointers to the cached packets, (*iii*) for matched fingerprints, replaces their byte subsequences with the pointers, (*iv*) inserts the new packet into the packet cache and updates the signature table. The decompression procedure is straightforward: the egress end simply follows the pointers and replaces them with byte sequences in the cache. The algorithm involves two parameters:

---

[2]　http:// www. gzip. org, http:// bzip. org,
　　http:// www. 7-zip. org

the packet cache size n, and the sampling rate for fingerprint generation p^3. Selecting their values involves trading off the compression ratio and the processing speed.

5   Measurement Results

We apply the aforementioned RE techniques to our dataset to study their effectiveness.

5.1   Evaluation Methodology

We perform RE in the following order. In the remainder of this paper, we refer to a web object (*e.g.*, an HTML document) carried by an HTTP response as a *file*.

Step 1: Web Caching. We eliminate redundant transfers due to problematic caching behaviors by assuming a good HTTP caching implementation that *(i)* strictly follows the protocol specification [11], and *(ii)* has a non-volatile LRU cache shared by all applications. The cache size is assumed to be 256 MB. As long as the cache size is not too small (*e.g.*, >50 MB), it has little impact on the RE effectiveness, as shown in [17].

Step 2: Delta Encoding. Assume a handset has requested for file f, and there is already a copy of f in the cache (a file is keyed by its full URL including query strings). If the content of f has changed, we use VCDIFF to encode the delta between the new and the old version, to save the bandwidth. If f is not expired or not changed, the standard caching procedure (Step 1) is used although VCDIFF can also handle two identical inputs and output a delta of zero.

Step 3: File Compression. The file is compressed by an off-the-shelf compression technique such as gzip, unless it is already compressed in the trace or by Step 2.

Step 4: Packet Stream Compression. We use MODP to compress all the IP packets in both directions between the cellular gateway and the handset.

Steps 1 to 3 are object-level RE schemes. In theory these general techniques can be applied to any application-level objects. However, here we apply them to only HTTP traffic that dominates smartphone traffic usage [8][12]. In particular, encrypted HTTPS traffic over TCP port 443 accounts for 11.2% of the bytes – we are unable to apply objected-based RE techniques to them (the data collector runs below the SSL library). Hence the reported RE effectiveness is an *underestimation* of the actual possible gains. Also, Step 1 and 3 are already part of the HTTP specification [11] but today's smartphones and web servers may not strictly follow or fully utilize them. *We quantify the additional benefits that can be gained if they do so.*

The Ordering of the Four Steps is justified as follows. We consider caching (Step 1) first since it can potentially avoid transferring the entire file. If Step 2 is performed, then Step 3 will be skipped, because delta encoding usually yields a more compact output than compressing a single file does. Note that in Step 2, the output of VCDIFF (*i.e.*, the delta) is always compressed (using gzip by default). Step 4 is applied at the end of the pipeline because packet stream compression is performed on a network path after packets leave the server.

---

[3] Fingerprints are indexed probabilistically since indexing all is computationally impractical.

Table 1. Compression Ratios (CR) for caching, file compression, and delta encoding, when each of them is individually applied. The "HTTP" row and the "All" row correspond to CR values computed for only HTTP traffic, and the overall traffic, respectively.

	1. Caching	2-4. File Compression (lv 1–9)			5-7. Lower Bound (lv5)			8-9. Δ Encoding	
		gzip	bzip2	7-zip	gzip	bzip2	7-zip	T & NT*	NT only
HTTP	79.8%	83.9–84.5%	84.4–84.9%	82.5–82.5%	80.4%	78.9%	71.7%	77.8%	98.0%
All	82.7%	86.3–86.8%	86.7–87.1%	85.1–85.1%	83.3%	82.0%	75.8%	81.0%	98.3%

* "T": trivial cases (two versions are identical); "NT": non-trivial cases (two versions are different).

Implementation of RE Techniques. Step 1 was realized by a standard web caching simulator correctly following the HTTP protocol. Step 2 and 3 were implemented by using open-source projects of xdelta 3.0 (http:// xdelta. org/, for VCDIFF), LZMA SDK 9.20 (for 7-zip), bzip2 1.0.6, and gzip 1.2.4, all having a tunable parameter between 1 (least compact but fastest) and 9 (most compact but slowest) allowing users to balance between compression ratio and speed. We implemented the MODP algorithm in C++ based on a recent paper [14] that improves the original algorithm [19].

The Key Evaluation Metric is the *Compression Ratio* (CR), defined as the ratio of traffic volume after compression to the traffic volume of the original trace. A smaller CR indicates more effective compression. CR is consistently used in Tables 1 to 4.

5.2 Applying Individual RE Approaches

We first examine each individual RE approach.

Overall Statistics. The dataset consists of 118 GB of packet traces dominated by downlink traffic (93% of the bytes go from the Internet to handsets). As identified by the HTTP parser, 85.4% of all traffic is HTTP that can be potentially optimized by the object-based RE techniques described in §5.1.

TCP/IP Headers. We exclude all TCP/IP headers from our analysis because they can be effectively compressed by mobile networks (*e.g.,* UMTS uses the Packet Data Convergence Protocol [2] for header compression) but in our data collected on handsets they were captured as uncompressed.

We discuss key results in Table 1. As indicated by the "Caching" column (Column 1), good web caching implementation reduces the overall traffic volume by 17%.

File Compression. In Columns 2 to 4, all three file compression techniques effectively achieve compression ratios (CR) between 82.5% and 84.9% for HTTP traffic. Neither the algorithm nor the compression level impacts the CR significantly. This can be explained as follows. We first note that compression is likely to yield more gains for *smaller* files, which tend to be uncompressed text files. In contrast, large files are usually audio, video, or files already compressed in the data. Compressing them further brings little additional benefits regardless of the compression method (Table 2). This is validated by the fact that the overall CR value (gzip level 5) for all responses under 100KB (they account for 33% of the total HTTP response volume) is 71%, compared to 93% for all responses of at least 100KB. This confirms the intuition that most

Table 2. Effectiveness of gzip compression (lv 5) on different content types. Content types with CR values less than 30% (*i.e.*, compression is under-utilized) are highlighted.

Content-Type	% bytes	% NC*	CR (gzip)	Content-Type	% bytes	% NC*	CR (gzip)
video/mp4	19.34%	100.00%	97.84%	video/x-flv	4.65%	99.85%	98.64%
app/octet-stream	13.14%	99.44%	95.21%	text/html	3.74%	70.11%	23.49%
(App market)	12.46%	100.00%	86.83%	text/javascript	2.57%	58.17%	27.44%
image/jpeg	10.20%	99.47%	88.90%	image/png	2.40%	97.77%	90.86%
audio/mpeg	8.14%	99.99%	97.07%	app/x-javascript	2.34%	59.48%	29.45%
video/3gpp	6.34%	100.00%	96.86%	video/flv	1.61%	100.00%	97.86%
text/xml	5.23%	98.18%	14.59%	text/css	1.27%	85.84%	19.34%

* "NC": The fraction of bytes that are *Not Compressed*.

gains come from small files. Secondly, most reasonable compression techniques tend to perform similarly for small files – probably because redundancy patterns in smaller files are usually easier to discover so even using a lightweight compression technique less aggressively (*e.g.*, gzip with a small dictionary) can achieve a reasonable CR.

Under-utilization of compression can be caused by either a handset or the server. Specifically, 60% of HTTP requests, whose responses account for 79% of the total HTTP response traffic[4], do not contain an **Accept-Encoding** header field, making it impossible for the server to transfer a compressed file. Compressing the responses using gzip yields a CR of 82% for the corresponding 79% of the HTTP response traffic. Also 26% of HTTP requests do have **Accept-Encoding** header fields but their responses are not compressed by the server. Compressing them reduces their HTTP response traffic volume by 10%.

Table 2 lists the top **Content-Type** strings appearing in HTTP responses (Column 1), their contribution to the overall HTTP traffic volume (Column 2), the fraction of bytes that are not compressed in the original data (Column 3), and their CR values (Column 4). For example, for all bytes in the original trace belonging to **text/xml** files, they are responsible for 5.23% of the total HTTP traffic volume, and 98.18% of such bytes belong to files that were not compressed in the original trace. By compressing those files, the transferred **text/xml** data size can be reduced to 5.23%*14.59%=0.76% of all (unoptimized) HTTP traffic volume. Table 2 indicates a bimodal distribution of CR values across content types. Compression is under-utilized in the original trace for most text files (html, xml, javascript, and css) accounting for 15% of all HTTP traffic. For each of such content types, 58% to 98% of the response data is not compressed. If compression is used, more than 70% of their bytes can be saved. In contrast, images, videos and most binary data already have compact file formats so further compression brings marginal benefits.

To understand the limits of the effectiveness of the file compression techniques, we combine all HTTP requests and responses for each of the 20 users into a single large file, run compression for each file, and then compute a CR value across all these 20 files. The gaps between these lower bounds (Columns 5 to 7 in Table 1) and their corresponding CRs of object-based compression (Columns 2 to 4) vary between 3.5% and 10.8%, depending on the compression technique. Also, HTTP/1.1 does not compress HTTP

---

[4] Unless otherwise specified, a percentage such as "$x\%$ of HTTP traffic" and "$x\%$ of all traffic" refers to the percentage of traffic in the original data *before* being optimized by RE techniques.

	$p=1/4$	$p=1/8$	$p=1/16$	$p=1/32$
$n=512k$	70.2%	71.9%	73.7%	75.3%
$n=256k$	71.8%	73.4%	75.2%	76.8%
$n=128k$	73.1%	74.7%	76.4%	78.0%
$n=64k$	74.3%	75.8%	77.5%	79.0%
$n=512k$ (no loss)	69.3%	71.0%	72.8%	74.4%

Table 3. Applying the MODP algorithm on all traffic

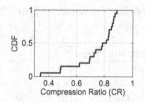

Fig. 1. CR distribution across users (caching+gzip+delta)

headers [11], which account for 5% of the total HTTP bytes in the trace. Compressing them reduces CR of HTTP traffic by about 1.4% (considered by Columns 2 to 4). This is performed by SPDY [3] that has been implemented in the Google Chrome browser.

Delta Encoding. Consists of two scenarios: a trivial case where the two versions are identical (*i.e.,* the delta is zero), and a non-trivial case where they are different. The trivial case is already handled by today's HTTP caching. Column 8 in Table 1 includes both cases while Column 9 in Table 1 only considers *additional* benefits brought by handling non-trivial cases using VCDIFF, a feature not widely deployed. We observe that doing so only slightly outperforms using only standard caching because trivial cases are much more prevalent than non-trivial cases. Specifically, 19.0% of HTTP bytes belong to cacheable files whose previous instances remain unchanged. Requests for these files can be served either by the local cache before expiration, or by a **304 Not Modified** response after expiration. In contrast, only 4.7% of HTTP bytes belong to files whose previous instances (with the same URL) differ. But for those 4.7% of HTTP bytes, VCDIFF does make them more compact than gzip does: VCDIFF achieves a CR value of 57.4%, while using gzip without leveraging similarities between the two versions yields a much higher CR of 72.4%.

Packet Stream Compression. Table 3 quantifies the effectiveness of MODP by changing two critical parameters n, the size of the packet cache in terms of the number of packets, and p, the sampling rate for fingerprint generation (§4). The overall CR is encouragingly good, between 70.2% and 79.0%. Exponentially decreasing p from 1/4 to 1/32 does not dramatically increase CR because the similarity between an input packet and a cached packet is often high so generating fingerprints less frequently can still yield a reasonably high matching rate. Decreasing n from 512k to 64k causes limited increase of CR as well due to the temporal locality of cache access [5].

Table 3 considers packet loss, which may hinder the MODP algorithm from functioning correctly. Consider a packet P that is lost after entering the ingress end's cache. The egress end thus cannot decode any subsequent packet that is compressed using the reference packet P. To address this issue, we assume that if the receiver cannot decode a packet, it immediately requests that the sender retransmit the lost reference packet(s) to synchronize the two packet caches [14].

We measured the overall retransmission rate of TCP traffic, which accounts for 98% of the overall traffic volume, to be 2.1% (1.8% for Wi-Fi and 2.2% for 3G). For all but the last row in Table 3, we conservatively treat all TCP packets that are later retransmitted as lost packets. The last row corresponds to a hypothetical scenario

Table 4. Jointly applying multiple RE techniques

	caching +gzip	caching +bzip2	caching +7-zip	caching +gzip +delta	caching +bzip2 +delta	caching +7-zip +delta	All * n=512k p=1/4	All * n=256k p=1/8	All * n=128k p=1/16	All * n=64k p=1/32
HTTP	71.4%	71.6%	70.4%	71.1%	71.3%	70.1%	-	-	-	-
All	75.5%	75.8%	74.7%	75.3%	75.5%	74.5%	68.1%	68.6%	69.2%	69.9%

* All = caching + gzip (lv 5) + delta + MODP (for all traffic). n and p are MODP parameters.

with no loss. In that ideal case, the CR decreases by about 1% due to the eliminated retransmission overhead of reference packets, implying that the impact of packet loss observed in the five-month dataset on CR is small.

5.3 Combining Multiple Approaches

We now apply multiple RE techniques together by following the order described in §5.1. The left seven columns in Table 4 indicate that jointly employing caching, file compression, and delta encoding is beneficial in that it reduces the CR to as low as 70.1% (for HTTP traffic) and 74.5% (for all traffic). Caching and file compression are complementary schemes: the former makes traffic due to multiple requests of the same file more efficient, while the latter improves the efficiency of a single file transfer.

Figure 1 plots the CR distribution (for all traffic) across the 20 users, assuming caching, gzip (lv 5), and delta encoding are jointly used. The CR for each user ranges from 34% to 89%, implying the heterogeneity of traffic generated by diverse users (§3). Clearly, the effectiveness of RE techniques depends on traffic content that differs across users, but the incurred bandwidth savings are unanimously non-trivial ($>$ 10%).

We then take a further step by applying MODP in addition to the three object-based RE techniques. By further looking at the right four columns in Table 4, we learn the additional CR reduction due to MODP is non-trivial (ranging from 5.4% to 7.2%) but is much smaller than the saving brought by using MODP alone (21.0% to 29.8% as depicted in Table 3). This implies that object-based RE techniques have already eliminated most redundancies for the HTTP traffic that dominates the trace. In fact, MODP further reduces the HTTP traffic volume by 6.2% to 7.8%, most of which comes from cross-file redundancy of non-cacheable files. In contrast, MODP results in much more reduction of CR for non-HTTP traffic, between 16.1% and 21.7%.

5.4 Performance

We measure the performance of each RE technique on a real server and a smartphone device. Our equipment includes a Dell PowerEdge server with an Intel Xeon E5620 quad-core CPU at 2.4 GHz and a Motorola Atrix 4G smartphone with a Tegra 2 dual-core CPU at 1 GHz. The server ran Ubuntu 11.04 and the phone used Android 2.2.

Two Macro-benchmarks were employed to evaluate the file compression and the packet stream compression technique, respectively. The *file benchmark* consisted of 1000 HTTP responses randomly sampled from the dataset. The *packet stream benchmark* was a 2GB packet trace generated by a random user. We produced five instances

Table 5. Throughput (in Mbps) of object-based RE techniques on the *File Benchmark*

	gzip (level 1 – 9)		bzip2 (level 1 – 9)		7-zip (level 1 – 9)		VCDIFF (δ 10%–90%)	
	comp	decomp	comp	decomp	comp	decomp	comp	decomp
Server	80–132	380–392	24–25	57–60	14–17	20–20	5.4–5.5	479–808
Phone	19–37	223–231	5.2–5.6	18–21	4.4–5.4	10–10	1.9–1.9	231–392

Table 6. Throughput (in Mbps) of MODP on the *Packet Stream Benchmark*

Compress	n=128k p=1/16	n=64k p=1/32	Decompress	n=128k p=1/16	n=64k p=1/32
Server	19	41	Server	320	348
Phone	4.2	8.9	Phone	40	41

of this benchmark, all yielding very similar performance results. We report the results for one instance.

We measured the in-memory compression/decompression time (excluding disk I/O) for the two benchmarks on both the server and the phone, using binaries compiled from the same source code. Table 5 shows the results for the *file benchmark*. Each file was compressed (decompressed) separately and the measured throughput is the total file size divided by the sum of the processing time of all files. For VCDIFF, we artificially generated a previous version of each file by randomly changing its content by a fixed percentage of δ. Table 6 summarizes the *packet stream benchmark* results. We measured the processing time of the second-half data of the 2GB packet trace, whose first-half data of 1GB was used to fill the packet cache and the signature table (for compression). Changing this 1GB to 0.5GB or 1.5GB has negligible impact on the results.

In Table 5 and Table 6, the throughput was estimated in an extreme case where the data was fed into the compressor/decompressor as fast as possible without any interruption. We repeated each test 10 times and measured the average running time, from which we derived the throughput value. The standard deviation of the running time across 10 runs was always less than 2% of the average.

The benchmark results deliver several observations. *(i)* As expected, compression is slower than decompression. But compressed files can be cached by servers to avoid having to repeat the compression for each incoming request for the same file. *(ii)* gzip is much faster than the more sophisticated bzip2 and 7-zip (for both compression and decompression) while its achieved CR is only slightly higher for small files from which most benefits of compression come (§5.2). *(iii)* VCDIFF is more expensive than all three file compression techniques, because it involves heavy computation for comparing *two* versions of a file. *(iv)* For gzip, bzip2, VCDIFF, and MODP, their low decompression overheads make it possible to keep up with a high data rate (*e.g.,* 15Mbps), incurring very small impact on page processing/rendering time on a handset. *(v)* MODP is quite efficient for small n and p. Exponentially increasing n and p worsens the performance (not shown in Table 6), and doing so provides little additional traffic savings when object-based RE is performed beforehand (Table 4). The performance could be further improved by enhancements of MODP, such as MAXP and SAMPLEBYTE [5].

6   Summary and Recommendations

We summarize our main findings and recommendations as follows.

1. Under-utilization of compression contributes to significant redundancy, *i.e.*, 15% of the overall traffic volume for our trace. It is imperative that the content providers utilize the compression feature supported by all mainstream Web servers. Handsets should use the `Accept-Encoding` header field, which appeared in only 40% of HTTP requests within the dataset, to enable compression.

2. Considering both effectiveness and performance, gzip is the best compression approach for small files from which most benefits of compression come (yet the traffic volume contribution of such small files is considerable, see §5.2). Applying delta encoding on non-trivial cases (§5.2) brings limited benefits, because less than 5% of HTTP bytes belong to files with a different previous version. Except for 7-zip, decompression performance is generally not an issue on mobile devices, leading to very small impact on page processing/rendering time.

3. Special emphasis should be put on html, xml, javascript, and css files. They account for 15% of the HTTP traffic in the dataset (17% reported in [12] for hand-held traffic in campus Wi-Fi networks), but are usually (58% to 98% bytewise) not compressed. More than 70% of their bytes can be saved using compression.

4. Using packet stream compression alone, represented by the MODP algorithm, effectively reduces the traffic volume by up to 30%. If object-based RE techniques, which are already part of the HTTP specification, are applied beforehand, the benefit of MODP decreases but is still non-trivial, *i.e.*, a reduction of 5.4% to 7.2% of all traffic. In that case, the impact of the aggressiveness level on CR is much less significant. We therefore recommend that MODP be deployed in a less aggressive manner, *e.g.*, $n \le 64$k packets and $p \le 1/16$ for downlink. This achieves most of the bandwidth savings possible from MODP while limiting the performance overhead for compression as well as decompression. Note that packet stream compression provides benefits despite idiosyncrasies in application implementations.

5. A judicious combination of all RE techniques achieves an overall reduction of the smartphone traffic studied in this measurement by more than 30% with acceptable computational overhead. This is even more interesting and somewhat surprising given that a major fraction of the traffic is video, audio, or image that are already compressed. In comparison, caching by itself only saves 17% of the overall traffic (§5.2).

Acknowledgements. This work is partly funded by NSF grants CNS-1059372, CNS-1050157, CNS-1039657 and Navy grant N00014-09-1-0705. We thank Emir Halepovic and the shepherd Marios Iliofotou for their valuable comments on the paper. We would also like to thank anonymous reviewers whose comments improved the final version.

References

1. Invest in Cell Phone Infrastructure for Growth in 2010 (2010), http://pennysleuth.com/invest-in-cell-phone-infrastructure-for-growth-in-2010/
2. Packet Data Convergence Protocol (PDCP) specification. 3GPP TS 25.323

3. SPDY: An experimental protocol for faster web, `http:// dev. chromium. org/ spdy`
4. Cisco Visual Networking Index (2012), `http:// newsroom. cisco. com/ press-release-content? type=webcontent& articleId=668380`
5. Aggarwal, B., Akella, A., Anand, A., Balachandran, A., Chitnis, P., Muthukrishnan, C., Ramjee, R., Varghese, G.: EndRE: An End-System Redundancy Elimination Service for Enterprises. In: NSDI (2010)
6. Anand, A., Gupta, A., Akella, A., Seshan, S., Shenker, S.: Packet Caches on Routers: The Implications of Universal Redundant Traffic Elimination. In: SIGCOMM (2008)
7. Anand, A., Sekar, V., Akella, A.: SmartRE: An Architecture for Coordinated Network-wide Redundancy Elimination. In: SIGCOMM (2009)
8. Anand, A., Muthukrishnan, C., Ramjee, R.: Redundancy in Network Traffic: Findings and Implications. In: SIGMETRICS (2009)
9. Deutsch, P.: DEFLATE Compressed Data Format Specification version 1.3. RFC 1951 (1996)
10. Erman, J., Gerber, A., Hajiaghayi, M., Pei, D., Sen, S., Spatscheck, O.: To Cache or not to Cache: The 3G case. IEEE Internet Computing (2011)
11. Fielding, R., Gettys, J., Mogul, J., Masinter, H.F.L., Leach, P., Berners-Lee, T.: Hypertext Transfer Protocol - HTTP/1.1. RFC 2616 (1999)
12. Gember, A., Anand, A., Akella, A.: A Comparative Study of Handheld and Non-handheld Traffic in Campus Wi-Fi Networks. In: Spring, N., Riley, G.F. (eds.) PAM 2011. LNCS, vol. 6579, pp. 173–183. Springer, Heidelberg (2011)
13. Korn, D., MacDonald, J., Mogul, J., Vo, K.: The VCDIFF Generic Differencing and Compression Data Format. RFC 3284 (2002)
14. Lumezanu, C., Guo, K., Spring, N., Bhattacharjee, B.: The Effect of Packet Loss on Redundancy Elimination in Cellular Wireless Networks. In: IMC (2010)
15. Mogul, J., Douglis, F., Feldmann, A., Krishnamurthy, B.: Potential benefits of delta encoding and data compression for HTTP. In: SIGCOMM (1997)
16. Mogul, J., Krishnamurthy, B., Douglis, F., Feldmann, A., Goland, Y., van Hoff, A., Hellerstein, D.: Delta encoding in HTTP. RFC 3229 (2002)
17. Qian, F., Quah, K.S., Huang, J., Erman, J., Gerber, A., Mao, Z.M., Sen, S., Spatscheck, O.: Web Caching on Smartphones: Ideal vs. Reality. In: Mobisys (2012)
18. Sanadhya, S., Sivakumar, R., Kim, K.H., Congdon, P., Lakshmanan, S., Singh, J.P.: Asymmetric Caching: Improved Network Deduplication for Mobile Devices. In: Mobicom (2012)
19. Spring, N.T., Wetherall, D.: A Protocol-Independent Technique for Eliminating Redundant Network Traffic. In: SIGCOMM (2000)
20. Zohar, E., Cidon, I., Mokryn, O.O.: The Power of Prediction: Cloud Bandwidth and Cost Reduction. In: SIGCOMM (2011)

Modeling Cellular User Mobility Using a Leap Graph

Wei Dong[1], Nick Duffield[2], Zihui Ge[2], Seungjoon Lee[2], and Jeffrey Pang[2]

[1] The University of Texas at Austin
[2] AT&T Labs – Research

Abstract. User mobility prediction can enable a mobile service provider to optimize the use of its network resources, e.g., through coordinated selection of base stations and intelligent content prefetching. In this paper, we study how to perform mobility prediction by leveraging the base station level location information readily available to a service provider. However, identifying real movements from *handovers* between base stations is non-trivial, because they can occur without actual user movement (e.g., due to signal fluctuation). To address this challenge, we introduce the *leap graph*, where an edge (or a *leap*) corresponds to actual user mobility. We present the properties of leap based mobility and demonstrate how it yields a mobility trace more suitable for mobility prediction. We evaluate mobility prediction on the leap graph using a Markov model based approach. We show that prediction using model can substantially improve the performance of content prefetching and base station selection during handover.

1 Introduction

Mobile network providers have a strong desire to optimize network resources due to the scarcity of radio frequency spectrum and the rapidly increasing bandwidth demands of mobile users. The ability to predict short-term user mobility can be useful in optimizing these resources. For example, at the network layer, accurate prediction can inform the choice of basestation(s) used to communicate with a mobile device. At the application level, different delivery strategies in the network based on expected movement (e.g., prefetching) could improve both the user experience and network efficiency.

A recent body of work has examined user mobility prediction from data collected on user devices, e.g., by using GPS or Wi-Fi associations readings [10,15,16,19]. However, the spatial information most relevant from a provider's perspective would be the cellular basestations that mobile devices associate with. This data is readily and ubiquitously available to mobile operators without requiring additional instrumentation of devices, and does not pose the coverage, energy-consumption, and privacy concerns of GPS and Wi-Fi association based techniques. Thus, this paper takes a novel provider-centric approach: we study how to perform mobility prediction by using the base station-level location information readily available to a cellular service provider. This data reports the *active set* of basestations with which a given mobile device is currently associated, and, in particular, a data record is generated for each *soft handover* event that changes a user's active set.

Despite the advantages of handover traces, there are a number of challenges that make it non-trivial to use handover data directly as a mobility trace. First, while it seems natural to use the active set to define a user's location, fine granularity of the coverage intersections is unachievable or unreliable due to the dynamic nature of radio environment. Using the active set to define location can also suffer from the state-explosion

M. Roughan and R. Chang (Eds.) PAM 2013, LNCS 7799, pp. 53–62, 2013.
© Springer-Verlag Berlin Heidelberg 2013

problem, since a mobile device may see any combination of tens of sectors in densely covered regions. Secondly, not all handovers happen due to user mobility. Other causes include radio signal and workload fluctuations. In these cases, it is not obvious how to distinguish fluctuations from real user mobility.

To address these challenges, we introduce a *leap graph*, where an edge (or a *leap*) between two sectors denotes that moving from one sector to the other requires actual user mobility. A leap consists of two or more sector-level transitions. We use a data driven approach to identify sectors that overlap, and find leaps in the handover data between non-overlapping sectors. We then design procedures to effectively leverage the transitions that are not leaps and fully extract the leap information. The resulting leap graph differs significantly from the direct handover graph in terms of the number of state changes and degree. It effectively reduces fluctuations, yielding a mobility trace more suitable for mobility prediction. We study mobility prediction on the leap graph using a Markov-based approach. We also show the performance of our mobility prediction in two example applications: prefetching and handover optimization. Using a month of handover data from a cellular service provider, we show that our approach can improve content prefetching hit-rate to 84%, compared with 40% for a popularity-based approach. We also show that our approach can potentially reduce the number of handovers by 38% on average.

The rest of the paper is organized as follows: Section 2 introduces background on cellular handovers and discusses the challenges of using handover data for mobility prediction in detail; Section 3 describes our approach to extract the leap based mobility; in Section 4 we study properties of leap traces and evaluate leap based mobility prediction; we study prediction performance in real applications in Section 5; we review related works in Section 6 and conclude in Section 7.

2   Background and Challenges

2.1   Soft Handover and Active set

To maintain a data connection in a UMTS cellular network, each mobile device connects to several cell sectors when it is actively sending or receiving. A cell sector is defined by an antenna on the base station and the frequency that it transmits in. There are typically 1–3 sectors pointing in each of three directions on each macrocell base station. The set of sectors to which a mobile device is connected is called the *active set*. The size of active set typically varies from 1 to 4 sectors depending on the quality of the radio channel and the load on the base stations. In a UMTS network, any or all of these cell sectors may transmit to the device at once, depending on the radio technology used. Most modern devices use HSPA technology and only receive data from a single *serving sector* in the active set at a time although this serving sector can change very quickly.

The process of adding or removing sectors from the active set is called *soft handover* and is controlled by the radio network. A sector is added if its signal strength is greater than a threshold and the sector has not already admitted the maximum number of connections, while a sector is removed if its signal strength falls below another threshold [17]. Hence, the active set typically contains the sectors with the highest signal strength with respect to the mobile device. Since signal strength falls off with the square of the distance from the antenna, the active set cells are usually close to the mobile device in geographic space as well. We leverage this fact to use soft handover traces to predict a device's mobility.

```
17:46:59.296  S1 S2        13:22:32.012  U0        Trace 1  13:22:32.012  U0
17:46:59.976  S2           13:22:47.795  U1                 13:22:56.088  U2
17:47:00.936  S1 S2        13:22:56.088  U2                 13:24:56.118  U3
17:59:41.395  S3 S2        13:23:57.005  U1
17:59:43.195  S2           13:24:56.118  U3        Trace 2  13:22:47.795  U1
17:59:43.875  S3 S2        13:24:59.625  U4                 13:24:59.625  U4
17:59:46.995  S2           13:25:38.340  U5                 13:36:38.473  U7
17:59:48.355  S3 S2        13:25:38.775  U6
18:00:35.194  S4 S5        13:25:40.593  U3        Trace 3  13:23:57.005  U1
18:04:09.481  S6           13:36:38.473  U7                 13:24:59.625  U4
                                                            13:36:38.473  U7
```

Fig. 1. Example records of timestamp and active set for a stationary device

Fig. 2. Example raw trace. Each pair of adjacent sectors overlap. In addition, U3, U4, U5, and U6 mutually overlap.

Fig. 3. 3-hop leap traces for Figure 2

2.2 Challenges

As described in Section 1, modeling user mobility through handover traces offers many advantages. Yet there are several rather unique challenges with this approach. The first challenge is on how to define users' location. Different cell sectors have overlapping coverage areas, and a mobile user is located within the intersect of the coverage areas of all the sectors in the active set. It seems natural to use the active set to define the user's location as it may offer high precision. However, it turns out that the radio environment dynamics and sectors' workload variability can lead to significant fluctuation in the active set, making the fine granularity of the coverage intersects unachievable or unreliable. In addition, the combinatorial nature of the active set can potentially create a state-explosion problem in densely covered regions where tens of sectors are visible to a mobile device. Another approach is that we cluster/partition the geo-space into regions and take the union of sectors in the region to define the location. However, we lose the precision with this approach. In this work, we choose to use the serving cell in the active set as the representative for location as we find it achieving a good balance between precision and accuracy.

Another major challenge of examining the handover trace is to identify real user mobility from handovers due to radio signal fluctuations. To understand this aspect, we performed a controlled experiment where a stationary phone owned by a cellular provider is set up to transmit data packets periodically. We obtained the handover logs shown in Figure 1. We observe that handovers occur even when a user is stationary. We also see a diverse set of sectors in the active sets. While we present more details later in Section 4.2, it is clear that these handovers are inherently different from the ones induced by user movement and hence present noise for mobility modeling. Signal strength triangulation does not help in identifying which handover is due to real user movements as signal strength at a single location can vary a lot [14].

Before describing our solution, we examine the limitations of two heuristics:

Loop Detection and Elimination: Stationary users are much more likely to alternate among a small set of sectors than mobile users. Hence, one simple approach to eliminate non-mobility handovers would be to remove trace segments between repeated occurrences of the same serving sector. However, not all stationary traces manifest a loop, and thus this approach does not eliminate superfluous handovers. Moreover it is possible that a users comes back to the same location after making real movements in a short period of time, in which case the real movements will be discarded.

Low-Pass Filter: Low-pass smoothing is a principled approach to suppress membership fluctuations in the active set among near-by sectors. For example, we can pass the the sectors in each consecutive active set through a queue. If a sector is already in queue, we move it to the tail of queue. When the queue is full, we evict the oldest member and produce a "smoothed" trace using the eviction sequence. However, the number of sectors visible to a user varies, making it difficult to determine a single fixed queue size. When we apply this approach to real traces with a fixed queue size, we find that it admits superfluous handovers as mobility-induced and misses true user movement.

3   Mobility and Leaps

Individual changes in the active set do not in themselves indicate whether a handover was due to user mobility. Thus in trying to infer mobility from the handovers, we try to eliminate handovers involving changes whose interpretation is ambiguous, and focus instead on minimal groups of successive handovers which together likely indicate mobility. The boundaries of these groups will be termed a *leap*, and a set of successive adjacent leaps together constitute a *leap trace*. These are constructed in a two step procedure.

Step One: Identifying Overlapping Sectors
Informally, two sectors overlap if a handover can take place between them. Although overlap could in principle be inferred from auxiliary sector configuration data (such as sector antenna locations, directions and powers), this would be a complex task in general. Instead we designate two sectors s_i and s_j as overlapping (written $s_i \sim s_j$) if at least one of the following two criteria holds: (i) Configurational: s_i and s_j are based at the same cell tower; (ii) Empirical: s_i and s_j appear within an active set reported in the handover trace during a specified time period (3 weeks in our evaluation). We considered alternate ways of determining overlap (e.g., considering serving sector transitions), and they yielded marginal performance differences and thus are not discussed further.

Step Two: Creating Leap Traces
We partition the handover trace by user, then further extract the sequence of serving sectors reported for each such user. We call each such sequence a *raw trace*. A *segment* is a maximal ordered subset of a raw trace in which the time between handovers does not exceed a specified timeout value. A *leap* is a pair $s_i s_j$, $i < j$ of sectors within a segment such that $s_i \not\sim s_j$ but $s_i \sim s_k \, \forall i < k < j$. A *leap trace* on a segment $\{s_1, s_2, \ldots, s_m\}$ is a maximal set of some number ℓ of adjacent leaps $s_{i(1)} s_{i(2)}, s_{i(2)} s_{i(3)}, \ldots, s_{i(\ell)} s_{i(\ell+1)}$. A first leap trace constructed by finding a leap with initial node $s_{i(1)} = s_1$ and then using that leap's final node as the initial node for the next leap, and so on until reaching the end of raw segment. As many as $m - 2$ further leap traces may be constructed from the segment by the same procedure, taking each s_k, $k = 2, \ldots, m-1$, as the initial node $s_{i(1)}$ of the initial leap. But in order to avoid double counting of leaps, we stipulate that if a leap trace starts to repeat leap segments already identified in trace from a previous starting sector, we ignore the remaining trace after including at most some number n of further leaps. The n is determined by the mobility modeling requirement. For example, $n = 1$ for first order Markov model and $n = 2$ for second order Markov model.

To illustrate, we show an example raw trace in Figure 2, where all adjacent sectors overlap (e.g., U0~U1, U1~U2, etc.). In addition, U3, U4, U5, and U6 overlap with each other. Starting from U0, we can get Trace 1 in Figure 3. There can be multiple leap traces from the same raw trace. For example, starting from U1, we can get Trace 2 in Figure 3. In fact, the number of different leap traces can be exponentially large to the length of raw trace. Moreover, leap traces from different starting sectors may become identical after a few leaps since they are derived from the same raw trace. In this case we only keep the useful information and discard the repeated part as described above.

The leap trace ignores handovers due to signal fluctuations or user movements in small areas, while focusing on longer trips. This is sufficient for our target applications because we focus on improving handovers or prefetching in larger areas. We study application specific performance in section 4.

4   Properties of Leap Traces and Leap-Based Mobility Prediction

4.1   Data Set

We use anonymized event logs collected from several RNCs (Radio Network Controllers) in a major U.S. cellular operator in December 2011. These RNCs control a significant fraction of the base stations in a large U.S. city. The logs record soft handover events, i.e., additions and removals from each device's active set. Each log entry has a timestamp, and devices are anonymously identified by an irreversible hash of the device's IMSI, which is unique per SIM card. All device and subscriber identifiers are anonymized to protect privacy without affecting the usefulness of our analysis. Furthermore, the data set does not permit reversing the anonymization or re-identification of subscribers. We use the data of the whole month (the first 3 weeks are considered known and used for training, the last week is considered unknown for testing purpose) and include all users from the trace. The logs recorded 67 million soft handover events for 413K users distributed over 5K sectors. The logs are generated only for active devices transmitting data, but not for idle devices. In our evaluation, if two subsequent soft handover records for a given device is apart by more than 30 minutes, we assume that the device has been idle, and start a new mobility segment using the latter record.

Our data set contains proprietary information and cannot be made public.

4.2   Characteristics of Leap Traces

We extract the leap traces from the above data set. In this subsection, we present a high-level characterization of the aggregate leap traces.

We first compare the length of raw trace segments and leap segments. Figure 4(a) plots their CDF. We can see that leap segments are much shorter than raw segments. Specifically, over 80% of the raw segments generate no leap at all, indicating limited or no user mobility. In contrast, around 20% of raw segments contain only 1 active set report. This result illustrates that many soft handovers in raw traces either do not involve serving sector transition or the transition happens between close-by sectors and are likely not due to user mobility. This highlights the importance of our approach in separating the different causes for handovers. In Figure 4(b), we compare the inter-leap time and inter-handover time. We observe that the inter-leap time is much longer than inter-handover time. Specifically, the median of inter-leap time is 636 seconds, while for inter-handover time the number is 2.8 seconds.

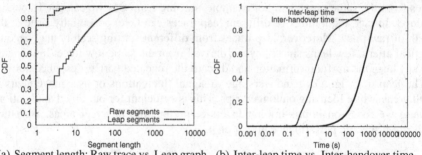

(a) Segment length: Raw trace vs. Leap graph   (b) Inter-leap time vs. Inter-handover time

Fig. 4. Segment Characteristics

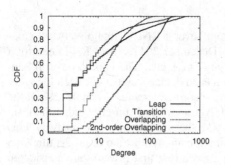

Fig. 5. Degree distribution comparison

Fig. 6. Prediction accuracy. S and T denotes second- and third- order Markov models, respectively.

We define the **leap graph** as the graph of sectors in which the edges represent the presence of a leap transition in any of the leap traces. Similarly, we also consider graphs obtained from serving sector changes, from overlapping sets, and from second-order overlapping sets[1]. In Figure 5, we compare their degree distributions. We first observe that the size of overlapping set can be quite large (e.g., more than 20 for around 30% of cases), while the second-order overlapping set is even larger. Compared to the second-order overlapping set, the degree of leap graph is significantly low (e.g., 10 or less for more than 60% of cases). For many sectors, it is even smaller than the number of serving sectors they can transition to (marked as "Transition"), which suggests that people follow similar patterns (e.g., along a highway) and only move out of a region with very limited choices of ways. While fewer choices can make the mobility prediction using the leap graph easier, we also observe in the tail part that the leap degrees may approach the size of second-order overlapping, indicating that areas with dense cellular coverage tend to have more mesh-like transportation paths (e.g., downtown areas) – posing a challenge for mobility prediction. A very small fraction of sectors have larger leap degree than the degree of second-order overlapping, that is because a leap may happen between two sectors more than two hops away, *e.g.*, when a user stops using his phone for a short period of time while he is still moving.

---

[1] u is in the second-order overlapping set of s if s and u are not overlapping, and there exists t that overlaps with s and u.

4.3 Mobility Prediction on Leap Graph

In this subsection we study mobility prediction on the leap based graph. We adopt Markov-based approaches for prediction, as it has been proven effective in the literature [12, 19]. We consider two variants: second-order Markov model using one leap as a state and third-order Markov model using two consecutive leaps as a state. Using a higher-order model allows us to make predictions based on not only the user's current location but also the recent path trajectory. We further consider a variant where we assume the knowledge of the destination of a segment, to understand how such additional information can help with mobility prediction. This is motivated by the observation that many people have highly predictable daily routine and that the destination may be projected simply based on the time of day [8, 9]. In the data trace, we estimate the probability of state s being the next state as $P(s|d, o)$ where d is the destination (the last sector in trace segment) and o is the current state.

We train our prediction models with the first 3 weeks' data and evaluate them with the leap segments extracted from the last week's data. Given the current state o, we predict m next sectors using the m highest-probability leaps, while we vary m from 1 to 3. We evaluate how often we can correctly predict the next leap. We adopt two accuracy measures: (1) the predicted sector exactly matches the actual sector in the testing data, and (2) the predicted sector is in the overlapping set of the actual sector. We also count how often we cannot make a prediction and report the result. To form a base for comparison, we also employ a naive scheme (denoted by "Popular"), where among all possible next leaps, we pick m leaps with the most transitions.

In Figure 6, we compare the prediction accuracy of the popularity based approach, second- and third-order Markov models (with and without destination information). We select $m=2$ and report both accuracy measures. In the figure, the accuracy of predicting any one among the overlapping set is significantly higher than predicting the exact match, which is well expected. We make three observations. First, the Markov models significantly outperform the simple popularity-based approach. Specifically, when using the overlapping set of the actual sector, the accuracy of the popularity-based approach is 68%, while the accuracy of Markov models is 80% or higher. Second, the knowledge of destination information can further improve the prediction accuracy of the exact sector (e.g., from 33% to 46% in second-order Markov model) but helps little when we use the overlapping set of the predicted sector to measure accuracy. Finally we observe that the accuracy gain from using longer history in the third-order Markov models is marginal. On the other hand, the probability of being able to predict a sector is lowest with the third-order Markov model with destination information (62%). This is because training data is often unavailable for consecutive leap transitions with a particular destination. In contrast, the popularity based approach, due to its simplicity, can make a prediction for 99.5% of the cases, and the second-order Markov model without destination information can make a prediction for 98.4% of the cases. In practice, we can start with as much information as possible and fall back to less demanding settings if needed [16].

5 Applications

There are many potential applications of future sector prediction. In this section we focus on two example applications, namely prefetching and handover optimization, and quantify the application specific performance of our prediction schemes.

5.1 Prefetching

In this application scenario, we prefetch user requested content to a predicted future cell tower, such that the user can retrieve the content upon entering the range of the cell tower. The content a user is going to request is often predictable [5, 18]. Users can also request for prefetching since it saves time for them.

Once a prefetching request is made, a prediction is made based on the user's current mobility history. One complication here is that at a given sector in a raw trace, there could be multiple different leap traces leading to it as well as multiple different leap traces "leaping over" it, e.g., depending on which sector we start with in the raw trace. We lose information by considering only leap trace and ignoring the rest. In this paper we combine the predictions made with these different leap traces using the following simple heuristic (assuming second order Markov model).

We extract all possible leap traces and from them we get the different ending leaps. Let $L_{ij} = (s_i, s_j)$ be one of the ending leaps, where s_i and s_j are sectors. Let $P(S|L_{ij})$ be the probability vector predicted using L_{ij}, where S is a vector of potential future sectors. The final prediction is then computed as $P(S) = << P(S|L_{ij}) >_i >_j$ ($<>_i$ means taking average over all i).

For prefetching, the criteria for a good prediction is that the cell tower of the predicted sector become within reach later. In our evaluation we consider a prediction correct if the sectors on the predicted cell tower appears in the active set in the future.

Due to space limit, we only present herein the result using second order Markov model without assuming destination knowledge. We make a prediction in the middle of the segment, and we choose the segments that have more than 3 leaps after the prediction is made to ensure that the user remains active after our prediction point. Then we prefetch the content to the cell tower of the top m predicted sectors. We vary m from 1 to 3. We run 10k tests and record how many times the prefetched content become available to the user after the prediction. We find that we can make a prediction for 99.6% of the times, which is slightly higher than the leap-based case (98.4%) because we effectively combine the predictions of different ending leaps. Out of the predictions we make, the accuracy is 84.7% when $m = 1$, suggesting 84.7% of the times the prefetched content becomes available to the user. Increasing m to two and three increase the number to 91.3% and 94.4%, respectively. We also find that 97% of the time the content becomes available within an hour. In comparison, prefetching to the cell tower at the most popular leap achieves lower than 40% accuracy.

5.2 Handover Optimization

Next we use future sector prediction to optimize handovers. The idea is based on the predicted leap, we can suggest which sector to hand over to, such that we reduce the total number of handovers. Detailed simulation of handovers is not trivial, as it requires a detailed modeling of signal strength variations, traffic load, load changes, etc. In this paper we only consider an idealized scenario to demonstrate the potential gain we can achieve. Specifically, after each leap we make a prediction of the next leap. Based on the prediction we first rank the sectors in the active set by giving preference to sectors that overlap with the predicted sector. Then we break ties using physical distance to the predicted sector (the closer the better). We use the highest ranked sector as the suggested handover target. To evaluate how many handovers we can potentially save, we count how many consecutive future handovers in the real trace have the suggested sector in the active set before the next leap actually happens, as these handovers can potentially be replaced by one handover to the suggested sector. In our evaluation we only consider the traces that have at least 2 leaps. We predict the second leap based on the first one using second-order Markov model without assuming destination information. We run the test for 10k times and we find that less than 0.1% of the times the suggested sector does not appear in future handovers, which means the prediction is wrong and may cause extra handovers; 59% of the times we can save at least one handover by using the suggested sector, and 32% of the times we can save three or more. On average, our handover optimization reduces the handover count by 38%.

6   Related Work

Despite the plethora of work in mobility modeling, we believe that this is the first work to address the unique challenges of mobility prediction using cellular handover traces and to present an approach that works well on real data. We survey a key selection of prior work here.

An important body of work focused on predicting locations as defined by Wi-Fi associations [10, 15, 16, 19]. Much of this work focused on evaluating the effectiveness of well known location predictors such as Markov-models [19], compression-based predictors [16], and CDF predictors [15]. Others have focused more on modeling [10]. In contrast to cellular handover traces, which include many handovers that occur when a user is stationary, changes in Wi-Fi associations represent real movement in most cases. Thus, our work is unique in addressing the inherent challenge of ambiguity in predicting future cell sectors in cellular traces. Nonetheless, we build upon the same principled predictors, such as Markov-models.

There have been previous proposals on location prediction in cellular networks [1, 3, 4, 11, 13]. However, they either make unrealistic assumptions (e.g., that basestations are mobile [13] or a prefect sector structure [4]), require information that is not typically available to a cellular operator (e.g., reports of device location and velocity [1, 11]), or are designed for different purposes (e.g., to limit cell updates [3] and paging [6]). As a result, all of these approaches have only been evaluated on synthetic data. Our approach is the first to be evaluated on real cellular handover traces.

Finally, there have been studies on the predictability of wireless attributes, such as cellular connectivity [7], Wi-Fi connectivity [12], and commute routes [2]. The predictors for them use similar data to our work, but are orthogonal in design and purpose.

7   Conclusion

In this paper we introduced a novel leap based approach to extract user mobilities from soft handover data, which is readily available but also contains significant fluctuations even for a stationary device due to signal strength change or load balancing. Our study showed that our approach can effectively reduce fluctuations in the raw handover data while maintaining real user mobility pattern. In our experiments, we demonstrated significant gain in prediction accuracy using our leap based approach, and performance improvement in two example applications that we considered. While our approach is provider-centric, a service provider can potentially make location prediction for a user available to selected applications on the user's device, so that the applications can provide a better service to the user. In the future, we plan to apply our approach to real world location based services to find further application specific optimizations and see its benefit in real systems.

References

1. Akyildiz, I.F., Wang, W.: The predictive user mobility profile framework for wireless multimedia networks. IEEE/ACM Trans. Netw. 12(6), 1021–1035 (2004)
2. Becker, R.A., Caceres, R., Hanson, K., Loh, J.M., Urbanek, S., Varshavsky, A., Volinsky, C.: Route classification using cellular handoff patterns. In: UbiComp 2011, pp. 123–132. ACM, New York (2011)
3. Bhattacharya, A., Das, S.K.: Lezi-update: an information-theoretic approach to track mobile users in pcs networks. In: MobiCom 1999, pp. 1–12. ACM, New York (1999)
4. Chellappa, R., Jennings, A., Shenoy, N.: The sectorized mobility prediction algorithm for wireless networks. In: In Proc. ICT (2003)
5. Chen, X., Zhang, X.: A popularity-based prediction model for web prefetching. Computer 36(3), 63–70 (2003)
6. Das, S., Das, S.K., Sen, S.K.: Adaptive location prediction strategies based on a hierarchical network model in cellular mobile environment. The Computer Journal 42, 473–486 (1996)
7. Deshpande, P., Kashyap, A., Sung, C., Das, S.R.: Predictive methods for improved vehicular wifi access. In: MobiSys 2009, pp. 263–276. ACM, New York (2009)
8. Gonzalez, M.C., Hidalgo, C.A., Barabasi, A.-L.: Understanding individual human mobility patterns. Nature 453(7196), 779–782 (2008)
9. Isaacman, S., Becker, R.A., Cceres, R., Kobourov, S.G., Rowland, J., Varshavsky, A.: A tale of two cities. In: HOTMOBILE 2010, pp. 19–24 (2010)
10. Kim, M., Kotz, D.: Extracting a mobility model from real user traces. In: Proceedings of IEEE INFOCOM (2006)
11. Liang, B., Haas, Z.J.: Predictive distance-based mobility management for multidimensional pcs networks. IEEE/ACM Trans. Netw. 11(5), 718–732 (2003)
12. Nicholson, A.J., Noble, B.D.: Breadcrumbs: forecasting mobile connectivity. In: MobiCom 2008, pp. 46–57. ACM, New York (2008)
13. Pathirana, P.N., Savkin, A.V., Jha, S.: Mobility modelling and trajectory prediction for cellular networks with mobile base stations. In: MobiHoc 2003, pp. 213–221. ACM, New York (2003)
14. Schulman, A., Navda, V., Ramjee, R., Spring, N., Deshpande, P., Grunewald, C., Jain, K., Padmanabhan, V.N.: Bartendr: a practical approach to energy-aware cellular data scheduling. In: MobiCom 2010, pp. 85–96. ACM, New York (2010)
15. Song, L., Deshpande, U., Kozat, U.C., Kotz, D., Jain, R.: Predictability of wlan mobility and its effects on bandwidth provisioning. In: INFOCOM. IEEE (2006)
16. Song, L., Kotz, D., Jain, R., He, X.: Evaluating location predictors with extensive wi-fi mobility data. In: Proceedings of INFOCOM, pp. 1414–1424 (2004)
17. Su, S.-F.: The UMTS Air-Interface in RF Engineering. McGraw-Hill (2007)
18. Su, Z., Yang, Q., Zhang, H.-J.: A prediction system for multimedia pre-fetching in internet. In: MULTIMEDIA 2000, pp. 3–11. ACM, New York (2000)
19. Yoon, J., Noble, B.D., Liu, M.: Building realistic mobility models from coarse-grained traces. In: In Proc. MobiSys, pp. 936–5983. ACM Press (2006)

Understanding Mobile App Usage Patterns Using In-App Advertisements

Alok Tongaonkar[1], Shuaifu Dai[2,3], Antonio Nucci[1], and Dawn Song[3]

[1] Narus Inc, USA
[2] Peking University, China
[3] University of California, Berkeley, USA
{alok,anucci}@narus.com, daishuaifu@pku.edu.cn, dawnsong@cs.berkeley.edu

Abstract. Recent years have seen an explosive growth in the number of mobile devices such as smart phones and tablets. This has resulted in a growing need of the operators to understand the usage patterns of the mobile apps used on these devices. Previous studies in this area have relied on volunteers using instrumented devices or using fields in the HTTP traffic such as `User-Agent` to identify the apps in network traces. However, the results of the former approach are difficult to be extrapolated to real-world scenario while the latter approach is not applicable to platforms like Android where developers generally use generic strings, that can not be used to identify the apps, in the `User-Agent` field. In this paper, we present a novel way of identifying Android apps in network traces using mobile in-app advertisements. Our preliminary experiments with real world traces show that this technique is promising for large scale mobile app usage pattern studies. We also present an analysis of the official Android market place from an advertising perspective.

1 Introduction

In recent years, there have been dramatic changes to the way users behave, interact and utilize the network. More and more users are accessing the internet via mobile devices like smart phones and tablets. According to recent statistics by Canalys [1], 488 million smart phones have been sold in the year 2011, compared to 415 million personal computers. Users of these devices typically download applications (commonly called mobile apps) that provide specific functionality. A majority of these apps access the internet. For example, 84% of the 55K Android apps in the official Android app market [2] that we randomly picked, required permission for Internet access. This has led to a burgeoning interest amongst network operators in understanding the mobile app usage patterns in their networks.

Recent years have seen an increasing number of research works that analyze network traffic to understand usage behaviors of mobile apps ([3,4]). However, these papers rely on techniques for app identification which are not applicable for Android apps or rely on having access to the Android devices and monitoring the specific devices. For example, Xu et al [3] and Maier et al [5] use `User-Agent`

M. Roughan and R. Chang (Eds.) PAM 2013, LNCS 7799, pp. 63–72, 2013.
© Springer-Verlag Berlin Heidelberg 2013

field in the HTTP header to identify the app. Apple has a guideline for iOS which requires that this field contain app identifier. However, this guideline is not strictly enforced. For Android apps the situation is even worse since developers generally put some generic string (not unique to the app but identifying the Android version and such) in this field. On the other hand the approach taken of making some users use apps on specific devices to collect network trace and profile app usage does not give real-world data ([4,6]). Moreover, manual execution of apps suffers from the problems of scalability. The approach of using Host field in the HTTP header for identifying the apps does not work all the time because the same host may serve multiple apps. This is typically true when the same app developer such as Zynga publishes multiple apps. Also many platforms, such as Facebook mobile app development platform support apps from different developers. The apps which are developed on these platforms typically use the servers from the platform provider to provide their service. For instance, m.facebook.com hosts diverse apps such as *Pirates Mobile*, a gaming app, and *Squats*, a personal training app.

In this paper, we present a new technique of identifying app usage patterns based on the advertising traffic originating from the apps. This technique is based on the observation that mobile apps may communicate with many different servers for different purposes. A typical Android app may contact the web site of the app provider to obtain the API information, connect to a cloud service like Amazon EC2 for downloading some files, contact sites such as doubleclick.com and mobclix.com to retrieve ads, and provide usage stats to sites such as googleanalytics.com. We can classify network traffic from an app into three main categories similar to the classification used by Wei et al [6] as follows: (i) Origin: traffic that comes from the servers owned by the app provider (e.g. pandora.com for *Pandora*). (ii) Content Distribution Network (CDN)+Cloud: traffic that comes from servers of CDNs (e.g., Akamai) and cloud providers (e.g. Amazon AWS). (iii) Third-party: traffic from various advertising services (e.g., AdMob) and analytical services (e.g., Omniture).

Previous studies of mobile app usage have focused on either origin traffic ([3]) or CDN+cloud traffic ([7]). We present a different approach by studying usage behavior of mobile apps based on advertising traffic. Advertising is a critical component of the mobile app ecosystems from a financial perspective. We believe that usage patterns studies based on advertisements will be very valuable in future. Many mobile apps use one or more advertising services as a source of revenue. To use these services, developers must register their apps with the advertising service provider. Developers bundle third-party, binary-only libraries (called ad libraries) from the advertising service providers into their apps. The information about the ad libraries being used by an app is usually present in the meta-data provided in the installable package of the apps. We can use this information to understand the distribution of advertisements in the apps.

Another interesting observation is that typically an advertising service provider identifies the app using the app name provided by the developer or unique app identifier generated by the service provider at the time of the registration.

These app names or identifiers are present in network flows to the advertising service providers. We can use these identifiers to study the patterns of mobile app usage from real world network traces.

Mobile in-app ad libraries have been studied before in the context of security and privacy [8,9,10] and energy consumption [11]. This is the first work to present a systematic study of usage patterns of mobile apps using ad flows. We believe that considering the critical role of advertisements on mobile app ecosystems, our research paves the way for new studies which can be very useful for a variety of players like network operators, advertising service providers, advertisers, and mobile app developers. We focus on understanding the app usage patterns on the Android platform in this work. However, the ideas and techniques presented here are equally applicable to iOS and Windows Mobile platforms.

The main contributions of this work are as below.

- We present a systematic study of advertising libraries on the Android platform.
- We present results of analyzing more than 50K Android apps from an advertising perspective.
- We present results from evaluating the network traces from a Tier 2 cellular service provider.

The rest of the paper is organized as follows. In Section 2 we present our analysis of advertisements in apps in the official Android market. In Section 3 we present mobile app usage behavior patterns from real world network traces. We discuss the limitations and future work in Section 4. Finally we present the conclusions in Section 5.

2   App Market Analysis

In this section we present an analysis of the official Android app market, Google Play Store, with respect to the different categories of apps. Note that our goal is not to do a comprehensive study of all apps in the store but give a flavor of the kinds of analysis possible with the advertising information.

2.1   Background

Google Play Store is the most popular Android app market with over 500K apps which includes both free and paid apps. Developers of many of the free apps rely on advertisements (ads) for generating revenue so we focus only on free apps in this paper. Android apps are distributed as special files, called Application Package File (APK), with .apk file extension. Along with the application binaries and resources, each APK file contains an AndroidManifest.xml file. The manifest file is an XML file that contains meta-data about the app such as the name of the app, permissions required, resources used, libraries used, etc.

Developers of free apps typically use third-party advertising service providers such Google Ads or Smaato to display ads in the app. Ad service providers may differ in the way that ads are provided to the app but they have some common characteristics. Most ad networks provide libraries for user-interface

```
<manifest ... package="net.zedge.android" ...>
    <uses-permission android:name="android.permission.INTERNET" />
    ... ...
    ... ...                                              Ad Library
    <activity android:name="com.google.ads.AdActivity" ../>
    <activity android:name="com.inmobi.androidsdk.IMBrowserActivity" .../>
    <activity android:name="com.mopub.mobileads.MoPubActivity" ... />
    ... ...
    ... ...                                       App Identifier for Ad Library
    <meta-data android:name="ADMOB_PUBLISHER_ID" android:value="a14d2b448c73a08" />
    <meta-data android:name="ADWHIRL_KEY" android:value=
    "523e4ae0705248b0b2b770a91d33d1c6" />
    ... ...
</manifest>
```

Fig. 1. Sample of Zedge Manifest File

code (to present their ads) and network code (to request ads from the ad networks servers). The libraries are designed to be tightly bundled with host apps to make it more difficult to disable the ad functionality or defraud the ad network. When a developer registers an app with an ad service provider, she may receive a developer identifier or app identifier. The SDK for the ad library contains instructions, on how to embed the ad library in the app, such as the permissions required by the ad library and the mechanism used by the ad service provider to identify the app or the developer. The ad service provider may use either app name or an identifier generated at registration time to identify the app or the developer.

To understand how ad libraries are used, consider *Zedge*, which is a very popular app (more than 1M downloads) that is used for downloading wallpapers and ringtones. We use a tool for reverse engineering third-party, closed, binary Android apps, called `apktool` [12], to extract the manifest file in the .apk file into a human readable form. Figure 1 shows the manifest file for *Zedge*. We can see that the manifest file lists three ad libraries that are embedded in *Zedge* - (i) Google Ads, (ii) InMobi, and (iii) MoPub. Many (but not all) of the ad service providers require the identifier to be mentioned explicitly in the manifest file. For instance, in Figure 1, the identifier of *Zedge* for Google Ads (a14d2b448c73a08) is provided in the meta-data field for AdMob (owned by Google). An interesting point to note is that even though AdWhirl is not explicitly mentioned in the activity list there is an identifier of *Zedge* (523e4ae0705248b0b2b770a91d33d1c6) for AdWhirl. The package name for *Zedge* is `net.zedge.android`. Users can search for an app in the Google Play Store using its package name. Google Play Store provides a lot of information regarding the app such as the developer name, the number of downloads, and the category of the app. We can make use of this information to perform in-depth analysis of the app market from an advertising point of view.

2.2 Dissecting Google Play Store

We downloaded 55K free apps from Google Play Store. These apps were chosen randomly to avoid any bias towards the most popular apps or any particular category of apps. 46K of the apps asked for the `android.permission.INTERNET`

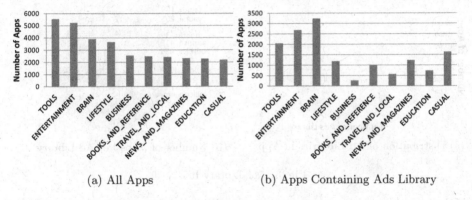

(a) All Apps   (b) Apps Containing Ads Library

Fig. 2. Top 10 Categories for Apps

which is needed by any app that needs to access the network. We obtained the category of each app by querying the Play Store. We identified 30 different categories to which the apps belonged. Our analysis showed that the top 10 categories accounted for ≈60% of the apps. Figure 2a shows the distribution of the apps in these top 10 categories.

We picked 30 popular ad libraries on Android platform [8] and generated rules for identifying these libraries from the manifest files. For 19K of these 46K apps we were able to identify the ad libraries that were being used. Figure 3a shows the number of ad libraries used by each app. We can see that a majority of the apps (≈15K) use only 1 ad library and less than 0.3% of the apps use more than 5 ad libraries. Figure 3b shows the most popular ad libraries in these apps. We can see that Google Ads is the most popular ad library as it is embedded in close to 12K apps, followed by Millennial Media (1.7K apps) and Mobclix (1.3K apps). The long tailed nature of the distribution suggests that, in practice, studying any data with respect to the top 50-100 ad libraries would result in high coverage in terms of apps.

We categorized the 19K apps which contained identifiable ad libraries. Figure 2b shows the distribution of the apps in the top 10 categories that we identified above. We see that of the 5.5K apps in the Tools category only 2K contained ads. On the other hand the percentage of Entertainment apps containing ads is much higher (2.6K out of 5.2K). Brain apps (related to puzzles and such) have the highest proportion of apps containing ads (3.2K out of 3.9K). The proportion of apps containing ads in other categories which have similar number of apps in our dataset such as Business, Books and Reference, Travel and Local, News and Magazines, Education, and Casual, shows a large variance. Such information is very useful for new developers looking to pick a category to develop apps in or for ad providers to target development community in any particular category. We can further drill down into the distribution of categories per ad library or popularity of different ads library in a given category. Figure 4a and Figure 5 show the distribution of apps in three of the most popular ad networks in our data set: Google Ads, Mobclix, and Millennial Media. We can see that Google Ads is quite evenly spread amongst various app categories while Millennial Media and

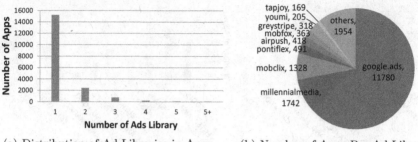

(a) Distribution of Ad Libraries in Apps   (b) Number of Apps Per Ad Library

Fig. 3. Ads Library Info

Mobclix ad libraries are very unevenly distributed amongst the categories. The top 2 categories for Mobclix are Entertainment and Casual, while for Millenial Media they are Brain and News and Magazines.

The popularity of an app is commonly measured in terms of the number of downloads of the app. Having the information about the ad libraries in an app allows us to obtain many different perspectives from the downloads data. For instance, for each ad network, we can determine the number of downloads for each app. Figure 4b shows the downloads data for apps containing Google Ads. We can see that the maximum download numbers are for 10K-50K downloads (3K of the 12K apps). We can plot similar graphs for other ad networks or even include app category dimension in these graphs. This information is useful to various entities such as network providers or developers looking to select an ad library.

3   Network Trace Analysis

In this section we present the analysis of real-world network traces from a Tier 2 cellular service provider. We collected the HTTP headers for all users in the network for a week (June 18-25, 2011). Here we present our analysis of the traces from two days in the week - one a weekday (June 21) and the other a weekend (Jun 24). We note that due to company non-disclosure agreements we can not release our dataset/tools. However, this paper contains sufficient details to perform similar analysis on any publicly available trace containing mobile data.

3.1   Methodology

We have developed a system for analyzing Android apps that installs and runs each Android app in a separate emulator running in a virtual machine [13]. Here we describe the parts of the system relevant for collecting ad flows. We can identify an ad flow from the Host field in the HTTP header field. We created a database of the host names used by different ad networks as follows. For each ad library we picked a few apps using the library. We used tcpdump to collect all the network traffic from the virtual machine. We ported the strace utility to Android to log each networking system call performed by the app. We identified all the threads started

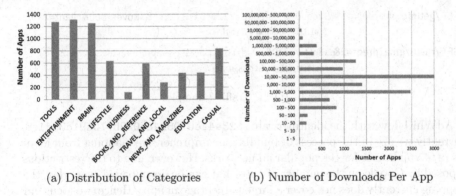

(a) Distribution of Categories   (b) Number of Downloads Per App

Fig. 4. Google Ads

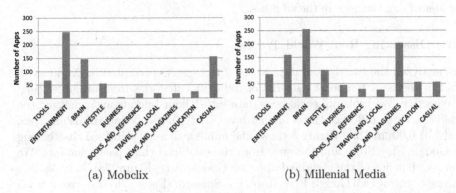

(a) Mobclix   (b) Millenial Media

Fig. 5. Distribution of Categories

by the app using the process id (pid) of the app. Based on this thread information, we can filter out the traffic that does not origin from the app. We extracted the host names for the ad library by manually inspecting these traces and identifying the host names that contain parts of the ad library name.

The main challenge in performing any meaningful analysis on real-world traces is to identify the app from the ad flow. As mentioned in Section 2.1, ad networks identify the app using either app name or an identifier that is unique to the app or the developer. It is easy to identify an app from an ad flow that uses app name to identify the app. All we need to know is the key name used in the query. We can do that by running a single app, that contains the given ad library, as explained above, and obtain the key name that is used for the identifier. For instance, for Google Ads flows, the app name is stored in the query parameter with the key msid. So we can just look for msid= for any flow to Google Ads and the value of the parameter will give the app name such as net.zedge.android. Figure 6b shows a Google Ads flow. We can see that the flow belongs to the app with the package name com.portugalemgrande.LiveClock. For the ad networks that use unique alphanumeric strings as identifier, the identifiers may be present in the manifest files. We can download all apps from any market, extract the manifest file, and generate a mapping of the identifier for each app for each ad library. Figure 6(a) shows

GET /getInfo.php?appid=523e4ae0705248b0b2b770a91d33d1c6&appver=300&client=2

(a) HTTP Traffic of AdWhirl

GET /mads/gma?preqs=2&...&u_w=320&msid=com.portugalemgrande.LiveClock&...

(b) HTTP Traffic of Google Ads

Fig. 6. HTTP Traffic Examples

an AdWhirl flow with the identifier value 523e4ae0705248b0b2b770a91d33d1c6. Currently we are in the process of building a comprehensive mapping from identifiers to app names for the popular ad networks. However, due to the restrictions imposed by Google on the number of apps that can be downloaded every day, the mapping currently does not cover a large percentage of apps. Hence, we focus our analysis on two popular ad networks (Google Ads and Smaato) that use app names for identifying the apps in the ad flows.

3.2   Dissecting Real World Traces

We analyzed the two days of data to see if the results presented by Xu et al [3] hold in terms of temporal patterns of different categories from an advertising perspective. We broke up each day's data into 1 hour buckets and analyzed the traffic at three different times of the day - (i) 6.00am-7.00am, (ii) 12pm-1pm, and (iii) 6.00pm-7pm. Figure 8 shows the number of apps identified that belong to Google Play Store and the ones from the unofficial third-party markets. We can see that out of the identified apps for Google Ads (Figure 7a), only 35-38% belong to the official Google Play Store. For Smaato, (Figure 7b), we have a much smaller number of identified apps, but the percentage of those apps belonging to Google Play Store is much higher (70-80%). What this seems to indicate is that Google Ads is a popular choice for many of the app developers for the unofficial third-party app markets.

Xu et al [3] had observed some interesting diurnal patterns in different app categories. For example, they report that the weather and news apps are used most frequently in the morning while sports apps peak in the early evening. Similarly, an ad network provider, or a network operator, or a developer is likely to find the patterns of usage of apps containing ads very insightful. Figure 8a shows the top 5 categories of apps present in the traffic at different times for Google Ads. We see that the app usage goes down at noon compared to early morning and early in the evening. This is true for both weekday and weekend. Another interesting observation is that the top 5 categories for apps using Google Ads remains same irrespective of the time of the day or the day of the week. What changes is the proportion of apps being used in one of these categories. For instance, maximum number of Arcade apps are used on a weekend evening. The top category differs for Smaato (Arcade) from Google Ads (Brain) but surprisingly it remains the same over time just as for Google Ads. Figure 8b shows the usage patterns for the same categories over 12 hours on 21st June for Google Ads. Again, we see the number of apps vary through the day but the mix of categories remains more or less same.

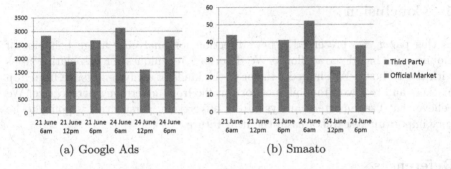

(a) Google Ads   (b) Smaato

Fig. 7. Apps Belonging to Official Market in Network Traffic

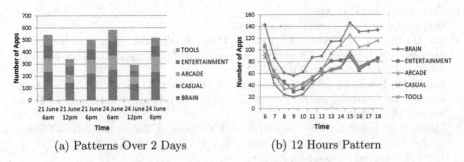

(a) Patterns Over 2 Days   (b) 12 Hours Pattern

Fig. 8. Apps Containing Google Ads in Network Traffic

4 Limitations and Future Work

Many of the free apps have corresponding paid apps that do not show any ad. These paid apps can not be identified using our ad flow based technique. However, we observe that many flows to third-party platforms like Facebook and analytical services such as Google Analytics also contain identifiers that can be used to identify the apps. We plan to extend our technique to include these flows in the future studies. However, we just like to point out that 73% of the apps in Google Play are free [10].

A limitation of this technique is that some of the ad networks require developer identifiers which can be shared by different apps from the same developer. We have observed that queries from many apps have certain unique patterns (such as certain key-value parameters in the URL query) that can be used to identify them [13]. In the future we plan to analyze patterns in the URL queries in ad flows to form fingerprints that can be used to correctly attribute the flow to the originating app.

Grace et al [8] have observed that many of the ad libraries require user's location for targeted advertising. We confirmed that many of the ad flows contained location information. In future, we plan to use this location information to identify spatial patterns in app usage. Moreover, if the traces contain information about users, then we can build app usage profiles for each user which can be used in applications such as targeted app recommendation.

5   Conclusion

In this paper, we presented a new direction for analyzing usage behavior of mobile apps based on ad flows. We described techniques for associating apps with the ad flows. We showed a flavor of the kinds of analysis possible from app markets and real world mobile network traffic from advertising perspective. We believe that usage pattern analysis from advertising perspective is going to be very important research area in the near future.

References

1. http://www.canalys.com/
2. https://play.google.com/store/apps/
3. Xu, Q., Erman, J., Gerber, A., Mao, Z., Pang, J., Venkataraman, S.: Identifying diverse usage behaviors of smartphone apps. In: Proceedings of the 11th Internet Measurement Conference, IMC (2011)
4. Falaki, H., Lymberopoulos, D., Mahajan, R., Kandula, S., Estrin, D.: A first look at traffic on smartphones. In: Proceedings of the 10th Internet Measurement Conference, IMC (2010)
5. Maier, G., Schneider, F., Feldmann, A.: A First Look at Mobile Hand-Held Device Traffic. In: Krishnamurthy, A., Plattner, B. (eds.) PAM 2010. LNCS, vol. 6032, pp. 161–170. Springer, Heidelberg (2010)
6. Wei, X., Gomez, L., Neamtiu, I., Faloutsos, M.: Profiledroid: Multi-layer profiling of android applications. In: Proceedings of the 18th Annual International Conference on Mobile Computing and Networking, MobiCom (2012)
7. Aioffi, W.M., Mateus, G.R., Almeida, J.M., Mendes, D.S.: Mobile dynamic content distribution networks. In: Proceedings of the 7th ACM International Symposium on Modeling, Analysis and Simulation of Wireless and Mobile Systems, MSWiM (2004)
8. Grace, M.C., Zhou, W., Jiang, X., Sadeghi, A.R.: Unsafe exposure analysis of mobile in-app advertisements. In: Proceedings of the 5th ACM Conference on Security and Privacy in Wireless and Mobile Networks, WISEC 2012 (2012)
9. Pearce, P., Felt, A.P., Nunez, G., Wagner, D.: Addroid: Privilege separation for applications and advertisers in android. In: Proceedings of the 7th ACM Symposium on Information, Computer and Communications Security, ASIACCS (2012)
10. Leontiadis, I., Efstratiou, C., Picone, M., Mascolo, C.: Don't kill my ads!: Balancing privacy in an ad-supported mobile application market. In: Proceedings of the 13th Workshop on Mobile Computing Systems and Applications, HotMobile (2012)
11. Vallina-Rodriguez, N., Shah, J., Finamore, A., Grunenberger, Y., Papagiannaki, K., Haddadi, H., Crowcroft, J.: Breaking for commercials: Characterizing mobile advertising. In: Proceedings of the 12th Internet Measurement Conference, IMC (2012)
12. http://code.google.com/p/android-apktool/
13. Dai, S., Tongaonkar, A., Wang, X., Nucci, A., Song, D.: Networkprofiler: Towards automatic fingerprinting of android apps. In: Proceedings of the 32nd IEEE International Conference on Computer Communications, INFOCOM (2013)

A Measurement of Mobile Traffic Offloading

Kensuke Fukuda[1] and Kenichi Nagami[2]

[1] National Institute of Informatics, Japan
[2] INTEC, Inc, Japan

Abstract. A promising way to use limited 3G mobile resources efficiently is 3G mobile traffic offloading through WiFi by the user side.
However, we currently do not know enough about how effective the mobile traffic offloading is in the wild. In this paper, we report the results
of a two-day-long user-based measurement of mobile traffic offloading by
over 400 android smartphone users in Japan. We first explain that the
variation of aggregated traffic volume via WiFi is much greater than that
via 3G in our dataset. Next, we show that the traffic volume offloading
through WiFi is common over whole weekend and weekday night, though
weekday rush hours have less chance of traffic offloading. Our results
emphasize that a small fraction of users contribute to a large fraction of
offload traffic volume. In fact, our per-user level analysis reveals that the
top 30% of users downloaded over 90% of their total traffic volume via
WiFi. However, bottom 20% of users stuck to 3G only and over 50% of
users turned off the WiFi interface in business hours. Also, 17.4% of the
total traffic volume was generated by users whose WiFi traffic volume was
less than 1MB. We observed that some hybrid users downloaded most of
their traffic volume via WiFi in shorter durations. In this sense, there is
more room to improve the current traffic offloading by promoting users
to use WiFi more effectively. Furthermore, we demonstrate that WiFi
offloading is mainly performed by access points (APs) in homes while
the use of public WiFi APs is still uncommon in our dataset.

1 Introduction

Smartphones, intelligent mobile phones, are becoming ever more popular around
the world. The Ministry of Internal Affairs and Communications of Japan reports that 3G mobile network traffic is now doubling every six months in Japan
[13]. This rapid increase in the mobile 3G traffic is a big problem for 3G carriers,
because the frequency and bandwidth of the 3G network are limited resources
that largely differ from residential FTTH access lines. In addition to the increasing number of users, another reason for this growth is that the monthly fee for
a mobile phone is basically a flat-rate. Some 3G carriers have started to force
bandwidth capping to heavy-hitters on the basis of their traffic. Furthermore,
the 3G carriers promote migration of 3G mobile traffic to high-capacity and less
congested fixed networks. For this reason, the offloading of 3G traffic through
WiFi (IEEE 802.11{a,b,g,n}) has been attracting more attentions. There are
two main usage scenarios of traffic offloading by WiFi. One is to use public
WiFi access points (APs) provided by 3G carriers or other WiFi providers in

M. Roughan and R. Chang (Eds.) PAM 2013, LNCS 7799, pp. 73–82, 2013.

downtown areas (e.g, cafes, stations, airports) to avoid congestion at 3G base stations. The total number of such public APs provided by 3G carriers is estimated to be over 300,000 APs in Japan according to their web pages. The other is APs in homes where the high-speed network has been rapidly deployed. In particular, increasing penetration of the fiber access in residential users (over 40%) is reported in Japan [3]. Some 3G carriers started to provide customized WiFi APs to non-professional users so they can easily use WiFi at home. The deployment of WiFi APs in homes accounts for roughly 65% of the total number of residential broadband users.

However, it becomes more and more difficult to understand the behavior of such mobile traffic by traffic offloading, because 3G carriers cannot track such offloaded traffic at their backbone network. Even ISPs providing FTTH services cannot distinguish traffic volume generated by smartphones and others in homes. Thus, in this paper, we intend to characterize the usage of the 3G and WiFi of smartphones in terms of the traffic offloading. We developed special software for android smartphones to measure its usage and collected two day's worth of traffic data from over 400 smartphone monitor users using the measurement software in Japan. The main findings of our measurements are as follows: (1) The traffic offloading in homes is common in our dataset. The total amount of traffic volume via WiFi is much larger than that via 3G. The average traffic offload ratio (i.e., ratio of penetration to WiFi) is 0.64 and the peak traffic offload ratio could reach 0.95, indicating that offloading is effective in terms of traffic volume. (2) However, a small fraction of users contributed a large fraction of traffic offloading. The top 30% of users downloaded over 90% of their traffic volume via WiFi, though 20% of users only used 3G networks. Also, 17.4% of the total traffic volume was generated by users whose WiFi traffic was less than 1MB. In particular, over 50% of users turned off their WiFi interface in business hours, and some hybrid users downloaded most of their traffic volume via WiFi in shorter durations. These results indicate that there is more room for improving the offload by promoting the use of WiFi. (3) WiFi offloading was mainly done by APs at home while public WiFi APs are still not commonly used in our dataset.

2   Dataset and Preprocessing

We developed special software to measure the traffic volume via the 3G network and WiFi for android smartphone. It reports the values of the byte and packet of network interfaces of a smartphone to an external server every 10 minutes, as well as the WiFi information (e.g., ESSID, BSSID), 3G network information (e.g., base station information), and device information (e.g., hardware and OS types). For privacy reasons, it does not collect user IDs, GPS information, or application usage. We recruited 435 monitor users who own android smartphones in Japan that were sampled from a thousand potential candidates, considering demography and the market share of the 3G carriers in Japan. Moreover, over 90% of monitor users reported that they have WiFi APs at home. In this sense, the results we will present are likely biased to the behavior of advanced users who have less difficulty using WiFi. The measurement experiment was performed on May 13th (Sun) and 14th (Mon), 2012 (48 hours long).

For preprocessing, we removed the traffic volume by tethering, which means a smartphone simply relays traffic from other devices (i.e., laptop PC) to the Internet, from the dataset. This is because we intended to focus on traffic patterns generated by the smartphone itself, though tethering is a promising application of smartphones. Also, some smartphones have a mobile WiMAX interface (IEEE802.16e) more than 3G and WiFi interfaces, but we removed their traffic.

3   Results

3.1   Global View

Figure 1 displays the variation of aggregated traffic volumes and that of the aggregated number of packets in 30-minute bins. Each plot indicates a different type of media: mRx (3G received), mTx (3G sent), wRx (WiFi received), and wTx (WiFi sent). The direction of the traffic is from the view of users (i.e., "received" corresponds to user's download). First, we observed higher WiFi traffic volumes than 3G ones, and the peak of the traffic volume is 1.5 times larger than that of mRx. In particular, the volumes on Sunday are higher than those on Monday, though Monday night is also characterized by high WiFi traffic volume. Thus, the availability of the WiFi network is lower on the weekday in our dataset. Second, we emphasize that peaks in both traffic volumes are not always synchronized, meaning that some users switch the media appropriately depending on the availability. In particular, we confirmed a sharp peak of mRx traffic volume at 6pm on Monday, corresponding to the rush hour in Japan. This peak does not appear in wRx, suggesting that WiFi was hard to use during the rush hours. The same type of non-synchronized peak appears at 9pm on Sunday. The correlation coefficient of time series of mRx bytes and wRx bytes is 0.03, and that of packet based time series is 0.11. Although each user switches between two interfaces exclusively, the variations of aggregated traffic volumes neither positively nor negatively correlate.

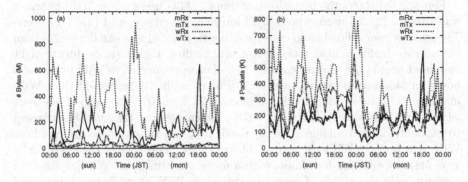

Fig. 1. Traffic variation (bin size = 30 min): (a) bytes and (b) packets

The Tx volumes are lower than Rx volumes, likely due to the typical application type of smartphone (i.e., server-client type). In addition, the traffic pattern of Tx resembles that of Rx in 3G packets, while that in WiFi is synchronized but with some gaps. This suggests that typical usage and application of 3G and WiFi are likely different. These results are consistent with the observation that most application traffic is server-client in 3G smartphone traffic [14,15].

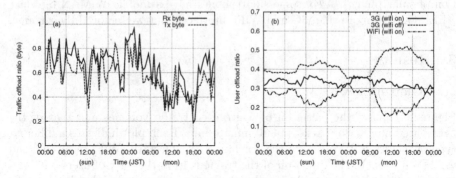

Fig. 2. WiFi offload ratio (bin size = 30min) (a) bytes and (b) users

Next, we investigate the degree of traffic offloading. We define a *traffic offload ratio* as the ratio of WiFi traffic volume to the total volume and a *user offload ratio* as the ratio of the number of WiFi users to the total number of users in 30-minute bins. The ratio closer to 1.0 means the penetration to a WiFi network while that closer to 0.0 means the penetration to a 3G network.

Figure 2 (a) represents the traffic offload ratio over time. The average traffic offload ratio was 0.64 though it varied largely depending on the usage of smartphone; the peak and bottom ratios are 0.97 and 0.19, respectively. The figure highlights the fact that the offloading ratio on Sunday is relatively higher than that on Monday. The average ratio was 0.70 on Sunday and 0.58 on Monday. The lower offloading ratio in the morning and afternoon on Monday suggests fewer opportunities to connect to the Internet via WiFi during work time. As expected, again, the ratio increased on Monday night.

Figure 2 (b) shows the breakdown of users: (1) 3G users whose WiFi interface was also up, (2) 3G users whose WiFi interface was down, and (3) WiFi users. The average user offload ratio corresponding to case (3) was smaller (0.22) than the average traffic offload ratio. We, again, confirm higher ratios during night and lower ones in the afternoon. Only 15% of users connected to WiFi in business hours on Monday, moreover, over 50% of users explicitly turned off their WiFi interface in business hours as shown in case (2). Similarly, the ratio of 3G users whose WiFi was also up is stable (≈ 0.3), indicating that they had few chances to encounter any available APs. In particular, the ratios of 3G users whose WiFi was up and WiFi users in night are closer. This means that WiFi APs were actually effective for almost half of users who turned on WiFi in night. In contrast, only about 35% of users who turned on WiFi interface could download data via WiFi in business hours.

Comparing both figures, we can conclude that the traffic offload was mainly exploited by a relatively smaller number of users. In other words, such heavy users switched their network interfaces explicitly.

3.2 Per-User View

Here, we focus on a microscopic view of traffic offloading. Figure 3 displays the scatter plot of 3G traffic and WiFi traffic volume per user for two days. We confirm horizontal dots in the bottom and vertical dots in the left of the figure, corresponding to the users who only used 3G and WiFi respectively. The former did not use WiFi even at home, and the latter likely saved the fee for 3G network access. A diagonal line in the figure represents users who used 3G and WiFi equally. A non-negligible number of dots below the diagonal, i.e., 3G traffic volume is greater than WiFi traffic volume, show that there is a possibility of increasing traffic offloading. For example, the traffic volume of 3G-only users accounted for 9.6% of the total traffic volume, while that of users whose WiFi traffic is less than 1MB accounted for 17.4% of the total volume.

In addition, Figure 4 displays the cumulative user distribution of the ratio of using WiFi and 3G per user. As explained before, a high (or low) traffic offload ratio corresponds to the penetration of WiFi (or 3G) usage. From the figure, we observe that the 3G-only users accounted for approximately 20% of all users and the WiFi-only users accounted for 10%. The median of users used more WiFi than 3G (0.62). Notably, the top 30% of users switched 90% of traffic volume to WiFi. These results are consistent with the previous results that revealed a relatively small portion of users penetrate to WiFi offloading.

Similarly, Figure 5 shows the relationship between total download traffic volume per user and its traffic offload ratio. We confirm a positive correlation (0.35) between two metrics, indicating that heavy-hitters consume more bandwidth via WiFi and that 3G-only users received less data than offloading users. We conclude that heavy-hitters efficiently use WiFi for their download traffic.

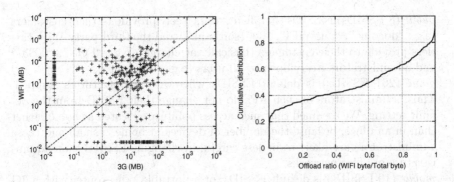

Fig. 3. Scatter plot of 3G and WiFi download traffic volume per user

Fig. 4. Cumulative distribution of offload ratio per user

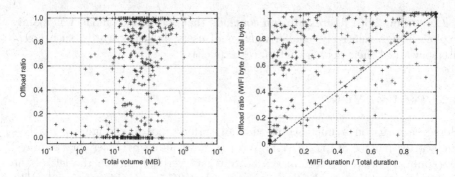

Fig. 5. Total traffic volume and traffic offload ratio

Fig. 6. Ratio of WiFi duration and traffic
offload ratio

Finally, we examine the traffic penetration to WiFi and the duration using
WiFi interface. Figure 6 displays the scatter plot of the ratio of duration using
WiFi to the total duration and the traffic offload ratio per user. The diagonal
in the figure indicates the users whose WiFi traffic volume is proportional to its
duration. As expected, we see plots concentrated near $(0, 0)$ (i.e., 3G only user)
and $(1, 1)$ (i.e., WiFi only user). A notable point, however, is that we still observe
plots scattered around lower ratios of the duration and higher offload ratios. This
means that these hybrid users downloaded most of their traffic volume via WIFI
in shorter periods, consistent with the macroscopic observation in Figure 2.

3.3   WiFi Usage

Here, we investigate the location where users associate with WiFi APs. SSID is
an identifier of AP in WiFi, and administrators of APs could set their name by
themselves, or it could also be left as the default setting. Thus, by categorizing
the names of ESSIDs, we could infer the types of location of APs with which
users associated. We gathered all SSIDs appearing in the dataset (418 unique
ESSIDs) and manually classified them into the following four categories.

- *public* (8 ESSIDs) is SSIDs that 3G carriers freely provide to their customers
  (e.g., "docomo", "au_WIFI", "0001softbank") and the third-party WiFi carriers provide to their customers (basically at charge) (e.g., "FON", "0033")
  and administrators freely open to all users (e.g., "freespot").
- *home* (261 ESSIDs) is default ESSIDs when AP manufacturers shipped.
  Thus, administrators of such APs do not change their ESSID from the default setting. We assumed that such access points are located at home rather
  than in an office, because the number of devices at home is small and these
  administrators are likely to be less careful in changing ESSIDs than administrators in office networks.
- *mobile* (19 ESSIDs) is default ESSIDs for a portable WiFi router with a 3G
  uplink and WiFi down link provided by 3G carriers. The user's smartphone
  connects to this router via WiFi to obtain an Internet connection.

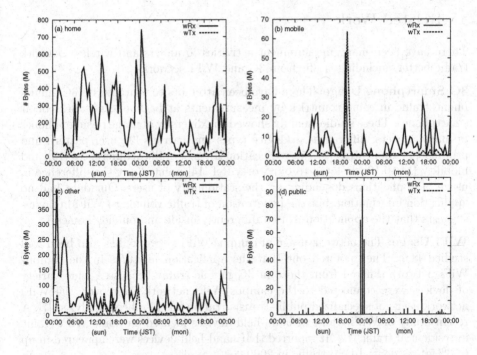

Fig. 7. WiFi traffic usage patterns

- *other* (130 ESSIDs) is named ESSIDs, i.e., administrators of APs explicitly changed their ESSIDs. This can be located in homes, offices, shops, etc. Also, it included unclassified ESSIDs.

Figure 7 indicates the variation of traffic volumes for different categories of SSIDs users associated with: (a) home, (b) mobile, (c) other, and (d) public. We confirm that the variation of traffic volume in home dominates the total amount of the WiFi traffic volume shown in Figure 1. Similarly, the traffic variation of the other category is similar to that of home users, indicating that most of these APs are also likely located at home. One interesting point in the mobile category is that its traffic pattern was closer to that of 3G traffic shown in Figure 1 than that of the home category; high traffic in the morning and evening on Sunday and the evening on Monday. The usage pattern of a portable WiFi router is similar to that of the 3G device, indicating that such users save 3G traffic costs by paying the cheaper monthly fee for a portable WiFi router as an alternative. Indeed, the correlation coefficient of wRx bytes of the mobile category and mRx bytes is higher (0.16) than that of wRx bytes of the mobile category and wRx bytes of the home category (−0.01) Also, one unexpected result is a much smaller traffic volume in public WiFi. Sharp and discrete spikes indicate that a small number of users generate traffic volume in a short time; indeed, the biggest peak of the spikes was traffic volume via a FON AP.

In summary, traffic offloading in homes currently works well, though that in public WiFi APs is not very high in our dataset.

4   Related Work

There have been many measurement activities to understand wireless network traffic better, including traffic from 3G and WiFi networks.

3G Smartphone Usage: There have been attempts to characterize 3G smartphone traffic in some countries by measurements at backbone networks or at smartphones. These studies mainly showed the diversity of usage of smartphones in many aspects; differences in device types and carriers [9], user pattern and protocol [4], application [14,15], geolocation [1], geographical differences [15], and mobility [14,10,16]. Related to our work, Ref [14] pointed out the difference in usage of applications depending on the stationarity of users. Our data had no application information, but the penetration of traffic volume to WiFi in homes suggests that the application is used differently inside and outside homes.

WiFi Usage: The network usage of campus WiFi networks has also been well studied [8,6]. They pointed out that the application mixtures in the campus WiFi network differed from those in 3G mobile traffic because a wide variety of devices were connected to the campus WiFi network. Moreover, the WiFi network usage of specialized public transportation has also been analyzed [7]. A recent study of WiFi traffic of hand-held devices focused on home WiFi traffic in residential traffic [12]. It reported that hand-held devices were appeared in up to 3% of residential DSL traffic in 2009.

Availability of 3G and WiFi: 3G and WiFi availability and performance have been compared in [2,11,5]. They investigated availability and performance by vehicle and/or walking based measurements. However, some studies only discussed availability of the WiFi network by the appearance of APs rather than actual connectivity.

The originality of our work to others is to characterize the 3G traffic offloading through WiFi on the basis of a large-scale device-based measurement and analysis of a combination of 3G and WiFi traffic.

5   Discussion

Our monitors were recruited by a web-based application and most have APs at home. This means that they are more familiar with using the Internet and smartphones than the average user. Thus, our results are likely biased towards the behavior of such advanced users, and the user and traffic offloading ratios of the current average users will be smaller than in our results. However, these results can be interpreted as corresponding to the situation in the very near future if 3G carriers successfully promote to average users the option of offloading more of their traffic volume to WiFi, considering the fact that the majority of residential users have high-speed Internet connections at home. Even in the current results, the high usage of WiFi was only by a relatively small number of users, and still 17.4% of the total volume was generated by users whose WiFi traffic volume was less than 1MB. In addition, over 50% of users turned off their

WiFi interface in business hours, and most of the traffic volume of some hybrid users was downloaded via WiFi in shorter durations. Therefore, the traffic and user offloading ratios could have been higher if the promotion by 3G carriers had been more effective.

Different from the high traffic offload ratio in homes, we observed lower traffic volumes in public WiFi. We cannot currently identify the exact reason for this low availability of public WiFi, but there are several plausible reasons: (1) Most users turned off WiFi connectivity outside the home to save energy. (2) Handover of WiFi APs did not work well due to fast movement of users. (3) Outside of downtown areas, the availability of public WiFi may be not very high. (4) There is wave interference due to a large number of APs at downtown areas. Our results at least demonstrated the possibility of reason (1) being true as shown in Figure 2(b). In particular, the advanced users may proactively save the battery by turning off the WiFi interface. Also, considering the usage of WiFi and 3G networks outside homes and offices, users likely need Internet connection only for e-mail checking or simple web browsing, rather than rich bandwidth applications such as streaming. Such short and simple usage of smartphones generates a smaller amount of traffic volume. In this sense, the availability and connectivity are likely more important than bandwidth for such public WiFi.

Connecting a user's private smartphone to APs at offices is currently not common in Japan because of security policies of companies, and we also confirmed a low traffic volume of named WiFi in office hours. However, some companies have started to allow their employees to connect their private smartphone to APs at offices. In future, WiFi offloading at offices may become more common.

6   Conclusion

We reported the results of our measurement of mobile traffic offloading. We first pointed out that the variation of aggregated traffic volume via WiFi is much greater than that via 3G in our dataset. The average traffic offload ratio was 0.64 and the peak traffic offload ratio could reach 0.95 at midnight. On the other hand, the user offload ratio stayed lower, meaning that a small fraction of users contributed to a large fraction of traffic offloading. In fact, our user level data revealed that the top 30% of users downloaded over 90% of their total traffic volume via WiFi, while 10% of users only used WiFi. However, 20% of users only stuck to 3G, whose traffic volume accounted for 9.4% of the total traffic volume, and over 50% of users turned off their WiFi interface in business hours. Moreover, we observed that some hybrid users downloaded most of their traffic via WiFi in shorter durations. In this sense, there is more room to improve the current situation of traffic offloading by promoting users to use WiFi more effectively. We also showed that WiFi offloading was mainly performed by APs in homes, and public WiFi APs are still not very commonly used in our dataset.

Acknowledgements. We would like to thank Kenjiro Cho, Romain Fontgune, and the anonymous reviewers for their helpful comments. Also, we thank the Ministry of Internal Affairs and Communications of Japan for its support.

References

1. Balakrishnan, M., Mohomed, I., Ramasubramanian, V.: Where's that phone?: Geolocating IP addresses on 3G networks. In: IMC 2009, Chicago, IL, pp. 294–300 (November 2009)
2. Balasubramanian, A., Mahajan, R., Venkataramani, A.: Augmenting mobile 3G using WiFi. In: MobiSys 2010, San Francisco, CA, pp. 209–222 (June 2010)
3. Cho, K., Fukuda, K., Esaki, H., Kato, A.: Observing slow crustal movement in residential user traffic. In: ACM CoNEXT 2008, Madrid, Spain, p. 12 (December 2008)
4. Falaki, H., Mahajan, R., Kandula, S., Lymberopoulos, D., Govindan, R., Estrin, D.: Diversity in smartphone usage. In: MobiSys 2010, San Francisco, CA, pp. 179–194 (June 2010)
5. Gass, R., Diot, C.: An Experimental Performance Comparison of 3G and Wi-Fi. In: Krishnamurthy, A., Plattner, B. (eds.) PAM 2010. LNCS, vol. 6032, pp. 71–80. Springer, Heidelberg (2010)
6. Gember, A., Anand, A., Akella, A.: A Comparative Study of Handheld and Non-handheld Traffic in Campus Wi-Fi Networks. In: Spring, N., Riley, G.F. (eds.) PAM 2011. LNCS, vol. 6579, pp. 173–183. Springer, Heidelberg (2011)
7. Hare, J., Hartung, L., Banerjee, S.: Beyond deployments and testbeds: Experiences with public usage on vehicular WiFi hotspots. In: MobiSys 2012, Low Wood Bay, UK, pp. 393–405 (June 2012)
8. Henderson, T., Kotz, D., Abyzov, I.: The changing usage of a mature campus-wide wireless network. In: MobiCom 2004, Philadelphia, PA, pp. 187–201 (2004)
9. Huang, J., Xu, Q., Tiwana, B., Mao, Z.M., Zhang, M., Bahl, P.: Anatomizing application performance differences on smartphones. In: MobiSys 2010, San Francisco, CA, pp. 165–178 (June 2010)
10. Jang, K., Han, M., Cho, S., Ryu, H.-K., Lee, J., Lee, Y., Moon, S.: 3G and 3.5G wireless network performance measured from moving cars and high-speed trains. In: MICNET 2009, Beijing, China, pp. 19–24 (October 2009)
11. Lee, K., Rhee, I., Lee, J., Chong, S., Yi, Y.: Mobile data offloading: How much can WiFi deliver? In: CoNEXT 2010, Philadelphia, PA, p. 12 (December 2010)
12. Maier, G., Schneider, F., Feldmann, A.: A First Look at Mobile Hand-Held Device Traffic. In: Krishnamurthy, A., Plattner, B. (eds.) PAM 2010. LNCS, vol. 6032, pp. 161–170. Springer, Heidelberg (2010)
13. Ministry of Internal Affairs and Communications. Growth of Mobile Traffic in Japan (2011),
http://www.soumu.go.jp/johotsusintokei/field/tsuushin06.html
14. Trestian, I., Ranjan, S., Kuzmanovic, A., Nucci, A.: Measuring serendipity: Connecting people, locations and interests in a mobile 3G network. In: IMC 2009, Chicago, IL, pp. 267–279 (November 2009)
15. Xu, Q., Erman, J., Gerber, A., Mao, Z., Pang, J., Venkataraman, S.: Identifying diverse usage of behaviors of smartphone apps. In: IMC 2011, Berlin, Germany, pp. 329–344 (November 2011)
16. Zhu, Z., Cao, G., Keralapura, R., Nucci, A.: Characterizing data services in a 3G network: Usage, mobility and access issues. In: ICC 2011, Kyoto, p. 6 (2011)

Estimating TCP Latency Approximately
with Passive Measurements

Sriharsha Gangam[1], Jaideep Chandrashekar[2], Ítalo Cunha[3], and Jim Kurose[4]

[1] Purdue University
sgangam@purdue.edu
[2] Technicolor Research
jaideep.chandrashekar@technicolor.com
[3] UFMG, Brazil
cunha@dcc.ufmg.br
[4] Univ. of Massachussetts, Amherst
kurose@cs.umass.edu

Abstract. Estimating per-flow performance characteristics such as latency, loss, and jitter from a location other than the connection end-points can help locate performance problems affecting end-to-end flows. However, doing this accurately in real-time is challenging and requires tracking extensive amounts of TCP state and is thus infeasible on nodes that process large volumes of traffic. In this paper, we propose an *approximate* and *scalable* method to estimate TCP flow latency in the network. Our method scales with the number of flows by keeping approximate TCP state in a compressed, probabilistic data structure that requires less memory and compute, but sacrifices a small amount of accuracy. We validate our method using backbone link traces and compare it against an exact, baseline approach. In our approximate method, 99% of the reported latencies are within 10.3 ms of the baseline reported value, while taking an order of magnitude less memory.

1 Introduction

Latency is a key determinant in the performance of a network flow and large values can adversely affect bulk transfers, increase buffering, and make interactive sessions unresponsive. Thus, tracking flow latency is a critical tool in monitoring the performance of TCP-based applications; these form the bulk of Internet traffic today. While estimating this latency is an intrinsic part of TCP and thus trivial at the end-points of a connection, it is extremely challenging in the middle of the network, *i.e.,* at a network node along the path connecting the end-points. At the same time, the ability to infer the flow latency at such locations would be extremely valuable to users and network operators. Consider a typical WiFi-enabled home network with DSL broadband connectivity. Today, when applications underperform or latencies to destinations are larger than usual, it is extremely difficult to reason about where the bottleneck is. Is the increased latency occurring inside the wireless network? or is the server slow to respond? Answering this seemingly simple question directly is quite difficult (even if we could query the end-points for their estimates). This question is easy to answer if the home gateway could

M. Roughan and R. Chang (Eds.) PAM 2013, LNCS 7799, pp. 83–93, 2013.

estimate latencies of the connections on the wireless link. Similar applications could be imagined at data center borders or egress routers in enterprise networks.

This area has attracted a lot of attention in the past and several methods have been proposed; these broadly fall into two categories—active or passive. Active methods rely on probing the destination(s) independent of the TCP flow (various flavors of ping exist), or else by inserting a transparent TCP proxy on the path of the TCP flow [4]. This has the effect of terminating one half of the connection, and creating a new connection from the midpoint. Clearly, this is impractical for large numbers of concurrent flows. Moreover, terminating the flow in the middle of the network *alters* the flow and may not be acceptable. The other set of methods is based on passive observations of the traffic. A single RTT estimate can be obtained by matching SYNs and ACKs in the beginning of a TCP connection [11]; this is useful, but of limited utility since latency can change considerably over the connection duration. Another idea is to infer the RTT by computing the delay between the transmission of two consecutive congestion windows [10,12,15]. In [2, 10], the TCP state machine is emulated *offline*, using passively recorded traces, to infer RTT estimates by matching ACKs and TCP sequence numbers. Some of these methods can track latency over the entire duration of a connection in the middle of the network; however, they are not scalable and are not designed to be run in real-time.

The challenge in *accurately* estimating TCP latency *in the network* centers on the amount of state that needs to be maintained. Packets going in one direction need to be stored and matched with acknowledgements coming back the other way. In measurement points that handle a large number of flows (routers in ISP networks, data center switches) or embedded devices that are resource constrained, it is generally infeasible to store sufficient TCP state information, or to process it fast enough to support very accurate TCP latency estimates in real-time. The key observation we make is that when estimating latency, a strict accuracy constraint limits how well a solution can scale. There are applications that need to measure latency accurately and with a high degree of precision (electronic trading systems, B2B applications). Correspondingly, there are particular solutions that target these markets, relying on specialized hardware and multiple vantage points (see [13, 14]). However, most other applications, particularly those that focus on troubleshooting or performance diagnosis, are more interested in tracking whether latencies are within a specified range or if they have exceeded a threshold. Importantly, such applications can tolerate approximate answers and a certain amount of error. Take for example an application that monitors VoIP call quality; acceptable quality might require that accuracy not exceed 150ms [9]. Similar latency thresholds are associated with other applications: 100ms for online first person shooter and racing games [6], and in the same region for video streaming applications [16]. In such applications, tracking approximate latencies is good enough.

In this paper we investigate the problem of performing scalable and approximate latency estimation in real-time inside the network. We describe such a method, called ALE (Approximate Latency Estimator), present its key ideas and introduce two variants ALE-U (Uniform) and ALE-E (Exponential). These methods work by sacrificing accuracy, which requires (exactly) tracking a great deal of TCP state, and instead keeping approximate state, which uses far less memory, but have a certain inherent amount of error. Importantly, this loss of accuracy can be controlled by using more (or less) memory. These methods were implemented and compared against `tcptrace` [2], a well established, *offline* analysis tool for TCP. We carried out a validation study using two different traces obtained from CAIDA. On these traces, we show that ALE can achieve accuracy very close to tcptrace, while using far less memory and requiring less computation. In the best performing latency estimator, 99% of the reported latencies are within 10.3 ms of the actual value and over 97% of the median flow latencies reported are within 10.2 ms of the actual medians; all while taking about one thirtieth of the memory used by the baseline.

2   TCP Latency Estimation

TCP estimates RTT by matching ACKs against a set of *data segments* sent (but not yet acknowledged). For example, suppose host A is sending data to host B on a path that goes through M. At time t_1, A sends a data segment with k bytes of data to B. This segment contains a sequence number range $[s, s+k]$ (bytes are individually numbered). After B processes this segment, it sends back an acknowledgement to A which explicitly indicates the next byte in the stream it expects to receive, *i.e.*, $s+k+1$ (this is exactly one more than the last sequence number in the packet sent by A), and this reaches A at t_2. Since the acknowledgement can be matched with the segment sent previously, A estimates the RTT as $t_2 - t_1$. Now, node M can also perform a similar estimation by matching data segments with acknowledgements (ACKs, in short) seen in flight. The RTT estimate for the path segment $M \leftrightarrow B$ is $t_a - t_d$, where t_d and t_a are when the data segment and the acknowledgement were observed at M. Note that there is not enough information to estimate the RTT on the path segment $A \leftrightarrow M$; this requires B sending data to A and receiving ACKs back. To obtain accurate RTT estimates at M, for either side of the path, we need to remember all the unacknowledged data segments seen in one direction, and match them against ACKs coming back the other way. This makes straightforward RTT estimation infeasible at nodes that handle a large flow volume, or at memory constrained embedded devices of the type used in home and small business gateways. That being said, if we are willing to tolerate a small amount of error in the RTT estimates or a few missed RTT estimates, we significantly reduce the amount of memory required.

In our approach, we exploit the following two observations: (i) storing the exact timestamp associated with each TCP segments is overkill. It is sufficient to remember having seen it in a particular time interval, and (ii) we can avoid storing the sequence number *range* and just store a single sentinel value instead. Following the first observation, we can divide time into discrete intervals and just associate the segments with particular intervals. Thus, with each interval, we now associate a (possibly) large set of segments that arrived in that interval (specifically, the sequence number ranges and flowids). The second observation does away with having to store the sequence number *range* and lets us store a single number for each unacknowledged segment. Specifically, this number is just one larger than the end of the sequence range in the segment, *i.e.*, the number that is expected to be returned in the acknowledgement. We note that this is not guaranteed to always be the case; the TCP specification permits partial segments to be acknowledged. However, this is not the norm and when it does happen, it is an indication of a performance bottleneck at the receiver. If we overlook this corner case, we can simply record the *expected* acknowledgement number for each segment (this is exactly one larger than the last sequence number in the segment) and match this against incoming ACKs. By exploiting this "most likely behavior" in TCP, the problem of searching through a number of ranges or intervals now becomes that of set membership queries which can be done very efficiently with probabilistic data structures (such as Bloom filters).

Approximate Latency Estimator (ALE). Looking into the recent past, we divide time into fixed size discrete intervals, $[w_0, w_1], [w_1, w_2], \ldots, [w_{n-1}, w_n]$, over a sliding window. Here, $[w_0, w_1]$ is always the most recently elapsed interval, the sliding window covers a span of $W = w_0 - w_n$ seconds, and each interval is of length $w = w_i - w_{i+1}$ (we use *interval* and *bucket* interchangeably). This time discretization is shown in Fig. 1. We denote by B_i the data structure *currently* associated with interval i. Apart from the buckets associated with the sliding window, we use another bucket B to hold state for the immediate present. At the end of every w seconds, we move B (to the left in the figure) into the past and into the sliding window. The data structures B_i and B are Counting Bloom Filters (CBF) [7], a variation that supports set member deletions.

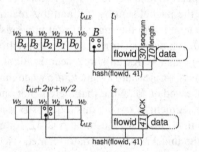

Fig. 1. Operation of the ALE Algorithm

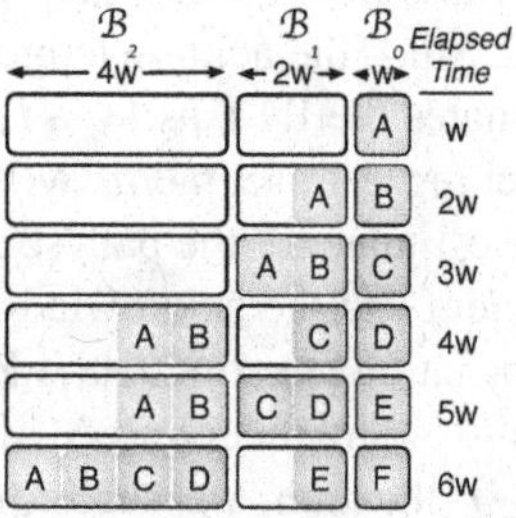

Fig. 2. Buckets Being Shifted and Merged in ALE-E

The TCP segment insertion operation in ALE records the flow identifier and the expected sequence number into a bucket by hashing the concatenation of the two and incrementing the appropriate counters (see [7] for details). Deletion proceeds the same way, but with the counters decremented. Set membership reads the counters indexed by the hash functions and reports 'yes' if all of them are non-zero, and 'no' otherwise.

We use the diagram in Fig. 1 to walk through an example. The upper half demonstrates a just arrived TCP segment being recorded. The TCP data segment that arrives at t_1 is recorded into B (with sequence number 30 and containing 10 data bytes). After every w seconds, the data structure associated with each interval is shifted to the left, *i.e.*, $B_{i+1} \leftarrow B_i$. Thus, the contents of the current window B move to B_0, the most recently elapsed interval in the sliding window, and B is reset. At the same time, B_n reaches the end of the sliding window and is discarded. Rather than keep track of each of the interval boundaries (which have fixed size), we use a single running timestamp t_{ALE} that points to the end of the sliding window, *i.e.*, corresponds to w_0. After every w seconds t_{ALE} is incremented by w. Thus, an entry stored in B_i would have arrived in the time interval $t_{\text{ALE}} - wi$ and $t_{\text{ALE}} - w(i+1)$.

Now, suppose an acknowledgement arrives (possibly piggybacked on a data packet) at time t_2 (see lower half of Fig. 1): we need to look backwards in time and find the (first) bucket where the corresponding segment was recorded. We first check B (and if there is a match, the RTT is just $(t_2 - t_{ALE})/2$). Then we check $B_0, B_1, \ldots, B_n$ until we find a match. In the figure, we find a match in the window $[w_2, w_3]$. We estimate the RTT as $t_2 - t_{ALE} + 2w + w/2$. More generally, when a match is located in B_i, the RTT is $t - t_{ALE} + (2i + 1)w/2$. If there is no match after checking the last bucket B_n, ALE does not return an RTT estimate.

Notice that there are two parameters, w and W, that control accuracy and coverage. For a given span W, increasing the accuracy requires smaller w; thus, more buckets and associated data structures. A similar argument holds if we were to hold accuracy fixed (*i.e.,* fix w) but increase W. Rather than require accuracy to be uniform in each bucket (necessitating a lot of buckets), one could also use non-uniform buckets. We now introduce a variation of the estimator just introduced that we call ALE-E, which employs exponentially increasing intervals. ALE-E attempts to support *relative accuracy* for the same number of buckets *i.e.,* better accuracy for smaller latency samples and lesser accuracy for larger latencies. To differentiate the two, we use ALE-U to denote the use of uniform sized buckets.

ALE with Exponential Buckets. ALE-E follows the same general idea of moving the contents of buckets to its older neighbor. However, the buckets follow a slightly different rule for the shift operation. Like before, bucket B_0 shifts its contents to B_1 after every w seconds. However, bucket B_i is shifted (and merged) into B_{i+1} every $2^i w$ seconds. This is illustrated in Fig. 2. Here, we see that every w seconds, B_0 is merged with B_1; B_1 is merged with B_2 every $2w$ seconds; B_2 is merged with B_3 every $4w$ seconds (not shown) and so on. Whenever the buckets are merged, we adjust their starting and ending times appropriately. The actual merging is trivial if B_i is maintained as a CBF: we simply add up the corresponding counters. Intuitively, the size of each interval is twice as long as the one preceding it. That is to say the i-th interval is of size $2^i w$. If the width of the smallest bucket is w, monitoring the span W requires $1 + \lfloor \log_2(W/w) \rfloor$ buckets. ALE-E can cover the same range using fewer buckets. However, this comes at a price: larger buckets cause larger errors in RTT estimate. Moreover, the merging of bloom filters causes them to attenuate with each merge, *i.e.,* the bitmaps get more "crowded" and prone to false positives. Thus, ALE-E makes the estimation of longer latencies inaccurate in return for parsimonious use of memory and better accuracy for smaller latencies.

Other Sources of Error. When multiple data segments are acknowledged by a single cumulative acknowledgement (*e.g,* a delayed ACK), we can only match (and remove) the last data segment and generate a single RTT sample. The other data segments are not removed from the CBFs until they drop out of B_n. The same phenomenon occurs if the ACKs are not flowing (or flowing fast enough) towards the sender. If this persists over time, the counting bloom filter becomes saturated and exhibits a high false positive rate. We can deal with this by increasing the size of the CBFs.

Since ALE does not maintain the state for the TCP segments, we cannot identify reordered packets. When this does happen, ALE will return an incorrect answer (rather than discarding the RTT sample). Retransmitted packets also pose a source of error. In general, retransmitted segments can be identified (and excluded from the RTT estimation) in ALE by first checking through all the buckets *before* recording the segment. If a copy is found, one of the segments being matched is a duplicate and they should both be discarded. However, this additional check makes the TCP segment insertion operation go to $\mathcal{O}(n)$ from $\mathcal{O}(1)$.

Accuracy and Overhead Bounds. ALE has simple discretization error bounds on the estimated latencies. Let w denote the width of the bucket B_0. For ALE-U, the worst case error is $w/2$ and the average case error is $w/4$. In ALE-E, when an ACK has a match in bucket i, the worst case error is $2^{i-1}w$ and the average case error is $(3w/16)2^i$. We omit the proofs due to a lack of space.

ALE with h hash functions takes $\mathcal{O}(h)$ time to insert an expected acknowledgement number in the CBF of bucket B. Matching an ACK takes $\mathcal{O}(hn)$ time (answering CBF membership queries on n buckets). For every time interval w, shifting buckets takes $\mathcal{O}(1)$ time, if the buckets are implemented as a linked list. Additionally, ALE-E takes $\mathcal{O}(C)$ time to add counters of two CBFs (merging). Finally, ALE takes $n \times C \times d$ bits of memory, where d is the number of bits in each counter of the CBFs.

ALE Parameters. The sliding window size, or span (W) should be chosen to ensure that most of the *normal* latencies observed fall inside of it. It is a limitation of ALE to use a preconceived estimate of the maximum latencies in the network. Interval width (w), the other ALE parameter, is mainly dictated by accuracy requirements. In an application like VoIP, which needs latencies lower than 150 ms, an error of 20 ms is acceptable to identify problematic scenarios. This requires setting w to 40 ms in ALE-U.

We use CBFs with 4 hash functions. For m entries and C counters, the optimal number of hash functions h is given by $h = (C/m)\ln 2$ and the corresponding false positive rate is $\approx (2^{-\ln 2})^{C/m}$ [5]. With 4 hash functions, this false positive probability is 0.0625. One can estimate C based on the traffic rate, the time interval w, and the number of hash functions h. The traffic rate R in our traces varies between 350,000 and 600,000 TCP packets per second [1]. For $w = 20$ ms, $h = 4$, and $m = R \times w$, the constraint for optimal h $(h = (C/m)\ln 2)$ yields $C = 40396$. In practice, we require fewer counters (30000) as the matched ACK numbers are deleted from the CBFs. We use CBFs with 4-bit counters as they work well in practice [7].

3   Evaluation

We compare different ALE variants against `tcptrace` as the baseline solution. The terms tcptrace and baseline are interchangeable. We use two 60-second traces captured at a backbone link of a tier-1 ISP obtained from CAIDA. The traces capture headers of all packets in both directions of the link. Trace 1 starts on 07-21-2012 at 13:55 UTC, contains 2,115,802 TCP flows, and 50,022,761 TCP packets; Trace 2 starts on 02-17-2011 at 13:01 UTC, contains 2,423,461 TCP flows, and 54,089,453 packets. We find that only 1.8% and 2.1% of the captured flows are bidirectional, a result of most Internet paths being asymmetric at the core [8]. However, closer to the network edge (home gateways and even most access networks), traffic is bidirectional. Since we do not handle unidirectional flows in our current implementation, we pre-processed the traces to

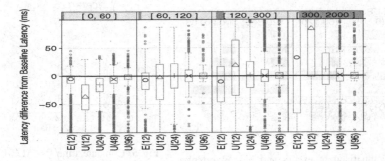

Fig. 3. Distribution of estimation error ($RTT_{baseline} - RTT_{ALE}$) over all samples

filter out unidirectional flows. We point out that it is indeed feasible to filter out such flows in an online fashion, but this discussion out of the scope of this paper. In the rest of the section, unless explicitly stated, we show results from Trace 1, but results for Trace 2 are qualitatively similar.

We compare 4 different configurations of ALE-U with $n = 12, 24, 48$, and 96 buckets; we refer to these configurations as ALE-U(n). Using `tcptrace`, we find that the majority of RTTs in Trace 1 are less than 100 ms and only 0.5% are larger than 2 s. We thus configure ALE with a window span of two seconds, *i.e.,* $W = 2$ s. This results in intervals w ranging from 167 ms (when $n = 12$) to 21 ms (when $n = 96$). Finally, we configure ALE-E with 12 intervals and we refer to this configuration as ALE-E(12). To accommodate the high traffic rates in our traces, we use CBFs with $C = 30000$ counters and 4 hash functions.

RTT Estimation Accuracy. We first report on the per-sample RTT estimation accuracy across the various methods. While this is not a very natural metric of comparison—most applications would be in interested in some statistic over these—it does serve to illustrate some of the intuition for why ALE performs comparably, and talks to its suitability for certain situations. Fig. 3 presents a box and whisker plot of the *differences* between the RTT reported by each method and `tcptrace`. In other words, it shows the distribution of $RTT_{tcptrace} - RTT_{ALE}$ over all RTT samples in Trace 1 for different ALE configurations. Recall that the size of the interval bounds the accuracy for ALE. To draw out how ALE might perform at different regimes, the plot is partitioned into four latency regions (unrelated to w): $(0, 60]$ ms, $(60, 120]$ ms, $(120, 300]$ ms, and $(300, 2000]$ ms. For example, the first group (left) plots the distribution for all samples where the baseline approach reported a latency between 0 and 60 ms. The horizontal line in the center of the figure marks the region where the difference is zero (the values reported by the baseline and ALE are identical). The height of the box spans the inter-quartile range of the differences in the RTT estimate and the point in the box is the median difference.

Not surprisingly, across all latency ranges, increasing the number of buckets improves accuracy. We also note that ALE-U(96), which almost completely agrees with the far more expensive baseline approach. There are a few rare large differences, but this may be quite acceptable considering the savings in memory; especially keeping

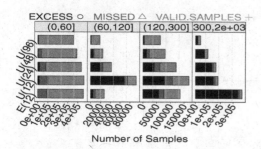
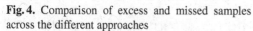

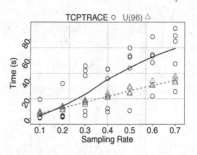

Fig. 4. Comparison of excess and missed samples across the different approaches

Fig. 5. Compute time for ALE-U(96) and tcptrace and for different thinned traces

in mind that per-sample RTT estimates are rarely used directly. In Fig. 3, we note that ALE-E(12) does almost as well as ALE-U(96) for latencies less than 60 ms even though ALE-E(12) uses 8 times less memory. The price, however, is reduced accuracy for latencies above 60 ms.

Excess and Missed Samples. As discussed previously, the ALE algorithms sometimes miss RTT samples reported by the baseline approach (RTT *misses*, *e.g.,* when CBF false positives decrement counters prematurely); and sometimes report RTTs *not* reported by the baseline (*excess* RTTs, due to, *e.g.,* CBF false positives or reordered packets). We plot the absolute numbers of each, separated by latency regions in Fig. 4. We observe that adding more memory (buckets) reduces both missed and excess RTTs. With respect to ALE-E, we see that missed and excess RTTs are few when latencies are small, but the excess samples are common for large latency values. As the CBFs for each bucket in ALE-E are shifted and merged, they are increasingly attenuated and have higher false positive rates. Nevertheless, ALE-E is still accurate up to 120 ms, which may be enough for interactive applications.

Fig. 4 can qualitatively explain the contribution of the different sources of error. For example, when ALE-U uses sufficiently large memory (*e.g.,* U(96)) the effects of false positives and negatives are mitigated. U(96) has few misses and excess values indicating that there are few retransmitted and reordered packets in the CAIDA traces. If the results in Fig. 3 and Fig. 4 do not improve with additional memory, one can conclude that the errors are due to re-ordered and retransmitted packets.

Errors in Flow Latency Properties. Typical flow performance monitoring applications track some *statistic* of the flow latencies, rather than use the RTT samples directly. Consider the example of VoIP quality tracking, very sensitive to jitter. This involves monitoring and tracking the variation in latencies of a flow, relating this to the user perceived quality of the session. We study the impact of the approximations native to ALE on two relevant flow statistics: (i) median latency of a flow, which impacts the quality of interactive applications (network games, web browsing), and (ii) jitter (latency variation) in a flow, which impacts the perceived quality of most real-time streaming applications (VoIP, video conferencing).

Fig. 6a plots the distribution of differences in the median latency computed by the baseline and ALE. Each curve is a distribution of the values of $median_{baseline} - median_{ALE}$

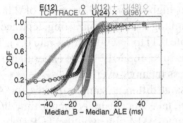
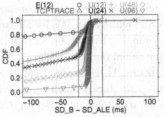

(a) Difference in median latency.   (b) Difference in latency std. dev.

Fig. 6. Accuracy for latency statistics over all flows

over all flows. The vertical black line in the middle represents perfect agreement with the baseline. In the figure, we note that ALE-U(96) performs best over the other instances: at least 97% of the flows have medians within 10 ms of the baseline (shown by the vertical red lines). To put this in context, the acceptable latency for VoIP is between [20, 150] ms: being off by 10 ms does not affect the monitoring application to a large degree. The other ALE-U instances perform as expected: larger number of buckets tends to make the curve steeper (and more aligned with the center line). We also note that ALE-E performs reasonably well: about 65% of the flows have median latency estimate within 15 ms of the actual value. Since the median is robust to outliers, some of the large errors that ALE-E reports for individual samples are filtered out. Thus, along with ALE-U(96) and perhaps ALE-U(48), ALE-E might be effective as a lightweight method to monitor the quality of low latency sessions.

In a similar comparison, Fig. 6b plots the CDF of disagreement in the standard deviations of flow latencies, $i.e.$, $\sigma_{baseline} - \sigma_{ALE}$. The vertical black line (at $x = 0$) marks the region where the std. dev. reported by ALE matches that of the baseline perfectly. Firstly, we notice that the baseline approach in general reports lower variance than the ALE approaches (the cases when the difference is negative). This is because the latencies are dispersed over a time interval w. In the figure, the red vertical lines indicate the 20 ms boundary from zero. We again see that ALE-U(96) performs better than any of the others, and 95.7% of the flows have delay variance that differ from the baseline reported version by at most 20 ms. We also see that ALE-E performs poorly on this comparison. About 80% of the flows disagree with the baseline reading by at least 20 ms. This is most likely due to CBF attenuation in the larger intervals leading to a large number of false positives.

Memory and Compute Overhead. We thin out the trace by sampling flows uniformly at random at rates 0.1, 0.2, ... 0.7, such that there are 5 pcap sub-traces at each rate. For a given rate, all the 5 pcap sub-traces have about the same number of flows. A sub-trace with higher sampling rate requires processing of more packets and flows per unit time. Using these sub-traces, we run ALE-U(96) and tcptrace (both implemented in GNU C), on an AMD quad core 512 KB cache, 2.6 GHz, 8 processor machine with 32 GB RAM to study the overhead. We use tstime [3] tool which leverages the GNU Linux taskstats API to get user time, system time, high water RSS (resident segment size) memory and high water VSS (virtual segment size) memory of a process.

As expected, ALE-U(96) takes constant high water RSS memory of 2.0 MB and high water VSS memory 9.8 MB for all sampling rates. In contrasting, tcptrace requires RSS memory ranging from $\approx$ 64 MB (at rate 0.1) to $\approx$ 460 MB (at rate 0.7). The VSS memory requirement ranges from $\approx$ 74 MB to $\approx$ 468 MB. These experiments confirm our hypothesis that ALE has significantly less memory overhead.

Fig. 5 shows the times taken to process at different sampling rates for ALE and tcptrace. As the data rates increase, tcptrace takes increasingly longer time than ALE. tcptrace has higher variability in compute times. ALE, by avoiding TCP state, has less variability and takes constant per-packet processing time (on average) at all traffic rates.

4 Discussion

Though our implementation does not incorporate computational optimizations, we hope that a performance-focused implementation (*e.g.,* parallelizing ACK lookups in the n buckets) would be even faster. An optimized implementation can fit the data required by a wide range of ALE configurations in the caches of low-end Atom and ARMv8 processors (currently between 256 KiB and 1 MiB). The evaluated configuration with 48 buckets and 30,000 4-bit counters per bucket would require about 700 KiB of memory for processing 10 Gbit/s links. We note that ALE lends itself well to implementation in hardware: ALE's basic building blocks are hashing functions, 4-bit accumulators, and 4-bit comparators.

Current home DSL gateways usually run local area networks that run at 100 Mbit/s and connect to the Internet with connections up to 28 Mbit/s. In an heavy-loaded scenario with an Internet download at 28 Mbit/s and a local transfer at 100 Mbit per second, the gateway would receive 11000 full-size (1500 B) packets/s (the absolute number of flows does not impact ALE in any way). Configuring ALE-U(12) with 12 buckets and $W = 200$ ms would require bucket sizes of 1058 counters per bucket, for a total memory utilization of $12 \times 1058 \times 4 \div 8 \div 1024 = 6.2$ KiB. This fits easily in the cache of current MIPS and ARM processors used in home DSL gateways.

References

1. CAIDA: Passive network monitors,
   http://www.caida.org/data/realtime/passive/
2. tcptrace, http://www.tcptrace.org/
3. tstime, https://bitbucket.org/gsauthof/tstime/
4. Web10G, http://www.web10g.org
5. Bonomi, F., Mitzenmacher, M., Panigrahy, R., Singh, S., Varghese, G.: An Improved Construction for Counting Bloom Filters. In: Azar, Y., Erlebach, T. (eds.) ESA 2006. LNCS, vol. 4168, pp. 684–695. Springer, Heidelberg (2006)
6. Dick, M., Wellnitz, O., Wolf, L.: Analysis of Factors Affecting Players' Performance and Perception in Multiplayer Games. In: Proc. ACM Netgames (2005)
7. Fan, L., Cao, P., Almeida, J., Broder, A.Z.: Summary cache: a scalable wide-area web cache sharing protocol. IEEE/ACM Trans. Netw. 8(3), 281–293 (2000)
8. He, Y., Faloutsos, M., Krishnamurthy, S., Huffaker, B.: On Routing Asymmetry in the Internet. In: Proc. IEEE GLOBECOM (2005)
9. ITU-T. Recommendation G.114: One-way Transmission Time (May 2000)

10. Jaiswal, S., Iannaccone, G., Diot, C., Kurose, J., Towsley, D.: Inferring TCP connection characteristics through passive measurements. In: Proc. IEEE INFOCOM (2004)
11. Jiang, H., Dovrolis, C.: Passive estimation of TCP round-trip times. SIGCOMM Comput. Commun. Rev. 32(3), 75–88 (2002)
12. Lance, R., Frommer, I.: Round-trip time inference via passive monitoring. SIGMETRICS Perform. Eval. Rev. 33(3), 32–38 (2005)
13. Lee, M., Duffield, N., Kompella, R.R.: Not all microseconds are equal: fine-grained per-flow measurements with reference latency interpolation. In: Proc. ACM SIGCOMM (2010)
14. Lee, M., Duffield, N., Kompella, R.R.: Leave them microseconds alone: Scalable architecture for maintaining packet latency measurements. Technical report, Purdue Univ. (2011)
15. Veal, B., Li, K., Lowenthal, D.: New Methods for Passive Estimation of TCP Round-Trip Times. In: Dovrolis, C. (ed.) PAM 2005. LNCS, vol. 3431, pp. 121–134. Springer, Heidelberg (2005)
16. Xiu, X., Cheung, G., Liang, J.: Delay-cognizant interactive streaming of multiview video with free viewpoint synthesis. IEEE Trans. on Multimedia 14(4), 1109–1126 (2012)

Effect of Competing TCP Traffic
on Interactive Real-Time Communication

Ilpo Järvinen[1], Binoy Chemmagate[1], Aaron Yi Ding[1], Laila Daniel[1],
Markus Isomäki[2], Jouni Korhonen[3], and Markku Kojo[1]

[1] University of Helsinki
[2] Nokia
[3] Nokia Siemens Networks

Abstract. Providing acceptable quality level for interactive media flows
such as interactive video or audio is challenging in the presence of TCP
traffic. Volatile TCP traffic such as Web traffic causes transient queues to
appear and vanish rapidly introducing jitter to the packets of the media
flow. Meanwhile long-lived TCP connections cause standing queues to
form which increases the one-way delay for the media flow packets. To
get insights into this problem space we conducted experiments in a real
high-speed cellular network. Our results confirm the existence of issues
with both Web-like traffic and long-lived TCP connections and highlight
that current trend of using several parallel connections in Web browsers
tends to have high cost on media flows. In addition, the recent proposal
to increase the initial window of TCP to ten segments, if deployed, is
going to make the jitter problem even worse.

1   Introduction

Introducing delay sensitive end-to-end media flows such as interactive video and
audio between Internet users introduces a number of challenges with congestion
control. These challenges involve two interrelated problems. First, how to ensure
that real-time communications behave fairly with other competing Internet traffic. Second, how to ensure good quality to the interactive media, in particular
with the other competing traffic that the users potentially generate to share the
bottleneck(s) on the end-to-end path. In this paper we focus on the latter challenge. In a common case the bottleneck resides in the access network of the end
user, where most of the traffic, if not all, is that generated by the user. When we
consider the link speed in developing or underdeveloped areas, we can see that,
most of the users are still using residential access such as DSL or mobile broadband as the primary Internet access. Even in developed areas the link capacity
for residential Internet access is quite often not more than a few megabits per
second.

Web traffic in general is very bursty and easily creates transient queues at bottlenecks in front of slow and moderate speed access links. These queues interfere
with any competing traffic by introducing delay spikes that delay sensitive flows

M. Roughan and R. Chang (Eds.) PAM 2013, LNCS 7799, pp. 94–103, 2013.

encounter as harmful jitter. Moreover, a browser of today is quite aggressive using many parallel TCP connections to speed up retrieval of the Web pages [2,15]. At the same time, websites "optimize" the end user experience by taking advantage of the parallel TCP connections feature of the browser. The "optimized" Web pages contain objects that seem to reside in different domains but are instead coming from the same server. Such fake domains trick the browser to allow more parallel connections as browsers limit the number of parallel connections per domain. The use of a large number of parallel TCP connections with typical Web traffic tends to intensify queuing effect and may dramatically increase the effect of the delay spikes, which is likely to be particularly harmful to delay sensitive traffic such as interactive audio and video. Moreover, in the recent years some efforts have been made to increase the initial window of TCP from three to ten segments [3,5]. Such increase together with the large number of parallel TCP connections introduces rapidly changing environment for any traffic competing with the parallel TCP flows.

While solutions such as Low Extra Delay Background Transport (LEDBAT) [14] that attempt to keep queuing delay low exist, their use for Web traffic would be controversial as the Web traffic is certainly not less than best effort type. Quite contrary, the browsers and websites aim to minimize the latency in Web page transmission which is in direct conflict with the carefulness that approaches such as LEDBAT need. Considering that current browsers and websites disregard advice on number of concurrent connections [6] to shorten latency, it is unlikely that browser makers or website administrators would find LEDBAT or similar approach an acceptable solution. Besides, deployment of a new TCP variant in large scale would be a challenge in itself. On the other hand, if such TCP variant would be used only on-demand when a threat to harm media flows exists, additional signalling between the end hosts would be required as LEDBAT is implemented at the sender. Such signalling again would face deployment challenges.

On the network side, phenomenon called bufferbloat [8,11] has recently attracted some attention. Because of bufferbloat, devices in the network can end up buffering enormous amount of traffic such as the initial windows of all parallel web responses. Active queue management (AQM) and its most prominent representative Random Early Detection (RED) [7] is often proposed as a solution to the bufferbloat but that is challenging to realize in practice. The access network devices that are typically bottlenecks lack support for AQM/RED, and even if available, RED does not work with the default settings as it is "too gentle to handle fast changes due to TCP slow start when the aggregate traffic is limited" [10]. As tuning of the RED parameters requires modifications on the intermediate network nodes, it is not deployable in the short run on large scale even if RED itself is supported by the devices.

Media flows are typically reduced in size for transmission by a codec which tries to retain human observable properties of the original content while removing information where human senses cannot detect the changes. Usually codecs can conceal sporadic losses quite well, but when more losses occur consecutively, quality deteriorates and distortions become noticeable. A jitter buffer between the receiving codec and the network absorbs jitter that occurs in the packet transmission over the network. The codec needs the data on time because the media playback is time bound. If a sudden delay increase occurs in the network, the media packet might not arrive in time for the playback and needs to be discarded unused. Selecting a larger jitter buffer size is a tradeoff as it would allow larger jitter to occur but at the same time it increases the total end-to-end delay, potentially resulting in unacceptable interactive media quality.

Another problem for media flows are long-lived TCP connections such as software updates and file downloads. A long-lived TCP connection tends to create long queues that occupy the bottleneck buffers for a long period of time. The long term queues often cause high end-to-end one-way delay for interactive media, resulting in unacceptable interactive media quality.

Some studies explored media flows and Web Traffic in 3G/3.5G network [9,16]. In these studies, however, the different traffic types might not be competing with each other over the cellular data channel. In this study we focus on the effect of simultaneous TCP flows on interactive media, and also on the effect of the larger TCP initial window [3]. To our best knowledge, neither effect has been explored in a 3G/3.5G environment before. Although cellular access is used in the experiments, we believe that the results are representative for any access with similar moderate link capacity because deep buffers are a widespread phenomenon [8]. TCP performance and the interactions between parallel TCP connections are out of scope for this study.

In this paper we measure the effect of competing TCP traffic to interactive media flows in a real high-speed cellular network environment. The rest of this paper is organized as follows. In Section 2 we introduce the test setup and workloads for the experimentation. In Section 3 we analyze how TCP traffic affects the one-way delay and delay variation of a media flow. In Section 4 we analyze the transient effect of jitter-induced loss periods on a media flow and in Section 5 we conclude our findings.

2   Test Setup and Workloads

The experiments have been carried out over a real cellular Internet access using emulated traffic flows to allow full control over the workloads and more accurate analysis of the results. The test system comprises of a mobile host and fixed server, as presented in Figure 1.

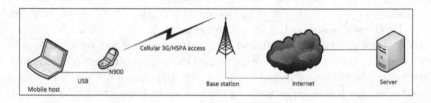

Fig. 1. Test environment

In order to get the baseline for interactive media flow behavior without competing traffic in the test environment we first measure the performance of an emulated audio only workload. We then focus on the two major workloads that roughly mimic two typical TCP traffic loads competing with an interactive media flow: (1) Software update during a voice call (*Audio+Bulk*) and (2) Web browsing when a voice call is ongoing (*Audio+n short TCP flows*). In the *Audio+Bulk* workload, an emulated audio flow starts first and then a Bulk TCP transfer of 28 MB starts. Bulk TCP's start time is distributed uniformly between 10 to 12 seconds after the start of the audio flow. In the *Audio+n short TCP flows* workload, an emulated audio flow starts first and then n short TCP flows start at the same time, the start time being distributed uniformly between 10 to 12 seconds after the start of the audio flow. The n short TCP flows can be one TCP flow, two TCP flows or six TCP flows. The total size of the short TCP flows is 372 kB. In both scenarios the audio flow is ongoing while TCP traffic is starting in the middle of the audio flow. The audio flow lasts long enough to cover the whole duration of the TCP transfer.

The direction of traffic in all test cases is from the fixed server to the mobile host. We also send enough warming up packets right before each test run to ensure that a dedicated channel (DCH state) is allocated for the actual test data, and thereby radio state changes are not affecting the results. The n short TCP flows are tested with initial window of three (IW3) and initial window of ten (IW10). The audio flow is a constant bit-rate (CBR) type with bit-rate of 16 kbps yielding 32 kbps total bit-rate with IP, UDP, and RTP headers, that is, an IP packet of 80 bytes is transmitted every 20 ms. We run 50 replications with each different combination of test parameter values. All the test traffic is captured using tcpdump [17] on both the mobile host and the fixed server. We carefully synchronized the end host clocks prior each test run using Network Time Protocol (NTP) [13] allowing initially enough time for the clocks to be slowly adjusted towards almost equal rates. This enabled us to measure one-way delay [1] for each media packet with reasonable accuracy by taking the difference in timestamps found in the tcpdump logs at each end.

3   Effects on One-Way Delay and Delay Variation

In the conducted experiments, the HSPA network introduced hardly any losses during the observed period. Therefore, the effect of competing TCP traffic is mainly due to the delay and the changes in the delay. While analyzing the results, we noticed that on a few occasions the wireless link introduced very long delays to packet delivery ranging from 3 seconds to rare occurrences with more than 60 seconds of delay. Also a large number of consecutive losses, reordering, or packet duplication occurred during such events. We choose to filter out the cases where clear symptoms of such event occurred because we are interested in how TCP affects media flow rather than wireless link problems. As we do not have access to the cellular operator network to collect traces, we cannot confirm the exact cause for this "wireless phenomenon" but in most of the cases they are likely to be caused by the cellular access deciding to switch access technology.

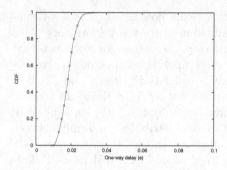 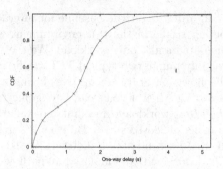

Fig. 2. CDF of one-way delay for 15 secs audio only workload, 50 replications

Fig. 3. CDF of one-way delay for an audio flow with a competing Bulk TCP connection, 50 replications

Figure 2 shows the cumulative distribution function (CDF) of end-to-end one-way delay [1] for 15 secs audio only workload. The one-way delay is good enough for inter-active audio conversation. The loss-rate is only 0.05 %. The delays remain below 40 ms except for a handful of packets, the median and maximum measured one-way delay being 18.0 ms and 70.4 ms, respectively.

Figure 3 shows the CDF of one-way delay for the media flow packets during a bulk TCP transfer. With the competing bulk TCP transfer interactive audio is impossible because the one-way delays during the TCP transfer are prohibitive. Already the 25th percentile of the one-way delay is 0.5 secs and the median is 1.42 secs. We confirmed from the traces that deep buffering is the main cause for the delay increase; soon after the bulk TCP transfer starts the delay increases and remains around 1.5-2.5 secs consistently for the duration of the TCP transfer. Such a delay increase was not present in audio only results. Few values especially in the highest end, however, might be due to wireless network phenomena on top of the deep buffering.

Figure 4 shows CDF of the one-way delay for the media flow with short TCP flows when different number of TCP connections and different TCP initial window sizes are in use. The one-way delay with one competing TCP flow using initial window of three segments is reasonably low and seems to allow smooth packet delivery for interactive media. Increasing the number of TCP connections from one to two causes only a moderate increase in the end-to-end delay. However, increasing the TCP connection count to six introduces larger one-way delays, and the sharp knee transition with one or two flows is transformed into an earlier increase in the one-way delay affecting roughly 40 % of the packets. However, in all cases with competing TCP traffic using IW3 the one-way delay remains below 150ms all the way up to 75th percentile.

The one-way delay with competing TCP traffic using initial window of ten segments is notably higher than when using initial window of three in all corresponding cases. In all cases with the initial window of ten the one-way delay is higher than with the case of six TCP connections using the initial window of three. The median one-way delay with six competing TCP flows using IW10

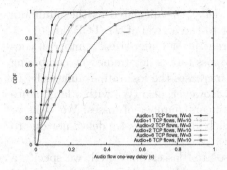
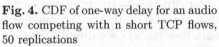

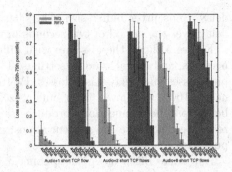

Fig. 4. CDF of one-way delay for an audio flow competing with n short TCP flows, 50 replications

Fig. 5. Loss rate with different jitter buffer sizes for Audio+n short TCP flows workload

approaches 200ms but remains below 150ms even with one and two competing TCP flows.

IP Packet Delay Variation (IPDV) [4] for the media flow is shown in Table 1. As the high-end values seemed to correlate well with the increase in the size of the combined initial windows of parallel TCP flows, we extracted from the packet traces those TCP data packets that are received between two audio packets and confirmed that the large IPDV values typically occur when the TCP initial windows are among those TCP packets. In particular, with IW10 the large IPDV values are mostly introduced when the TCP flows inject the initial windows into the network.

4 Estimated Delay Induced Loss Period Effects

In order to explore the transient effect of the delay jitter on the media flow, we introduce a jitter filter to mimic receiving codec behavior in dropping late arriving media flow packets. First, there are "pure losses" when a packet is dropped in the network, either due to congestion or link errors. With interactive media, there is also "delay-based loss" when a media flow packet delay exceeds the jitter buffer limit and thereby misses the deadline for codec to decode and play the transmitted content. Such a packet is unusable similar to the pure loss. Delay-based losses are flagged when one-way delay of the packet exceeds "base

Table 1. CDF of IPDV for an audio flow competing with n short TCP flows, 50 replications

IW	n	Min	25%	Median	75%	90%	95%	96%	97%	98%	99%	Max
3	1	-0.020107	-0.011373	-0.000206	0.009194	0.020072	0.029445	0.031174	0.034697	0.043296	0.070158	0.111526
3	2	-0.020102	-0.011242	-0.000281	0.008824	0.018924	0.028301	0.029892	0.039526	0.050787	0.100523	0.182076
3	6	-0.020107	-0.011696	-0.000588	0.001666	0.012330	0.025413	0.031916	0.059762	0.081594	0.125042	0.282826
10	1	-0.020414	-0.012084	-0.000482	0.001835	0.016195	0.020696	0.029253	0.030297	0.050413	0.172464	0.242798
10	2	-0.020128	-0.019264	-0.000919	0.003032	0.019432	0.030032	0.031393	0.041291	0.070785	0.160448	0.322197
10	6	-0.020098	-0.019541	-0.009664	0.000454	0.018741	0.030004	0.040417	0.069099	0.121090	0.220447	0.589717

delay" plus jitter buffer size. The "base delay" is calculated as the minimum delay over the period of two seconds prior to the arrival of the TCP flows.

Figure 5 shows the loss rate with different jitter buffer sizes, number of connections, and initial window settings. The loss rate is determined by combining pure losses and delay-based losses. IW10 increases the loss rate dramatically to nearly 100% with lower jitter buffer sizes. However, also IW3 with a large number of parallel connections produces significant number of losses. We want to reiterate that these losses occur almost solely due to excessive delay, not due to pure losses.

As codecs often are able to conceal isolated losses quite well, we specify a metric to estimate loss period effect on the interactive media from codec and end user perspective. The estimate is based on loss periods [12] that are encountered by the codec when several consecutive media flow packets are dropped due to jitter delay. We combine also pure losses into this metric though pure losses occur infrequently in our experiments. For a given jitter buffer size, each data packet carrying interactive media (Audio) is assigned a loss period level according to the definition in Table 2.

We intentionally chose to use minimum delay as base delay in order to report the worst-case behavior. As a real codec might choose higher value, it is reasonable to assume that the loss period effect is unlikely to be worse than that indicated by the loss period level.

In order to better understand transient effects that are hidden with CDF, Figures 6a, 6b, and 6c estimate the loss period effect in a function of time for a media flow using 40 ms jitter buffer size and competing with 1, 2, and 6 short TCP flows, respectively. 50 replications are included in each test case. The loss period level values are filtered to only include the media flow packets that overlap with the TCP transfers and therefore the number of samples starts to decline around 1 second when the TCP flows in individual test replications start to complete.

Almost immediately when the TCP flows start the TCP traffic generates significant loss period effect on the media flow packets, as the SYN handshakes complete and the TCP flows inject their initial windows into the network. We note that the arrival of the initial windows causes the worst effect during the whole transfer. When only a single TCP connection is competing with the media

Table 2. Loss period level definition for estimating loss period effects

Value	Description
0	no loss
1	20 ms gap in the stream, no adjacent packet lost
2	40-60 ms of the stream was lost
3	80-100 ms of the stream was lost
4	120-180 ms of the stream was lost
5	200+ ms of the stream was lost

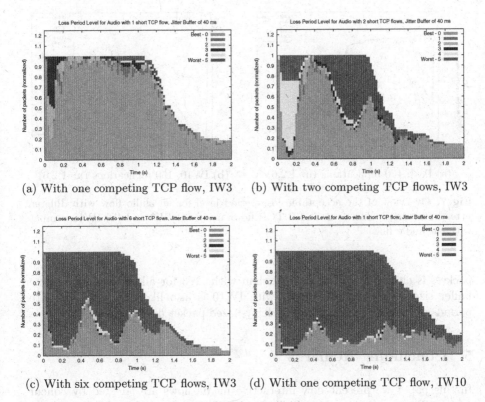

(a) With one competing TCP flow, IW3   (b) With two competing TCP flows, IW3

(c) With six competing TCP flows, IW3   (d) With one competing TCP flow, IW10

Fig. 6. Estimated loss period levels for audio packets when an audio flow using 40 ms jitter buffer competes with TCP transfers, 50 replications

flow the loss period effect is not falling to the worst level and the level is rapidly restored after the initial window around 0.2 seconds. With two TCP flows the initial window injection causes much worse effect than with one concurrent flow but still the media flow is able to restore better level once the initial windows have been transmitted. However, as the two TCP flows start to open up their window resulting in more jitter the loss period effect again becomes notable. With six concurrent connections the loss period level is very bad right from the beginning and affects almost the whole duration of the TCP transfers. Figure 6d shows the loss period level with one competing TCP flow using IW10. The worst loss period level immediately becomes dominant like in case of six TCP flows with IW3 and remains dominant all the way until the completion of the TCP flows.

Figure 7 summarizes the estimated loss period effect on the media flow with n competing TCP flows when different IW sizes are used. The loss period levels 0 and 1 are combined to determine "acceptable" level (i.e., no lost packet has an adjacent packet lost) and all the cases with one, two, or six short TCP flows are considered together. We observe that the number of acceptable media flow

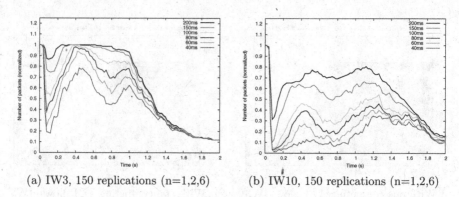

(a) IW3, 150 replications (n=1,2,6)   (b) IW10, 150 replications (n=1,2,6)

Fig. 7. Overview of the acceptable loss period level for an audio flow with different jitter buffer sizes when 1, 2, and 6 TCP flows using (a) IW3 and (b) IW10 compete with the audio flow

packets is clearly lower with IW10 than with IW3 for all corresponding jitter buffer sizes. The aggressive start with IW10 is also likely to make the later periods of transfer to trigger more delay-based packet discarding at the codecs.

5   Concluding Remarks

In this paper we present how interactive media flows are affected by concurrent TCP transmissions in a high-speed cellular network. Our measurements show that the packets of the media flow are heavily delayed when competing with TCP connections, which is likely to prevent a codec from using significant portion of the packets before the playback deadline. Even a moderate number of parallel TCP connections that are typically used for carrying Web page responses, for example, causes irreparable harm for a concurrent interactive media transfer. Startup dynamics for individual TCP connections may vary between the browsers and Web pages but we believe that our current measurements captured the major effect regardless of different mechanisms in browsers for launching parallel connections. Such variations are just likely to result in numerous variants of similar behavior.

Our experiments also indicate that during a short TCP transmission the worst effect on the media flow is measured during the burst of packets that occur because of the initial TCP window transmission, and that initial window of ten segments is worse for the competing media flow than initial window of three segments. With a competing bulk TCP transfer, the media stream becomes unusable for interactive purposes.

As the media flow performance degradation is caused by the behavior of Web traffic and deep buffers, we believe that the results are representative also for other than cellular access. The performance data is available at: http://www.cs.helsinki.fi/group/wibra/pam2013-data/.

References

1. Almes, G., Kalidindi, S., Zekauskas, M.: A One-way Delay Metric for IPPM. RFC 2679 (September 1999)
2. Browserscope, http://www.browserscope.org/?category=network&v=1
3. Chu, J., Dukkipati, N., Cheng, Y., Mathis, M.: Increasing TCP's Initial Window. Internet Draft (November 2012) (work in progress)
4. Demichelis, C., Chimento, P.: IP Packet Delay Variation Metric for IP Performance Metrics (IPPM). RFC 3393 (November 2002)
5. Dukkipati, N., et al.: An Argument for Increasing TCP's Initial Congestion Window. ACM SIGCOMM Computer Communications Review 40(3), 26–33 (2010)
6. Fielding, R., et al.: Hypertext Transfer Protocol – HTTP/1.1. RFC 2616 (June 1999)
7. Floyd, S., Jacobson, V.: Random Early Detection Gateways for Congestion Avoidance. IEEE/ACM Transactions on Networking 1(4), 397–413 (1993)
8. Gettys, J.: IW10 Considered Harmful. Internet Draft (August 2011) (work in progress)
9. Huang, J.: et al.: Anatomizing Application Performance Differences on Smartphones. In: Proceedings of the 8th International Conference on Mobile Systems, Applications, and Services (MobiSys), pp. 165–178 (June 2010)
10. Järvinen, I., Ding, Y., Nyrhinen, A., Kojo, M.: Harsh RED: Improving RED for Limited Aggregate Traffic. In: Proceedings of the 26th IEEE International Conference on Advanced Information Networking and Applications (AINA) (March 2012)
11. Jiang, H., Liu, Z., Wang, Y., Lee, K., Rhee, I.: Understanding Bufferbloat in Cellular Networks. In: Proceedings of the Workshop on Cellular Networks: Operations, Challenges, and Future Design (CellNet) at SIGCOMM 2012 (August 2012)
12. Koodli, R., Ravikanth, R.: One-way Loss Pattern Sample Metrics. RFC 3357 (August 2002)
13. Mills, D., Martin, J., Burbank, J., Kasch, W.: Network Time Protocol Version 4: Protocol and Algorithms Specification. RFC 5905 (June 2010)
14. Shalunov, S., Hazel, G., Iyengar, J., Kuehlewind, M.: Low extra delay background transport (LEDBAT). RFC 6817 (December 2012)
15. Souders, S.: Roundup on Parallel Connections (March 2008), http://www.stevesouders.com/blog/2008/03/20/roundup-on-parallel-connections/
16. Tan, W., Lam, F., Lau, W.: An Empirical Study on the Capacity and Performance of 3G Networks. IEEE Transactions on Mobile Computing 7(6), 737–750 (2008)
17. TCPDUMP/LIBPCAP public repository, http://www.tcpdump.org/

A Comparative Study of Android and iOS for Accessing Internet Streaming Services

Yao Liu[1], Fei Li[1], Lei Guo[2], Bo Shen[3], and Songqing Chen[1]

[1] Dept. of Computer Science, George Mason University
{yliud,lifei,sqchen}@cs.gmu.edu
[2] Dept. of CSE, Ohio State University
lguo@cse.ohio-state.edu
[3] Vuclip
bshen@vuclip.com

Abstract. Android and iOS devices are leading the mobile device market. While various user experiences have been reported from the general user community about their differences, such as battery lifetime, display, and touchpad control, few in-depth reports can be found about their comparative performance when receiving the increasingly popular Internet streaming services.

Today, video traffic starts to dominate the Internet mobile data traffic. In this work, focusing on Internet streaming accesses, we set to analyze and compare the performance when Android and iOS devices are accessing Internet streaming services. Starting from the analysis of a server-side workload collected from a top mobile streaming service provider, we find Android and iOS use different approaches to request media content, leading to different amounts of received traffic on Android and iOS devices when a same video clip is accessed. Further studies on the client side show that different data requesting approaches (standard HTTP request vs. HTTP range request) and different buffer management methods (static vs. dynamic) are used in Android and iOS mediaplayers, and their interplay has led to our observations. Our empirical results and analysis provide some insights for the current Android and iOS users, streaming service providers, and mobile mediaplayer developers.

1 Introduction

Mobile devices are gaining increasing popularity among common users. While the market competition between different devices has been intense, iOS devices (such as iPhone, iPad, and iPod Touch) and Android devices (such as Galaxy Nexus, Motorola Droid, and Kindle Fire) are most popular today. It is reported that iOS and Android devices comprise more than 79% of all existing mobile devices [1].

Today more and more mobile users use their devices for Internet streaming accesses. While various streaming protocols are supported, Pseudo Streaming [2] is the most popular among mobile devices. Both iOS and Android have native support for Pseudo Streaming from the very beginning. YouTube [3], Dailymotion [4], and Veoh [5] all support Pseudo Streaming for mobile devices to access their video content.

As streaming accesses typically involve a large amount of data transferring in a continuous fashion for a relatively long duration, two aspects are of particular concerns to a mobile device user. The first is about the battery power consumption. Today the limited

M. Roughan and R. Chang (Eds.) PAM 2013, LNCS 7799, pp. 104–114, 2013.

battery power supply is still the Achilles' heel of all mobile devices, and a breakthrough of the battery technology is still not on the horizon yet. On the other hand, for most common mobile users, their mobile traffic amount is closely related to the monetary cost that they need to pay to the cellular service provider. Streaming accesses often involve bulk data transmission, resulting in more traffic than other routine activities. Thus it is of a user's greatest interest if a less amount of traffic is delivered while the service quality remains unchanged.

In this work, focusing on Internet streaming accesses, we set to analyze and compare the performance when Android and iOS devices are accessing Internet streaming services. We start with the analysis of a server-side workload collected from a top mobile streaming service provider. In this workload, about 26,713,708 HTTP requests were observed to access 15,725 video clips in 28 days, generating a total of 27.4 TB video traffic. Analyzing this workload, we find that Android and iOS devices use different approaches to request media content, leading to a different amount of received traffic on Android and iOS devices when a same video clip is accessed.

To figure out the underlying causes, we further conduct client-side experiments with the state-of-the-art iOS and Android devices. Through extensive experiments and by delving into the source code of the Android mediaplayer, we find that the current Android and iOS mediaplayers employ different data requesting approaches (standard HTTP request vs. HTTP range request) and different playout buffer management methods (static vs. dynamic). These contrasting approaches and methods lead to a significant amount of redundant traffic received on iOS devices but not on Android devices. Intuitively, this causes more battery power consumption on iOS devices and potentially results in more monetary cost to iOS users.

Our study provides some insights for common users when they access online streaming services. In addition, our experiments and analysis show that different mediaplayer frameworks have been used in Android and iOS with different media content requesting approaches and playout buffer management methods. These insights can help the future mediaplayer development as well as streaming service providers. The client-side trace is available for download at [6].

2   Server-Side Observations

The server log we have collected is from a top mobile streaming video site, Vuclip, which serves worldwide mobile users. The workload is collected from Feb 1st to Feb 28th, 2011. In this workload, about 26,713,708 HTTP requests are observed to access 15,725 video clips in 28 days, generating a total of 27.4 TB video traffic.

Vuclip supports both iOS and Android. Users can install an application [7] on their mobile devices from iOS AppStore or Google Play. The application provides the same user interface to both iOS and Android users, and allows them to access the same pool of videos via WiFi or cellular connections. Thus, it provides a good base for our study.

Vuclip allows users to watch videos on their mobile devices using Pseudo Streaming. With Pseudo Streaming, a client can download the video file via HTTP requests, and can start video playback without waiting for the file being completely downloaded. It can also support a user's request to jump to a certain position for playback by downloading the desired part of the file directly via HTTP range requests – HTTP requests with properly specified range headers. In order to provision for the variance of network speed during playback, Pseudo Streaming usually requires a buffer, often referred to as playout buffer, on the client side to store video data to be played. Typically, downloading should be faster than the playback for good user experience, and it is very common that the entire video file has been downloaded while the playback just proceeds to an earlier part of the video.

We use the *User-Agent* string to examine whether a request comes from an iOS device or an Android device. For example, when sending HTTP requests, iOS devices use `AppleCoreMedia/1.0.0` for its User-Agent string, while Android devices identify themselves with `stagefright/1.x (Linux;Android x.x.x)`. In the workload, we extract 397,940 unique video sessions from iOS devices and 884,648 unique video sessions from Android devices. Each session may consist of multiple HTTP requests. In these sessions, the users do not necessarily watch the entire video from the beginning to the end. Users may find the video uninteresting, and terminate the playback in the middle.

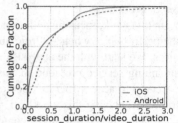

Fig. 1. Ratio Between Session Duration and Video Duration (CDF)

Figure 2 shows the distribution of downloading session duration for both iOS and Android accesses[1]. Note that the downloading session duration may be shorter than the user's actual viewing duration, because in Pseudo Streaming, the download-ing is often faster than the playback. Comparing the accesses from iOS with these from Android devices,

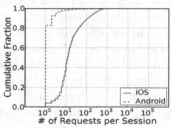

Fig. 2. # of HTTP Requests per Session (CDF)

we find that the patterns of session duration as opposed to the video duration are quite similar (although Android devices generally have a slightly longer session duration than that of iOS devices). This indicates similar accessing behaviors of Android and iOS devices to this streaming service.

More Requests Are Sent Out by iOS Devices. Figure 2 shows the distribution of the # of HTTP requests that were sent to the server from mobile devices in these sessions. We find that more than 80% of Android sessions consist of only one single HTTP request, and only less than 2% sessions consist of more than 10 HTTP requests. On the contrary, iOS devices always send more HTTP requests. The median number is 13 HTTP requests per iOS session. This is quite surprising because intuitively, only one HTTP request is needed, which happened to most Android sessions. We are interested in why so many more HTTP requests have been used in iOS sessions.

Based on the log, we find that the MediaPlayer on a mobile device can request the video file in two ways: (1) it requests the entire video file with a standard HTTP request, and the server responds with `HTTP 200 OK`, or (2) it requests a portion of the video file using an HTTP range request, and the server responds with `HTTP 206 Partial`

---

[1] iOS and Android accesses (or sessions) refer to accesses (or sessions) originated from an iOS or Android device. They are used for brevity.

Content. Typically an HTTP range request is used when a user wants to skip part of the video, and jump to the desired content directly. However, in this server log, we find that iOS devices always use HTTP range requests, even for the first request. But Android devices always use standard HTTP requests, and only use HTTP range requests to fetch desired content directly if the user decides to jump to another part of the video. Table 1 shows the percentage of different types of HTTP requests that have been used by iOS and Android devices, respectively. As shown in the table, more than 80% Android traffic is delivered using standard HTTP responses (200), while almost all iOS traffic is delivered using HTTP partial content response (206). Note that although the percentage of HTTP range requests in Android sessions seems also high, it is mainly because once a user starts to use interactive functions, a sequence of range requests often have to be used. Nevertheless, over 80% of Android traffic is delivered via standard HTTP connections.

More Traffic Is Received at iOS Devices. We further sum up the size of HTTP responses that belong to the same video session, and examine if such different content requesting approaches on Android and iOS devices have any impact on the traffic delivered to them. Figure 3 shows the result. As we can observe from this figure, for Android devices, about 55% Android sessions downloaded the same amount of traffic as the video file size, and only a very small percentage of the sessions downloaded more data than the video file size. This could be caused by user re-watching the video. The rest (about 43%) only downloaded partial video content and terminated earlier.

On the other hand, for iOS devices, about 72% iOS sessions terminated earlier before the entire file is downloaded. But the most surprising result is that for about 28% iOS sessions, the downloaded traffic is larger than the video file size. Because we are comparing the requests of Android and iOS devices from a same streaming service, it is reasonable to assume that the users' interest

Table 1. HTTP Request/Reply (Number and Traffic Amount)

HTTP 200		
Name	#Requests	Traffic Amount
iOS	0.01%	0.001%
Android	27.30%	80.594%

HTTP 206		
Name	#Requests	Traffic Amount
iOS	99.99%	99.999%
Android	72.70%	19.406%

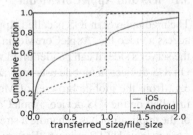

Fig. 3. Ratio Between Received Traffic and File Size (CDF)

and access patterns are similar. Thus, among the 28% sessions that iOS devices downloaded more data than the actual video file size, only a very smaller portion is likely due to users' real re-watching activities. We are interested in about 28% iOS sessions that have received extra traffic (than the actual file size).

3   Analysis of Android and iOS Mediaplayers

While the server-side workload has provided us a high-level overview of different content requesting approaches of iOS and Android devices when accessing Internet streaming services as well as different amounts of traffic received, the workload cannot provide

Table 2. Devices Used

Name	OS version	Memory Size
iPod Touch	iOS 3.1.2	128 MB
iPhone 3G	iOS 4.2.1	128 MB
iPhone 3GS	iOS 5.0.1	256 MB
iPhone 4S	iOS 5.1	512 MB
Nexus One	Android 2.3.4	256 MB
Kindle Fire	Android 2.3.4	512 MB

Table 3. iOS Devices Accessing a 36.7 MB YouTube Video

Name	# of HTTP Connections	Received Traffic (Bytes)	Re-downloaded (Bytes)
iPod Touch	261	83,410,351	26,450,851
iPhone 3G	301	82,616,828	37,449,911
iPhone 3GS	105	63,713,281	11,523,915
iPhone 4S	67	51,625,429	9,292,410

more details for us to explore the underlying reasons. Thus, in this section, we further investigate these observations using the state-of-the-art Android and iOS devices.

For iOS, because we cannot access its source code, we mainly conduct client-side experiments in a controlled environment to infer how it works by analyzing the captured traffic. For Android, in addition to the client-side experiments, we are able to get a better idea of how it works by accessing the source code of its mediaplayer.

The client-side experiments are conducted in our lab with a dedicated 802.11 b/g access point (AP). We use six different mobile devices running different mobile operating systems and different versions of the mobile OS. Table 2 lists these devices. We use 4 different iOS devices and 2 different Android devices. Note that although Kindle Fire uses a customized version of Android, it uses the same mediaplayer framework as other Android devices including the Nexus One we use in our experiments.

In order to examine all the incoming and outgoing traffic to/from our testing devices, we set up Wireshark [8] running on a laptop computer to listen on the same channel as the AP in promiscuous mode. Packets are captured in real-time and processed offline.

3.1 iOS and AppleCoreMedia

The mediaplayer in iOS is called AppleCoreMedia. When Pseudo Streaming is used to access a video file, AppleCoreMedia will send out HTTP requests for the video file. On the server's side, it can be identified with User-Agent of `AppleCoreMedia/1.0.0`. On iOS devices, a mobile user may access the video streaming service in various ways, e.g., from the mobile browser of MobileSafari, or a third party streaming application installed on the iOS device. AppleCoreMedia will be called when the mobile browser or the application has to handle a streaming request. AppleCoreMedia usually specifies a range in its HTTP requests. For example, if it is requesting the entire video file, it will send out an HTTP request with the range specified from 0 to filesize-1.

To study the behavior of AppleCoreMedia in downloading media content, we use our testing devices to access a same 480-second YouTube video via their mobile browsers. The file size of that video is 38,517,389 Bytes. In each experiment, we let an iOS device watch the entire video (8 minutes) from the beginning to the end without any manual activities. Figure 4 shows the accumulative traffic pattern of 4 different iOS devices accessing this video along time as well as the playback progress. Note the total traffic in this figure only includes the media content. That is, protocol headers are all excluded. We find that during the first 30 seconds of each session, AppleCoreMedia downloads with a high speed, and slows down afterwards. Clearly, this is the initial buffering phase of a video streaming session, which is also called *fast start* [9]. More interestingly, we notice that the amount of received traffic by iOS devices is larger than the video file size

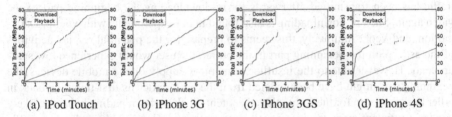

(a) iPod Touch   (b) iPhone 3G   (c) iPhone 3GS   (d) iPhone 4S

Fig. 4. Traffic Pattern of iOS Devices Accessing a YouTube Video

(36.7 MBytes). For iPod Touch and iPhone 3G, the total received traffic amount is even more than twice of the actual video file size.

Table 3 summarizes the amount of total traffic received during these sessions by 4 iOS devices. Note that these sessions are normal sessions without early terminations or any replays. Analyzing the corresponding packet-level workload we have captured, we find that multiple HTTP range requests are issued to download the streaming content. That is, instead of using a standard HTTP request, iOS devices always issue multiple range requests to download media content. This is consistent with what we have observed from the server-side workload shown in Figure 2. It is noticeable that iPhone 3G even issued more than 300 HTTP requests to download the video file. For devices with an increased memory size, such as iPhone 3GS and iPhone 4S, the number of HTTP requests is reduced to 105 and 67, respectively.

The above results show that the multiple HTTP range requests used by iOS are not due to Vuclip, as the same phenomenon has been observed in other popular streaming services as well. Besides YouTube, we have also tested against two other popular sites Dailymotion and Veoh, we have found similar patterns.

In addition, we also find in Table 3 that the received traffic amount on these iOS devices is significantly larger than the actual file size. Recall that we have observed different amounts of traffic delivered to Android and iOS devices in the server-side log. We are interested in whether such extra traffic received on iOS devices is related to the content requesting approach, i.e., the multiple HTTP range requests.

Inspecting the packet-level workload we have captured for these experiments, we find that while AppleCoreMedia always starts with an HTTP range request instead of a standard HTTP request, it constantly terminates the HTTP connection spontaneously before the full response to that range request is received. Subsequently, it will issue another HTTP range request. Having carefully studied the workload, our conjecture is that such behaviors are closely related to the available memory space in a mobile device. Our packet level traces across all these experiments consistently show that AppleCore-Media always resets (via TCP-RST) the active connection used for the HTTP request. The most likely reason is due to the lack of the memory space for the playout buffer. With a small amount of available memory, AppleCoreMedia has to frequently abort the current connection because the playout buffer is going to overflow.

Besides highly frequent connection aborts (which also necessitates multiple HTTP range requests after aborts), we also find that AppleCoreMedia always re-downloads the beginning part of the video after it has received the entire video file. Recall that with Pseudo Streaming, the entire file is usually received before the user finishes the playback. However, as shown by the last column in Table 3, a significant amount of traffic has been transmitted afterwards for re-downloading the beginning part of the video again. Such re-downloading is also found in our experiments with Vuclip, Daily-motion, and Veoh. Intuitively, this seems to prepare for the potential re-play activities of the user. With the beginning part in the buffer, the user would experience low start-up delay. However, due to the insufficient memory supply on the mobile devices, the beginning part might have been evicted from the buffer after its first-time playback in order to make room for the to-be-played content. Such re-downloading behavior, likely due to insufficient memory size as well, apparently contributes to the redundant traffic we have observed in Figure 3.

For the same reason, for iOS devices with a larger memory size (such as iPhone 3GS and iPhone 4S), the re-downloading traffic amount is much smaller as shown in Table 3. This indicates that with more available memory, AppleCoreMedia can get more buffer space, and put a larger portion of the video file in its buffer.

We further examine the impact of the memory size by instructing our testing de-vices to access different video files with an increasing file size. We use three different YouTube videos. Videos are of different du-rations but are encoded with the same data rate. Table 4 shows the results we have ob-tained. These results are the average results over multiple experiments. This table shows that devices with different physical memory

Table 4. Transferred Traffic vs. File Size (Bytes)

	Video1	Video2	Video3
Duration (sec)	360	480	657
File Size	29,503,221	38,517,389	53,405,910
iPod Touch	42,379,164	57,176,659	90,445,044
iPhone 3G	42,322,498	74,442,375	86,933,886
iPhone 3GS	37,702,143	47,460,396	72,388,936
iPhone 4S	32,248,384	44,538,836	61,731,408

sizes have different traffic efficiency. If we compare the results in a same row, we can see that when the video file size becomes larger, the amount of redundant traffic would also increase. For example, from Table 4 we can see that the redundant traffic for iPhone 4S is increased from 9% when accessing Video1 to more than 15% when accessing Video2 and Video3.

3.2 Android and Stagefright

The study of iOS and AppleCoreMedia shows that the memory available to the playout buffer of the mediaplayer is dynamically changing and it plays a critical role in the entire streaming session. In this subsection, we examine if a different type of buffer management method has been used in Android as Android devices have shown different behaviors in accessing streaming media.

Starting from Android 2.3 Gingerbread, a new mediaplayer framework called Stage-fright is used in Android. Similar to AppleCoreMedia, Stagefright also supports Pseudo Streaming by using HTTP for requesting video data. On Android devices, a mobile user can access video streaming services from either the mobile browser or applications installed, similar to that on iOS devices. Stagefright is called when a video request needs to be handled. From the server's side, it can be identified with User-Agent of stagefright/1.x (Linux;Android x.x.x). As we shall show later, Stage-fright results in a completely different traffic pattern from that of AppleCoreMedia.

To examine how Stagefright works on Android devices, we use our testing devices to access the same 480-second YouTube video (36.7 MBytes) via their native browsers. Again, for each experiment, we let the Android devices watch the entire video for 8

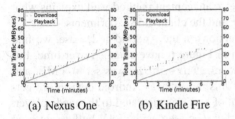

(a) Nexus One   (b) Kindle Fire

Fig. 5. Traffic Pattern of Android Devices Accessing a YouTube Video

Table 5. Android Devices Accessing a 36.7 MB YouTube Video

Name	# of HTTP Connections	Received Traffic (Bytes)	Re-downloaded (Bytes)
Nexus One	1	38,517,389	0
Kindle Fire	1	38,517,389	0

minutes without any manual activities. Figure 5 shows the accumulative traffic pattern of our 2 different Android devices, Nexus One and Kindle Fire, with the corresponding playback speed. We find that downloading is explicitly and periodically paused during the 8-minute playback. With multiple experiments conducted, we find that although the data burst length is different across Nexus One and Kindle Fire, such pausing and resuming behaviors can be consistently observed.

Further inspection of the corresponding packet level workloads reveals that only one single HTTP request is used to download the video file by both Nexus One and Kindle Fire as shown in Table 5. When the downloading is paused, instead of terminating the current TCP connection as AppleCoreMedia does, Stagefright sets the TCP window size to 0, so that the server would not send any more packets to it. When it wants to resume the downloading, it will send a TCP window update message, and the server will start to deliver the data again. Moreover, we find that the total traffic amount is always equal to the video file size, indicating no re-downloading of the beginning part. This is also different from AppleCoreMedia.

Such different behaviors observed on Stagefright in these experiments and in the server-side log motivate us to explore the underlying reasons. Next, we study the Android source code to better understand how Stagefright works.

In the libstagefright framework, the underlying media playout buffer is handled by `NuCachedSource2.cpp`. Basically, it sets a `HighWaterThreshold`. When the total buffer size reaches this threshold, the

```
enum {
    kPageSize              = 65535,
    kDefaultHighWaterThreshold = 20 * 1024 * 1024,
    kDefaultLowWaterThreshold  = 4 * 1024 * 1024,
    kDefaultKeepAliveIntervals = 15000000,
};
```

Fig. 6. Code Snippet From /libstagefright/include/NuCachedSource2.h

downloading would be paused. As the playback progresses, the buffer depletes. When the to-be-played data in the buffer drops below another pre-defined threshold `LowWaterThreshold`, the downloading will be resumed. Figure 6 shows some code snippet from the latest Stagefright source code we extract from the Android base. We can see that buffer space is allocated in terms of 65,536 Bytes (64 KB). When the total buffer size reaches 20 MB, downloading would be paused; when the remaining not-played data is less than 4 MB, Stagefright will resume the downloading. As the downloading is paused, in order to keep the connection with the server, it would temporarily resume to download a PageSize (64 KB) of data every 15 seconds and pause the downloading after that. This buffer management method well explains what we have observed in both the server-side log and the client-side experiments.

Further studying the history of earlier versions in the Android code base, we find that the value of these 4 parameters shown in Figure 6 have changed over time. For example, in the earliest version, the HighWaterThreshold was set to 3 MB, and the LowWaterThreshold was 512 KB. This indicates as Android devices are getting more physical memory, a larger amount of buffer is allocated to the mediaplayer. Nevertheless, the HighWaterThreshold can be seen as the total buffer size used by Stagefright on Android devices. That is, Stagefright would only use a fixed amount of memory despite different video file sizes, and that only a fixed amount of video data would be kept in the buffer. Compared to iOS, this is a simple and static buffer management method.

In addition, different Android devices may use different values for these parameters in their out-of-factory settings. For example, based on Figure 5, we can estimate that the HighWaterThreshold for Nexus One is around 5 MB, while Kindle Fire uses a larger value of about 13 MB. By analyzing the debugging log from these Android devices, we are also able to get the accurate value of LowWaterThreshold, which is 768 KB for Nexus One and 10 MB for Kindle Fire, respectively.

3.3 Comparisons

Through client-side experiments, we confirm that Android devices often use a single HTTP connection to download the video file unless there is manual interruption of current playback. On the contrary, iOS devices always use multiple HTTP range requests to download the video file. Buffer management wise, by analyzing the source code of Android mediaplayer, we find that Stagefright always uses a fixed/preset amount of memory for the playout buffer, while AppleCoreMedia of iOS devices always adjust the playout buffer dynamically at runtime.

We believe such different buffer management policies have caused iOS and Android devices to exhibit different behaviors when they are used to access streaming videos. Stagefright would always and only store a fixed amount (set by HighWaterThreshold) of video data, and may download at most this amount of video data ahead of the playback. If the user stops watching the video in the middle, at most HighWaterThreshold amount of data may be wasted. But in normal streaming sessions with few user manual inter-activities, Stagefright on Android devices always downloads the exact amount of data as the video size, while AppleCoreMedia on iOS devices always tries to keep as much video data as possible in the buffer for user's experience, including re-downloading the beginning part. This results in a significant amount of redundant traffic delivered to iOS devices.

4 Related Work

With the increasing video accesses from mobile devices, a lot of research has been conducted to examine Internet mobile streaming, from the client's perspective [2] [10], the video server's perspective [11], and the ISP's perspective [12] [13]. For example, in our prior work, we conduct extensive measurements from the client's perspective about the energy-efficiency of various streaming protocols used by mobile devices today [2].

Li et al. present a detailed analysis of user behaviors and access patterns in mobile video streaming from a server's perspective [11].

Researchers have also studied how accesses from mobile devices and desktop computers are served differently by the video service providers. For example, Rao et al. characterize the traffic pattern of YouTube and Netflix on both desktop computers and mobile devices [10]. Finamore et al. [12] compare the playback performance of PC-players and mobile-players accessing YouTube, and examine the potential causes for the inferior performance of mobile-players.

Different from prior work, in this study, we focus on the streaming access performance of two dominant types of mobile systems Android and iOS. We find that the different content requesting patterns and different playout buffer management policies have caused these devices to have sharply different behaviors.

5   Conclusion

Internet mobile streaming has attracted significant attention from both industry and research community, due to the dominant streaming traffic volume in the entire mobile data traffic. In this work, we focus on the Internet mobile streaming delivery to Android and iOS devices, with an aim to investigate their performance when receiving Internet streaming content. With both server-side log analysis and client-side experiment-based investigations, we find that Andriod and iOS mediaplayers are using different content requesting approaches and different buffer management methods when accessing streaming content, which result in a non-trivial amount of redundant traffic received by iOS devices. This would lead to extra battery power consumption on iOS devices and additional monetary cost if cellular networks have been used. Our study not only provides some guidelines for common mobile device users, but also offers some insights for Internet streaming service providers and mobile mediaplayer developers.

Acknowledgements. We appreciate constructive comments from anonymous referees and our shepherd Edmond W. W. Chan. The work is partially supported by NSF under grants CNS-0746649, CNS-1117300, CCF-0915681, CCF-1146578.

References

1. Mobile/Tablet OS Market Share,
   http://marketshare.hitslink.com/
   operating-system-market-share.aspx?qprid=8&qpcustomd=1
2. Liu, Y., Guo, L., Li, F., Chen, S.: An Empirical Evaluation of Battery Power Consumption for Streaming Data Transmission to Mobile Devices. In: Proc. of ACM Multimedia (2011)
3. YouTube, http://m.youtube.com/
4. Dailymotion, http://touch.dailymotion.com/
5. Veoh, http://www.veoh.com/iphone/
6. Trace, http://cs.gmu.edu/~sqchen/open-access/pam13-trace.tgz
7. Vuclip-Chinese Cinema, http://www.vuclip.com/
8. Wireshark, http://www.wireshark.org
9. Fast Start,
   http://www.microsoft.com/windows/windowsmedia/howto/articles/
   optimize_web.aspx#performance_faststreaming

10. Rao, A., Legout, A., Lim, Y.-S., Towsley, D., Barakat, C., Dabbous, W.: Network Character-
    istics of Video Streaming Traffic. In: Proc. of ACM CoNext (2011)
11. Li, Y., Zhang, Y., Yuan, R.: Measurement and Analysis of a Large Scale Commercial Mobile
    Internet TV System. In: Proc. of ACM IMC (2011)
12. Finamore, A., Mellia, M., Munafo, M., Torres, R., Rao, S.G.: YouTube Everywhere: Impact
    of Device and Infrastructure Synergies on User Experience. In: Proc. of ACM IMC (2011)
13. Erman, J., Gerber, A., Ramakrishnan, K.K., Sen, S., Spatscheck, O.: Over The Top Video:
    The Gorilla in Cellular Networks. In: Proc. of ACM IMC (2011)

Performance Implications
of Unilateral Enabling of IPv6

Hussein A. Alzoubi[1], Michael Rabinovich[1], and Oliver Spatscheck[2]

[1] Case Western Reserve University
[2] AT&T Research Labs

Abstract. While some IPv6-enabled Web sites such as Google require an explicit opt-in by IPv6-enabled clients before serving them over the IPv6 protocol, we quantify performance implications of *unilateral* enabling of IPv6 by a Web site. In this approach, the Web site enables dual-stack IPv4/6 support and resolves DNS queries for IPv6 addresses with the IPv6 addresses of its Web servers, and legacy DNS queries for IPv4 addresses with the IPv4 addresses. Thus, clients indicating the willingness to communicate over IPv6 are allowed to immediately do so. Although the existence of the end-to-end IPv6 path between these clients and the Web site is currently unlikely, we found no evidence of performance penalty (subject to 1sec. granularity of our measurement) for this unilateral IPv6 adoption. We hope our findings will help facilitate the IPv6 transition and prove useful to the sites considering their IPv6 migration strategy.

1 Introduction

The address space of IPv4 is practically exhausted: the last block was allocated to regional Internet registries in February 2011. While registries can still distribute their allocated addresses internally, the last allocation brought the issue of IPv6 transition into stark focus. With the revived efforts for IPv6 transition, many clients are now dual-stack, that is, are capable to using both IPv4 and v6 protocols. High profile Web sites, e.g., Google, started to likewise deploy IPv6 platforms to serve these clients [6]. However, as the overall Internet transition to IPv6 is lagging, the network paths between these clients and the Web site commonly do not support IPv6, in which case the two end-hosts cannot communicate over IPv6 even if they both are IPv6-enabled. Despite a recent recommendation on how end-hosts should handle this situation [19], in practice the lack of end-to-end IPv6 path may expose the user to excessive delays or outright connectivity disruption. The possibility of these delays can influence the Web site's IPv6 transition strategy – e.g., Google only directs clients to its IPv6 servers if they have verified the end-to-end IPv6 connectivity and explicitly opted in [6].

This paper quantifies the basis for such a conservative strategy. In other words, it asks an important question: what are the implications of a Web site *unilaterally* switching to a dual-stack mode, whereby it would simply send IPv6-enabled

M. Roughan and R. Chang (Eds.) PAM 2013, LNCS 7799, pp. 115–124, 2013.
© Springer-Verlag Berlin Heidelberg 2013

clients to an IPv6 server, and IPv4 clients to an IPv4 server? We found no evidence of any performance penalty (subject to 1 sec. granularity of our measurement) and an extremely small increase in failure to download the object (from 0.0038% to 0.0064% of accesses). This suggests the feasibility of the unilateral IPv6 deployment, which could in turn spur a speedier overall IPv6 transition.

2 Background

A user access to a Web site is usually preceded with a DNS resolution of the site's domain name. An IPv6-enabled client would issue a DNS query for an IPv6 address (an AAAA-type query) while an IPv4 client would send an A-type query for an IPv4 address. Our goal is to assess the implications of a unilateral enabling of a dual-stack IPv4/6 support by the Web site. In this setup, the Web site would deploy both the IPv6 and IPv4 HTTP servers. It would then resolve AAAA DNS queries to the IPv6 address of the IPv6 server, and A-type queries to the IPv4 address of the IPv4 server. Thus, clients indicating the willingness to communicate over IPv6 are allowed to immediately do so.

The danger of this approach is that, given the current state of IPv6 adoption in the core networks, the likelihood of the valid end-to-end IPv6 path or tunnel between any host-pair is low, even if both end-points are IPv6-enabled. When the IPv6 path does not exist, plausible scenarios for IPv6-enabled clients can be grouped into two categories. In the first scenario, the client follows the recent IETF recommendation [19] to avoid any delay in attempting to use an unreachable IPv6 Web server. Basically, clients would issue both AAAA and A queries to obtain both IPv6 and IPv4 addresses, then establish both the IPv4 and IPv6 HTTP connections at the same time using both addresses; if the IPv6 connection advances through the TCP handshake, the IPv4 connection is abandoned through an RST segment. The other scenario is that the client attempts to use IPv6 first and then, after failure to connect, resorts to IPv4, which leads to a delay penalty.

The macro-effects of dual IPv4/6 Web site deployment are the result of complex interactions between behaviors of browsers, operating systems, and DNS resolvers, which differ widely, leading to drastically different delay penalties (see [5] for an excellent survey of different browser and OS behaviors). Consequently, to avoid the possibility of high delay penalty, high-profile Web sites, such as Google, only resolve AAAA DNS queries to IPv6 addresses for clients that have verified the existence of an end-to-end IPv6 path between themselves and Google and explicitly opted-in for IPv6 service. This procedure is valuable as a demonstration and testbed for IPv6 migration but it does not scale as making a client network to duplicate this procedure for every Web site is infeasible.

Note that the client typically resolves DNS queries through a client-side DNS resolver (commonly referred to as "local DNS server", or "LDNS"), which is often shared among multiple clients. It is possible that the resolver submits AAAA queries even if some (or all) of its clients are not IPv6-enabled. A Web site that unilaterally deploys IPv6 as described above has no way of knowing the status of IPv6 support of the actual client when the AAAA query arrives - it simply responds with the IPv6 address. Our measurement methodology captures any possible effects of this uncertainty. Thus, unless it may cause confusion, we refer to all clients behind the resolver that sends AAAA queries as IPv6-enabled or, interchangeably, dual-stack.

3   Methodology

We used the following methodology to measure the performance implications of unilateral IPv6 deployment when the client cannot reach the IPv6 server due to the lack of the end-to-end IPv6 path or tunnel. We registered the domain `dns-research.com` and built a specialized DNS server to act as its authoritative DNS server (ADNS) as well as a specialized Web server to host a single object (a one-pixel image) from subdomain *sub.dns-research.com*. Assume for a moment that we can reliably associate a given DNS query with the subsequent HTTP request (we describe the approach we use to accomplish this shortly). We configured our specialized DNS server to respond to IPv6 queries (type-AAAA requests) for any hostname from domain *sub.dns-research.com* with a non-existent IPv6 address, and to any IPv4 DNS queries (type-A requests) with the valid IPv4 address of our Web server. Responding to IPv6 queries with a non-existent IPv6 address mimics the situation where there is no end-to-end IPv6 path between the client and server and thus the server is unreachable[1]. We then measure the delay penalty as the time between when we send the unreachable IPv6 address to the client's DNS resolver and when the client falls back to IPv4 (i.e., the corresponding HTTP request from the client arrives over IPv4). We deployed both our ADNS and Web servers on the same host so that we could measure time intervals between DNS and HTTP events without clock skew.

Our setup is illustrated in Figure 1. As mentioned, we need to associate a given DNS query with the subsequent HTTP request. To do so, we first associate a DNS query with the originating client using the approach from [14]. Our Web server hosts a special image URL, `dns-research.com/special.jpg`. When a user accesses this image, their browser first sends a DNS query for dns-research.com (we refer to this as a "base domain" and "base query") to the user's DNS resolver (step 1 in the figure), which then sends it to our ADNS server (step 2). An IPv6-enabled client network is likely to send both A and AAAA DNS queries. Since the base DNS queries can not be reliably associated with the clients, our ADNS responds with NXDOMAIN ("Non-Existent Domain") to the AAAA query and with the proper IPv4 address of our Web server to the A query (step 3). The resolver forwards the response to the client (step 4), which then sends the HTTP request for this image to our server (step 5). Our Web server returns an HTTP 302 ("Moved") response (step 6) redirecting the client

---

[1] Indeed, attempting to communicate with our non-existent address has the same effect as an attempt to communicate with an existing IPv6 destination over a non-existent path, which is the same as a path that is not end-to-end IPv6-enabled.

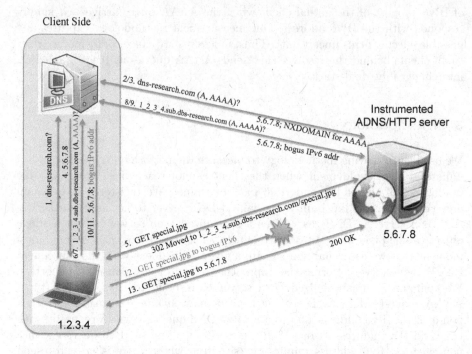

Fig. 1. Measurement Setup. Presumed interactions are marked in blue font.

to another URL in the `sub.dns-research.com` domain[2], but with the host name that embeds the client's IP address (we refer to these queries as "sub" requests). The client needs to resolve this name through its resolver again (steps 6-9). This time the DNS query can be reliably attributed to the HTTP client through the client's IP address embedded in the hostname.

Having associated the DNS query to the originating client, we measure the delay between the arrival of AAAA query in step 8 and the first subsequent HTTP request from the same client in step 13 as the delay penalty for unilateral IPv6 deployment. To eliminate HTTP requests that utilized previously cached DNS resolutions (as their time since the preceding DNS interaction would obviously not indicate the delay penalty) we measure the incidents of IPv6 delays for an HTTP request only if it was immediately preceded (i.e., without another interposed HTTP request) by a full DNS interaction, including both A and AAAA requests, for that client. We contrast these delays with the delays for non-IPv6 enabled clients, whose resolvers did not send AAAA queries. We use the same technique to associate these HTTP clients with DNS queries, and measure the delays as the time between a type-A DNS query in step 2 and the first subsequent HTTP request in step 13.

---

[2] In reality our setup involved more redirections to enable other measurements; we omit these details for clarity as they are unrelated to the present study.

Table 1. High-level dataset characterization

LDNS IP addresses	278,559
Client IP addresses	11,378,020
Unique Client/LDNS IP Pairs	21,432,181

We have collaborated with a major consumer-oriented Website to embed our image starting URL into their home page. Whenever a Web browser visits the home page, the browser downloads the linked image and the interactions in Figure 1 take place. We used a low 10 seconds TTL for our DNS records. This allowed us to obtain repeated measurements from the same client without overwhelming our setup. Further, our Web server adds a "cache-control:no-cache" header field to its HTTP responses to make sure we receive every request to our special image. Unfortunately, the conditions for this collaboration prevent us from releasing the datasets collected in the course of our experiment.

4   The Dataset

We have collected the DNS logs (including the timestamp of the query, LDNS IP, query type, and query string) and HTTP logs (request time, User-Agent and Host headers) resulting from the interactions described in the previous section. Our experiment lasted 28 days, from Jan 5th, 2011 to Feb 1st, during which we collected over 34.4 million DNS *"sub"* requests and around 56 million of the HTTP downloads of the final image (step 13 in Figure 1).[3]

Table 2. The basic IPv6 statistics

	Base DNS Requests	"Sub" DNS Requests
# Requests	19,945,037	2,398,367
LDNS IP addrs	59,978	32,291
Client IP addrs	No data	1,134,617

Table 1 shows high-level characteristics for our dataset. We have collected over 21M client/LDNS associations between 11.3M unique client IP addresses from 17,778 autonomous systems (ASs) and almost 280K LDNS resolvers from 14,627 ASs.

---

[3] While one could have expected the number of final HTTP downloads to be roughly equal to the number of "sub" DNS requests since each client access would normally generate a "sub" DNS request and one final HTTP download, the number of these HTTP downloads in our dataset is much greater than that. We verified that this is due to clients and LDNSs caching our replies to "sub" queries for much longer than our specified TTL value. These wide-spread TTL violations were first reported in [15].

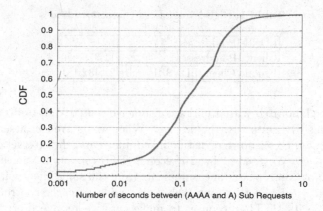

Fig. 2. Time difference between A and AAAA "sub" requests

Table 2 summarizes the general statistics about IPv6 requests, as well as clients and LDNSs behind them. Out of the 278,559 LDNSs we observed during our experiment, almost 22% were IPv6-enabled (i.e., sent some AAAA queries). However, only around 54% of the latter sent AAAA "sub" requests, and the number of "sub" requests was much lower than that of the base queries. This is because some LDNS servers seem to cache the NXDOMAIN response (which, as discussed earlier, our DNS server returns to the IPv6 queries for the base domain) and not issue queries for subdomains of the base domain, while other LDNS servers seem to not cache NXDOMAIN responses at all and send repeated base queries even when serving subsequent "sub" requests from the cache.

5   The Results

We now present our measurement results. We first consider if unilateral IPv6 enabling entails any penalty clients' DNS resolution, and then report our measurements of the overall delays.

5.1   DNS Resolution Penalty

Our first experiment investigates any potential delays in obtaining the IPv4 DNS resolution given that our IPv6 Web server is unreachable. If clients failover to IPv4 only after being unable to connect to the IPv6 Web server, then it could be that the DNS A-type query would only arrive after the corresponding timeout. To test for this behavior, we consider the time between A and AAAA "sub" request arrivals from the same client. Our immediate observation is that almost 88% out of the 2.3 Million AAAA "sub" requests were received *after* their corresponding A request. This says that not only do these clients/LDNSs perform both resolutions in parallel but, between the two wall-to-wall DNS requests, they most likely send the A query first. For the remaining 12% of requests, Figure

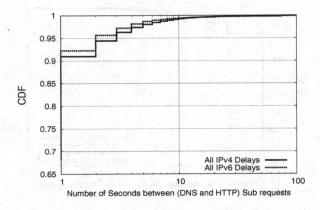

Fig. 3. Comparison of all IPv6 and IPv4 delays

2 shows the CDF of the time difference between A and AAAA "sub" requests. The figure indicates that even among these requests, most clients did not wait for a failed attempt to contact the IPv6 Web server before obtaining the IPv4 address. Indeed, even assuming an accelerated default connection timeout used in this case by Safari and Chrome (270ms and 300ms respectively [5] - as opposed to hundreds of seconds for regular TCP timeout [1]), roughly 70% of type-A queries in these requests came within this timeout value. We conclude that a vast majority (roughly $88 + 0.7 \times 12 \approx 95\%$) of requests do not incur extra DNS resolution penalty due to IPv6 deployment.

5.2   End-to-End Penalty

Our first concern is to see whether unilateral IPv6 enabling can lead to disruption of Web accesses, that is, whether the IPv6-enabled clients successfully fail over to IPv4 for HTTP downloads. We compare the rate of interactions where HTTP request fails to arrive following the AAAA DNS query, either until the next DNS interaction from the same client or until the end of the trace. For IPv6-enabled clients, these lost HTTP requests amounted to 154 out of 2,398,367 total interactions, or 0.0064%. For IPv4-only clients, this number was 1217 lost requests out of the total (34.4M-2.4M), or 0.0038%. Although the rate of lost requests in IPv6-enabled clients is higher, both rates are so extremely low that they can both be considered insignificant.

Turning to assessing the upper bound on the overall delay for IPv6-enabled clients, we measure the time between the arrivals of the AAAA "sub" DNS request (a conservative estimate of when the client receives the unreachable IPv6 address) and the actual subsequent HTTP request by the client. As a reminder, to eliminate HTTP requests that utilized previously cached DNS resolutions, we measure the incidents of IPv6 delays for an HTTP request only if it was immediately preceded (i.e., without another interposed HTTP request) by a full DNS interaction, including both A and AAAA sub requests for that client.

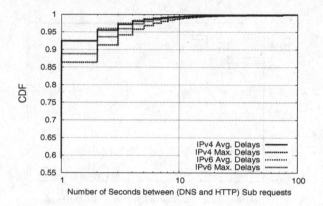

Fig. 4. IPv4 and IPv6 delays per client

Applying this condition resulted in 1,949,231 instances of IPv6 delays from 1,086,323 unique client IP addresses. Our HTTP logs provide timestamps with granularity of one second; thus we can only report our delays at this granularity.

Figures 3 and 4 compare delays incurred by IPv6-enabled and IPv4-only clients. Figure 3 shows CDFs of all delays across all clients in the respective categories (i.e., multiple delay instances from the same client are counted multiple times) and Figure 4 shows the CDFs of average and maximum delays observed per client. Both figures concentrate on delays within 100s. There were 0.063% of IPv6 delays and 0.076% of IPv4 delays exceeding 100s, with the maximum IPv6 delay of 1.2M sec and IPv4 delay of 1.8M sec. We attribute exceedingly long delays to a combination of clients commonly violating DNS time-to-live (as first observed in [15]) with corner cases such as duplicate DNS requests resulting from a single client interaction (the behavior that we directly observed in a different study). For instance, one HTTP request on January 7 was surrounded by 6 DNS queries, two of which arrived after the HTTP request; since there were no more DNS requests until the next HTTP request on January 27 (presumably due to a TTL violation), this scenario contributed a delay of 1.7M sec.

Neither figure shows significant differences in delay between the two categories of clients. In fact, where one can discern the difference, the delay distributions actually show *lower* delay penalty for IPv6-enabled clients. The maximum per-client delays shows the most discernible difference; this could be explained by the fact that there are an order of magnitude more IPv4-only interactions, thus there is a higher chance of an outlier value of maximum delay. While the one-second measurement granularity is clearly a limitation of this experiment, our study finds no evidence of delay penalty and in any case provides the upper bound of 1 sec. for any penalty that could not be measured.

6 Related Work

Much effort has been devoted to IPv6 transition. A number of transition technologies have been proposed that help construct end-to-end IPv6 paths without the need for ubiquitous deployment of IPv6 network infrastructure (see, e.g., [2,18,12,4,8]). We look at another aspect of IPv6 migration, namely, the penalty for unilateral IPv6 enabling when the end-to-end path does not exist. A number of studies have reported on the extent of IPv6 penetration from a variety of vantage points. In particular, Shen et al. [17] used netflow data from a Chinese tier-1 ISP, Savola [16] and Hei and Yamazki [7] analyzed data collected on 6to4 relays, Kreibich et al. [11] employed user-launched measurements, Malone [13] and Huston [9] studied IPv6 traffic attracted to IPv6-connected Web sites, and Karpilovsky et al. [10] considered IPv6 penetration from several vantage points including netflows in core networks, address allocations, and BGP route announcements. A general conclusion of these studies is that IPv6 deployment remains low. For example, Huston found that in 2009, end-to-end IPv6 connectivity was only available to around 1% of the clients of the two Web sites he considered. These findings motivate our study by showing that most clients receiving an IPv6 address from a unilaterally IPv6-enabled Web site would have no end-to-end IPv6 connectivity to the site.

Several studies considered the performance of the current IPv6 network infrastructure. Zhou and Van Mieghem [20] compared the end-to-end delay of IPv6 and IPv4 packets between selected end-hosts and observed that IPv6 paths had higher variation in delay. Colitti et al. [3] compared latency experienced by clients accessing the Google platform over IPv4 and IPv6 and found little difference once the effect of processing at tunnel termination points is factored out (otherwise the IPv6 latency was slightly higher). While this study considered performance of the IPv6 clients that had the end-to-end IPv6 path to their platform, we focus on the performance implications for IPv6-enabled clients that do not have this connectivity.

7   Conclusion

While many end-hosts have become IPv6-enabled, the overall IPv6 adoption in the network is lagging and thus it is common for two IPv6-enabled hosts to have no end-to-end IPv6 network path between them. Consequently, Web sites such as Google that pioneer IPv6 adoption only direct those clients to their IPv6 servers that previously verified their end-to-end IPv6 connectivity to the IPv6 servers in question and explicitly opted in. This paper studies the performance implications of a *unilateral* enabling of IPv6 by a Web site, without requiring any verification or opt-in from the clients. We found no evidence of performance penalty for such unilateral IPv6 adoption and an extremely small increase in failure to download the object (from 0.0038% to 0.0064% of accesses). While the one-second measurement granularity is clearly a limitation of our study, it in any case provides the upper bound of 1 sec. for any penalty that could not be measured. We hope these findings will help sites as they consider their IPv6 migration strategy.

References

1. Al-Qudah, Z., Rabinovich, M., Allman, M.: Web Timeouts and Their Implications. In: Krishnamurthy, A., Plattner, B. (eds.) PAM 2010. LNCS, vol. 6032, pp. 211–221. Springer, Heidelberg (2010)
2. Carpenter, B., Moore, K.: Connection of IPv6 domains via IPv4 clouds. RFC 3056 (2001)
3. Colitti, L., Gunderson, S.H., Kline, E., Refice, T.: Evaluating IPv6 Adoption in the Internet. In: Krishnamurthy, A., Plattner, B. (eds.) PAM 2010. LNCS, vol. 6032, pp. 141–150. Springer, Heidelberg (2010)
4. De Clercq, J., Ooms, D., Prevost, S., Le Faucheur, F.: Connecting IPv6 islands over IPv4 MPLS using IPv6 provider edge routers (6PE). RFC 4798 (2007)
5. Dual stack esotropia, http://labs.apnic.net/blabs/?p=47
6. Google over IPv6, http://www.google.com/intl/en/ipv6/
7. Hei, Y., Yamazaki, K.: Traffic analysis and worldwide operation of open 6to4 relays for ipv6 deployment. In: IEEE Int. Symp. on Applications and the Internet, pp. 265–268 (2004)
8. Huitema, C.: Teredo: Tunneling IPv6 over UDP through network address translations (NATs). RFC 4380 (2006)
9. Huston, G.: IPv6 Transition. Presentation at the 3d Meeting of the Australian Network Operators Group (2009),
   http://www.potaroo.net/presentations/2009-09-01-ipv6-transition.pdf
10. Karpilovsky, E., Gerber, A., Pei, D., Rexford, J., Shaikh, A.: Quantifying the extent of IPv6 deployment. In: Passive and Active Measurement Conf., pp. 13–22 (2009)
11. Kreibich, C., Weaver, N., Nechaev, B., Paxson, V.: Netalyzr: illuminating the edge network. In: The 10th ACM Conf. on Internet Measurement, pp. 246–259 (2010)
12. Lee, Y., Durand, A., Woodyatt, J., Droms, R.: Dual-Stack Lite broadband deployments following IPv4 exhaustion. RFC 6333 (2011)
13. Malone, D.: Observations of IPv6 addresses. In: Passive and Active Measurement Conf., pp. 21–30 (2008)
14. Mao, Z.M., Cranor, C.D., Douglis, F., Rabinovich, M., Spatscheck, O., Wang, J.: A precise and efficient evaluation of the proximity between web clients and their local DNS servers. In: USENIX Annual Technical Conference, pp. 229–242 (2002)
15. Pang, J., Akella, A., Shaikh, A., Krishnamurthy, B., Seshan, S.: On the responsiveness of DNS-based network control. In: The 4th ACM Conf. on Internet Measurement, pp. 21–26 (2004)
16. Savola, P.: Observations of IPv6 traffic on a 6to4 relay. SIGCOMM Comput. Commun. Rev. 35(1), 23–28 (2005)
17. Shen, W., Chen, Y., Zhang, Q., Chen, Y., Deng, B., Li, X., Lv, G.: Observations of IPv6 traffic. In: ISECS Int. Colloq. on Computing, Communication, Control, and Management, vol. 2, pp. 278–282. IEEE (2009)
18. Townsley, M., Troan, O.: IPv6 Rapid Deployment on IPv4 Infrastructures (6rd)–Protocol Specification. RFC 5969 (2010)
19. Wing, D., Yourtchenko, A.: Happy eyeballs: Success with dual-stack hosts. IETF draft (October 2011),
    http://tools.ietf.org/html/draft-ietf-v6ops-happy-eyeballs-05
20. Zhou, X., Van Mieghem, P.: Hopcount and E2E delay: IPv6 versus IPv4. In: Passive and Active Measurement Conf, pp. 345–348 (2005)

Measuring Occurrence of DNSSEC Validation

Matthäus Wander and Torben Weis

University of Duisburg-Essen, Duisburg, Germany
dnssec@vs.uni-due.de
http://dnssec.vs.uni-due.de

Abstract. DNSSEC is a security extension that adds public-key signatures to the Domain Name System for the purpose of data authenticity
and integrity. While DNSSEC signatures are being deployed on an increasing number of name servers, little is known about the deployment
advancements of client-side DNSSEC validation. In this paper we present
a methodology to determine whether a client is protected by DNSSEC
validation. We applied our methodology over a period of 7 months collecting results from different data sources. After data cleaning, we gathered
131,320 results from 98,179 distinct IP addresses, out of which 4.8% had
validation enabled. The ratio varies significantly per country, with Sweden, the Czech Republic and the United States having the largest ratios
of validating clients in the field.

1 Introduction

The original Domain Name System (DNS) specification did not provide any security measures to protect from forged domain names. As DNS heavily relies
on UDP messages, an attacker can send spoofed DNS responses, as e.g. demonstrated by Kaminsky in 2008 [1]. In order to mitigate DNS spoofing, senders currently encode random entropy into DNS messages without breaking the message
format, e.g. random transaction ID and source port. This lowers the attackers'
spoofing success rate, but still attacks remain feasible for insistent remote attackers and trivial for local attackers, e.g. when eavesdropping on a public Wi-Fi
hotspot. Cryptographic DNS protocol extensions have been proposed to make
DNS spoofing infeasible, most notably DNSSEC [2] which is being deployed right
now. DNSSEC utilizes public-key cryptography to sign and verify public DNS
data. For verification, the public key of the root zone must be known beforehand
to the resolver (DNS client). A delegation signer (DS) record indicates whether a
child zone is signed and contains the fingerprint (hash value) of the child zone's
public key. The resolver can thus securely retrieve the public key of the child
zone when needed.

Apart from establishing secure name resolution, DNSSEC deployment implies
some side effects. The cryptographic enhancement increases CPU and network
load on name servers and validating resolvers. Distributed denial of service attacks which abuse the public DNS infrastructure for traffic amplification become
more effective with large DNSSEC responses. Rogue DNS redirects become impossible for malicious attackers but also for governments and ISPs which may

M. Roughan and R. Chang (Eds.) PAM 2013, LNCS 7799, pp. 125–134, 2013.
© Springer-Verlag Berlin Heidelberg 2013

act legitimated by national law or company policy. This includes redirects to governmental censorship or legal notices, DNS injection [3] and redirects to advertisement web pages [4]. Unlike e.g. SSL/TLS certificate failures, there is currently no application-level handling of DNSSEC validation failures [5]. When validation fails on a DNSSEC-enabled resolver, it passes a general name resolution error back to the application (e.g. web browser) which is indistinguishable from a network error.

Our contribution in this paper is a methodology to measure the occurrence of client-side DNSSEC validation and an analysis of such a measurement in practice. Different validation measures are possible, e.g. the number of clients protected by validation, the number of resolvers performing validation or the number of responses received by validating resolvers. We chose to count the number of clients because from this measure one can deduce the amount of users protected by DNSSEC.

2   Methodology

We set up a DNS zone VERTEILTESYSTEME.NET, signed it and added a DS record to the .NET zone. Two domain names in our zone return an A record, SIGOK with a valid signature and SIGFAIL with a placeholder signature, which is syntactically correct but fails to validate. We are using two test types: a scripted test that provides user feedback [6] and a hidden test that can be embedded into other web pages.

2.1   Scripted Test

The web-based scripted test uses client-side JavaScript to load an image from the SIGFAIL domain name. When loading the image succeeds, the resolver does not validate DNSSEC signatures as it failed to recognize the invalid signature. When loading fails, the script attempts to load an image from the SIGOK domain name. This happens to rule out other error sources, e.g. a stalled network connection or an unrelated DNS resolution fault. If the second image has been loaded, the resolver correctly validates DNSSEC signatures. Should the second image fail to load as well, then the test was inconclusive. The result is displayed to the user and posted to our web server in background.

2.2   Hidden Test

The web-based hidden test uses two <img> tags which can be embedded into existing web pages (Fig. 1). The two image URLs redirect the client browser to a transparent 1×1 pixel image at ID.SIGOK and ID.SIGFAIL. ID is a hexadecimal number 0000 to FFFF used to identify the client. As most clients do not resolve domain names by themselves, the client IP address seen by our web server usually differs from the resolver IP address seen by our name server. The ID number relates browser queries to resolver queries and enables us to analyze

```
<img src="http://dnssec.vs.uni-due.de/r/a" alt="" height="1" width="1">
<img src="http://dnssec.vs.uni-due.de/r/b" alt="" height="1" width="1">
```

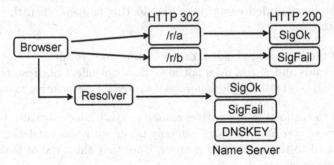

Fig. 1. Static HTML code block and queries of hidden test

their coherent behavior. This method is similar to the one used by Mao et al. in 2002 [7] but instead of embedding the IP address a 16 bit hash value is derived from the IP address. The rationale behind this method is as follows:

1. By using an HTTP redirect we can embed a static HTML code snippet into existing web pages and track the queries by client ID. When including the ID directly into the image URLs this would require to dynamically generate the HTML code.
2. The DNS zone is moderately sized when using 16 bit for the ID. As we need to deliver valid and invalid signatures, we pre-generate the DNS zone, sign it and then replace the SIGFAIL signatures with broken placeholders. This results in an 88 MB zone file with 2^{19} resource records (A and RRSIG, NSEC and RRSIG, for both SIGOK and SIGFAIL). If we dynamically created and signed the resource records as needed, this would require either a customized name server or an unusual zone layout which might pose a pitfall for some resolvers.
3. By deriving the ID number from the client IP address we get a simple stateless mapping which does not change while the same client is visiting multiple web pages and is unlikely to collide with another client at the same time.

DNSSEC validation is enabled if there were HTTP GET requests for the two redirect URLs and the SIGOK image but none for the SIGFAIL image. It is disabled if there were HTTP GET requests for the redirect URLs and both images.

2.3   Accuracy

For a positive test result we require the client to load an image from the signed SIGOK domain name. This is meant to catch faults that could spoil the result, e.g. blocking our signed domain name, not automatically loading images, not following cross-domain HTTP redirects or failing to receive EDNS0 messages

> 512 bytes. The responses for SIGOK and SIGFAIL are nearly the same size with a packet size of < 1000 bytes. Nevertheless, one of the images could fail to load for an unrelated reason, e.g. temporary network fault or user closes web page before it has been loaded completely. Should this happen, then the following faults are possible:

1. None of the images are loaded: does not affect our results.
2. SIGFAIL loads and SIGOK does not load: does not affect our results.
3. SIGOK loads and SIGFAIL does not load: causes a false positive in our results.

To estimate the ratio of false positives caused by case 3, we calculate the number of occurrence of case 2. Both cases can only occur with non-validating resolvers and correspond to the same fault pattern. Note that this type of fault can not cause false negatives.

Another possible fault source is caching. All tests mentioned above use a time to live (TTL) value of 60 seconds for the SIGOK and SIGFAIL resource records. To minimize the impact of browser caching, we return *no-cache* headers in image responses. Caching can spoil the result if the validation configuration has changed, i.e. when the resolvers have been reconfigured or when a client has moved to another network.

3   Analysis

We logged 3,387,622 DNS and HTTP requests over a period of 7 months starting in May 2012. This comprises three data sources: 1) participants of our scripted test 2) visits from *autosurf* websites which generate page views[1] in exchange for community credits 3) visits from websites which kindly included our hidden test. The results were evaluated offline by parsing the web server and name server logfiles. We grouped the requests together by ID into Bernoulli trials when the time delta between two requests was < 30s. Larger time deltas were grouped into different trials which resulted in 419,747 trials.

3.1   Data Cleaning

We removed 146,786 invalid trials which were lacking the minimum required set of requests. A valid trial requires at least both HTTP redirects to SIGOK and SIGFAIL, both DNS queries and an HTTP query to the SIGOK image. Fig. 2 shows the occurrence of invalid trials. Most are caused by a client browsing a website over a couple of minutes, loading the hidden test URLs with each page view. While the HTTP redirects are intended to be cached, web browsers also excessively cache DNS responses in disregard of their low TTL values. Another cause for invalid trials are web crawlers or similar noise. As explained in Section 2.3, incorrectly missing SIGFAIL image queries are causing false positives in

---

[1] Visits are mostly unattended but in end user environment and thus serve our purpose.

Missing query	Both	SIGOK	SIGFAIL
HTTP redirect	55,052	4,431	5,010
DNS query	74,560	3,673	2,050
HTTP image	1,634	376	-

Filter condition	Count
12h duplicates	141,433
ID hash collision	11
DNSKEY missing	425

Fig. 2. Invalid trials   **Fig. 3.** Filtered trials (overlapping)

our measurement. The equivalent fault pattern of a missing SIGOK image query occurred in 376 trials, which makes an estimate of 0.14% false positives of all valid trials.

We then applied different filters to the remaining trials to remove duplicate or dubious results. In total one or more filter conditions applied to 141,641 trials (Fig. 3). Most trials are filtered by ignoring duplicate results: we consider each client IP address only once every 12h. When users browse a participating website for a couple of minutes, they leave several trials, one for each page view. The deduplication period should be long enough to cover the whole browsing session of the user but not longer than the assignment of a dynamic IP address. Dynamic IP addresses cause two problems in combination with deduplication: 1. the same client may be counted twice with different IP addresses (unlike clients with static IP addresses) 2. another client may be filtered when assigned the same IP address. Xie et al. estimated the time interval between two different users on the same dynamic IP address to be >12h in 80% of all cases [8]. With a period of 12h we expect to filter duplicates without adding significant bias due to differences between dynamic and static clients. Experiments with different deduplication periods from 2h to 7d show a minor influence on the overall validation ratio (±0.3% points).

A negligible amount of trials (<0.01%) became useless because a hash collision occurred in our IP address to ID mapping. 425 trials (0.16%) were filtered because they were classified as positive but lacked a DNSKEY query. This indicates a false positive and is comparable to the estimate above. We do not count these as negative results because there is a possible scenario in which we might mistakenly include an actually true positive. When a validating resolver uses two or more non-validating forwarders[2], we may receive queries for SIGOK and SIGFAIL from one IP address and a query for DNSKEY from another IP address. The DNSKEY query would be missing in this trial because we correlate DNSKEY queries by IP address and not by ID. This limitation could be improved in future by including the ID into DNSKEY records.

We did not attempt to identify single users behind the same public NAT IP address because clients within a local network typically share the same DNS configuration. In some cases we observed inconsistent client IP addresses. The HTTP redirects need to be queried from the same client IP address, otherwise this would result in two different IDs and thus invalid trials. The HTTP images may be queried from a different IP address as they are correlated by ID. This

---

[2] Such setup is debatable as it limits the ability to scatter retries when validation fails.

happened in 1.4% of all valid trials, often clearly by the same user with multiple client IP addresses due to enterprise NAT. We also identified a German regional ISP which operates carrier-grade NAT for broadband customers. As we did not find any unwanted effect on our results, we kept trials with inconsistent client IP addresses in our result set.

3.2   Results

After data cleaning there are 131,320 remaining trials from 98,179 distinct client IP addresses. According to HTTP referers, most clients originate from the website CRYPTOOL.ORG (67%) and from the autosurf communities TRAFFICSPAMMER (10%) and EBESUCHER (9%). We consider a trial as negative if it contains an HTTP query to SIGFAIL or if all DNS queries are sent without DNSSEC OK flag. In contrast, a positive result does not contain any SIGFAIL HTTP query and at least one DNS query was sent with EDNS0 and DNSSEC OK flag.

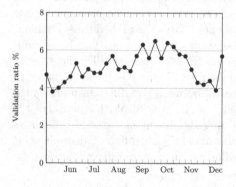

Fig. 4. Overall validation   **Fig. 5.** Data sources

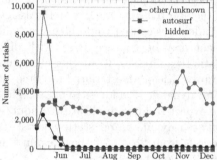

AS	$\frac{V}{V_{total}}$	$\frac{V}{V+N}$	cli=dns
Comcast 7922	29.1%	69.0%	0.5%
KabelBW 29562	14.3%	86.4%	0.3%
M-Net 8767	6.1%	46.6%	3.9%
Telia SE 3301	3.3%	73.8%	1.5%
O2 CZ 5610	3.0%	69.2%	0.5%
Telenor 2119	2.2%	54.1%	0.7%
pt.lu 6661	1.7%	83.5%	0.0%
rub.de 29484	1.6%	34.1%	0.0%
TELE2 1257	1.5%	52.4%	0.0%
DFN 680	1.5%	3.3%	4.3%
other	35.9%	1.9%	17.8%

Fig. 6. Top 5 participating countries   **Fig. 7.** Top 10 validating ASes

#	Country	Trials	Validation ratio	#	Country	Trials	Validation ratio
1.	SE	1099	56.3% ± 1.5	11.	GR	1939	3.7% ± 0.4
2.	CZ	957	31.1% ± 1.5	12.	IT	1537	3.5% ± 0.5
3.	US	15368	13.1% ± 0.3	13.	ID	1332	2.6% ± 0.4
4.	HU	526	9.9% ± 1.3	14.	PT	602	2.5% ± 0.6
5.	CH	2975	5.6% ± 0.4	15.	UA	1922	1.9% ± 0.3
6.	FR	3043	4.8% ± 0.4	16.	AU	1053	1.5% ± 0.4
7.	BR	1319	4.5% ± 0.6	17.	CA	1562	1.4% ± 0.3
8.	NL	2076	4.1% ± 0.4	18.	GB	4312	1.3% ± 0.2
9.	PL	2107	3.9% ± 0.4	19.	AR	577	1.2% ± 0.5
10.	DE	46624	3.8% ± 0.1	20.	RS	983	1.1% ± 0.3

Fig. 8. Validation ratio per country (± standard deviation in binomial distribution)

Overall 6,323 trials were positive (4.8%) and Fig. 4 shows the results per week. The dips in May and November correlate with the distribution of data sources (see Fig. 5) and can be explained by differences per country. The autosurf communities have a broad user base from various countries while the hidden website test was accessed mainly from Germany (43% of all "hidden" accesses) and the United States (12%). Changes in the country participation ratio (Fig. 6), e.g. fewer accesses from the U.S. in November, influence the overall validation ratio. The results per country are hence more meaningful than the overall ratio which is inclined towards the DE and US numbers.

There are 79 countries in the data set with >100 trials and 40 countries with >500 trials. Fig. 8 shows the top validating countries out of the >500 trials subset, sorted by validation ratio. Half of the countries in the >500 trials subset have a validation ratio of ≤1%.

Fig. 7 shows the top validating autonomous systems (AS) by absolute number of trials. $\frac{V}{V_{total}}$ is the fraction of the positive results of one AS to all ASes. $\frac{V}{V+N}$ is the fraction of positive to all results within one AS. While some are fairly high, no AS is fully protected by DNSSEC. The last column cli=dns is the fraction of trials in which the client IP address equals at least one DNS resolver being used. The low number indicates that most validating clients use the DNS infrastructure of the AS operator as forwarder.

2,150 trials are negative results despite containing a DNSKEY query, suggesting that a single DNSKEY query is an unsuitable validation indicator. This comprises trials with one and with multiple resolver IP addresses. Using multiple resolvers (or forwarders) is quite common, though mostly within the same AS. In 4,991 trials DNS resolvers appeared from different ASes. Most commonly seen AS numbers for resolvers outside of the client AS were AS15169 (Google), AS36692 (OpenDNS) and AS3356 (Level 3). The complete anonymized data set grouped into trials is available for public download [6].

4 Related Work

There exists thorough work on measuring and analyzing the server-side DNSSEC deployment advances [9] [10], i.e. the number and status of signed zones. Our scope in this paper is the client-side DNSSEC deployment, i.e. the number of clients protected by validators.

4.1 Passive Measurements

Public statistics from RIPE NCC [11] indicate that about 70% of all queries at the K-root name server are coming from resolvers that are capable of parsing DNSSEC answers. However, one can not deduce from this indicator whether validation is actually enabled. Another number measured at K-root are the queries for DNSKEY resource records which was about 2 queries/s in August 2012. Validating resolvers are expected to refresh the root DNSKEY within specified intervals [12] but the total number of resolvers querying K-root is unknown and so is the amount of extra DNSKEY queries due to pollution [13]. Hence, this measurement allows for observing the validation tendency but not the actual validation ratio.

Gudmundsson and Crocker [14] measured the validation ratio in 2010/11 by analyzing network traces from authoritative name servers for .ORG. Capturing and processing network traces is resource-intensive, therefore they were limited to 50 min traces from a subset of name servers. As resolvers do not distribute evenly across redundant name servers but instead prefer low latency, this subset might pose an incomplete view. They applied different criteria and found out that looking for DS queries is more effective in their scenario than looking for DNSKEY queries. The ratio of validating resolvers was 0.8% (mistakenly stated as 1.2%) which accounted for 8–10% observed queries to .ORG, though part of the queries may have been pollution due to dropped EDNS0 packets or amplification attacks. The geographical distribution and the number of clients served by these resolvers is unknown.

Fujiwara performed a similar measurement for .JP over a period of one year [15] [16]. He acquired 2 day network traces from all authoritative name servers for .JP on selected dates and interpolated interjacent numbers by analyzing partial log files. The number of resolvers querying for DNSKEY rose from 3,000 (0.2%) in March 2011 to 10,000 in February 2012.

4.2 Web-Based Tests

VeriSign runs a web-based project to quantify validating resolvers [17]. It uses the link prefetching feature of web browsers but does not require any HTTP requests. The target domain name resolves to an unsigned record, though there is a DS record indicating that it ought to be signed. A non-validating resolver will accept this response while a validating one will retry several times. The query pattern observed is used to fingerprint the resolver implementation. Despite using a different measure—counting resolvers not clients—the overall validation

Test	JavaScript	Images	Criteria
dnssec.vs.uni-due.de	yes	yes	image loads
dnssec.vs.uni-due.de (hidden)	no	yes	image loads
test.dnssec-or-not.net	no	no	3× query retry
dnssectest.sidn.nl	yes	yes	DNSKEY

Fig. 9. Comparison of web-based test methods

ratio is comparable to our results. The geographic distribution confirms our top two results for Sweden and the Czech Republic. The U.S. result is much lower, presumably because the large user base of AS7922 (Comcast) is served by few resolvers. VeriSign also provides a web page TEST.DNSSEC-OR-NOT.NET for users to check their validation status.

Another web-based DNSSEC test is provided by SIDN [18]. The client loads a web page DNSSECTEST.SIDN.NL which embeds an <img> tag pointing to a 1×1 pixel image. The domain name of the image URL contains a random ID and is signed with a valid chain of trust. Validating and non-validating resolvers both resolve the domain name, but only the validating resolver is expected to retrieve the DNSKEY record. When the image has been loaded, the JavaScript code queries the SIDN database whether the DNSKEY was retrieved and displays the result to the user. SIDN does not provide public statistics.

Fig. 9 shows an overview of all tests described above. As the tests use different mechanics, they may return different results under certain conditions. We confirmed this for mixed validation when a client uses validating and non-validating resolvers. The VeriSign and SIDN tests are positive if the pattern of one validating resolver is found, even if the client falls back to a non-validating secondary resolver and actually resolves the domain name without validation. Our tests are positive, if all resolvers queried by the client reject the incorrectly signed domain name.

5 Conclusions

We presented a web-based methodology to determine whether a client uses DNSSEC validation. After applying this methodology in a practical measurement, we identified and eliminated various effects that could distort the results. DNSSEC validation does occur in practice but there are major differences in the adoption between countries. Most countries covered in our measurement have a validation ratio of less than 5%. A remaining issue is the investigation of using mixed validating and non-validating resolvers. We expect our test to yield a negative result in case of mixed validation but the effect on the client application is not well understood yet.

References

1. Kaminsky, D.: Black ops 2008: It's the end of the cache as we know it. Black Hat USA (August 2008)

2. Arends, R., Austein, R., Larson, M., Massey, D., Rose, S.: DNS Security Introduction and Requirements. RFC 4033 (March 2005)
3. Anonymous: The collateral damage of internet censorship by dns injection. SIGCOMM Comput. Commun. Rev. 42(3), 21–27 (2012)
4. Weaver, N., Kreibich, C., Paxson, V.: Redirecting DNS for Ads and Profit. In: USENIX Workshop on Free and Open Communications on the Internet (FOCI), San Francisco, CA, USA (August 2011)
5. Hirsch, T., Lo Iacono, L., Wechsung, I.: How Much Network Security Must Be Visible in Web Browsers? In: Fischer-Hübner, S., Katsikas, S., Quirchmayr, G. (eds.) TrustBus 2012. LNCS, vol. 7449, pp. 1–16. Springer, Heidelberg (2012)
6. Wander, M., Weis, T.: Dnssec resolver test, http://dnssec.vs.uni-due.de
7. Mao, Z.M., Cranor, C.D., Bouglis, F., Rabinovich, M., Spatscheck, O., Wang, J.: A precise and efficient evaluation of the proximity between web clients and their local dns servers. In: Proceedings of USENIX Annual Technical Conference, pp. 229–242. USENIX Association (2002)
8. Xie, Y., Yu, F., Achan, K., Gillum, E., Goldszmidt, M., Wobber, T.: How dynamic are ip addresses? In: Proceedings of the 2007 Conference on Applications, Technologies, Architectures and Protocols for Computer Communications, SIGCOMM 2007, pp. 301–312. ACM, New York (2007)
9. Osterweil, E., Massey, D., Zhang, L.: Deploying and monitoring dns security (dnssec). In: Proceedings of the 2009 Annual Computer Security Applications Conference, ACSAC 2009, pp. 429–438. IEEE Computer Society, Washington, DC (2009)
10. Deccio, C., Sedayao, J., Kant, K., Mohapatra, P.: Quantifying and improving dnssec availability. In: 2011 Proceedings of 20th International Conference on Computer Communications and Networks (ICCCN), July 31- August 4, pp. 1–7 (2011)
11. RIPE NCC: Status for k.root-servers.net, http://k.root-servers.org/statistics/ROOT/daily/ (accessed September 2012)
12. St.Johns, M.: Automated Updates of DNS Security (DNSSEC) Trust Anchors. RFC 5011 (September 2007)
13. Castro, S., Wessels, D., Fomenkov, M., Claffy, K.: A day at the root of the internet. SIGCOMM Comput. Commun. Rev. 38(5), 41–46 (2008)
14. Gudmundsson, Ó., Crocker, S.D.: Observing dnssec validation in the wild. In: Securing and Trusting Internet Names, SATIN (2011)
15. Fujiwara, K.: Dnssec validation measurement. In: DNS-OARC Workshop, San Francisco, CA, USA (March 2011)
16. Fujiwara, K.: Number of possible dnssec validators seen at jp. In: IEPG Meeting @ IETF 83, Paris, France (March 2012)
17. Yu, Y., Wessels, D.: Quantifying dnssec validators. In: DNS-OARC Workshop, Toronto, Canada (October 2012)
18. SIDN: Dnssec test, http://dnssectest.sidn.nl (accessed August 2012)

On the State of ECN and TCP Options on the Internet[*]

Mirja Kühlewind[1], Sebastian Neuner[1], and Brian Trammell[2]

[1] Institute of Communication Networks and Computer Engineering (IKR)
University of Stuttgart, Germany
[2] Communication Systems Group, ETH Zürich, Switzerland

Abstract. Explicit Congestion Notification (ECN) is a TCP/IP extension that can avoid packet loss and thus improve network performance. Though standardized in 2001, it is barely used in today's Internet. This study, following on previous active measurement studies over the past decade, shows marked and continued increase in the deployment of ECN-capable servers, and usability of ECN on the majority of paths to such servers. We additionally present new measurements of ECN on IPv6, passive observation of actual ECN usage from flow data, and observations on other congestion-relevant TCP options (SACK, Timestamps and Window Scaling). We further present initial work on burst loss metrics for loss-based congestion control following from our findings.

1 Introduction

Since the initial design of TCP, there have been a number of extensions designed to improve its throughput and congestion control characteristics. Explicit Congestion Notification (ECN) is a TCP/IP extension that allows congestion signaling without packet loss. Though it has been shown to have performance benefits [1] and has been a standard since 2001 [2,3], ECN deployment lags significantly. Initial deployment problems where middleboxes cleared the ECN IP bits or even dropped packets indicating ECN-capability, as well as firewalls that would reset ECN-capable connections [4], led to mistrust of ECN.

In this work, we examine how much this situation has improved, adding another datapoint to a series of active measurements of ECN usage going back a decade. We also measured the usage of three other congestion-control-relevant TCP options: Selective Acknowledgment (SACK) [5], Timestamps (TS), and Window Scale (WS) [6]. SACK allows more precise signaling of loss, TS improves round-trip-time estimation, and WS allows a larger receiver windows.

Our measurement methodology consists of active probing of the ECN-readiness of a large set of popular web-servers (section 3.1) as well as passive measurement of ECN usage from flow data collected on a national-scale research and education network (section 3.2).

---

[*] This work is partly funded by ETICS and mPlane, FP7 research projects supported by the EU. Thanks to SWITCH for the flow data used in this study.

M. Roughan and R. Chang (Eds.) PAM 2013, LNCS 7799, pp. 135–144, 2013.
© Springer-Verlag Berlin Heidelberg 2013

Table 1. ECN implementation status

year	OS	version
2007	Microsoft Windows	Server 2008, 7, Vista
2007	Mac OS X	10.5
2006	Cisco IOS	12.2(8)T
2001	Linux	2.4 (full support)
1999	Linux	2.3 (router support)

Table 2. History of ECN and options deployment

Reference	Date	ECN	SACK	TSOPT
Medina ea. [7]	2000	1.1%	28%	-
Medina ea. [7]	2004	2.1%	68%	30%
Langley ea. [8]	2008	1.06%	-	-
Bauer ea. [9]	2011	17.2%	-	-

Deployment of ECN and related TCP options has been periodically studied in the literature over the past decade [7,8,9]; the most relevant results for the present work are summarized in Table 2. Bauer *et al* [9] probed the same set of servers as in the present work, so these results are directly comparable. Also related are measurements on TCP extensibility, which focus on middlebox treatment of packets with TCP options. Here findings vary between 0.17% [8] and 70% [9] of hosts dropping packets with unknown options, and 4–14% of middleboxes dropping such packets [10].

We find a recent acceleration in deployment of ECN-capable servers (section 4.1) and greater ECN support on IPv6-enabled servers (section 4.2). We compare this to actual ECN usage, passively measured from flow data captured from the border of a national-scale network, and find that while ECN is more frequently deployed, it is still seldom used (section 4.3).

In section 5, we define a metric for *burst loss* taking into account the peridic probing of congestion-control algorithms, and show that different types of traffic have different burst loss characteristics. Given the continued lag of ECN usage, we advance this initial work as a way to better understand loss dynamics and its relation to application behavior. Section 6 presents our conclusions.

2   Explicit Congestion Notification (ECN): A Review

ECN allows routers using active queue management (AQM) (e.g., Random Early Detection (RED)) to mark packets in case of congestion instead of dropping them. Two bits in the IP header provide four possible marks: No-ECN (00), Congestion Experienced (CE, 11), and two codepoints for ECN-Capable Transport (ECT(0), 01; and ECT(1), 10). An ECN-capable sender sets ECT(0) or ECT(1), which can be changed to CE by a router to signal congestion.

ECN uses two additional flags in the TCP header: ECN-Echo (ECE) is set on all packets from the receiver back to the sender to signal the arrival of a CE-marked packet until the sender sets Congestion Window Reduced (CWR) to acknowledge the ECE. These flags are also used to negotiate ECN usage: a connection initiator requests ECN by setting ECE and CWR on the initial SYN, and the responder acknowledges by setting ECE on the SYN/ACK. After successfully completing the negotiation, the senders can set an ECT codepoint on all subsequent packets over the connection.

Today, ECN is implemented in most operating systems (see Table 1). However even if enabled by default, it is often in "server mode" only: ECN will be negotiated if requested by a remote node initiating a connection, but connections opened by the node will not attempt to negotiate ECN usage.

3 Measurement Methodology

3.1 Active Probing of Web Servers

We measure ECN-readiness and usage of options by sending a TCP SYN with ECN negotiation and the SACK, TS, and WS options enabled to a target server, immediately closing the connection by sending a FIN. The resulting SYN/ACK responses are captured using tcpdump and evaluated offline using scapy[1], an open source Python-based framework for manipulation and evaluation of TCP packets. The target servers were selected from the Alexa Top 100,000 webservers list, as resolved by the Google public DNS server. If more than one IP address was resolved, we choose the first under the assumption that all servers operated by one provider have the same configuration.

We implemented a tool, also based on scapy, to determine whether ECN is usable on a path to a target. First, it generates a SYN with ECN negotiation. If the target is ECN-capable, it then sends one data segment with the CE codepoint set, and evaluates whether ECE was set on the corresponding ACK.

We evaluated the IP Time-to-Live (TTL) of the response as an estimate of the operating system in use at the target. When the TTL is smaller than 64, we assume Linux/BSD, 128 for Windows, and 255 for Solaris. Moreover, we checked the number of hops to be smaller than 64 based on ICMP traceroute. Anyway, this is not a reliable indication, as the initial TTL is configurable; one conspicuous exception is Google, which generally uses Linux but a TTL of 255.

The measurements were performed on a Linux host located in the University of Stuttgart network, connected via the Baden-Württemberg extended LAN (BelWü) to the DE-CIX Internet exchange in Frankfurt. We also performed these measurements over two German mobile network providers (O2 and Vodafone) and got similar results for both.

3.2 Analysis of Aggregated Flow Data

Though active measurement shows increasing deployment of ECN-ready web servers, this gives no information on the actual use of ECN in the network. To measure this, we examine NetFlow version 9 flow data collected from the border of SWITCH[2], the Swiss national research and education network. This network originates about 2.4M IPv4 addresses (the rough equivalent of a /11), with typical daily traffic volumes on the order of 100 TB, and contains both client machines as well as servers for universities.

---

[1] http://www.secdev.org/projects/scapy
[2] http://www.switch.ch/

Table 3. April 25, 2012, 77969 unique hosts (of 93573 responding hosts)

	All	TTL < 64	64 ≤ TTL ≤ 128	TTL > 128
hosts	77969 (100.00 %)	57610 (73.89 %)	12794 (16.41 %)	7590 (9.73 %)
hosts	77969 (100.00 %)	57610 (100.00 %)	12794 (100.00 %)	7590 (100.00 %)
ECN	19616 (25.16 %)	18954 (32.90 %)	521 (4.07 %)	143 (1.88 %)
SACK	69037 (88.54 %)	52409 (90.97 %)	11506 (89.93 %)	5145 (67.79 %)
TSOPT	65307 (83.76 %)	49667 (86.21 %)	10729 (83.86 %)	4928 (64.93 %)
WSOPT	68419 (87.75 %)	53137 (92.24 %)	10047 (78.53 %)	5258 (69.28 %)

Table 4. August 13, 2012, 77854 unique hosts (of 93756 responding hosts)

	All	TTL < 64	64 ≤ TTL ≤ 128	TTL > 128
hosts	77854 (100.00 %)	57651 (74.05 %)	12471 (16.02 %)	7769 (9.98 %)
hosts	77854 (100.00 %)	57651 (100.00 %)	12471 (100.00 %)	7769 (100.00 %)
ECN	22948 (29.48 %)	22193 (38.50 %)	616 (4.94 %)	145 (1.87 %)
SACK	69334 (89.06 %)	52783 (91.56 %)	11226 (90.02 %)	5353 (68.90 %)
TSOPT	65220 (83.77 %)	49749 (86.29 %)	10379 (83.23 %)	5112 (65.80 %)
WSOPT	68684 (88.22 %)	53420 (92.66 %)	9846 (78.95 %)	5446 (70.10 %)

Our methodology focuses on counting distinct sources, to give us a number comparable to that produced by active measurements. Our flow data unfortunately does not include the TCP flags used for ECN negotiation[3]; however, it does include the ECN Field in the IP header for the first packet observed in each flow record. Since the first packet in a ECN TCP flow is not ECN-capable, we observe *continued* flows: records created after an existing record for a long-lived flow is exported on active timeout (in the measured data, 300s). These capture the ECN field from mid-flow. So, in a given time interval, we count any source address appearing in at least one continued TCP flow record with either the ECT(0) or ECT(1) codepoint set as an *ECN-capable source*. We note this presents only a lower bound for ECN-capable sources, as it will not count any source which never sends a flow longer than the active timeout.

4   Results

4.1   ECN and TCP Option Deployment

We first measured ECN and TCP option support in web servers in April 2012. As shown in Table 3, 25.16 % of web servers negotiated ECN, a substantial increase over that measured by Bauer [9] using a compatible methodology and comparable set of hosts. We measured again in August 2012 (Table 4) and found a further increase to 29.48 % using the current Alexa list, or 29.35 % using the set of targets probed in April. We presume that operating system upgrades are

---

[3] While the devices can be *configured* to export ECE and CWR, they are always *exported* as zero, due to apparent implementation faults.

the primary cause of increased ECN deployment, as ECN has been supported by all major OSes only since 2007 (see Table 1).

We find that ECN is still less supported than SACK, TS, and WS, though these latter three show no discernible trend between April and August. We also find that ECN is far better supported on Linux hosts (TTLs less than 64) than on Windows (TTL between 64 and 128) or Solaris (TTL greater than 128)[4].

To validate the start TTL estimates, we checked the path length of the top 10,000 servers to ensure less than 64 hops. The minimum path length was 10 hops, as there are 9 hops within the BelWü network; the median was 17.47 hops, the maximum 29, and the mode 13; further investigations are needed on this last point to check for caching or CDNs in Frankfurt.

With respect to ECN usability on the path, we tested 22487 hosts in August 2012 which had negotiated ECN. Of these, 20441 (90.9 %) sent an ECE in response to an CE. 1846 (8.2 %) replied with an ACK without ECE, and 200 (0.9 %) sent no ACK at all. These 9 % of cases where ECN is not usable represent middleboxes which clear CE, which drop packets with CE set, or implementation errors at the endpoints. Additionally, experiments on two UMTS network showed 100 % ECN support but 0 % ECN feedback; we presume due to an ECN-capable HTTP proxy setup and clearing of CE in the mobile network. In any case, these observations show that middleboxes can still significantly affect the end-to-end use of ECN in the network.

We observed one curiosity in our options measurements: with our latest measurement run in September 2012 (31.2 % ECN-capable), we also probed all servers without ECN or any options, to check general responsiveness. We found 429 more unique hosts responding to a SYN without any TCP extension. 828 out of 78204 unique hosts (1.06 %) attempted to use SACK in the SYN/ACK even if not requested. 294 (0.38 %) similarly attempted to use WS, most of them presumably Windows hosts. None responded with TS or ECT. Moreover, while probing facebook.com we observed oscillation in RTT between about 100 ms and 150 ms, with an irregular period on the order of hours. This is indicative of load balancing between data centers on the (US) east and west coasts.

4.2   ECN Deployment on IPv6

We investigated the use of ECN over IPv6, in April and August as well as during the World IPv6 Launch event on 6 June 2012; the results are shown in Table 5. Here we find more support for ECN (47.52 %) than over IPv4, as well as more support for other TCP options, but without a comparable increase over time. There was a significant increase in the proportion of Alexa Top 100,000 web servers supporting IPv6 after World IPv6 launch, though only 2.28% support IPv6 as of August 2012. Most IPv6 servers have been installed within the last two years, so we expect greater ECN support in IPv6: these systems should be more up-to-date than average.

---

[4] As noted above, Google uses an initial TTL of 255, but disables ECN.

Table 5. ECN and options deployment on IPv6

	IPv4 Aug'12		IPv6 April'12		IPv6 June'12		IPv6 Aug'12	
responding hosts	93573		980		1819		2132	
unique hosts	77854	(100.00 %)	785	(100.00 %)	1075	(100.00 %)	1208	(100.00 %)
ECN	22948	(29.48 %)	370	(47.13 %)	522	(48.56 %)	574	(47.52 %)
SACK	69334	(89.06 %)	733	(93.38 %)	1006	(93.58 %)	1093	(90.48 %)
TSOPT	65220	(83.77 %)	713	(90.83 %)	986	(91.72 %)	1049	(86.84 %)
WSOPT	68684	(88.22 %)	734	(93.50 %)	1011	(94.05 %)	1136	(94.04 %)

4.3 Passive Measurement of ECN Adoption

Using the methodology in section 3.2 we examine data for the full day Wednesday, August 29, 2012, from midnight local time, from four of six border routers. Our results are not particularly surprising: while hosts and devices supporting ECN are seeing increased deployment, we confirm that ECN is mostly not used.

We observed 11,039 total distinct ECN-capable IPv4 sources. This is 0.774% of 1,426,152 distinct sources of continued flows, or 0.161% of 6,837,387 distinct sources observed in all TCP traffic. We estimate the true proportion is somewhere between these measurements. ECN-capable sources were responsible for 1.77TB (3.01%) of 58.84TB of measured TCP traffic.

Of the top 50 ECN-capable sources, there are 19 public-facing web servers, 13 of which appear in the Alexa list used in section 3.1; 12 DHCP clients; 8 servers apparently used for development, testing, or other non-public services; 6 network infrastructure machines, 2 of which are part of an active network performance measurement system; and 5 cloud servers.

Notably, the count of observed ECN-capable sources is on the same order of magnitude as clear errors in ECN usage: 24,580 sources set ECT(0), ECT(1), or CE on a TCP SYN packet. Most of these (16,911 or 68.9%) can be traced to a single ISP which sets the CE codepoint on 99.1% of its outgoing traffic. That there are more sources of persistent misuse of the ECN field from a misconfiguration at a single operator than sources of ECN-capable traffic is a discouraging sign for ECN adoption. We did not observe a single continued flow whose first packet had CE set, other than from sources which set CE on all packets: the extent of use of ECN on routers is too small to measure using this method.

To estimate the historical trend in ECN capability, we count all ECN-capable sources between 13:00 and 14:00 UTC on the last Wednesday of each month on six-month intervals leading up to October 27, 2010, and monthly intervals from January 25 to August 29, 2012[5]. We see a general increase in the proportion of ECN-capable sources, from 0.02% in April 2008 to 0.18% in August 2012. In Figure 1 we compare this trend to our datapoints as measured in section 4.1 as well as to prior measurements summarized in Table 2.

---

[5] We do not have TCP flags data prior to July 2012; therefore, historical trends detect ECN-capable sources on all flows. This leads to overcounting, as some sources set the ECT bits on the SYN packet as well. We treat these numbers as comparable, as they are all subject to the same overcounting.

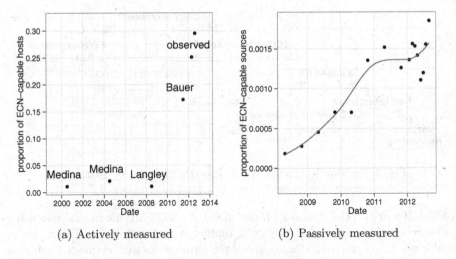

(a) Actively measured   (b) Passively measured

Fig. 1. Trends in ECN capability

5   Identifying Conditions of Congestion: Burst Loss Study

As ECN usage remains negligible, packet loss remains the only practical signal
for congestion control. We therefore turn our attention to loss patterns in typical Internet usage scenarios in order to identify conditions of congestion. This
information can be used to improve congestion control or network measurements.

In related work, Allman *et al* [11] showed that 0.6 % of connections experience
a loss rate of more than 10 % with a loss of at least 1 packet in more than 50 % of
the cases and a loss period, which is a number of losses in a row, of 1 packet in over
60 %. Mellia *et al* [12] measure an average total amount of anomalous segments,
including loss and reordering, of 5 % of outgoing traffic and 8 % for incoming
traffic on an enterprise network. However, these metrics are given independent
of usage pattern and algorithm. Additionally, usage of known TCP congestion
control algorithms has been investigated by [13,7,14].

Typically, the loss patterns depend not only on the usage scenario, as congestion control periodically induces overload to probe for available bandwidth.
Therefore, the observed loss patterns themselves are also algorithm-dependent.
Here we define a *burst loss* as an event consisting of all losses occurring on a
TCP connection within one RTT of the first loss; counting these events provides
a metric which captures packet loss in a congestion-control-aware way, as losses
occurring within a single RTT will be treated as a single event by TCP.

Moreover, application behavior does influence the loss pattern as well. Thus we
investigated three common classes of Internet activity – web browsing, download,
and YouTube – to study their loss patterns individually. In initial trials we
emulated these three types of network traffic on a residential access network
with a maximum measured datarate of 5.7 MBit/s: web browsing of 33 common
websites with a 12 second delay after each site, viewing of two YouTube videos

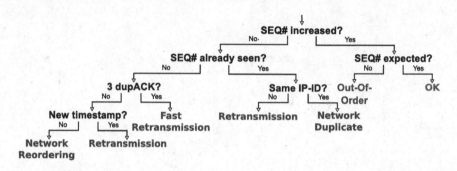

Fig. 2. Decision Diagram for TCP Loss/Retransmission Estimation

(4.62 MB and 11.59 MB), and FTP download of a 80.56 MB file from a host using cubic congestion control. 24 trials were conducted over a single day. The resulting traffic was captured, individual losses or retransmissions were estimated using an algorithm similar to those in the literature [11,15,12]; the decision tree is shown in Figure 2. Losses were then grouped into bursts.

Web browsing consists of many short flows; over all trials, we saw only 5.8% of flows experiencing any loss at all. 82.7% of bursts consists of only a single loss while also bursts of up to 71 losses occurred. The FTP download, on the other hand, involves one single, long flow, and a very regular loss pattern due to congestion control can be observed. As cubic congestion control was used, we observed 70.7% of single losses as well as frequent bursts of up to 12 losses. In our 24h measurement series we found three probes (at 3am, 10am and 5pm) with a very large number of small burst losses (4058, 3905, and 4157, respectively). Those cases presumably show an anomaly in the network or at the server side. Youtube presents an entirely different pattern, including regular, larger bursts due to its block sending behavior [16] even though YouTube uses TCP congestion control. In 18 of 24 trials, the longer video experienced exactly five bursts, while we always observed one burst for the smaller video. But, given the application behavior, in both cases the mean burst size was around 33. These results are summarized in Table 6.

Table 6. Active measurement from September 10, 2012 [mean number of packets (PKTS), of retransmissions (RET), of burst losses (B), of packets per burst loss (P/B); mean loss rate (RATE); time between burst losses (TBB)]

	PKTS	RET	RATE	B	P/B	TBB
Web-browsing	80779	533.96	0.66 %	227.88	2.37	-
Download (all)	58643	703.04	1.2 %	535	2.10	2.88
Download (21 of 24)	58639	76.14	0.13 %	34.29	2.23	3.28
YouTube1 (11.59 MB)	8469.2	176.29	2.08 %	5.58	31.72	27.31
YouTube1 (18 of 24)	8469.4	159.83	1.89 %	5	31.97	29.40
YouTube2 (4,62 MB)	3386.2	34.04	1 %	1	34.04	-

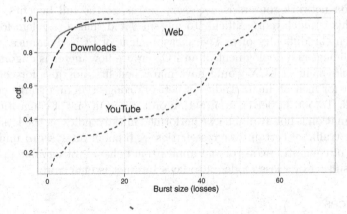

Fig. 3. Burst size (in losses) measured per scenario

These initial findings on loss patterns indicate burst losses to be a well-observable metric. As shown in the distribution of burst loss sizes in Figure 3, the burst loss sizes depend on the scenario. This distribution may therefore provide information to identify the origin of losses, not available with simple metrics such as average loss rate. E.g. a greedy flow using the Reno congestion control algorithm over different network paths (different available bandwidth and RTT) will lead to a different average loss rate but the same pattern in burst size and regularity. Further theoretical or simulation-based work is needed to develop a loss model for different traffic classes and then relate this model to the loss patterns observed in today's Internet to differentiate other sources of losses. Similar influence of congestion control and application behavior can be expected for ECN-based congestion marking, with the additional influence of the AQM at the bottleneck queue.

6   Conclusions and Future Work

This study has shown that deployment of ECN-capable hosts in the Internet continues: about 30% of the top 100,000 web servers can now negotiate ECN usage. We suspect this is due to normal upgrade and replacement cycles affecting the operating systems deployed. Of further interest is that Linux servers are far more likely to support ECN, as are IPv6 servers. Additionally we could measure a general increase in IPv6 support over the IPv6 Launch Day.

While we found 91% of paths to ECN-capable servers are ECN-capable, a failure rate of 9%, including 1% of paths where CE-marked or ECE-marked packets are lost in the network, indicates that earlier problems with ECN deployment are not completely solved. Further, passive measurements give a lower bound for actual ECN usage which was measured to be two orders of magnitude less common than ECN capability. Even worse: twice as many observed sources misused the CE codepoint as properly used the ECT codepoints. Of course, the ECN readiness on network routers is necessary to realize the full benefits of ECN, as well. This is much more difficult to measure, and thus a problem for future work. Given the difficulty of passive measurement of ECN dynamics, work on the development and deployment of an ECN-aware flow meter is ongoing.

The deployment of ECN would have many benefits, not just for congestion control but for measurement studies of network congestion and traffic engineering, as well. To obtain better information on the conditions of congestion when ECN information is not available, we performed initial studies on the loss pattern of Internet traffic of certain usage scenarios. A broader analysis to understand the effects of congestion control and application behavior observable in the loss pattern resulting in a loss model of today's Internet is underway.

References

1. Salim, J.H., Ahmed, U.: Performance Evaluation of Explicit Congestion Notification (ECN) in IP Networks. RFC 2884, IETF (July 2000)
2. Ramakrishnan, K., Floyd, S., Black, D.: The Addition of Explicit Congestion Notification (ECN) to IP. RFC 3168, IETF (September 2001)
3. Kuzmanovic, A.: The power of explicit congestion notification. SIGCOMM Comput. Commun. Rev. 35(4), 61–72 (2005)
4. Floyd, S.: Inappropriate TCP Resets Considered Harmful. RFC 3360 (Best Current Practice) (August 2002)
5. Mathis, M., Mahdavi, J., Floyd, S., Romanow, A.: TCP Selective Acknowledgement Options. RFC 2018, IETF (October 1996)
6. Jacobson, V., Braden, R., Borman, D.: TCP Extensions for High Performance. RFC 1323, IETF (May 1992)
7. Medina, A., Allman, M., Floyd, S.: Measuring the evolution of transport protocols in the Internet. SIGCOMM Comput. Commun. Rev. 35(2), 37–52 (2005)
8. Langley, A.: Probing the viability of TCP extensions (2008), http://www.imperialviolet.org/binary/ecntest.pdf
9. Bauer, S., Beverly, R., Berger, A.: Measuring the state of ECN readiness in servers, clients and routers. In: Proc. of Internet Measurement Conference (2011)
10. Honda, M., Nishida, Y., Raiciu, C., Greenhalgh, A., Handley, M., Tokuda, H.: Is it still possible to extend TCP? In: Proc. of IMC 2011, pp. 181–194. ACM, New York (2011)
11. Allman, M., Eddy, W.M., Ostermann, S.: Estimating loss rates with TCP. ACM Performance Evaluation Review 31 (2003)
12. Mellia, M., Meo, M., Muscariello, L., Rossi, D.: Passive analysis of TCP anomalies. Comput. Netw. 52(14), 2663–2676 (2008)
13. Padhye, J., FLoyd, S.: On Inferring TCP Behavior. In: Proceedings of ACM SIGCOMM, pp. 287–298 (2001)
14. Yang, P., Luo, W., Xu, L., Deogun, J., Lu, Y.: TCP Congestion Avoidance Algorithm Identification. In: 31st International Conference on Distributed Computing Systems (ICDCS), pp. 310–321 (June 2011)
15. Benko, P., Veres, A.: A passive method for estimating end-to-end TCP packet loss. In: Global Telecommunications Conference, GLOBECOM 2002, vol. 3, pp. 2609–2613. IEEE (November 2002)
16. Ghobadi, M., Cheng, Y., Jain, A., Mathis, M.: Trickle: Rate limiting YouTube video streaming. In: Proc. of the USENIX Annual Technical Conference (2012)

Measuring Query Latency
of Top Level DNS Servers

Jinjin Liang[1,2], Jian Jiang[1,2], Haixin Duan[1,2], Kang Li[3], and Jianping Wu[1,2]

[1] Institute for Network Science and Cyberspace, Tsinghua University
[2] Tsinghua National Laboratory on Information Science and Technology
[3] Department of Computer Science, University of Georgia

Abstract. We surveyed the latency of upper DNS hierarchy from 19593 vantage points around the world to investigate the impact of uneven distribution of top level DNS servers on end-user latency. Our findings included: 1) generally top level DNS servers served Internet users efficiently, with median latency 20.26ms for root, 42.64ms for .com/.net, 39.07ms for .org; 2) quality of service was uneven, Europe and North America were the best while Africa and South America were 3 to 6 times worse; 3) most of the root servers performed well in Europe and North America, but only F, J, L roots showed low query latency in other continents; 4) query latency of F and L roots showed that only about 60% resolvers were routed to the nearest anycast instances. We also revealed two problems that lead to constantly large query latency (6s~18s) for resolvers. One was buggy implementation of some resolvers on IPv4/IPv6 dual-stack hosts, the other was misconfigured middle-boxes that filtered large or fragmented DNSSEC packets.

1 Introduction

The Domain Name System (DNS) is a fundamental component of Internet which translates domain names into IP addresses for most of the Internet applications. This makes DNS query latency a critical factor that affects the quality of Internet experienced by end-users.

Essentially, DNS is a distributed database organized as a hierarchical tree. On the top of the hierarchy are root zone and some top level domain (TLD) zones such as .com and .net. DNS authority servers of top level zones are crucial for Internet operation since these servers serve Internet users all over the world as the start points of the whole domain name space. Their performance is also important to end-users as some popular implementations could still visit top level DNS servers frequently even with the local caches [10].

A common technique to increase DNS robustness and performance is DNS zone replication, in which one DNS zone can be served by multiple authority servers in various locations. For example, root zone is currently served by 13 logical root servers and hundreds of anycast instances.

An important issue of deploying replications of top level zones is geographic distribution. Historically, most of the root servers were located in the

M. Roughan and R. Chang (Eds.) PAM 2013, LNCS 7799, pp. 145–154, 2013.

United States. Internet users of other regions inevitably stood longer DNS query latency due to geographic distance. Previous research indicated that Europe and Asia were underprovisioned while North America was overprovisioned [7], suggesting that some root servers should be relocated.

Recently, the deployment of replication instances for top level zones grows massively with wide adoption of anycast, which further allows multiple instances in different locations to use a same IP address. Publicly available information [1] shows 319 anycast instances for 13 root servers have been deployed all over the world. Our curiosity is that how Internet users from different regions experience this progress and whether the uneven quality of service has been improved. One recent article compared the number of root instances and the population served in different continents and concluded that the distribution of root servers was still very uneven [1]. However, the conclusion of [1] is based on simplistic statistics of users served per root server. We hope to have a more technical and comprehensive evaluation of the quality of services of upper DNS servers.

We probed 19,593 open recursive resolvers to query top level servers using a method we called *NXDOMAIN-Query* and King technique [5]. *NXDOMAIN-Query* could obtain the overall latency from resolvers to root or TLD level while King technique could measure the latency between a resolver and an arbitrary nameserver. With the measured latency, we compared the DNS performance in different regions and further analyzed the current state of top level zones' replication deployment. We find: 1) generally top level DNS servers serve Internet users efficiently, with median latency 20.26ms for root, 42.64ms for .com/.net(they share the same infrastructure), 39.07ms for .org; 2) quality of service is still uneven: Europe and North America are the best while Africa and South America are 3 to 6 times worse; 3) in Europe and North America, most of the root servers perform well, but in other continents only F, J, L roots show low query latency; 4) query latencies of F and L roots show that only about 60% resolvers are routed to the nearest anycast root instances.

Along with the results for initial motivation, we also observed anomalous large latency from a group of resolvers, ranging from 6s to 18s. Our further investigation revealed two reasons. One was buggy implementation of some resolvers on IPv4/IPv6 dual-stack hosts. The other was misconfigured middle-boxes on certain paths which filtered large or fragmented DNSSEC responses.

2   Methodology

We collect plenty of open recursive resolvers and then drive these resolvers to query our targets. Using the round trip times (RTTs) observed from these resolvers, we further estimate DNS query latency between these resolvers and the targets. This approach has two advantages: 1) we do not need the direct control of our vantage points, which allows us to scale our study extensively; 2) probing open resolvers triggers *real* DNS lookup behaviors in the wild, which helps us to observe anomalous behaviors and further identify the causes.

---

[1] http://www.root-servers.org

2.1 Collecting Open Recursive Resolvers

We collect 19593 open resolvers in total by three ways: 1) extracting open resolvers from the query log of a busy DNS authority nameserver (42%); 2) probing DNS authority servers of Alexa top 1M sites (42%); 3) inquiring help from other researchers (16%). [2] It is worth to note that we must exclude DNS forwarders since they would query their upper resolvers rather than query authority servers directly. The geographic distribution of these resolvers is detailed in Table 1.

Table 1. Distribution of Open Resolvers (Based on GeoIP database)

Continent	# of countries	# of ASes	# of resolvers	% of total
Europe	45	2821	7169	36.59
North America	25	1837	5525	28.20
Asia	40	940	6056	30.91
South America	11	173	426	2.17
Oceania	7	131	248	1.27
Africa	26	77	149	0.76
Unknown	-	-	20	0.10
Total	154	5979	19593	100.00

2.2 NXDOMAIN-Query Technique

We utilize a method called *NXDOMAIN-Query* to indirectly measure the query latency from a resolver to a domain level. The main idea of NXDOMAIN-Query is leveraging non-existent domain names to control recursive resolvers to stop at specified domain levels. Besides, *NXDOMAIN-Query* uses a fresh non-existent domain name for each request to avoid cached negative responses. For example, to measure the query latency from a resolver to root level, we issue the resolver with a DNS query containing a fresh non-existent TLD from a client. When the resolver receives this query, it asks one of the root servers, then receives a *NXDOMAIN* response and replies to the client with the *NXDOMAIN* answer. Assume T_{c-root} is the whole query latency observed from the client, T_{r-root} is the latency between the resolver and the root server, T_{c-r} is the latency between the client and the resolver which can be measured by issuing the resolver with a non-recursive query. Then we can estimate T_{r-root} by $T_{r-root} = T_{c-root} - T_{c-r}$. Similarly, we can also measure DNS lookup latency from resolvers to TLD level.

The limitation of *NXDOMAIN-Query* is that this method only allows us to measure the overall latency from selected resolver to a group of DNS servers serving a specified level of DNS domain, rather than to a certain DNS server. The reason is that different resolvers implement different server selection strategies which cannot be controlled indirectly.

---

[2] The limitation of using open resolvers as vantage points is that query latency may be affected by network condition of the resolvers. However, our exploration verifies that about 70% of these resolvers are also authority servers, thus we believe networks may only have limited influence on our measurement results.

2.3 King Technique

We leverage King technique [5] to indirectly measure DNS lookup latency from selected resolver to one certain DNS server, as a complement to the above *NXDOMAIN-Query*. The basic idea of King technique is tricking recursive resolver to query any designated IP address through pointing the nameserver of a controllable domain to that IP address, and then estimating latency between the resolver and the designated IP with the observed RTTs. Please refer to the original paper [5] for more technical details.

3 Measurements and Results

Using methods introduced above, we investigated the impact of geographic distribution of top level DNS servers by measuring overall query latency of both root and TLD level, as well as the individual query latency of each of the 13 root servers from different regions. We also analyzed anycast proximity of F and L roots and compared the differences among continents [3].

3.1 Query Latency of Root and TLD Hierarchy

We assessed the overall query latency of root level and popular TLDs through *NXDOMAIN-Query* approach. For each open resolver we collected, we measured its query latency to root, .com/.net, .org respectively. To reduce measurement noises, we continuously measured the latency over 500 times during a two days period for each resolver and used median value as a resolver's final latency.

Figure 1 shows the CDF of all resolvers' query latency to the three measured top DNS zones. We can see that generally these three zones serve global users efficiently. For most of the resolvers the latency are small, and the median latency for all three zones are less than 50ms. Specifically, root zone has the lowest overall query latency and the median latency is about 20.26ms. .org slightly outperforms .com/.net, the median latency for .org is 39.07ms while for .com/.net is 42.64ms.

A surprising result from Figure 1 is that a few resolvers constantly show very large query latency, with the values mostly around 6, 8, 12, 18 seconds. We present our investigation for this strange behavior in Section 4.

We break down the measurement results to compare the differences among various continents. Figure 2 shows the quartiles of all resolvers' latency to the three zones in each continent. The results show that the cost of querying the three top DNS zones is uneven across continents. All six continents can be categorized into three groups. Most of the resolvers in Europe (EU) and North America (NA) have distinctly smaller latency than other continents, especially comparing to resolvers in South America (SA) and Africa (AF), the median latency of which are 3 to 6 times larger. Asia (AS) and Oceania (OC) are more complicated. While the median latency can be equal (OC) or slightly larger than those of

---

[3] The results are available at https://github.com/dnsmeasurement/latency.

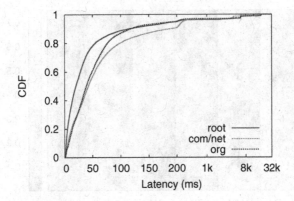

Fig. 1. Cumulative distribution of latency of root, `.com/.net`, `.org`

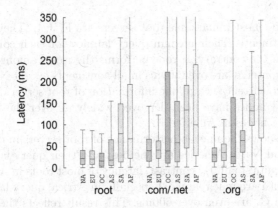

Fig. 2. DNS query latency of root, `.com/.net`, `.org`, breaking down by continent

EU and NA, the quartile values are usually much bigger. This indicates the quality of service of top level DNS servers varies greatly among countries or autonomous systems (ASes). We leave the detailed analysis of country-level or AS-level differences as our future work.

3.2   Query Latency of Thirteen Root Servers

Using King technique, we measured the query latency from each open resolver to each of the thirteen root servers. Same as above, we launched the measurement over 300 times in two days continuously and for each root server we extracted the median value as each resolver's final query latency.

We categorize the resolvers by continents and show all their query latency to the thirteen root servers in Figure 3. Since the number of resolvers in each continent is different, we normalize the results in Figure 3 before analyzing them.

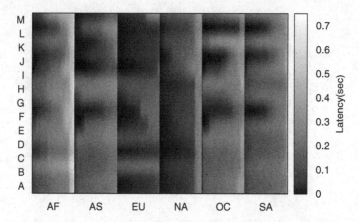

Fig. 3. Query latency of 13 root servers in different continents

In Figure 3, the most remarkable root servers are F, J, L. They perform well in all of the continents. Their median query latency for each continent are all below 200ms. On the contrary, B root performs the worst among all the roots. Most of its query latency are over 300ms in all continents except North America. The results are consistent with public information of root server deployment. F, J, L root anycast nodes have been deployed widely all over the world while B root only has one nodes in America.

Figure 3 also shows the uneven performance of root servers in different continents. Europe and North America are the best and their query latency to most root servers are quite small. By contrast, latency of most roots in Africa, Oceania and South America are much larger. Especially in Africa, query latency of some roots, like B and G, are even over 600ms. This result reflects the current state of root anycast deployment that Europe and North America deploy much more root instances than other continents do.

Compared with the result in Section 3.1, we observe that although not all the roots perform well in each continents, the overall latency of root level are relatively small. This results from the resolvers' server selection mechanisms which usually choose a best server to request.

3.3 Proximity of Root Anycast

Anycast instances of a logical root server share a same anycast address, but have different unicast addresses for management. Comparing query latency of anycast address with the minimum latency for all the unicast addresses could infer whether a resolver is indeed routed to the nearest anycast node. In previous research, this property was referred to as *anycast proximity* [2].

We used King technique to measure the anycast proximity of F and L roots, whose unicast addresses were publicly available. Our measurement repeated about 200 times in two days and used medians as the final latency for each

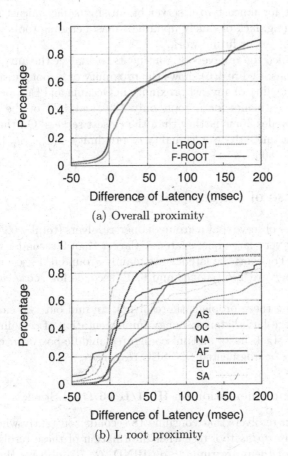

(a) Overall proximity

(b) L root proximity

Fig. 4. The proximity of root anycast

resolver. Finally, we computed the proximity of a root $T_{proximity}$ by $T_{anycast} - min(T_{unicast})$, where $T_{anycast}$ was the latency of a root's anycast address and $min(T_{unicast})$ was the minimum latency of all that root's unicast addresses.

Figure 4(a) shows the overall proximity of F and L roots. We find that a fair fraction of resolvers are not routed to the anycast nodes closest to them. For example, about 40% of the resolvers are routed to servers more than 50ms farther away from the nearest anycast nodes for both F and L roots. This is most likely caused by routing policies like BGP and the hierarchical deployment [4]. What's more, we observe that about 2% and 1% of resolvers whose $T_{proximity}$ are below -30ms for F root and L root, which means that the queries are routed to servers that are nearer than the closest nodes. Several possible reasons could lead to such strange phenomenon: errors in measurement results, paths for anycast are

---

[4] F-root are deployed hierarchically, only 2 of 49 nodes advertise the anycast prefix globally.

faster than that for unicast to a server or missing some unicast nodes in our experiment list (e.g. lack of timely update or masquerading roots [4]). We leave this investigation as our future work.

We also classified the resolvers by continents to analyze the anycast proximity in different regions. Figure 4(b) shows the proximity of L roots in six continents. We see that the quality of anycast proximity in Oceania and Europe outperforms those in other continents for L root, only 13% and 15% of the resolvers are directed to the nodes 50ms farther than the closest servers. On the other hand, resolvers in Asia suffer the worst quality of proximity, $T_{proximity}$ for 65% of its resolvers are over 50ms.

4   The Cause of Large Query Latency

In Section 3.1, we observe that a group of open resolvers (totally 664, 3.2% of all) constantly show very large query latency (larger than 2 seconds) when visiting root and TLDs. For root, the latency are mainly around 6, 18 seconds, while for TLDs, the latency are 4, 6 seconds and 6, 12 seconds for .com/.net and .org respectively.

After exploring these problematic resolvers, we find out two causes that are responsible for the large latency: buggy implementation of certain resolvers on IPv4/IPv6 dual-stack hosts and misconfigured middle-boxes on certain paths which filter large or fragmented DNSSEC responses.

4.1   Buggy Implementation on IPv4/IPv6 Dual-Stack

We first focus on resolvers that consume 18 seconds constantly when traversing root level. We use *fpdns* tool to gather information of these resolvers and find that nearly all of them are running on BIND 9.2. To observe these resolvers' resolution process, we set up a testing domain with three name servers and drive the problematic resolvers to visit our name servers through querying them for subdomains under the testing domain.

We find that everytime we put a new IPv6 address into the glue record, two seconds extra delay will be added. We infer that the large latency are related to the IPv6 address of name servers. 9 of the 13 root servers are configured with IPv6 addresses, so these resolvers need about 18 seconds to traverse the root level. Similarly, 2 .com/.net and 6 .org TLD servers use IPv6 addresses, which lead to 4 and 12 seconds latency respectively. Further investigation on source code confirms that BIND 9.2.x running on IPv4/IPv6 dual-stack host always prefers IPv6 authorities even if they are unreachable. New versions of BIND ($\geq$ 9.3) have fixed this problem.

4.2   Filtering of DNSSEC Response

Excluding large latency explained above, the rest ones are mostly around 6 seconds. Using fpdns tool again, we find that most of the rest problematic resolvers are BIND 9.3.x. We also drive them to query our name servers to observe their behaviors.

We notice that when we configure our testing domain with DNSSEC, the 6 seconds' resolution will occur. Observing from our name server, we find that resolvers firstly send 3 queries with EDNS0 every 2 seconds sequentially and then send a query without EDNS0 at last. Since DNSSEC is enabled, responses for the first three EDNS0 queries contain DNSSEC records which are larger than 512 bytes. We infer that large DNSSEC responses are dropped on the paths to these problematic resolvers, which eventually causes 6 seconds resolution latency.

5   Related Work

Quite a few measurements were carried out to study the DNS infrastructure. Brownlee *et al.* [3] and Lee *et al.* [6] investigated the performance indicators of root and some TLD nameservers, such as DNS response time and request loss rate. Liston *et al.* [8] and Lee *et al.* [7] analyzed the performance impact of top level nameserver placement. Our work measured the query latency to top level DNS servers from a large number of vantage points and tried to correlate the query latency with the current nameserver deployment. Yu *et al.* [11] measured the placement of top level DNS servers. While they focused on identifying the locations of nameservers and assessing their robustness, our work aimed at revealing the impact of nameserver deployment on performance. Sarat *et al.* [9] and Ballani *et al.* [2] measured the availability and the proximity of DNS root anycast, and also provided suggestions for deployment strategies. Our work focused on the proximity of F and L roots anycast and investigated the differences among various regions.

6   Conclusion

DNS is a public resource shared by Internet users all over the world. However, historically, top level DNS servers are unevenly deployed, which leads to unfair quality of DNS service in different regions. Recently top level DNS servers, especially root servers have been deployed massively with wide adoption of anycast. Our measurement shows that this progress improves the overall DNS performance. However the quality is still uneven among different regions. Nevertheless, the adoption of anycast enables rapid deployment of replication in underprovisioned areas. ISPs should be more proactive to deploy local root anycast instances to improve their DNS query performance.

Our measurement also observed anomalous large latency. While the cause of buggy implementation might not be an issue, the other cause of filtering large DNSSEC response is more important. With DNSSEC being a crucial protocol of Internet in future, large DNS response and IP fragment should be considered as regular rather than harmful traffic. The community should take more efforts to measure unexpected DNS packet filtering and discuss possible implications.

Acknowledgements. We are grateful to the anonymous reviewers and our shepherd Simon Leinen for their valuable comments. This work is supported by the National Basic Research Program of China (973 Project, Grant No. 2009CB320505) and National Natural Science Foundation of China (Grant No. 61161140454). Kang Li's research on this work is partially supported by US National Science Foundation (NSF) Office of Cyberinfrastructure grant 1127195.

References

1. The (very) uneven distribution of DNS root servers on the internet, http://royal.pingdom.com/2012/05/07/the-very-uneven-distribution-of-dns-root-servers-on-the-internet/

2. Ballani, H., Francis, P., Ratnasamy, S.: A measurement based deployment proposal for ip anycast. In: Proceedings of the 6th ACM SIGCOMM Conference on Internet Measurement, IMC 2006, pp. 231–244. ACM, New York (2006)

3. Brownlee, N., Claffy, K., Nemeth, E.: DNS root/gtld performance measurements. In: USENIX LISA, San Diego, CA (2001)

4. Fan, X., Heidemann, J., Govindan, R.: Identifying and characterizing anycast in the domain name system. Tech. rep. (2011)

5. Gummadi, K.P., Saroiu, S., Gribble, S.D.: King: estimating latency between arbitrary internet end hosts. In: Proceedings of the 2nd ACM SIGCOMM Workshop on Internet Measurement, IMW 2002, pp. 5–18. ACM, New York (2002)

6. Lee, B.S., Tan, Y.S., Sekiya, Y., Narishige, A., Date, S.: Availability and effectiveness of root DNS servers: A long term study. In: 2010 IEEE Network Operations and Management Symposium (NOMS), pp. 862–865 (April 2010)

7. Lee, T., Huffaker, B., Fomenkov, M., et al.: On the problem of optimization of DNS root servers' placement (2003)

8. Liston, R., Srinivasan, S., Zegura, E.: Diversity in DNS performance measures. In: Proceedings of the 2nd ACM SIGCOMM Workshop on Internet Measurment, IMW 2002, pp. 19–31. ACM, New York (2002)

9. Sarat, S., Pappas, V., Terzis, A.: On the use of anycast in DNS. In: Proceedings.15th International Conference on Computer Communications and Networks, ICCCN 2006, pp. 71–78 (October 2006)

10. Wessels, D., Fomenkov, M., Brownlee, N., Claffy, K.: Measurements and Laboratory Simulations of the Upper DNS Hierarchy. In: Barakat, C., Pratt, I. (eds.) PAM 2004. LNCS, vol. 3015, pp. 147–157. Springer, Heidelberg (2004)

11. Yu, Y., Cai, J., Osterweil, E., Zhang, L.: Measuring the placement of DNS servers in top-level-domain

IPv6 Alias Resolution via Induced Fragmentation[*]

Robert Beverly[1], William Brinkmeyer[1],
Matthew Luckie[2], and Justin P. Rohrer[1]

[1] Naval Postgraduate School, Monterey, CA
[2] CAIDA, University of California, San Diego, CA
{rbeverly,wdbrinkm,jprohrer}@nps.edu, mjl@caida.org

Abstract. Discovering router-level IPv6 topologies is important to understanding IPv6 growth, structure, and evolution and relation to IPv4. This work presents a fingerprint-based IPv6 alias resolution technique that induces fragmented responses from IPv6 router interfaces. We leverage the way in which IPv6 implements fragmentation to provide reliable inferences. We demonstrate perfect alias resolution accuracy in a controlled environment, and on a small subset of the production IPv6 Internet for which we have ground-truth. Internet-wide testing finds that over 70% of IPv6 interfaces probed respond to the test. Our promising results suggest a valuable technique to aid IPv6 topology discovery.

1 Introduction

IPv6, standardized nearly 15 years ago [6] as the successor to Internet Protocol version 4 (IPv4), is experiencing commercial deployment – primarily due to economic and business constraints, rather than any technical impetus [4]. Modern systems and hardware support IPv6, service and content providers are deploying IPv6 [17], and government networks are mandating IPv6 [13].

The number of global IPv6 BGP routing prefixes is growing exponentially [11]. More than 6,000 autonomous systems, approximately 15%, now announce IPv6 reachability [16]. Amid IPv6 measurement efforts underway [7] [22], understanding the evolution of the IPv6 router-level topology is an ongoing challenge.

This paper investigates IPv6 *alias resolution* – the process of determining if two IP addresses are assigned to different interfaces of the same physical router [12]. Alias resolution reduces an interface-level graph, e.g. discovered via active probing, into a router-level graph [3], thereby permitting a better understanding of the resilience and robustness properties of the network [21].

Taking inspiration from prior IPv4 alias resolution work, we present a fingerprint based IPv6 alias resolution technique that relies on eliciting *fragmented* responses from IPv6 router interfaces. Although IPv6 has no in-network fragmentation, sources can send large IPv6 packets in fragments. We find that, as with IPv4 routers, the IPv6 fragment identifier counter is frequently common across a

---

[*] The rights of this work are transferred to the extent transferable according to title 17 §105 U.S.C.

M. Roughan and R. Chang (Eds.) PAM 2013, LNCS 7799, pp. 155–165, 2013.
© Springer-Verlag Berlin Heidelberg 2013

router's interfaces. While all IPv4 control-plane packets sourced by a router require a unique fragment identifier, IPv6 fragment identifiers increase only when the router must source a fragmented packet. Thus, in contrast to fragmentation-based IPv4 alias resolution that is prone to false positives due to background control-plane traffic incrementing a small 16-bit counter, our IPv6 technique is highly accurate because control-plane messages are rarely fragmented.

This paper seeks to detail and validate a new IPv6 alias resolution algorithm; we leave Internet-wide alias resolution, scaling, and comparison against other techniques to future work. We make four primary contributions:

1. Development of a fingerprint-based IPv6 alias resolution technique[1].
2. Validation on a large virtualized testbed of common commercial routers.
3. Internet-wide probing of more than 49,000 distinct live IPv6 router interfaces where we discover approximately 70% respond to our test.
4. Validation of the technique on a small subset of the production IPv6 network for which we have alias ground-truth, where we obtain perfect accuracy.

2 Related Work

Significant prior research investigates IPv4 alias resolution; see [12] and [9] for an overview of major techniques. Design differences between IPv4 and IPv6 obsolete some techniques used in IPv4, while enabling new ones. For instance, the elimination of in-network fragmentation and the simplification of the IPv6 header prevents the trivial reapplication of IPv4 techniques that utilize the IPID field [19]. Alias resolution through IPv6 source-routing has been explored in Atlas [20], RPM [15], and the "option header method" [14]. Given a potential alias pair (x, y), Atlas performs a UDP traceroute to y via x with the hop limit set to expire at x and relies on the fact that routers will generally process the routing extension header before checking the hop limit. If x and y are aliases, "hop limit exceeded" and "port unreachable" ICMP6 messages are generated.

RPM finds that the source address of "hop limit exceeded" ICMP6 messages for packets that are not destined to the router at which the expiration occurs is frequently the ingress address. To discover aliases for address y, probes are sent from p via x and y destined to p, with the hop limit set to expire at y. Performing this probe for a large enough set of addresses x will result in ICMP6 "hop limit exceeded" messages originating from aliases of y. The option header method makes use of the fact that setting an invalid bit sequence in the IPv6 options header will generate an ICMP6 "parameter problem" message, originating from the ingress interface of the packet generating the response. By probing via multiple intermediate routers (similar to RPM), multiple aliases of the target address may be discovered. Our alias resolution method is distinct from those listed here in that it does not depend on IPv6 source routing and therefore is not defeated on hosts where source routing is disabled due to security concerns, as has become the norm in IPv4.

---

[1] A freely licensed prototype Python implementation is available from: [2].

Lastly, the THC IPv6 [10] toolkit employs false ICMP6 packet too big messages (discussed next) as part of its attack suite. However, the tool's goal is to maliciously reduce the MTU of a target rather than to resolve IPv6 aliases.

3   Methodology

Our technique is fingerprint-based: we require some identifier or signature that is both common to all interfaces on an IPv6 router, and is unique across routers such that we do not make false inferences. Further, it must be possible for a remote probing host to obtain the identifier without any privileged access.

We take inspiration from prior work in IPv4 alias resolution that relies on fragment identifiers [19]. The IPv4 header contains a 16-bit identifier that is used by an end-host receiving fragmented packets such that it can reconstruct the original packet. Prior research [19] has shown that packets originated by IPv4 routers often use a common counter, irrespective of physical interface, for the identifier field. Since this counter increases sequentially, it is possible to infer whether two interfaces are aliases by querying the router, e.g. via ping.

Two factors complicate IPv4 identifier-based alias resolution. First, the natural rate of counter increase as the router sends other control plane traffic implies that observed counters from two true aliases may have large gaps. Second, the 16-bit identifier space is small relative to the number of possible Internet router interface aliases, yielding false positives.

This section describes our IPv6 alias resolution technique and how we induce a remote router to send fragmented packets. We then describe our controlled environment for ground-truth testing where we show that our technique does not suffer from the false positive problems inherent in similar IPv4 approaches.

3.1   Eliciting Fragmented Responses

IPv6 does not permit in-network fragmentation, and the IPv6 header does not include any identifier field akin to IPv4. However, IPv6 supports end-host fragmentation. If a router's forwarding table entry for a packet is via an interface with a Maximum Transmission Unit (MTU) smaller than the size of the packet, the router drops the packet and sends an ICMP6 "packet too big" message to the source of the packet [5]. It is then the responsibility of the end-host to maintain state, typically in the destination cache, of the *path* MTU (PMTU) feasible for a particular destination. The host then sends packets smaller than the PMTU, or can fragment large packets by using the IPv6 fragment header [6].

Our approach, which we term the "Too-Big Trick" (TBT) induces a remote router to originate fragmented packets. Figure 1 is a timing diagram of TBT between a prober and an IPv6 interface. The prober first sends a 1300 byte ICMP6 echo request to a candidate IPv6 interface. The request is 1300 bytes – larger than the IPv6 minimum MTU of 1280 bytes, but small enough to pass most tunnels. The prober receives an 1300 byte ICMP6 echo response and then sends an ICMP6 packet too big message with its own source IPv6 address to the interface under test, and includes an MTU of 1280 along with the first 1184 bytes

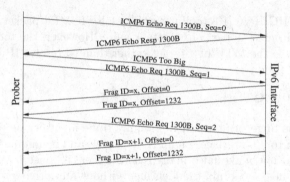

Fig. 1. TBT, the "Too-Big Trick:" A prober spoofs an ICMP6 too big message such that subsequent large ping responses are fragmented

of the original ICMP6 echo request ([5] states that the packet-too-big message include "as much of the invoking packet as possible without the ICMP6 packet exceeding the minimum IPv6 MTU."). This "false" too big message mimics a PMTU constraint coming from a router along the reverse path from the interface to our prober. While we use the prober's source IPv6 address for the too big message rather than an intermediate router, the receiving router is indifferent.

We then send a series of 1300 byte ICMP6 echo requests. These arrive at the interface without fragmentation, but the end IPv6 stack now has a cached PMTU of 1280 for packets destined to the prober. Each ping causes the router to send two fragments, each with the same fragment identifier, but different offsets. As we will show next (§3.2), popular commercial routers use a common counter for the fragment identifier, regardless of the physical interface. Further, in §4 we show that this counter frequently is monotonic and sequential.

A natural question is whether the ICMP6 too big packet is required. The prober could instead send a larger than typical MTU echo request packet, e.g. 2000 bytes. Once received and reassembled, the remote router should respond in-kind with a 2000 byte reply that would be fragmented. Thus, the echo packets would be fragmented in both the forward and reverse direction. However, as we find in our real-world testing in §4, such fragmented requests are frequently either blocked or not processed by the receiving router. Using TBT results in ≈ 6% more interfaces successfully identified than when sending large request packets, most likely due to destination hosts only being required to accept fragments with a reassembled size of 1500 bytes [6].

3.2 Ground-Truth Testing

To develop, test, and validate TBT, we employ the Graphical Network Simulator (GNS3) [8] to build virtual test topologies of routers and virtual hosts.

TBT emulates a normal operational mode whereby the forward path from the prober to an interface can carry full 1500 byte packets, while the reverse path is asymmetric and has a smaller, 1280 byte MTU. To understand the behavior of commercial routers in such situations, we implement the topology of Figure 2 in

GNS3. In this test, static IPv6 routes pin traffic from Host 1 to Host 2 to take the upper path from $R1 \to R2 \to R4$. Reverse traffic from Host 2 to Host 1 is statically configured to take $R4 \to R3 \to R1$. We set the MTU of all links to 1500 bytes, except for the $R1C \leftrightarrow R3A$ link which is set to 1280 bytes.

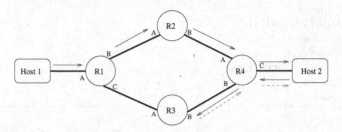

Fig. 2. GNS3 Test topology with asymmetric MTU paths inducing ICMP6 too big

A 1300 byte ICMP6 ping request from Host 1 to Host 2 induces a 1300 byte ping response (blue arrows). However, $R3$ sends an ICMP6 too big message to Host 2 (red arrows). Host 1 receives no reply to this first ping since the packet is dropped at $R3$. Host 2 records a new PMTU for traffic destined to Host 1 and maintains soft-state resulting in Host 2 fragmenting future responses to Host 1.

Next, we send 1300 byte ICMP6 ping requests from Host 1 to the router interface $R4A$. $R4$ receives the ICMP6 packet too big message from $R3$ upon sending the ping response to Host 1, and $R4$ updates its destination cache PMTU value. We observe that subsequent pings to $R4A$ results in fragments with sequential identifiers, with the first identifier after router boot being 1.

We then send ICMP6 ping requests to $R4B$ and $R4C$. Critically, we observe that identifiers come from a common counter, i.e. the fragment identifier is one more than the last identifier received from the other interface. Specifically, for a large ICMP6 echo request to $R4A$ that returns fragments with identifier x, a subsequent probe to $R4B$ returns $x+1$, and a third probe to $R4C$ returns $x+2$. Probing $R4A$ again returns $x + 3$. Thus, with the Cisco images we test, these routers use a *fragment identifier counter that is common across interfaces.*

Based on these findings, we reset all links to the standard Ethernet 1500 byte MTU. Here we seek to determine whether we can masquerade as an in-path router instructing the probed router to update its PMTU for traffic sent to Host 1. We first verify that large 1300 byte echo requests traverse the network to and from the target without fragmentation. We then repeat testing, but send an ICMP6 too big message with Host 1's source IPv6 address to the target. We verify that the ICMP6 too big message arrives at Host 2 and that Host 2 fragments subsequent echo replies, confirming that our technique is indeed able to induce remote interfaces to send fragmented traffic.

Lastly, we find that while the routers use a common fragment counter, the destination cache appears to be per-interface. After sending an ICMP6 too big message from host 1 to e.g. $R4A$, a large probe to $R4C$ does not return fragmented responses to host 1. In our testing, the ICMP6 too big message must be sent to each interface to reliably induce fragmentation.

Algorithm 1. $v6aliases(A, B)$: Determine whether A and B are IPv6 aliases

---

    $send(A, TooBig)$
2: $send(B, TooBig)$
    for i in range(5) **do**
4:      ID[0] ← $echo(A)$
        ID[1] ← $echo(B)$
6:      **if** (ID[0]+1) $\neq$ ID[1] **then**
          return $False$
8:      ID[2] ← $echo(A)$
        if (ID[1]+1) $\neq$ ID[2] **then**
10:        return $False$
    return $True$

3.3 IPv6 Alias Resolution Algorithm

Given the success in the controlled test environment, we develop an IPv6 alias resolution algorithm. There are several points of note. First, as we will detail in §4, more than 28% of live Internet interfaces we probed had sequential identifiers that start at either zero or one. In other words, prior to our probing these routers had sourced no fragmented IPv6 traffic. Therefore the alias algorithm must be careful to avoid false positives. Second, because the counter only increases when sending fragmented IPv6 traffic, which is a rare event, we can reasonably expect, in the absence of our probing, the counter to remain static.

Algorithm 1 provides the alias resolution pseudocode [2]. To determine whether two IPv6 addresses (A and B) are aliases, an initial echo request probe is sent to each destination, then the fake ICMP6 too big messages are sent. Next, a probe is sent to A. Once the fragment ID from A is received, B is probed (each step proceeds synchronously; no race condition exists). The fragment identifiers from A and B are compared. If at anytime the fragment IDs are not sequential, the test returns false to avoid generating needless traffic. Note that when performing $O(n^2)$ alias comparisons between all pairs of discovered interfaces, the common case will be a true negative where our algorithm quickly exits. Only if the fragment IDs are sequential are further probes sent to ensure no false positives. Based on the above observations, we ensure that, in each round of execution through the for loop, address A is probed a different number of times than B to avoid potential counter synchronization issues in the case that the addresses are not true aliases.

4 Results

To understand the real-world efficacy of our technique, we perform Internet-wide probing. For candidate IPv6 router interfaces, we utilize two traceroute datasets. The first dataset includes 23,892 distinct IPv6 interfaces discovered via traceroutes from 33 vantage points belonging to a commercial Content Distribution Network (CDN) to approximately 12,300 destinations. Interestingly, we find nine

Table 1. TBT Response Characteristics

	CDN		CAIDA	
ICMP6 responsive	18486/23892	77.4%	18959/25174	75.3%
Post-TBT unresponsive	235/18486	1.3%	66/18959	0.4%
Post-TBT nofrags	5519/18486	29.9%	5800/18959	30.6%
TBT responsive	12732/18486	68.9%	13093/18959	69.1%
TBT sequential	8288/12732	65.1%	9183/13093	70.1%
TBT sequential (1)	3455/12732	27.1%	3496/13093	26.7%
TBT random	4320/12732	33.9%	3789/13093	28.9%

link-local (`fe80::/10`) addresses included in this dataset, suggesting that these non-public IPv6 addresses are being used for a small number of public links. The second data set is from CAIDA [1] with 38,300 distinct IPv6 interfaces, 25,174 of which are not present in the CDN trace. For those traces that complete, we ignore the last hop IPv6 address of the target so as to only use router interfaces. Thus, we probe a total of ≈ 49k distinct live Internet IPv6 router interfaces, belonging to networks advertised by 2,617 different autonomous systems. The largest number of interfaces belonging to a single AS is 2,014 (from ASN 3356, Level 3), and the median number of interfaces per AS is 3. The CDN trace was collected on May 3 and 23, 2012, while the CAIDA traces were collected in August, 2012. We actively probed interfaces derived from the CDN trace on August 28, 2012, while the CAIDA interfaces were probed on August 29, 2012.

4.1   Efficacy of TBT

Our goal is two-fold, determine: i) *how many* live IPv6 interfaces respond to TBT; and ii) *in what way* these interfaces respond. We perform all testing from a single IPv6 vantage point. For each interface, we first send a 1300 byte ICMP6 echo request in order to determine if the interface is live and responding to pings. We then use TBT to send the ICMP6 message too big that will update the interface's PMTU to our vantage point. Finally, we send ten 1300 byte ICMP6 echo requests. Contemporaneous to our probing, we capture all IPv6 packets to disk for analysis; our packet monitor did not experience any packet loss.

Table 1 summarizes the responsiveness of our sample of Internet interfaces to TBT. We observe 18,486 of 23,892 (77.4%) and 18,959 of 25,174 (75.3%) interfaces respectively responding to "normal" ICMP6 pings. The unresponsive interfaces may be due to router behavior, or ICMP6 filtering. As these interfaces cannot be expected to respond to TBT, we exclude them from our analysis. Of the interfaces responding to our initial echo request, we find ≈ 70% returning fragmented echo replies after we send a packet too big to the interface. Thus, our technique works for a significant fraction of Internet IPv6 routers we probe.

Three primary conditions result from sending the TBT: subsequent ping responses are sent fragmented, subsequent ping responses are sent unfragmented, or the router stops responding to ping requests. We observe approximately 29% of the interfaces we probe continuing to send unfragmented responses after we send TBT. Between 1.3 and 0.4 percent of interfaces respond to the initial echo

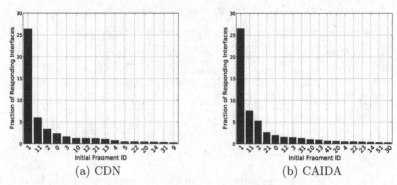

(a) CDN   (b) CAIDA

Fig. 3. Histogram of IPv6 Fragment Identifiers Occurring $\geq 0.3\%$

request, but then respond to no subsequent echo requests after the packet too big for a few minutes. We conjecture that these behaviors are due to paths that filter fragments or ICMP6 too-big messages, routers incorrectly implementing IPv6, or security measures. In future work we plan to more precisely understand the root causes of such non-responsive behavior.

Next, we characterize the sequence of returned fragment identifiers. Recall that we send ten ICMP6 echo requests after the TBT, therefore we expect to receive ten responses where each response consists of two fragmented packets, i.e. 20 total packets with identifiers. As shown in Table 1, $\geq 65\%$ of interfaces that respond to TBT return sequential identifiers, e.g. 120, 121, ..., 130. However, as many as 34% return random identifiers, a behavior consistent with BSD systems and BSD-based routers [18]. While TBT works for these interfaces, it does not admit a fingerprint for alias resolution.

An interesting characteristic of those interfaces with sequential identifiers is that a significant fraction (27.1% and 26.7% respectively) had an initial identifier of one. This suggests that, in the uptime of the router, it had sent no fragmented IPv6 packets prior to our probing. As discussed in §3, we take into account non-alias interfaces that begin with correlated counters; our algorithm advances them at different rates to prevent false positives.

To understand the initial values of fragment counters in the wild, Figures 3(a) and 3(b) are histograms of initial fragment identifiers that occur with at least a 0.3% frequency. We see that one is the most common initial identifier for every sequence echoed and that all common identifiers are less than 50.

While this paper presents and validates a new technique for IPv6 alias resolution, we leave large-scale alias resolution on the IPv6 Internet for future work. However, we observe that the second most common initial identifier within a returned identifier sequence is 11, while there are modes at 21, 31, and 41. These modes are due to our probing naturally encountering aliases. Since we probe each interface 10 times, if we happen to later probe an alias, the counter will have advanced to 10 and we expect to receive 11.

Finally, a natural question is whether we can induce routers to send fragmented responses without TBT. Instead, we experiment with sending large

ICMP6 echo requests that are themselves fragmented, such that the receiving IPv6 router interface must reassemble the fragments to respond, and then send a fragmented response. We again probe our two datasets of IPv6 interfaces and find that this method results in 64.2% and 65.1% of interfaces successfully responding. However, using TBT results in over 5% more responses, which can equate to significantly more absolute interfaces. More importantly, sending large, fragmented probes results in much more traffic whereas our technique is more efficient. For these reasons, we focus on TBT for alias resolution.

4.2   Accuracy of TBT Alias Resolution

Imperative to understanding the performance of our TBT alias resolution technique is having known ground-truth. In this subsection we test the inference accuracy of our tool on both a virtual network topology in GNS3 [8], as well as on a small subset of the live IPv6 Internet for which we have ground-truth.

First, we construct a virtual network topology in GNS3 [8] consisting of 26 Cisco routers, each containing up to four interfaces. Using our TBT tool, and Algorithm 1 as implemented in our publicly available ScaPy tool [2], we run a complete test comparing each interface to every other interface in the topology, i.e. the $O(n^2)$ all pairs testing that would be performed in the wild, and verify the results against known truth. The test results provide a count of identified aliases and identified non-aliases. This controlled test results in 92/92 alias matches and 1584/1584 non-alias matches for a total accuracy of 100 percent with perfect precision and recall. The results, although constrained by the virtual topology and simulation available in GNS3, help validate the ability of our tool in identifying IPv6 aliases and non-aliases.

Finally, we obtain a list of IPv6 interfaces from eight physical production routers of a commercial IPv6 service provider. This small ground-truth dataset includes 72 interfaces with each router having between 2 and 21 interfaces. Using TBT we correctly identify 808/808 true alias pairs with no false positives. Given this encouraging result, we plan more extensive probing in the future.

5   Conclusion

This research develops and tests a new method for IPv6 alias resolution. Our technique, the "Too-Big Trick" (TBT), elicits a fragment identifier fingerprint from a significant fraction of production IPv6 router interfaces. We demonstrate that our alias resolution algorithm, a prototype of which is publicly available, is highly accurate among networks for which we have ground truth.

To understand instances where TBT fails, we plan to use multiple vantage points to help distinguish between path and host filtering of fragments. We plan to test additional routers, both in hardware and within GNS3 to better understand the variety of behaviors we observe in Table 1.

We leave to future work the task of leveraging TBT to perform Internet-wide IPv6 alias resolution. An important step is making the algorithm robust to packet loss, or another TBT-like process causing the fragment counter to increase. Toward this goal, we are investigating sequential hypothesis detection to provide a bounded confidence in the alias pair. Further, at scale, we must modify the algorithm to be more intelligent than pair-wise resolution.

As IPv6 grows and gains importance, understanding its router-level topology and relationship to the IPv4 topology is increasingly important. In particular, our current research examines how TBT compares with and compliments existing resolution schemes, while generating router-level IPv6 topologies. Comparing these topologies to those previously inferred will yield valuable insights into the structure of the IPv6 network, and how it differs from the IPv4 topology.

Acknowledgments. We thank Arthur Berger and Geoff Xie for invaluable early feedback, and Ítalo Cunha for shepherding. Special thanks to Aaron Hughes and 6connect for operational support and insight. This work supported by collaborative NSF grant CNS-1111445 and CNS-1111449. Views and conclusions are those of the authors and should not be interpreted as representing the official policies, either expressed or implied, of the U.S. government.

References

1. The CAIDA UCSD IPv6 Topology Dataset (2012), http://www.caida.org/data/active/ipv6_allpref_topology_dataset.xml
2. Brinkmeyer, W.: Too-Big Trick prototype (2012), http://www.cmand.org/tbt/
3. Claffy, K., Hyun, Y., Keys, K., Fomenkov, M., Krioukov, D.: Internet mapping: From art to science. In: Conference For Homeland Security (March 2009)
4. Claffy, K.: Tracking IPv6 evolution: data we have and data we need. SIGCOMM Comput. Commun. Rev. 41(3), 43–48 (2011)
5. Conta, A., Deering, S., Gupta, M.: Internet Control Message Protocol (ICMPv6) for the Internet Protocol Version 6 Specification. RFC 4443 (March 2006)
6. Deering, S., Hinden, R.: Internet Protocol, Version 6 (IPv6) Specification. RFC 2460 (Draft Standard) (December 1998)
7. Dhamdhere, A., Luckie, M., Huffaker, B., Claffy, K., Elmokashfi, A., Aben, E.: Measuring the deployment of ipv6: topology, routing and performance. In: Proceedings of the 2012 ACM Internet Measurement Conference, pp. 537–550 (2012)
8. Grossman, J., Marsili, B., Goudjil, C., Eromenko, A.: GNS3 Graphical Network Simulator (2012), http://www.gns3.net/
9. Gunes, M.H., Sarac, K.: Resolving ip aliases in building traceroute-based internet maps. IEEE/ACM Trans. Netw. 17, 1738–1751 (2009)
10. Heuse, M.: THC-IPv6 tool suite (2012), http://www.thc.org/thc-ipv6/
11. Huston, G.: IPv6 BGP Statistics (2012), http://bgp.potaroo.net/v6/as2.0/
12. Keys, K.: Internet-scale IP alias resolution techniques. SIGCOMM Comput. Commun. Rev. 40, 50–55 (2010)
13. Mohan, R.: Will U.S. Government Directives Spur IPv6 Adoption? (September 2010)
14. Qian, S., Wang, Y., Xu, K.: Utilizing Destination Options Header to Resolve IPv6 Alias Resolution. In: GLOBECOM, pp. 1–6 (December 2010)
15. Qian, S., Xu, M., Qiao, Z., Xu, K.: Route Positional Method for IPv6 Alias Resolution. In: Computer Communications and Networks, ICCCN (August 2010)

16. RIPE-NCC: IPv6 Enabled Networks (2012), http://v6asns.ripe.net/v/6
17. Sarrar, N., Maier, G., Ager, B., Sommer, R., Uhlig, S.: Investigating IPv6 Traffic. In: Taft, N., Ricciato, F. (eds.) PAM 2012. LNCS, vol. 7192, pp. 11–20. Springer, Heidelberg (2012)
18. Silbersack, M.J.: Improving TCP/IP security through randomization without sacrificing interoperability. In: Proceedings of BSDCan (2006)
19. Spring, N., Mahajan, R., Wetherall, D.: Measuring ISP topologies with rocketfuel. SIGCOMM Comput. Commun. Rev. 32, 133–145 (2002)
20. Waddington, D.G., Chang, F., Viswanathan, R., Yao, B.: Topology discovery for public IPv6 networks. SIGCOMM Comput. Commun. Rev. 33, 59–68 (2003)
21. Willinger, W., Alderson, D., Doyle, J.C.: Mathematics and the internet: A source of enormous confusion and great potential. Notices of the AMS 56(5) (2009)
22. Zander, S., Andrew, L.L., Armitage, G., Huston, G., Michaelson, G.: Mitigating sampling error when measuring internet client ipv6 capabilities. In: Proceedings of the 2012 ACM Internet Measurement Conference, pp. 87–100 (2012)

Unveiling the Patterns of Video Tweeting: A Sina Weibo-Based Measurement Study

Zhida Guo[1], Jian Huang[1], Jian He[1], Xiaojun Hei[2], and Di Wu[1]

[1] Dept. of Computer Science, Sun Yat-Sen University, China
[2] Dept. of Electronics & Info. Engineering, Huazhong University of Sci. & Tech.,
China
{guozhida,huangj77,hejian9}@mail2.sysu.edu.cn, heixj@hust.edu.cn,
wudi27@mail.sysu.edu.cn

Abstract. Sina Weibo is the most popular Twitter-like microblog service in China. Contents, such as texts, pictures, music, videos, are propagated rapidly by tweeting and retweeting among users. In this paper, we conduct a measurement study on the patterns of video tweeting over the Sina Weibo system. We build a customized measurement platform to collect a huge amount of data (e.g., video tweets, user/video information, etc)[1] from 1 million Weibo users on the Sina Weibo system. Our measurements enable us to understand the sources and characteristics of tweeted videos, geographical distribution of viewers, distribution of viewing devices, popularity dynamics of tweeted videos, etc. We observe frequent flash crowds occur for popular tweeted videos due to social tweeting. We also analyze how social links among Weibo users impact video tweeting and it is found that the majority of viewers are within 3 hops from the original tweet publisher. Finally, we discuss potential implications of our measurement results on the design of future social video distribution infrastructures.

1 Introduction

Microblogging has emerged as a pillar application in the era of Web 2.0. Different from traditional blogs, a microblog user is only allowed to post messages with no more than 140 characters (referred to as "*tweets*"). A tweet can be propagated to a large number of followers timely via the underlying microblog platform. On Aug 14th, 2009, Sina Inc. launched its own Twitter-like microblog service called "*Weibo*". To date, Sina Weibo [1] has become the largest microblog service in China, with 300 million registered users by 2012 [2].

Sina Weibo allows the sharing of contents other than texts, such as pictures, music, videos, etc, by embedding a short encoded link (e.g., http://t.cn/z0fjzlL) in a tweet. Such a short link can be decoded into the original URL that points to the content using Weibo APIs. A tweet that contains a video link is often called a "*Video Tweet*". A Weibo user can post a video tweet either by directly uploading a

---

[1] Our dataset is currently made available at
http://netlab.sysu.edu.cn/$\sim$jhe/weibo-dataset-2012.rar.

M. Roughan and R. Chang (Eds.) PAM 2013, LNCS 7799, pp. 166–175, 2013.
© Springer-Verlag Berlin Heidelberg 2013

video clip or pasting an external URL in the tweet. Once a video tweet is published, the followers will see the tweet in a nearly real-time manner. They can watch the video embedded in the tweet, comment and retweet that video as they wish.

Such microblog-triggered video sharing is inherently different from the sharing model of traditional UGC (user-generated content) sites, such as YouTube, Youku, Tudou, etc. Instead of watching videos suggested by search engines or recommendation systems, Weibo users tend to watch videos pushed via video tweets, which are suggested by their friends, social stars, etc. Thus, the spreading of videos is much faster and happens in a granularity of minutes. For a social star with millions of followers, one video tweet may bring forth a flash crowd in triggering millions of video views in a very short period. Such kind of sudden surge of video traffic will pose great challenge to the underlying video distribution infrastructure. However, there has been little work to date on the measurement of video tweeting. It is of great significance to study the characteristics of video tweets/retweets and their implications on video distribution.

The main purpose of this paper is to investigate video tweeting by real measurements and unveil its impacts on the underlying distribution infrastructure. To the best of our knowledge, this is the first attempt to measure the patterns of video tweeting over the largest microblog system in China. We focus our measurements solely on video tweets as we are more interested in their impact on video distribution. We build a customized measurement platform to obtain tweet/video information from the Weibo system and other video-sharing sites. By analyzing the obtained data set, we have the following observations:

- We observe that most of tweeted videos are from third-party video-sharing sites instead of Sina Video itself. Due to the collaboration between Sina and Tudou, Tudou is the largest source of tweeted videos over Sina Weibo, in spite that Tudou's market share is much smaller than that of Yukou. The length of 80% tweeted videos is less than 10 minutes.
- Our results show that only 3% of viewers of tweeted videos are outside of China, which implies that Weibo is not an internationalized service as Twitter. We also find that over 30% of viewers are using mobile devices to watch tweeted videos, with iPhone and Android phones being the top two widely used devices. Due to the diversity of user devices, it is essential to provide multiple video versions or adopt realtime transcoding.
- We find that the popularity dynamics [2] of top tweeted videos exhibit a clear flash-crowd pattern, which is a direct consequence of social tweeting. For 87% of tweeted videos, the first viewing event occurs within ten minutes after the tweet is posted. By examining active periods of tweet videos, we observe that most of active periods are less than 10 hours.
- We measured the propagation distance of tweeted videos and find that the average propagation distance of 98% tweeted videos is within 3 social hops.

---

[2] The popularity of a video is defined as the number of users who have viewed that video. In our paper, the popularity is estimated by summing up the number of comments and the number of retweets.

It implies that prefetching videos according to social distance can be an effective approach to improve user experience.

In the above, we only present some preliminary results from our measurement. Further work is required to obtain more in-depth understanding. The remainder of the paper is organized as follows. Section 2 describes the methodology of our measurements. Section 3 shows the patterns of video tweeting. Section 4 introduces related work and explains the difference of our work. Finally, Section 5 summarizes this paper and discusses potential extensions.

2 Methodology

It is difficult if not impossible to obtain video tweets of all Weibo users due to the huge scale of Weibo users. Instead, we focus our analysis on a sample set of Weibo users and their posted video tweets to make the task tractable.

In the Weibo system, each registered user is randomly assigned a unique user ID (UID) with a length less than 12 digits. Therefore, we can obtain an unbiased sample of Weibo users by uniformly sampling in the UID space. To verify the existence of a user account, we develop an automatic HTTP querying program to query the Weibo system for a given UID. In case that the given UID has been assigned to a valid user, the system will return the status page of that user; otherwise, an error page will be returned. By repeatedly generating a random UID and checking its validness, we obtain a random sample set that consists of one million Weibo users. The whole sampling process takes nearly five days. During the process, all the invalid UIDs are eliminated from the sample set.

Next, we proceed to retrieve all their posted video tweets and analyze the patterns of video tweeting. Like Facebook, Sina Weibo also provides specific APIs to facilitate the development of third-party Weibo-based applications. A Weibo-based application can obtain tweets and user statistics information via Weibo APIs. For one third-party application in the development stage, at most 15 accounts are allowed to register for the testing purpose, and each account can only initiate 150 API queries per hour. To speedup the crawling of video tweets, we define 40 Weibo-based applications on the Weibo platform and register 15 accounts for each application. Meanwhile, we modify our crawling program to automatically switch the application and account when the quota of current account is exhausted.

Using our Weibo crawler, we retrieve the total video tweets posted or retweeted by one million users in the sample set during the period from *Jun 1, 2012* to *Jun 30, 2012*. Among all the tweets, there are totally 254,135 video tweets. By removing duplicated video tweets with same video links (by comparing tweet IDs and URLs) and unavailable video tweets (e.g., deleted by users themselves or Weibo administrators), we obtain 121,366 *root video tweets*. Here, a *root video tweet* refers to a video tweet directly posted by a user himself, instead of being retweeted from others' tweets. Next, we filter out root video tweets that have never been retweeted and finally obtain 87,699 active root video tweets, which also corresponds to 87,699 unique video links. Starting from these video links, we collect video-related information (including video length, view count, etc) from their corresponding video-sharing web sites, such as Youku, Tudou, Sohu, etc. We again build a customized crawler to conduct the crawling tasks. Finally, all the collected data are dumped into a mySQL database for data processing. The whole measurement platform contains around ten machines to enable parallel crawling and processing.

3 Patterns of Video Tweeting

Next, we will study the features of tweeted videos in the dataset.

3.1 Statistics of Tweeted Videos

By decoding the short video link embedded in the tweet, we are able to extract the original URL linked to the video. Thus, it is possible to know the source of tweeted videos. We develop a URL parser to automatically extract all the original video URLs and categorize videos according to their origins.

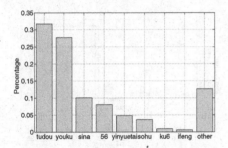
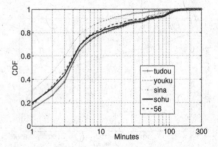

Fig. 1. Video source distribution   **Fig. 2.** Video length distribution

Fig. 1[3] shows where tweeted videos are originated. We observe that most of video sources are UGC sites, such as Tudou, Youku, Sohu, Ku6, etc., among which Tudou(32%),Youku(28%) and Sina Video(10%) are the top three sources of tweeted videos on Sina weibo. The statistics are different from the published information on the market shares of UGC sites [3], in which Youku and Tudou account for 39.1% and 20.3% of China's Internet video market respectively. We believe this is mainly caused by the collaboration agreement between Tudou and Sina [10], in which Sina provides Tudou with a privilege that allows Weibo users to upload their videos to Tudou via the Weibo interface directly. We also observe that, although YouTube is the largest UGC video site in the world, YouTube videos are rarely observed in the video tweets of our dataset, as YouTube is unaccessible in China if not using VPN or proxies.

---

[3] Fig.1 and Fig.2 are based on the dataset with 87,699 active root video tweets.

By using our video-sharing site crawler, we further retrieve video length information from multiple video-sharing sites, including Tudou, Youku, Sina video, Sohu video and 56.com. Fig. 2 shows the length distribution of tweeted videos. It is observed that most of tweeted videos are short videos. The length of videos from different video-sharing sites follows similar distributions. For Tudou, Youku, Sohu video and 56.com, the length of about 65% tweeted videos is less than 5 minutes and 80% is less than 10 minutes. For Sina video, nearly 30% of tweeted videos is less than 1 minute, and 80% is less than 5 minutes. It confirms well with the behaviors of typical Weibo users who are more likely to upload or share short video clips.

We use the sum of retweets and comments to estimate the popularity of a tweeted video. In our paper, we make a reasonable assumption that, a Weibo user will normally only retweet or comment after viewing the video in a tweet. However, it should be emphasized that the sum of retweets and comments can only serve as a lower bound of the number of views, as many Weibo users will not retweet or comment after viewing a video. We randomly select 6,500 videos from the 87,699 root video tweets and plot the distribution of video popularity in Fig. 3 [4]. Only 1.6% of tweeted videos have more than 10,000 views[5] and 85% of tweeted videos have less 1,000 views.

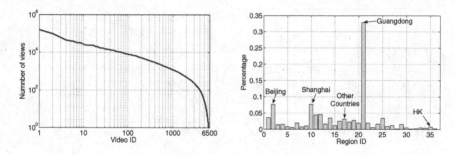

Fig. 3. Popularity distribution of videos   **Fig. 4.** Geographical distribution of viewers

3.2   Patterns of Viewer Behaviors

In the above, we conduct measurements from the perspective of tweeted videos. In the following, we will study the behaviors of viewers of tweeted videos.

We first describe how to obtain all the viewers for a tweeted video. For each root video tweet, which is the first tweet sharing a certain video, there are two associated lists: one is the *Root-level Retweet List (RRL)*, and the other is the *Root-level Comment List (RCL)*. For each retweet in the RRL, it can also have its own comment list, referred as *Secondary-level Comment List (SCL)*.

---

[4] Note that, all other figures (except Fig.1 and Fig.2) are based on the randomly selected 6,500 video tweets.

[5] In our paper, a view corresponds to a retweet/comment. We use the number of retweets/comments to estimate the number of views.

Each retweet will appear in the *RRL* and each comment will appear in either *RCL* or *SCL*. All the Weibo users who appear in one of the above three lists are most likely to have viewed the video; otherwise, they will not retweet or comment on that video. Our Weibo crawler can travel through the *RRL*, *RCL* and *SCL* of each video tweet, and aggregate all the viewers for that video. Later, the parser will remove all the duplicated viewers to avoid the issue of double counting.

For popular tweeted videos, the above process is time-consuming due to the limitation of Weibo APIs. Without impacting the conclusion, we randomly choose 6,500 tweeted videos from all the 87,699 videos and analyze their viewers' behaviors. Starting from these 6,500 tweeted videos, we finally obtain 5,512,130 viewers by crawling their *RRL*, *RCL* and *SCL* lists. For each viewer (also a Weibo user), we again query the Weibo system to retrieve the viewer's information, such as location, following/followed list, etc.

Fig. 4 depicts geographical distribution of 5.5 million viewers. Most of the viewers are from China, with only 3% of viewers are from other countries. Guangdong (35%), Beijing (7.6%) and Shanghai (7.6%) are the top three regions with the largest viewer population. Only 3% of viewers are outside of China.

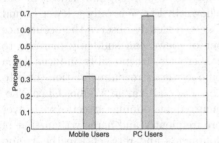 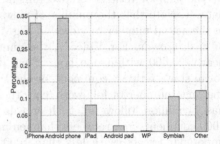

Fig. 5. Distribution of user devices   **Fig. 6.** Distribution of mobile clients

The retweet or the comment of a tweet also contains the device type of a Weibo user. Thus, we are able to know which devices Weibo users are commonly using to watch tweeted videos. Fig. 5 shows that 32% of viewers use mobile devices to watch videos, and the left 68% use personal computers. We further plot the distribution of mobile clients in Fig. 6, which shows that among all the mobile clients, iPhones and Android phones account for 32.7% and 34.2% respectively. For other devices, iPads, Android Pads, and Symbian devices account for 8%, 1.8%, and 10% respectively. The percentage of Windows Phones is less than 0.1%. In addition, there are 12% devices with unknown types. As the number of mobile users continues to increase, P2P-based solution may not be a practical approach considering the limited battery and bandwidth of mobile clients. In addition, due to the diversity of mobile clients (e.g., different screen sizes, video codec, etc), the video service provider should provide multiple versions of a video so as to be compatible with different devices.

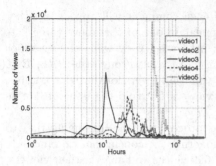
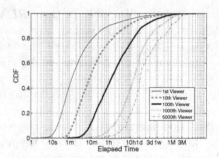

Fig. 7. Popularity dynamics of Top 5 popular videos

Fig. 8. Time lag between the original video tweet and its n-th view

For a Weibo user, we use the timestamp embedded in a retweet or comment to approximate the viewing time of a video. Such approximation is feasible as most Weibo users prefer to retweet/comment a video right after viewing the video. In Fig. 7, we show the evolution of the number of views (approximated by the sum of retweets and comments) for the top 5 popular videos in our dataset. Note that the number of views shown in Fig. 7 is only a lower bound of the actual number of views. In Fig. 7, we can clearly observe the occurrence of flash crowds. For Video 1, the number of views can suddenly increase to nearly 20,000 within one hour. Such flash crowds are possibly induced by a social star's retweet/comment, or the Weibo system's recommendation. Due to the huge number of followers (e.g., the top 1 social star in Weibo, Chen Yao, has 24 million followers), flash crowds incurred by popular tweets (with over 1000 comments and retweets) happen more frequently and fiercely than that of unpopular tweets (with less than 1000 comments and retweets) in the Weibo system. The underlying distribution infrastructure should be able to efficiently meet such sudden surging demand of video traffic.

In Fig. 8, we plot the distribution of time lag between the original video tweet and its n-th view. It depicts how fast the followers start to watch the tweeted videos. We observe that, for 87% of tweeted videos, the first viewing event occurs less than 10 minutes after the root video tweet is posted. For 60% of tweeted videos, the first 1000 views arrive within one day. It is largely due to the fast spreading nature of microblog service.

To further investigate the viewing patterns of tweeted videos, we define a new metric called k-active period, $k \in \mathbf{N}^+$. A period is composed of multiple consecutive time slots, and each slot lasts for one hour. A k-active period refers to a period in which each of its slot contains at least k views. For 6,500 tweeted videos, we identified 7,039 50-active periods, 4,974 100-active periods, 2,856 150-active periods and 2,186 200-active periods[6]. We plot the distribution of the number of k-active periods per video in Fig. 9. It is observed that most of tweeted

---

[6] Note that, small fluctuations of video activity may introduce bias to the statistics of k-active periods, but for $k \geq 50$ less than 2% of the active periods show fluctuations.

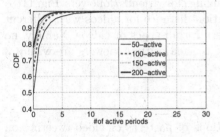 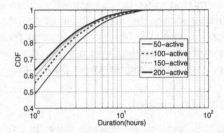

Fig. 9. Number of active periods   **Fig. 10.** Duration of active periods

videos are not highly active with 49% of them having no 50-active period. In the left 51%, around 39% of tweeted videos have less than three 50-active periods. Fig. 10 shows the distribution of the duration of active periods. 48% of 50-active periods, 55% of 100-active periods, 59% of 150-active periods and 63% of 200-active periods are no greater than one hour. Over 90% of all active periods are less than ten hours. It means that the popularity of tweeted videos cannot last for a long period.

3.3   Effects of Social Links

In this section, we will investigate how the social links among users impact video tweeting. For a tweeted video, we define the *Propagation Distance* between the original tweet publisher and the Weibo viewer as the number of social hops between them. For example, suppose A is the publisher of a root video tweet, B, who is A's follower, retweets that video, then we can think the propagation path is $A \rightarrow B$ and the associated propagation distance is one. For each video, we obtain all its viewers by crawling the video tweet's *RRL, RCL* and *SCL*, and then calculate the propagation distance between the publisher and viewers.

Fig. 11 depicts the distribution of propagation distance. We find that, for over 90% of viewers, their propagation distance is not greater than 3 (see Fig. 11(a)). It

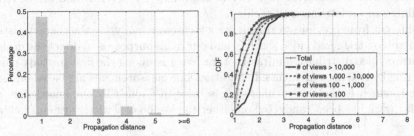

(a) Propagation distance of all viewers   (b) Propagation distance for videos
                                          with different popularities

Fig. 11. Distribution of propagation distance

means that video tweeting mostly occurs among close friends/followers. Fig. 11(b) further shows the distribution of propagation distance for videos with different popularities. We observe a common pattern for all types of videos. Namely, no matter the popularity of a tweeted video, the majority of viewers are within 3 hops from the original tweet publisher.

3.4 Discussion

In this section, we discuss a few implications of patterns of video tweeting on the design of future microblog-oriented video distribution platforms: (1) *Short video length*: Like UGC sites, most of the tweeted videos are short videos. The design of content distribution infrastructures should take the patterns of user-generated contents into account. (2) *Diverse user devices*: The diversity of user devices requires to distribute videos in different versions. A promising direction is to conduct real-time transcoding for different devices (e.g., cloud-based video transcoding). (3) *Frequent flash crowds*: Real-time tweeting enables many users to learn and watch a new video almost simultaneously. The induced flash crowds pose a large challenge to the video distribution platform. Online bandwidth provisioning strategies are needed to meet the unpredictable surging demand. (4) *Small propagation distance*: The majority of viewers are within 3 hops of the publisher. It is possible to perform efficient prefetching based on social distance to improve the user experience.

4 Related Work

In recent years, researchers have conducted extensive measurement work to understand the characteristics of popular Web 2.0 applications.

In the aspect of user-generated contents, most of previous work focused on the measurement of YouTube, including its video sharing patterns [4], traffic characterization[9], etc. To realize efficient distribution of user-generated contents, Liu et al. [8] proposed a peer-assisted approach to reduce the load on CDN servers. In [5], Cheng et al. conducted an online Web survey among tens of users and proposed a P2P-based design for video sharing. Krishnappa et al. [7] performed a measurement study of Hulu-like TV services and studied the feasibility of prefetching and caching.

Different from previous work, our work focuses on analyzing the characteristics of microblog-triggered video sharing, and our main purpose is to direct the design of future video distribution infrastructure. We are among the first to study video tweeting by real measurements. In addition, our measurements are based on Sina Weibo, which is the largest microblog service in China. To our knowledge, no similar work has been conducted on either the Weibo or Twitter systems before.

5 Conclusion

In this paper, we perform a measurement study on video tweeting over the Sina Weibo system. With a customized measurement platform, we collect the video tweets posted by 1 million Weibo users and further obtain video information from their corresponding web sites. We find that most of tweeted videos are short videos and there exist frequent flash crowds for video tweeting. Diverse mobile devices are used to watch tweeted videos. In addition, Weibo users mostly intend to only watch videos tweeted by their friends within a few hops. Next, we plan to extend our measurement to a larger scale, and to design efficient caching and prefetching strategies to further improve the effectiveness of social video distribution.

Acknowledgement. We thank anonymous reviewers and our shepherd, Bernhard Ager, for their valuable comments. This work has been supported by NSFC (60972014, 61003242, 61272397), Program for New Century Excellent Talents in University (NCET-11-0542), the Fundamental Research Funds for the Central Universities (12LGPY53, HUST:2011QN015), and Guangzhou Pearl River Sci. & Tech. Rising Star Project (No. 2011J2200086), and the National Technology Support Plan of China (No. 2009BAH51B00). Di Wu is the corresponding author.

References

1. Sina Weibo, http://weibo.com
2. Sina Weibo Has More Than 300 Million Registered Users, http://tech.ifeng.com/internet/detail_2012_05/16/14546599_0.shtml
3. China Online Video Market Update, http://www.chinainternetwatch.com/1041/online-video-q1-2011
4. Cheng, X., Liu, J., Dale, C.: Understanding the Characteristics of Internet Short Video Sharing: A YouTube-based Measurement Study. IEEE Transactions on Multimedia (2010)
5. Cheng, X., Liu, J.: Tweeting Videos: Coordinate Live Streaming and Storage Sharing. In: Proc. of ACM NOSSDAV (2010)
6. Xu, K., Li, H., Liu, J., Zhu, W., Wang, W.: PPVA: A Universal and Transparent Peer-to-Peer Accelerator for Interactive Online Video Sharing. In: The Proc. of IEEE IWQoS 2010 (2010)
7. Krishnappa, D.K., Khemmarat, S., Gao, L., Zink, M.: On the Feasibility of Prefetching and Caching for Online TV Services: A Measurement Study on Hulu. In: Spring, N., Riley, G.F. (eds.) PAM 2011. LNCS, vol. 6579, pp. 72–80. Springer, Heidelberg (2011)
8. Liu, Z., Ding, Y., Liu, Y., Ross, K.: Peer-Assisted Distribution of User Generated Content. In: IEEE P2P (2012)
9. Gill, P., Arlitt, M., Li, Z., Mahanti, A.: YouTube Traffic Characterization: A View From the Edge. In: Proc. of ACM IMC (2007)
10. Tudou Becomes The First Partner Of Sina Weibo On Video Upload, http://ir.tudou.com/releasedetail.cfm?ReleaseID=646038

Measuring Home Networks with HomeNet Profiler

Lucas DiCioccio[1,2], Renata Teixeira[2], and Catherine Rosenberg[3]

[1] Technicolor
[2] CNRS and UPMC Sorbonne Universités
[3] University of Waterloo

Abstract. This paper designs HomeNet Profiler, a software that runs on any computer connected inside a home network, to collect a wide range of measurements about home networks including the set of devices, the set of services (with UPnP and Zeroconf), and the characteristics of the WiFi environment. To attract a larger number of users, HomeNet Profiler runs one-shot measurements upon user demand. We evaluate this design choice against periodic measurements taken from six home networks. Data collected from these six homes and with HomeNet Profiler in more than 1,600 homes in France shed light on the diversity of devices that connect to home networks and of the WiFi neighborhood across home networks.

1 Introduction

The availability of cheap broadband Internet is popularizing Internet access from homes. A household today can have a variety of networked devices ranging from personal devices like laptops and smartphones to printers and media centers. These devices connect among themselves and to the Internet via a local-area network—the *home network*. Although there is increasing interest in home networking [1–3, 12, 19], there is yet little data on current home networks. Most prior work has focused on measuring and characterizing residential Internet access [4, 5, 9, 11, 13, 14, 17, 18]. The lack of data on home networks is partially due to the challenges of measuring home networks at large scales. The vast majority of home networks are behind network-address translators, so a device outside the home often cannot measure the characteristics of the home network itself. Some prior studies have deployed measurement points inside the homes of a few volunteers [10, 12, 15], but it is hard to get representative results from a few homes.

This paper designs HomeNet Profiler, a tool to measure home network configuration and performance (§2). Users run HomeNet Profiler on-demand from an end-system directly connected to their home network. HomeNet Profiler scans the local network for active devices and services advertised via protocols such as Universal Plug and Play (UPnP). It also measures the wireless environment per home. HomeNet Profiler incorporates features to help recruit a large number of volunteers. For example, it performs on-demand, one-time measurements, because many users feel uncomfortable downloading software that will run continuously in their machines. We evaluate this design choice with a periodic measurement from six homes in France (§3).

Between April 2011 and May 2012, users from 46 different countries ran HomeNet Profiler. This paper presents our analysis of home networks in France, where we have

M. Roughan and R. Chang (Eds.) PAM 2013, LNCS 7799, pp. 176–186, 2013.

data from over 1,600 homes. We analyze devices present in home networks (§4) and the WiFi environment (§5). Our results show that in 80% of homes, users connect less than a dozen devices to their home network. In addition, only a small number of these devices, mainly home gateways, are active at any given time. We also observe that the density of the WiFi neighborhood varies considerably across homes.

The main contribution of this paper is the design and evaluation of HomeNet Profiler. Our initial experience shows that HomeNet Profiler was able to reach a large number of users (2,432 homes worldwide). Our periodic measurements from six homes in Paris put HomeNet Profiler results into perspective by analyzing the dynamics of both the set of devices and the WiFi neighborhood, which we cannot study with HomeNet Profiler's one-shot experiments. As more users run HomeNet Profiler, we plan to conduct a larger characterization study to shed light on home networks performance and configuration worldwide.

2 Design

This section discusses the requirements of HomeNet Profiler as well as our design and implementation decisions.

2.1 Requirements

The primary requirement for a home network data collection tool is that it *runs from inside the home*. Measurements from outside the home cannot have visibility into the home network configuration and its devices. The goal of measuring a large diversity of home networks and the fact that it is not possible to collect data inside a user's home without explicit user participation impose the following additional requirements:

- **Ease of Use.** The tool should be simple to run, even for non-expert users.
- **Portability.** The tool should run on all home networks and end-systems.
- **Respect Users' Privacy.** Users are unlikely to run a measurement tool inside their homes if the tool collects information that they consider private or any personally identifiable information. Our data collection effort has to comply with the rules of the French National Commission of Informatics and Freedom.[1]
- **Light User Commitment.** We ask home users to do us a favor by allowing us to collect data in their homes. We cannot ask users to commit too much time or resources without running the risk of reducing the number of users willing to participate.
- **Incentive for Participation.** Some users will run research tools altruistically. However, if users can get something out of the experiment, then we are more likely to get a larger number of participants.

2.2 Design and Implementation Decisions

The design requirements outlined in the previous section lead to some high-level design and implementation decisions.

---

[1] Commission nationale de l'informatique et des libertés (CNIL):
http://www.cnil.fr/english/.

First, HomeNet Profiler runs on *end-systems*. We considered deploying measurements on the home router/gateway or on one of the end-systems connected to the home network. Although some home users deploy routers with measurement capabilities [18], a hardware deployment has higher cost and more complicated logistics.

Second, inspired by the success of Netalyzr [13], HomeNet Profiler runs *one-shot* measurements on user demand. On one hand, long term, periodic measurements would give us a complete picture of home networks. On the other hand, users may be uncomfortable with installing a permanent software on their machine for privacy concerns and because of the possible impact on machine performance. We evaluate one-shot measurements against periodic measurements in § 4.1 and § 5.1.

Third, HomeNet Profiler is a *Java executable JAR*. We considered implementing HomeNet Profiler as a signed Java applet similar to prior work [13, 16], but it is hard to load system libraries such as the Windows Native WiFi interface from an applet and we need sudo rights on some Linux distributions, which is not possible from an applet. Instead, a Java executable JAR can collect the datasets we want and yet it is portable and simple for users to run.

Finally, HomeNet Profiler takes the user perspective. We include a user survey to obtain information that would be hard to infer automatically from the measurements (such as finding devices which are turned off). To see the survey questions, we invite the reader to run HomeNet Profiler. As an incentive for users to run HomeNet Profiler, we output a detailed report of their home network.[2] Before the measurements begin, HomeNet Profiler lets the user select which measurements to execute. Hence, users who are uncomfortable with some measurements can still run HomeNet Profiler with a subset of the measurements.

System Overview. We design HomeNet Profiler as a client-server application. The server hosts the HomeNet Profiler website, which users visit to fetch and run the HomeNet Profiler client. HomeNet Profiler starts in a separate window. Users then complete the survey while the measurement modules run in the background. Upon completion, the client sends all collected data to the server and redirects the web browser to the report page. When HomeNet Profiler exits, it leaves a random identifier on the user's machine to track multiple runs from the same end-system. A *run* refers to one execution of HomeNet Profiler.

2.3 Measurement Modules

We select a broad range of measurements to learn as much as possible about the home network. At the same time, measurements should not take too long to execute, otherwise users might give up in the middle of the experiment. Our main goal is to discover the devices connected to the home network and the services they provide as well as the network technologies connecting the home to the Internet and inside the home. We also characterize the WiFi neighborhood by measuring the quality of all visible WiFi networks. In addition to these direct measurements, we collect the configuration of the machine running HomeNet Profiler as well as the list of applications running on the

---

[2] For an example report refer to: http://cmon.lip6.fr/hnp/example

machine. This extra information helps us interpret the results in case some configuration affects some of our measurements (e.g., a firewall or a VPN).

The HomeNet Profiler client has the following measurement modules.[3]

Device Scan: Searches the home network for active network devices. This module first populates the ARP cache by sending UDP packets on Port 9 (i.e., the discard port) to all IP addresses in the sub-network of the end-system. We force a 10 seconds timeout on the scan to avoid long delays when sub-networks are too large. Our data confirms that the vast majority of scans finishes before the timeout. This module then reads the ARP cache to collect the vendor ID (OUI) and the SHA1 hash of the MAC of each network interface on the LAN. If the associated IP address is private we also collect it, otherwise we just record the presence of a public IP.

WiFi Scan: Collects a list of access points found with one WiFi scan. For each access point we collect the ESSID (the network name), the BSSID (the MAC address of the access point), the channel number, and the Received Signal Strength Indicator (RSSI). We anonymize ESSIDs and BSSIDs. We distinguish between the *home WiFi*, which is the one the end-system is connected to, and *neighbor WiFis*. On MacOS, the airport command-line tool provides all this information. On Linux, we use *iwconfig* and *iwlist*. On Windows, we use the Win32 Native WiFi API, which is not available on windows XP prior to SP3. We also observe that some Linux WiFi drivers only report information for the network the end-system is associated to.

Service Scan: Queries two protocols commonly-used to advertise services in home electronics: Zeroconf and UPnP. We opt for querying these protocols instead of a port scan per device because a port scan is intrusive and may take too much time.

Netalyzr [13]: Performs a number of tests related to the access network configuration, security, and performance. At each execution, HomeNet Profiler downloads and runs the latest version of Netalyzr's command-line client.

Configuration of the UPnP Gateway: In cases where the home gateway supports UPnP, HomeNet Profiler collects the model of the gateway, the connection type, and the connection speed. It also tests traffic counters using UPnP queries.

Aside from these measurements taken from the client, when HomeNet Profiler's server receives the collected measurements, it maps the client's public IP address to its geographical location and AS number using the Maxmind database. We then discard the public IP address. HomeNet Profiler also sends meta-data such as the time taken by each module and whether HomeNet Profiler was running with sudo privileges.

This paper reports preliminary results on devices (§ 4) and WiFi (§ 5). We report on the Netalyzr and UPnP gateway configuration measurements in prior work [6].

3 Measurements

Testbed. In most cases, users run HomeNet Profiler once, but both the WiFi neighborhood and the devices connected to a home network vary over time. We thus complement HomeNet Profiler by instrumenting six different home networks in Paris. We installed laptops in homes of colleagues from Technicolor and UPMC Sorbonne Universités.

---

[3] To address privacy concerns and comply with French laws, we anonymize all personally-identifiable information using SHA1 hash.

The households have between one and three members. Each laptop runs the WiFi scan module every ten seconds using an Intel WiFi card. Every ten minutes, laptops also run the device scan module on an Ethernet adapter. We collect data from March 19, 2012 to July 31, 2012. These six homes are not representative of the population at large, but instrumenting a larger number of homes is a practical challenge. Nevertheless, this testbed allows us to evaluate HomeNet Profiler and put the collected data into perspective.

HomeNet Profiler Data. We announced HomeNet Profiler by email to family, friends, colleagues, and mailing lists of networking researchers as well as through grenouille.com, a French website for people who want to monitor their ISP performance. Between April 2011 and May 2012, a total of 2,721 distinct end-systems ran HomeNet Profiler 3,634 times. Some users run HomeNet Profiler multiple times on the same end-system or from multiple end-systems in the same home. Users may also run HomeNet Profiler when they are not at home. For our analysis, we select a single representative run per home using two heuristics described in our technical report [7]. After applying these heuristics, we infer that our data comes from a total of 2,432 distinct homes. Users ran HomeNet Profiler from home networks in 46 countries and 210 different ASes (more details in our previous work [8]). This paper focuses on the 1,682 homes in France. Two thirds of French users answering the survey say that they 'know Internet technology well'. Hence, our dataset is biased towards experts users. This bias may be an advantage because expert users may have home networks more representative of future trends than other users.

4   Set of Devices in Home Networks

This section studies the set of devices that connects to home networks. We first use our testbed to analyze the dynamics of devices over time. Then, we analyze differences in number of devices across homes in the HomeNet Profiler data.

4.1   Completeness of Device Scans

Some devices may be disconnected from the home network at the time when users run HomeNet Profiler. We evaluate whether HomeNet Profiler would benefit from additional device scans.

Repeated device scans in our testbed observe different sets of devices. Fig. 1 shows the presence of a given device during the four months of data collection. The x-axis is the time of each device scan. The y-axis represents individual devices measured in each home network (identified by their MAC address). We label the y-axis with the home-id and below each home-id, the number of devices observed in that home network during our measurements. We order devices per home based on their occurrence. The most prevalent device of all six homes is the home gateway. Note that there are gaps in the data collection because of maintenance or other measurement campaigns running on the same testbed. These gaps are easily identified by the vertical bars with no points per home. We ignore these gaps in the following discussion.

The number of devices measured per home in four months varies between 6 and 19 depending on the home. We ask each home user to manually label each device observed over the whole data collection period. We divide devices into types: *home devices*, which are those that belong to members of the household; and *visitor devices*,

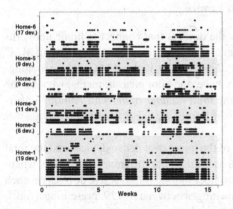

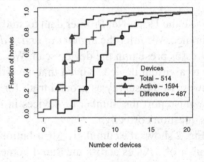

Fig. 2. Number of active devices versus the total number of devices per home. The number in the legend represents the number of homes included in the respective curve.

Fig. 1. Observed devices per home network

which belong to friends who are just using the home network for a short stay. The top-most devices of each home, those we only observed in a small fraction of the scans, correspond to visitor devices. We observe two types of home devices: always-on devices and on-off devices. *Always-on devices* are the ones users leave on all the time after the device first connects to the home network and until the device is decommissioned. These typically include home gateways and access points/routers. In Home-6 we also observe an IP printer and an IP security camera that were always on, and in Home-1 a network disk appears just before Week 5. *On-off devices* have prevalence between always-on home devices and visitor devices. We observe two types of on-off devices: personal mobile devices (such as laptops and smartphones) that leave the house with their owners; and devices that people turn on when needed (e.g., a weighing scale and a gaming console).

We compute the fraction of the home devices observed in a single scan over the total number of home devices. Given that HomeNet Profiler requires at least one user in the home to run the tool, we only count device scans when at least one laptop or desktop is on. Overall, we find that a single device scan only observes a small fraction of the home devices. For example, 92% of the scans with at least one laptop/desktop observe at most half of the home devices. Nevertheless, one single device scan captures all always-on devices more than 99.5% of the time. Hence, one-shot measurements are well-suited for studies that measure always-on devices such as home gateways [6].

We do not observe many more devices by aggregating the results of two scans made 10 minutes apart (85% of pairs of scans would still observe at most half of the home devices). Only periodic measurements of the home network can observe all the home devices. We find that it takes approximately eight days on average (and a median of four days) to discover all home devices in the six homes we measured. To alleviate the lack of periodic measurements, HomeNet Profiler's survey explicitly asks users to list the devices they typically connect to their home network.

4.2   Set of Devices in Home Networks in France

We use the HomeNet Profiler data to study the devices that connect to home networks in France. We infer the *number of active devices* in a home network by counting MAC addresses present in the device scan. We remove devices with a MAC address belonging to a virtual device.[4] Given that we only have one-shot measurements, we take the answers to the survey as ground truth for the *total number of devices*. Although users may misreport the number of devices in their home, we expect most users to answer this question correctly.

Fig. 2 shows the cumulative distribution of the number of active devices and the total number of devices across measured homes as well as the difference for homes where users selected both measurements (i.e., the number of total minus active devices for each home). The total number of devices per home ranges between 2 to 29, presenting a much wider spread than what we observe in our testbed. The range of the number of active devices, however, is smaller than that of the total number of devices. Approximately 75% of homes have at most four active devices during our measurements. This result is in agreement with our evaluation that shows that just a small fraction of home devices are on at any given time. The 'difference' curve confirms that many home devices are not connected when HomeNet Profiler runs.

The size of each household (i.e., the number of members living in a household) may explain the number of devices in a home network. However, some devices such as printers serve all members of a household. For the 400 homes for which users reported the size of their household, we find that the number of active devices and the size of the household have a Pearson correlation coefficient of only 0.18. The coefficient increases to 0.33 when considering the total number of devices and to 0.37 when considering only laptops and desktops. These results imply that the size of a household does have a moderate positive correlation with the total number of devices and hence it should be considered to model the total number of devices in the home.

5   WiFi Neighborhood

This section characterizes the WiFi neighborhood as seen by end-systems at home. We first study the dynamics of the results of WiFi scans in our testbed to evaluate the single WiFi scan in HomeNet Profiler. We then study the WiFi neighborhood of French homes.

5.1   Accuracy of Neighborhood Characterization in One-Shot Measurements

The set of neighbor WiFis can vary considerably even in short time windows (of seconds), because lost WiFi beacons prevent us from inferring the presence of an ESSID-BSSID pair. We study the short-term dynamics of the WiFi neighborhood of each of the six homes in two-minute intervals; during each two-minute interval we perform 12 consecutive WiFi scans. We assume that the aggregate set of measured ESSID-BSSID pairs in the 12 scans represents the complete WiFi neighborhood during the two-minute interval.[5] Then, we compute the *fraction of the WiFi neighborhood observed*, which is

---

[4] In our dataset, the OUI for virtual machines are VMWare, Hyper-V, and Parallels.
[5] It is practically impossible to get ground truth on the WiFi neighborhood.

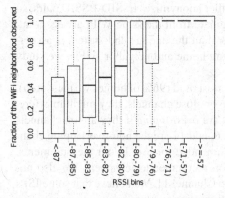

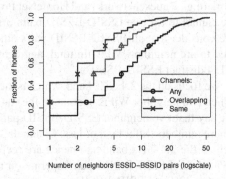

Fig. 3. Fraction of the WiFi neighborhood observed with one scan for different RSSI bins

Fig. 4. CDF of the number of neighbor ESSID-BSSID pairs

the number of ESSID-BSSID pairs observed in the first scan of a two-minute interval divided by the number of ESSID-BSSID pairs of the WiFi neighborhood in this interval.

Intuitively, the probability of a WiFi scan to observe an ESSID-BSSID pair will be lower if the pair has low RSSI. To better understand this effect, we group the ESSID-BSSID pairs into ten *RSSI bins* based on the mean RSSI of each pair during a two-minute interval. We pick bin boundaries at every 10th-percentile of the distribution of mean RSSI per two-minute interval for all ESSID-BSSID pairs to ensure that every RSSI bin has 10% of the points. Fig. 3 shows the boxplot of the fraction of the WiFi neighborhood observed. The x-axis presents the RSSI bins (note that the x-axis is not linear). Boxes represent the inter-quartile range of the distribution of the fraction of the WiFi neighborhood observed for ESSID-BSSID pairs in a given RSSI bin; the solid line inside the box is the median, the whiskers represent the minimum and maximum values. The 802.11 standards do not specify units for RSSI and each vendor may use a different scale. All machines in our testbed have the same hardware and software, so we can aggregate RSSIs from the six machines in our testbed.

Fig. 3 confirms the intuition that ESSID-BSSID pairs with stronger signals are easier to observe. For example, the leftmost bin shows that half the time, a single WiFi scan observes no more than 34% of the ESSID-BSSID pairs with RSSI lower than −87, whereas a single scan is sufficient to observe all ESSID-BSSID pairs with RSSI higher than −76. One scan is enough to collect all the ESSID-BSSID pairs with strong RSSI and to frequently get a large fraction of those with lower RSSI. This result implies that performing a single WiFi scan is a good compromise to speed-up the data collection. ESSID-BSSID pairs with strong RSSI are more likely to interfere with the home WiFi and are also the ones that home users could use for backup connectivity, for instance.

5.2   WiFi Neighborhood in France

HomeNet Profiler successfully collects WiFi results in 1,131 homes in France. Some end-systems do not have a WiFi interface or lack support from the OS to run the WiFi scan. Some WiFi access points broadcast ESSID-BSSID pairs for more than one network (e.g., a guest network) and HomeNet Profiler anonymizes ESSID-BSSID pairs, so we cannot tell if two ESSID-BSSID pairs originate from the same WiFi access point. We consider that all ESSID-BSSID pairs other than the one the end-system is associated to are neighbor WiFis. In total, aggregating home and neighbor WiFis, we study 7,154 distinct ESSID-BSSIDs.

We focus on the 2.4 GHz band, which is the most used (96% of homes we measured). When two neighbor WiFis operate on the same or close channels, they might interfere. We say that two neighbor ESSID-BSSID pairs are *overlapping* if they are on channels where numbers differ by 4 or less. Channels 1, 6, and 11 are the non-overlapping channels in the 2.4 GHz band and hence are recommended for use. In our measurements, 18% of the ESSID-BSSID pairs operate on non-recommended channels. We also notice that 39% of ESSID-BSSID pairs operate on Channel 11. We believe that some ISPs ship home gateways with hardcoded WiFi configuration.

WiFi neighborhoods are generally crowded in France. Fig. 4 plots the cumulative distribution of the number of neighbor ESSID-BSSID pairs across all measured homes. We present three distributions: for all neighbor WiFis; for ESSID-BSSID pairs that overlap with the home WiFi; and for ESSID-BSSID pairs on the same channel as the home WiFi. Overall, the number of ESSID-BSSID pairs of the WiFi neighborhood varies considerably across homes (from 1 to 52 neighbor WiFis) and more than 75% of homes have an overlapping WiFi neighbor. The actual number of WiFi neighbors is likely larger because HomeNet Profiler misses some WiFi neighbors with low RSSI.

The quality of the home WiFi also depends on the strength of the received signal. Since end-systems have different WiFi adapters, their RSSI measurements are not directly comparable. Thus we only compare RSSIs of different ESSID-BSSID pairs measured on the same end-system. Further, if the home access point broadcasts ESSID-BSSID pairs for a guest network, then their RSSI will be similar to the RSSI of the home WiFi. French ISPs offer country-wide community networks with well-known ESSIDs. After removing these ESSIDs, we find that in 13% of homes, the end-system has stronger RSSI to a neighbor WiFi that overlaps with the home WiFi. We have high confidence on this result because our testbed evaluation shows that we always observe WiFis with strong RSSI and here we are only studying the two strongest WiFis.

6   Conclusion

This paper designs HomeNet Profiler, a tool that home users run on an end-system to measure home networks. HomeNet Profiler scans the local network for active devices and services, observes the WiFi neighborhood, and complements measurements with a user survey. We design HomeNet Profiler as a one-shot measurement tool. Our testbed results show that one-shot measurements capture practically all always-on devices, but only a small fraction of on-off devices. As a result, HomeNet Profiler's survey is an important complement to understand the full set of home devices at a large number of homes. In addition, the testbed results show that one-shot measurements are sufficient to capture all WiFi neighbors with strong signal and a significant fraction of neighbors with lower signal. WiFi neighbors with strong signal are more likely to interfere with the home WiFi or to be useful as backup links. The biggest advantage of this one-shot approach is that it requires little effort/commitment from users and hence allow us to reach a large number of users. So far, users have run HomeNet Profiler from over 2,400 homes. Our analysis of 1,600 homes in France shows that the number of home devices vary considerably across homes and that only a small fraction of home devices are active at any given time. We also find that WiFi neighborhoods are crowded in France. We hope to attract more users in other countries in the near future to perform a larger scale characterization. We also plan to develop a service to query HomeNet Profiler data online and give an up-to-date view on home networks to the community.

Acknowledgment. We thank all HomeNet Profiler users. This work was supported by the European Community's Seventh Framework Programme (FP7/2007-2013) no. 258378 (FIGARO). Part of the work presented in this paper was carried out at LINCS (www.lincs.fr).

References

1. Calvert, K.L., Edwards, W.K., Feamster, N., Grinter, R.E., Deng, Y., Zhou, X.: Instrumenting Home Networks. In: ACM SIGCOMM HomeNets Workshop (2010)
2. Chetty, M., Banks, R., Harper, R., Regan, T., Sellen, A., Gkantsidis, C., Karagiannis, T., Key, P.: Who's Hogging The Bandwidth?: The Consequences Of Revealing The Invisible In The Home. In: Proc. ACM CHI (2010)
3. Chetty, M., Halsem, D., Baird, A., Ofoha, U., Summer, B., Grinter, R.E.: Why Is My Internet Slow?: Making Network Speeds Visible. In: Proc. ACM CHI (2011)
4. Choffnes, D.R., Bustamante, F.E., Ge, Z.: Crowdsourcing Service-Level Network Event Monitoring. In: Proc. ACM SIGCOMM (2010)
5. Croce, D., En-Najjary, T., Urvoy-Keller, G., Biersack, E.: Capacity Estimation of ADSL links. In: Proc. CoNEXT (2008)
6. DiCioccio, L., Teixeira, R., May, M., Kreibich, C.: Probe and Pray: Using UPnP for Home Network Measurements. In: Proc. PAM (2012)
7. DiCioccio, L., Teixeira, R., Rosenberg, C.: Characterizing Home Networks With HomeNet Profiler. Technical Report CP-PRL-2011-09-0001, Technicolor (2011)
8. DiCioccio, L., Teixeira, R., Rosenberg, C.: Measuring and Characterizing Home Networks (Poster). In: Proc. ACM SIGMETRICS (2012)
9. Dischinger, M., Haeberlen, A., Gummadi, K.P., Saroiu, S.: Characterizing Residential Broadband Networks. In: Proc. IMC (2007)
10. Dixon, C., Mahajan, R., Agarwal, S., Brush, A., Lee, B., Saroiu, S., Bahl, V.: An Operating System for the Home. In: Proc. NSDI (2012)
11. Han, D., Agarwala, A., Andersen, D.G., Kaminsky, M., Papagiannaki, K., Seshan, S.: Mark-and-Sweep: Getting the Inside Scoop on Neighborhood Networks. In: Proc. IMC (2008)
12. Karagiannis, T., Athanasopoulos, E., Gkantsidis, C., Key, P.: HomeMaestro: Order from Chaos in Home Networks. Technical Report MSR-TR-2008-84, MSR (2008)
13. Kreibich, C., Weaver, N., Nechaev, B., Paxson, V.: Netalyzr: Illuminating the Edge Network. In: Proc. IMC (2010)
14. Maier, G., Feldmann, A., Paxson, V., Allman, M.: On Dominant Characteristics of Residential Broadband Internet Traffic. In: Proc. IMC (2009)
15. Papagiannaki, K., Yarvis, M., Conner, W.S.: Experimental Characterization of Home Wireless Networks and Design Implications. In: Proc. IEEE INFOCOM (2006)
16. Ritacco, A., Wills, C., Claypool, M.: How's my Network? A Java Approach to Home Network Measurement. In: ICCCN (2009)

17. Siekkinen, M., Collange, D., Urvoy-Keller, G., Biersack, E.W.: Performance Limitations of ADSL Users: A Case Study. In: Uhlig, S., Papagiannaki, K., Bonaventure, O. (eds.) PAM 2007. LNCS, vol. 4427, pp. 145–154. Springer, Heidelberg (2007)
18. Sundaresan, S., de Donato, W., Feamster, N., Teixeira, R., Crawford, S., Pescapè, A.: Broadband Internet Performance: A View From the Gateway. In: Proc. ACM SIGCOMM (2011)
19. Yang, J., Edwards, W.K.: A Study on Network Management Tools of Householders. In: ACM SIGCOMM HomeNets Workshop (2010)

Characteristics of Real Open SIP-Server Traffic

Jan Stanek[1], Lukas Kencl[1], and Jiri Kuthan[2]

[1] Czech Technical University in Prague
Technicka 2, 166 27 Prague 6, Czech Republic
{jan.stanek,lukas.kencl}@fel.cvut.cz
[2] Tekelec
Am Borsigturm 11, 13507 Berlin, Germany
jiri.kuthan@tekelec.com

Abstract. Voice-over-IP (VoIP) is currently one of the most commonly used communication options and Session Initiation Protocol (SIP) is most often used for VoIP deployment. However, there is not a lot of general knowledge about typical SIP traffic and research in this area largely works with various assumptions. To address this deficiency, we present a thorough study of traffic of a real, free and publicly open SIP server. The findings reveal, among others, a surprisingly high overhead of SIP due to connection maintenance through Network Address Translation (NAT) nodes, differences from typical Web server Zipf's-law patterns and various unexpected creative uses of SIP servers.

1 Introduction

With proliferation of Voice-over-IP (VoIP) communication, its infrastructure – the signaling protocol (Session Initiation Protocol (SIP) [1, 2]) and the control nodes (SIP servers) – attracts much interest from the perspective of practical functioning within the Internet infrastructure. SIP traffic characteristics form a necessary basis for considerations of deployment in the light of emerging trends. SIP is lightweight, has easily understandable and human-readable structure and as a signaling protocol, it does not generate much traffic by itself. A lot of research is dedicated to VoIP improvement in reliability, stability, quality of service, security and other areas. However, publicly available analyses of SIP traffic are rare and thus not a lot of knowledge exists in the networking community about typical behavior of SIP servers (as opposed to, e.g. HTTP servers). Typically, a lot of assumptions are made about SIP traffic, but are they realistic?

The goal of this paper is to study properties of real SIP-server traffic. We analyze a freely accessible and open SIP server with a worldwide user base. Anyone can register and use this SIP server, free of charge and with no restrictions on the client device. A vibrant and multi-faceted community of users from all around the world form the user base, using various SIP devices, including proprietary ones. These often do not behave exactly as they should. This creates very interesting and sometimes non-standard SIP traffic that we also examine in this paper.

M. Roughan and R. Chang (Eds.) PAM 2013, LNCS 7799, pp. 187–197, 2013.

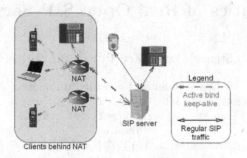

Fig. 1. Server-based connection maintenance through NAT

In more detail we study the problem of Network Address Translation (NAT) traversal, still not well-solved in SIP. The server and clients typically need to execute other mechanisms (STUN [3], TURN [4], ICE [5] etc.) to facilitate NAT traversal. The monitored server, too, uses its own mechanism to keep NAT connections alive (see Fig. 1).

The main contributions of this work are as follows:

- a thorough traffic analysis of three days of an operational SIP server, including geographic spread and time-series analysis;
- identification, measurements and demonstration of the large overhead in SIP traffic caused by NAT and keep-alive mechanisms;
- discussion of the findings and suggestion of possible remedies;
- analysis of geographic traffic distribution.

2   Related work

Sparks [6] and Prasad and Kumar [7] describe SIP basics and some typical extensions used. The problem of NAT traversal in SIP and its various solutions have been described in numerous papers e.g by Yeryomin et al. [8] and Song et al. [9]. Despite the many proposals for solving the NAT traversal issue, some of which are very popular (STUN, ICE), none of these was adopted generally as they impose strict extra requirements on the SIP clients and servers. Much work has also focused on identifying SIP anomalies. Heo et al. [10] studied the use of statistical distances for respective SIP message types, Cortes et al. [11] used performance metrics to identify SIP processing times and Kang et al. [12] used known profilers on various real SIP datasets. Ehlert et al. [13] used decision modules and Nassar et al. [14] vector machines to detect anomalous SIP traffic.

Significant amount of papers was dedicated to SIP security. Hentehzadeh et al. [15] used statistical approach to filter out potentially hazardous SIP traffic. Akbar et al. [16] proposed using evolutionary algorithms, able to adapt to the changing nature of SIP traffic. Sisalem, Kuthan and Ehlert [17] proposed some best practices for secure SIP deployment. Despite this body of works, many SIP deployments remain unprotected even against the simplest of attacks.

Considering cloud environment, deploying only SIP server itself in cloud is not economical due to its typical stable and continuous resource consumption. However, next to SIP there is a large body of related media traffic (typically in the form of RTP streams) and routing it through the best available paths is an important open problem. One solution, using anycast, was proposed by Andel et al. [18]. Considering the distributed nature of the cloud and its location-awareness, using it to deploy media relays might be beneficial.

3   SIP Server Setup and Dataset Description

We have analyzed SIP traffic from a publicly, globally and freely available SIP server a long time in operation. It is configured so that it expects user devices not to be able to do any advanced tasks and tries to solve any issues (such as maintaining the bindings for clients behind NAT) on the server side. Users are encouraged to use it for testing of their experimental set-ups and devices. Despite these differences from a typical commercial SIP server, analysis of its traffic is very useful as it exhibits many interesting and unexpected aspects of SIP traffic. Observations based upon this traffic are generally applicable since a lot of the "unexpectances" comes from client behavior or misconfiguration.

The respective iptel.org SIP server runs on a single host, located in Berlin, Germany. It is an instance of SIP Express Router (SER) [19], running on top of Linux on a Dell Poweredge 1850 server. The only services running on the server are SER, STUN (mystun) and a UDP relay for NAT traversal. The processing capacity is sufficient to process typical SIP-server traffic. About 3400 users are typically registered generating call rate between 2 and 50 concurrent calls.

We captured all network traffic on the server continuously for 67 hours using tcpdump [20]. The capture started on March 16 2012 at 13:00 GMT and ended on March 19 2012 at 8:00 GMT, its size is 40GB and it contains about 85 million packets. Of these, about 39GB are SIP and 1GB non-SIP packets, yet about 74 million are SIP and 11 million non-SIP packets. The difference in size and packet counts is caused by the non-SIP packets being mostly very small – TCP related, or UDP keep-alives.

Note that we focus solely on the signaling traffic. We do not analyze the media traffic as it is does not influence the signaling processing.

4   Data Analysis Methodology

We split the larger traffic dump so we could process it faster in parallel. We had 3 servers available so we split the dump accordingly – the first two parts corresponding to the first two days and the third to the remaining 19 hours. We used programs from the Wireshark [21] program suite for trace splitting and the various analyses. We divide the analysis into several phases:

Phase 1 - Load over time. We focused on the evolution of load over time. Using Wireshark we extracted the timestamp in unix time format from every packet.

We then imported these timestamps to Matlab and created a timeline for each part. As the timestamps in plaintext format consumed about 2GB of disk space, we aggregated them to blocks of 1 second for faster processing.

Phase 2 - SIP request types. We analyzed types of SIP requests and responses contained in the dump. We used tshark (a command-line version of wireshark) to produce SIP statistics (*tshark -z sip,stat*) i.e. a list of SIP message types with numbers of occurrences per each type observed. As the three blocks are still too large to be efficiently processed by tshark, we split them again to parts of 250000 SIP packets in size. The resulted reports were concatenated and an awk script was used to extract the necessary information. Final aggregation was executed in Matlab, producing a sorted lists of SIP requests and responses.

Phase 3 - Traffic sources. We analyzed the traffic according to its sources. We reused the parts from Phase 2 and analyzed them using tshark, now with -*z conv, udp/tcp* options. These options aggregate traffic between source and target locations (identified by IP address and port pair) and produce summary containing numbers of packets (bytes, frames) exchanged between every pair of locations that communicated with each other. These data were again aggregated and cleaned using awk and imported to Matlab for results generation.

Phase 4 - Geographic distribution. We analyzed the geographic spread of users. We used a userloc – text database of registered users containing all the user information the SIP server stores (including IP addresses). We extracted the IP addresses using awk and mapped them to their geographic locations using the WebNET77 Multiple IP address lookup tool [22].

Phase 5 - Geographic locations. Finally, we wanted to obtain geographic location for the caller and callee per every call observed. We did this by filtering the INVITE and REGISTER messages and extracting information about mapping of IP addresses to individual users. We also created a list of calls by separating unique INVITEs (e.g. filtering out re-INVITEs). Then we loaded the IP addresses into the webnet tool [22]. We saved the resulting IP to location mapping and replaced IP addresses with locations. Some calls were still unmappable since there were also reserved and local IP addresses present, but for the rest we obtained the list of calls in pairwise format (from country - to country).

5   SIP Server Traffic Analysis

5.1   General Properties

SIP traffic on the studied server is generated by about 3400 active SIP User Agents, mostly in Europe (41%), North America (25%) and Asia (22%). Other continents are less involved (South America 6%, Africa 3% and Oceania 3%).

Some of the clients are represented by bulk services, such as ipkall or virtualpbx. The User Agents are represented by about 280 distinct SIP client implementations. The distribution of client types can be seen in Fig. 2. The most frequently used SIP clients are AVM Fritzbox and Draytek (about 10% each).

Various Linksys devices represent a significant fraction (12%) as well. Another interesting aspect is the presence of mobile clients, representing about 12% of users. The most used mobile SIP client implementations are Comrex (7.7% of all clients), Acrobits(2.2%) and sipdroid(1.4%).

For this signaling-traffic analysis, we prefer to focus on the count of signaling messages rather than its (tiny) byte volume, as it is rather the former which influences SIP-server performance.

The split of traffic among TCP and UDP in numbers of packets is about 9:91 (less than 10% of traffic consists of TCP packets). Interestingly, only 150 out of the 3308 registered users were registered as using TCP (150/3308 = 4.5%), showing that the TCP clients generate more traffic than the UDP ones.

A graph of a typical one-day traffic can be seen in Fig. 3(a). About 8600 calls are made per day and there are about 3400 registered users (slight fluctuations, but no big changes if we do not count server outages that were observed in the traffic dumps - reason unknown, probably network failure). Calls express very strong 24-hour stability with just a small increases during prime-time. This is due to the high amount of options/keep-alives in the traffic (see Fig. 3(b)), caused by the deployed NAT traversal solution (notice that number of clients behind NAT does not fluctuate, so the generated keep-alive traffic is stable).

The division of load among the request and response message types can be seen in Fig. 4(a) and 4(b).

5.2 NAT Traversal

NAT traversal is still generally an unsolved problem of SIP. STUN is not reliable, ICE is often not implemented and usage of media-relays invokes notable overhead. Many clients and servers thus implement proprietary solutions – the most common one being periodic sending of "keep-alives" – messages with predefined content (OPTIONS and REGISTER being used most often). These messages are supposed to keep the NAT binding alive, thus solving the problem.

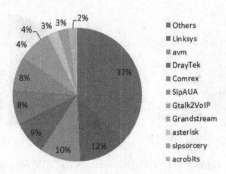

Fig. 2. Distribution of user devices

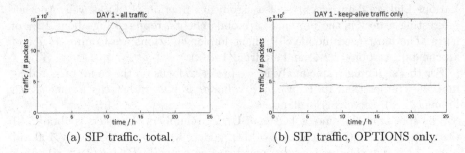

(a) SIP traffic, total.   (b) SIP traffic, OPTIONS only.

Fig. 3. Measurements of one day traffic

About 1500 out of the 3400 total users (44%) were detected to be behind NAT (from the view of the SIP server, actual number might be higher as some clients solve it on their own e.g. using ALGs). As the SIP server is open and supposed to support even proprietary SIP clients, it must use its own keep-alive messages to prevent eventual loss of NAT bindings. The clients, however, are not aware of this proactive server solution and run their own proprietary keep-alives. If the keep-alive messages were not sent in short intervals, NAT bindings would expire and clients would become unavailable for incoming calls. This results in an enormous part of the observed traffic (over 50%, see below for more detail) being just an exchange of proprietary keep-alive messages.

Considering the server-side NAT keep-alives only, every 15s there is one OP-TIONS message sent per every client detected as behind the NAT, resulting in roughly 8.64 million keep-alive requests per day. Not counting the responses to these requests, this corresponds to about 33% of the total server traffic (there are about 16.2 million requests and 9 million responses per day in total). Only about 10% of the clients were able to respond to them, meaning that about 90% of this excessive traffic was effectively useless.

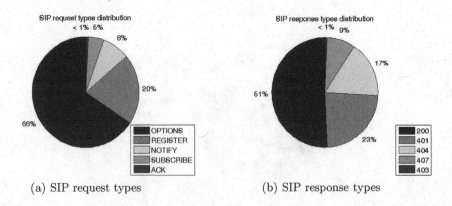

(a) SIP request types   (b) SIP response types

Fig. 4. Overall distribution of SIP message types

The REGISTER requests represent about 20% of total traffic. This is mainly due to every client re-registering after a predefined amount of time (default 600s) and some clients using the REGISTER requests as their NAT keep-alive mechanism. Note that a successful registration in SIP requires two REGISTER messages (first response indicates that authorization is necessary and provides necessary information) and a REGISTER request with the Expires attribute set to 0 is used for deregistration. Concretely, we have about 3400 clients, so counting two REGISTER requests per a successful registration this amounts to about 979200 REGISTER requests per day. In fact we observe about 3.3 million REGISTER messages per day, so probably the rest are client NAT keep-alives. The INVITE and BYE messages together represent only about 0.19% of all requests per day (30564 out of 16154468).

In summary, NAT traversal from the server causes overhead of 33%. The keep-alives from clients we can only estimate, but thanks to the high numbers of OPTIONS and REGISTERs we can conjecture that keep-alive messages may amount to over 50% of the total traffic.

5.3   HTTP Server / SIP Server Workload Comparison

It is a well known observation that typical network traffic follows Zipf's law. We analyzed this aspect in SIP traffic as well. For comparison, we have used data of HTTP traffic from a freely available source at [23]. These data show a very clear Zipf's law observable by a straight line in a graph on a log-log scale. We have created log-log graphs of SIP traffic of the first day of our capture, isolating the requests and responses, see Fig 5(a) and Fig.5(b).

Obviously, this traffic does not exhibit Zipf's law characteristics. The difference is caused by absence of sources with very low packet count ("mice"). This can be expected due to the periodic registration property of SIP that leads to periodically generated traffic and so one can hardly find a user sending only a few SIP packets (at least 2 packets are sent during registration and re-registration, occurring every 10 minutes).

SIP traffic thus does not generally follow Zipf's law and assumptions valid for network traffic should be handled with care when applied to SIP.

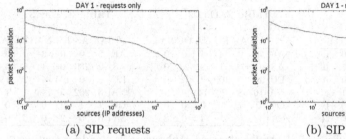 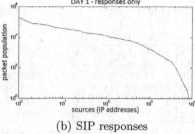

(a) SIP requests   (b) SIP responses

Fig. 5. Log-log scale graphs of captured SIP traffic, Day 1

5.4   Geographic Traffic Distribution

We have analyzed the division of traffic among countries and continents. Due to limited space in the paper, we present only the continental-level traffic division in Tables 1– 3. Clearly, the traffic is typically intra-continental (the non-zero numbers are on the diagonal in the tables). There is one large deviation though and that is traffic from North America to Asia. We scrutinized this unexpected phenomenon and found out a service called Virtualphoneline that offers American phoneline numbers and routes them via SIP anywhere the customers need. This way, for example a Chinese merchant can have an American helpline for his American customers automatically rerouted to his offices in China. Very useful and very unexpected to be run on a public, test-oriented SIP server. With Virtualphoneline traffic subtracted, however, the calls are basically carried-out intra-continentally, thus exhibiting geographic locality.

5.5   Registration Storms

Our analysis has shown that there is a big difference between normal traffic and traffic during an unexpected event such as a registration storm. Users are enforced to renew their registrations periodically (once each 600s). Considering a theoretical situation where every client re-registers exactly after 600s, then having 3400 clients one would expect traffic of approximately 12 REGISTER requests per second. Many users are however re-registering more often. Our data show that over 35% of the users have their re-registration interval set under 540s. When we measured the real registration load over a 600s period we obtained load of approx 65 requests per second (rps), much higher than the theoretical expectation. We have also observed a few server outages. When measuring load after an outage longer than 600s, it reached up to 900 rps after service renewal!

For a SIP service to be reliable, the server must be able to process the traffic even in the worst-case scenario of a registration storm. Filtering would not help as all the REGISTER requests are valid and must be processed. Overprovisioning is sure to help, but would be quite expensive. A highly distributed cluster might work, splitting outages to small parts served from different locations.

Table 1. Day 1

	AF	AS	EU	NA	OC	SA
AF	1	0	2	4	0	0
AS	1	169	4	26	5	0
EU	20	19	213	0	0	0
NA	19	355	18	114	1	1
OC	1	8	0	0	0	0
SA	0	0	0	0	0	11

Table 2. Day 2

	AF	AS	EU	NA	OC	SA
AF	1	0	4	4	0	0
AS	0	71	1	3	23	0
EU	10	0	109	2	12	0
NA	16	589	26	74	0	18
OC	0	7	11	0	0	0
SA	0	0	1	4	0	3

Table 3. Day 3

	AF	AS	EU	NA	OC	SA
AF	2	0	0	8	0	0
AS	2	289	0	1	5	0
EU	8	0	135	4	2	1
NA	3	202	5	148	1	1
OC	1	1	2	0	1	0
SA	0	0	2	0	0	0

Continental-level division of SIP traffic observed. Abbreviations stand for continents. AF Africa, AS Asia, EU Europe, NA N. America, OC Oceania, SA S. America.

6   Conclusion

The biggest issue we encountered, a large amount of "waste" traffic, stems from misconfiguration and poor implementation of user devices and improper use of NAT traversal mechanisms. Requests are often invalid, user devices unable to process valid but specific SIP messages. A large portion of the traffic is thus "wasted", as the requests are not properly handled (about 90% of servers' keep-alive traffic was effectively useless.). These results show that it is imperative to filter SIP traffic, whereby overall traffic could potentially be reduced by 60-70%. Note that in the case of the non-signaling, media traffic (e.g. VoIP calls), the overhead analysis might end-up differently, however, this paper focuses solely on issues of signaling.

Proper anomaly detection could help and it would also address another vital issue – security and protection of SIP infrastructure. Anomaly detection is generally hard – a lot of wasteful traffic and proprietary behavior complicates the analysis. A public SIP service must be very liberal in what traffic it receives, it must be prepared to deal with clients' imperfections and compensate for these, but at the same time it must not be prone to DoS attacks. Therefore anomaly detection should be carried out separately. These requirements should be always considered when deploying a SIP server as improper anomaly detection leads to unexpected problems. Some of the common security solutions, based on traffic limiting, might conflict with the "unexpected but harmless" behavior of misconfigured clients, thus blocking the service for legitimate clients. Service outage then exacerbates the problem as legitimate clients generate valid REGISTER requests which might create a false positive flood attack.

Our analysis showed that it not necessarily advantageous for SIP servers to be migrated into cloud datacenters, as SIP traffic is very stable and does not exhibit excessive spikes in terms of resources consumption. However, SIP traffic and, more importantly, media traffic, also exhibits strong geographic locality. This could be exploited using a cloud-based architecture since cloud providers usually allow the choice of a geographic location for running the services. Therefore we propose using distributed media relays in cloud. These could then be positioned according to the needs of the individual domains/zones and one could avoid the triangular routing introduced by UDP relays.

As future work we intend to analyze the registration storms and possibilities of minimizing their impact. We also plan to create a SIP-trace anonymizer so that our SIP traffic data can be made publicly available. Due to the nature of SIP, it is not possible to release the data simply IP-anonymized because it still contains interconnected personal information (usernames, domains, locations etc.) spread across different parts of multiple SIP messages. In spite of our every intention for public release of the data, proper anonymization that would maintain the analytical value appears to be a research problem on its own and will take some time to solve. Until the anonymizer is finished (we plan for Q2 2013 the latest) we can only share the data analyzed in this paper under NDA (please do not hesitate to contact us, if interested).

Acknowledgment. We thank iptel.org for generously providing access to its SIP-server traffic records. We also thank P. Kasparek and V. Kubart for help with data analysis.

References

1. Handley et. al. Sip: Session initiation protocol (rfc 2543), http://www.ietf.org/rfc/rfc2543.txt
2. Rosenberg et. al. Sip: Session initiation protocol (rfc 3261), http://www.ietf.org/rfc/rfc3261.txt
3. Rosenberg, J., et al.: Session traversal utilities for nat (stun), http://tools.ietf.org/html/rfc5389
4. Mahy, R., et al.: Traversal using relays around nat (turn): Relay extensions to session traversal utilities for nat (stun), http://tools.ietf.org/html/rfc5766
5. Rosenberg, J.: Ice: A protocol for network address translator traversal for offer/answer protocols, http://tools.ietf.org/html/rfc5245
6. Sparks, R.: Sip: Basics and beyond. Queue 5(2), 22–33 (2007)
7. Prasad, J.K., Kumar, B.A.: Analysis of sip and realization of advanced ip-pbx features. In: ICECT 2011, vol. 6, pp. 218–222 (April 2011)
8. Yeryomin, Y., Evers, F., Seitz, J.: Solving the firewall and nat traversal issues for sip-based voip. In: ICT 2008, pp. 1–6 (June 2008)
9. Song, M., Chi, J., Pi, R., Song, J.: Implementing an express sip nat traversal server. In: ICPCA 2007, pp. 527–529 (July 2007)
10. Heo, J., Chen, E.Y., Kusumoto, T., Itoh, M.: Statistical sip traffic modeling and analysis system. In: ISCIT, pp. 1223 –1228 (2010)
11. Cortes, M., Ensor, J.R., Esteban, J.O.: On sip performance. Bell Labs Technical Journal 9(3), 155–172 (2004)
12. Kang, H.J., Zhang, Z.-L., Ranjan, S., Nucci, A.: Sip-based voip traffic behavior profiling and its applications. In: MineNet 2007, pp. 39–44 (2007)
13. Ehlert, S., Wang, C., Magedanz, T., Sisalem, D.: Specification-based denial-of-service detection for sip voice-over-ip networks. In: Internet Monitoring and Protection, ICIMP 2008, June 29 -July 5, pp. 59–66 (2008)
14. Nassar, M., State, R., Festor, O.: Monitoring SIP Traffic Using Support Vector Machines. In: Lippmann, R., Kirda, E., Trachtenberg, A. (eds.) RAID 2008. LNCS, vol. 5230, pp. 311–330. Springer, Heidelberg (2008)
15. Hentehzadeh, N., et al.: Statistical analysis of self-similar session initiation protocol (sip) messages for anomaly detection. In: 2011 4th IFIP Conference on New Technologies, Mobility and Security (NTMS), pp. 1–5 (February 2011)
16. Ali Akbar, M., Farooq, M.: Application of evolutionary algorithms in detection of sip based flooding attacks. In: GECCO 2009 (2009)
17. Sisalem, D., Kuthan, J., Ehlert, S.: Denial of service attacks targeting a sip voip infrastructure: attack scenarios and prevention mechanisms. IEEE Network 20(5), 26–31 (2006)
18. Andel, L., Kuthan, J., Sisalem, D.: Distributed media server architecture for sip using ip anycast. In: IPTComm 2009, pp. 5:1–5:11 (2009)
19. Community of developers. The sip router project (developed from openser), http://sip-router.org/

20. Van Jacobson, Leres, C., McCanne, S., many later contributors: Tcpdump: Com-mandline packet analyzer, http://www.tcpdump.org/
21. Combs, G., contributors: Wireshark - network protocol analyzer,
    http://www.wireshark.org
22. WEBNet77. Ip to country multi-lookup tool,
    http://software77.net/geo-ip/multi-lookup/
23. ACM SIGCOMM partners. The internet traffic archive,
    http://ita.ee.lbl.gov/html/traces.html

Trying Broadband Characterization at Home

Mario A. Sánchez, John S. Otto,
Zachary S. Bischof, and Fabián E. Bustamante

Northwestern University
{msanchez,jotto,zbischof,fabianb}@eecs.northwestern.edu

Abstract. In recent years the quantity and diversity of Internet-enabled consumer devices in the home have increased significantly. These trends complicate device usability and home resource management and have implications for crowdsourced approaches to broadband characterization.

The UPnP protocol has emerged as an open standard for device and service discovery to simplify device usability and resource management in home networks. In this work, we leverage UPnP to understand the dynamics of home device usage, both at a macro and micro level, and to sketch an effective approach to broadband characterization that runs behind the last meter.

Using UPnP measurements collected from over 13K end users, we show that while home networks can be quite complex, the number of devices that actively and regularly connect to the Internet is limited. Furthermore, we find a high correlation between the number of UPnP-enabled devices in home networks and the presence of UPnP-enabled gateways, and show how this can be leveraged for effective broadband characterization.

1 Introduction

Over the last few years we have seen a dramatic increase in the quantity and diversity of Internet-enabled consumer devices in the home. Recent reports suggest that shipments of Internet-ready electronic devices – such as televisions and video game consoles – will surpass 500M units by 2013, triple the amount shipped in 2010.[1]

This unparalleled growth challenges home network usability and resource management, and has implications for broadband characterization behind the last mile [1, 7, 8, 10].

The Universal Plug and Play (UPnP) protocol has emerged as an open standard to address some of these challenges [11], with a growing number of devices supporting it. [2] In this work, we leverage UPnP to understand the

---

[1] http://www.isuppli.com/home-and-consumer-electronics/news/pages/
shipments-of-internet-enabled-consumer-devices-to-exceed-pcs-
in-2013.aspx

[2] http://realwire.com/releases/UPnP-Technology-Adoption-Continues-to-Soar
-With-New-Areas-of-Growth

M. Roughan and R. Chang (Eds.) PAM 2013, LNCS 7799, pp. 198–207, 2013.
© Springer-Verlag Berlin Heidelberg 2013

dynamics of home device usage and to sketch an effective approach to broadband characterization that runs behind the last meter. Previous studies have used UPnP data to better understand home networks, focusing on characterizing the number and type of devices present [5] or inferring network characteristics including bandwidth and packet loss rates [4]. However, these studies have typically been based on single snapshot tests. In contrast, our analysis is based on measurements collected *continuously* from over 13K Dasu [9] users and studies the implications of this on broadband characterization.

We use the collected data to show the complexity of home networks in terms of number and type of devices detected (Sec. 3). We classify the devices found based on their likelihood of generating cross-traffic on the access link and analyze the dynamics of devices usage both at a macro (when devices are on/off) and micro level (when turned-on devices exchange data). We demonstrate that while in many cases the number of devices in the network is high, only a few of them actively and regularly connect to the Internet, potentially interfering with network measurements (Sec. 4). Furthermore, we find a strong correlation between the number of UPnP-enabled devices in the home network and the presence of UPnP-enabled gateways and suggest how this can be leveraged for effective broadband characterization from the home (Sec. 5).

2 Data Collection and Dataset

We conduct our analysis using data collected with Dasu, a platform aimed at broadband characterization and network experimentation [9]. We use a combination of passive and limited active measurements gathered over a 6-month period between February 24, 2012 and August 23, 2012. This dataset includes traces of BitTorrent and overall home network activity collected by Dasu from 13,605 homes spanning 151 countries.[3]

Each Dasu client periodically (at 30s intervals) collected anonymized traffic traces from BitTorrent's activity, including the number of bytes uploaded and downloaded as well as the current transfer speed, the total number of bytes sent/received was also captured using `netstat`. Beyond this passively collected data, clients also scanned the local network in search of Internet gateway devices using UPnP, following an approach based on DiCioccio et al. [5, 6].

For each gateway device responding to UPnP discovery messages, Dasu pulled their device definition XML data and collected the following configuration parameters: (*a*) current state of NAT for this connection, (*b*) external IP address, (*c*) current connection type (Cable, DSL), (*d*) maximum upstream/downstream bit rate available, (*e*) device model name and version. At the same rate, clients also retrieved dynamic information from the gateway including (*f*) cumulative count of bytes and packets received and (*g*) sent, as well as (*h*) the connection status.

---

[3] The dataset is available to other researchers upon request.

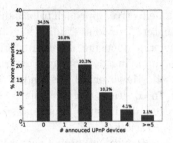

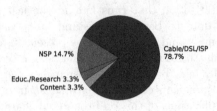

Fig. 1. UPnP-enabled devices in home networks

Fig. 2. Connection types for locations with ≥ 5 UPnP devices

A subset of clients periodically broadcasted UPnP discovery messages and recorded, for each responding device: (*a*) devices' uuid and UDN, (*b*) device type, (*c*) manufacturer, (*d*) model name and (*e*) model number.

Since Dasu is implemented as a BitTorrent client extension, there is a possible concern that our conclusions could be affected by some type of bias common to BitTorrent users, such as a particular set of countries, connection or user type. We argue that BitTorrent users can be seen as early adopters and thus, in a sense, worst-case scenarios in terms of the level of complexity in home networks. In the following section we show that the collected dataset comes almost entirely (93%) from clients in typical residential networks and spread over a diverse set of nearly 100 countries.

3 The Home Network – A Complex Environment

In this section, we examine the complexity of home networks in terms of number and diversity of connected devices. Given our end-goal of deriving an effective approach to crowdsourced broadband characterization from end-hosts, we present our findings in this context.

We first look at the number of networked devices found, which we estimate for a subset of $\approx$4.6K of our client's locations using UPnP discovery messages. Figure 1 shows the distribution of clients' locations by the number of UPnP announced devices found. While 34.5% of sampled locations have no UPnP devices announcing their presence, over 65% of them has at least 1 device, and over 16% have 3 or more devices.

We know of two possible sources of errors in this estimation. By relying on UPnP discovery messages, our measurement approach can miss devices that do not support UPnP. On the other hand, it is also possible that multiple UPnP services can be hosted by the same device, so that by counting each announced-service as a different "device" we might be over-counting the number of UPnP-enabled devices in the network. We plan to address both issues as part of our future work.

To evaluate potential biases in our dataset, we analyze the distribution of sampled locations based on type of network connection. Type of connection

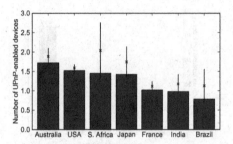

Fig. 3. Mean number of announced devices for homes across different countries

Table 1. Top ten countries with > 1% of homes

Country	%	Country	%
Italy	2.68%	Switzerland	4.62%
Austria	2.95%	Germany	4.91%
Portugal	2.95%	Great Britain	6.42%
Canada	4.17%	France	8.03%
Australia	4.35%	USA	25.61%

can indicate something other than a residential network (such as educational or enterprise) which could bias our results, especially for locations with large number of UPnP devices. We focus thus our attention on those locations in our dataset with five or more devices. There are 96 such locations distributed over 61 different autonomous systems (ASes). We map most of these ASes to their business type using the peeringDb[4] database and manually label those for which we could not find an entry. Figure 2 shows the percentage of location per business type (i.e. *Network Service Provider*, *Education/Research*, *Content*, and *Cable/DSL/ISP*). As the figure shows, the sampled dataset comes almost entirely from broadband providers (i.e., Cable/DSL/ISP and NSP). Interestingly, the average (and median) numbers of devices for each of these business types are very similar ranging between 5 and 6.5 devices.

We now analyze the adoption of UPnP across different countries by looking at the number of UPnP-enabled devices connected to the sampled locations in different countries. For this analysis we restrict our set to countries with more than 50 homes and select for each home the snapshot with the largest number of announced devices across all samples. In terms of potential biases due to the countries where our clients are located (such as an unexpected fraction of locations in a few high-income countries), we find that the sampled locations come from ≈100 different countries, with ten or more locations in nearly half of them. Table 1 shows the top ten countries in our dataset with more than 1% of sample locations.

Figure 3 plots the mean number of announced devices for homes across different countries. The bars show the lower bound on the 1-sided 95% confidence interval, the line shows the 2-sided 95% confidence interval, and the X plots the mean value across all samples. We used the Student's t-distribution to compute the confidence intervals (as the population's standard deviation is unknown). The figure shows that high(er) income countries tend to have a higher number of UPnP-enabled devices in the home network.

To study the diversity of home network devices we classify the found UPnP-enabled devices and study their prevalence. For common devices we use the

---

[4] https://www.peeringdb.com

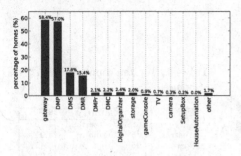

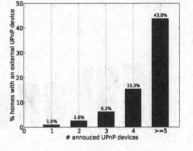

Fig. 4. The different UPnP devices and their popularity

Fig. 5. Percentage of homes with external devices based on number of UPnP-announced devices

DLNA's "Home Network Device" specification[5] to categorize them and divide the rest into functional classes such as *storage, cameras* or *television*. We labeled each device class as *Internal* and *External* based on their dominant network role – *externally-facing* devices that exchange traffic with the outside world (e.g. TV) or *internally-facing* devices that exchange traffic mostly within the home network (e.g. Storage). Given that the purpose of DLNA devices is to share media within the home (e.g. Digital Organizers, and Storage), each of these device classes are labeled as *Internal*. We classify the remaining classes of devices as external, including *Others*. We treat the *Gateway* category (e.g. DSL modems, WiFi routers) as its own class.

Table 2. Different classes of UPnP-enabled devices and their prevalence

Device Type	Connection	Perc.
Gateway	Gateway	36.7%
Digital Media Player (DMP)	Internal	34.7%
Digital Media Server (DMS)	Internal	10.2%
Digital Media Renderer (DMR)	Internal	9.5%
Digital Media Printer (DMPr)	Internal	1.2%
Digital Media Controller (DMC)	Internal	1.2%
Digital Organizer	Internal	1.3%
Storage	Internal	1.1%
Game Console	External	0.5%
TV	External	0.3%
Camera	External	0.2%
SetupBox	External	0.1%
House Automation	External	< 0.1%
Other	External	1.5%

Table 2 shows the different device classes identified in our traces. From the ≈6K devices seen across ≈3K peers the most popular device type are gateways (over 35%) followed by a large number of DLNA-compliant devices, including Digital Media Players (34.7%), Digital Media Servers (10.2%) and Digital Media

---

[5] http://dlna.org/dlna-for-industry/digital-living/
how-it-works/dlna-device-classes

Renderers (9.5%). Changing focus to the distribution of these devices in the sampled locations, Fig. 4 plots the popularity of each device type across the studied locations with at least one UPnP-enabled device in their network. We note the high popularity of Digital Media Players, Servers and Renderers.

In the context of broadband characterization, we are particularly interested in the distribution of *internally-* and *externally-facing* devices. Figure 5 shows the fraction of home networks within each group for which at least one externally-facing device was identified. Not surprisingly, as the number of announced devices in the network increases so does the probability that at least one of those devices be an external device.

3.1   Prevalence of UPnP-Enabled Gateways

UPnP-enabled gateways are helpful for managing resources and monitoring the state of the network. Although UPnP-enabled gateways are not always available, their presence is particularly important in home networks with high number of devices, where cross-traffic could interfere with characterization.

Figure 6a shows the availability of UPnP-enabled home gateways in our sample. The figure plots the fraction of homes, with a given number of UPnP devices, in which such a gateway is present. As the number of UPnP-enabled devices in the local network increases, so does the likelihood that the home gateway supports UPnP.

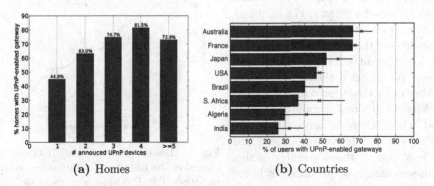

(a) Homes   (b) Countries

Fig. 6. Prevalence of UPnP-enabled gateways in sampled homes, clustered based on number of UPnP-enabled devices announced (6a) and (for a subset) by country (6b)

Last, we examine variations in the prevalence of UPnP-enabled gateways across countries. For this purpose, if a UPnP gateway is ever seen in a home network, we consider that sample as having a UPnP-enabled gateway. We group these homes by their ISP's country, giving us an estimate of each country's percentage of homes with UPnP-enabled gateways. We treat the data for each country as a sample from a binomial distribution and use the Wilson method to estimate confidence intervals.

Figure 6b plots the prevalence of UPnP-enabled gateways for several countries in our dataset. To account for different sample sizes across countries, we use the lower bound of the one-sided 95% confidence interval as a conservative estimate of the percentage of homes with UPnP in a given country. This means that there is a 95% chance that the actual percentage is *at least* the shown value. On the x axis, we show the proportion of samples having UPnP-enabled gateways and lines showing the extent of the two-sided 95% confidence intervals. In general, we find that more developed countries tend to have higher rates of UPnP-enabled gateways (as well as more complex home networks), hinting at a possible trend towards better environments for broadband characterization from end systems [2, 3].

4   Device Usage Dynamics

As the number of devices connected to the home network increases, so does the likelihood that the access link will be used by multiple devices simultaneously, potentially interfering with measurements looking to characterize the access link. In this section, we analyze the macro dynamics of network device usage – the frequency with which devices in the home network are active. We look at the micro dynamics – the rate and volume of traffic generated by these device – in the next section.

To study device dynamics, we leverage the fact that Dasu runs for long periods at a time (the median session time of a client is 178 minutes) and is thus able to take multiple snapshots of the active UPnP-enabled devices present on the network over time. We restrict the set of home networks to those for which we have at least 10 different sample snapshots and where there is more than one UPnP-enabled device announced and at least one of those is *outer-facing*. This set consists of 502 different home networks.

We rank all locations based on the percentage of measurement samples

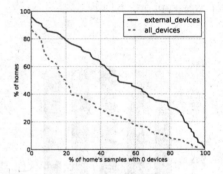

Fig. 7. Distribution of the fraction of homes vs the fraction of samples for which no other UPnP-device is present in the network

where we find no other device/no external device active other than the host machine. Figure 7 plots the CDF for both – any device active (labeled *all_devices*) and external device active (labeled *external_device*). As the figure shows, for nearly 85% of the locations, the host computer where our measurement client is running is the only active external device in the network for at least 10% of measurement samples. For the median location, about 20% of the measurement samples occur when the host computer is the only active device in the network and nearly 50% of them when there is no other external device present.

5   Broadband Characterization with UPnP Help

The following two sections sketch an approach for effective end-system-based broadband characterization that takes advantage of UPnP-enabled gateways and illustrate its use with specific traffic scenarios.

Two sources of concern for broadband characterization from end systems are the presence of cross-traffic from other applications in the hosting devices and from other devices in the home network. We use `netstat`, a network statistics tool available in most platforms, to capture the number of bytes sent and received from the host and compare it against the amount of traffic monitored by our client. This allows us to identify situations where significant amount of traffic is being generated by other applications in the host device.

The second type of cross traffic is the one generated by other devices in the network. To identify such cases we employ the technique described by DiCioccio et al. [4] where UPnP-enabled home gateways are periodically queried to measure traffic in the home network. In cases where the UPnP-supplied data is both available and accurate, the authors showed that this technique provides a rich source of information for inferring the presence of cross traffic in the home network. Thus, for homes with UPnP-enabled gateways, we periodically query for traffic counters across its WAN interface (the number of bytes and packets sent and received). When we identify times where the number of packets or bytes sent or received is high enough to affect our measurements we simply discard (if passive) or postpone (if active) our measurements. While gateway UPnP traffic counters are not always accurate [4], such instances can be easily identified and accounted for.

5.1   The Value of UPnP-Counters

We now present some concrete examples of how traffic counters from UPnP-enabled gateways allow us to disambiguate between different scenarios inside the home network. Using data collected from our Dasu users we show, for instance, how the presence of internal traffic can be identified and separated from traffic that uses the access link, both from the local host and other devices within the network.

No cross-traffic. As explained in Sec. 2, our traces contain the network activity as seen by each individual Dasu client at three different granularities. (*i*) Because Dasu runs as part of a network intensive application (BitTorrent) our traces contain traffic statistics about the number of bytes sent and received by the application alone. (*ii*) By using `netstat`, these traces also contain the overall traffic activity of the host, including the traffic generated simultaneously by all running applications at the time of collection. Finally, (*iii*) the client collects UPnP-supplied traffic data from the gateway which includes the number of bytes sent and received across the gateway's WAN interface.

Figure 8a shows the simplest scenario – where BitTorrent is solely responsible for the network traffic using the access link and the only source of traffic generated by the host. The figure plots the download activity of one Dasu client in a span of 15 hours in August 2012. Each of the three signals in the graph represents the number of downloaded bytes as reported by BitTorrent (blue), `netstat` (black), and the gateway counters (red), respectively, in intervals of 30 seconds increment. As the figure shows, all three signals overlap when Dasu' hosting application (BitTorrent) is the only network active application.

Local cross-traffic from other applications. Figure 8b plots the upload activity of another client, also for a span of 15 hours in June 2012. As before, the client is solely responsible for all the traffic present in the access link, but here BitTorrent is not the only network active application. As the figure shows, the signals that correspond to the local `netstat` counters (black) and the UPnP-counters at the gateway (red) overlap through the entire collection period (i.e., the client is the only device using the access link), but the signal that corresponds to BitTorrent traffic (blue) is much lower than that of `netstat` for the first five hours (300 minutes) of the session.

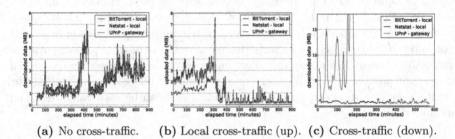

(a) No cross-traffic.   (b) Local cross-traffic (up).   (c) Cross-traffic (down).

Fig. 8. Traffic scenarios within the home network: (8a) download with no cross-traffic, (8b) local cross-traffic from other applications and (8c) download cross-traffic.

Cross-traffic from other devices. Figure 8c shows our last scenario, where there is significant cross-traffic from other devices in the home network. The figure plots download activity seen from a client over a span of five hours. In this case, there's no BitTorrent content being downloaded (the BitTorrent signal is a flat horizontal line around 0 bytes), but there is local traffic being generated by other applications in the host device (denoted by the black signal). However, for the first ≈ 200 minutes of the session, the traffic generated by the host devices represents only a small fraction of the total traffic present in the access link (red signal). The figure also shows the easily identifiable point at which the cross-traffic disappears.

6   Conclusion

The increasing complexity of home networks complicates device usability and home resource management and has implications for crowdsourced approaches to broadband characterization. In this work, we rely on UPnP measurements collected from over 13k end users study the complexity of home networks around the world. We presented a first look at the home network usage, both at a macro and micro level, and sketched an effective approach to broadband characterization that runs behind the last meter.

Acknowledgements. We would like to thank our shepherd, Aaditeshwar Seth, and the anonymous reviewers for their valuable feedback. We are always grateful to Paul Gardner for his assistance with Vuze and the users of our software for their invaluable data. This work was supported in part by the National Science Foundation through Awards CNS 1218287, CNS 0917233 and II 0855253 and by a generous Google Faculty Research Award.

References

1. Bischof, Z.S., Otto, J.S., Bustamante, F.E.: Up, down, and around the stack: ISP characterization from network intensive applications. In: Proc. of W-MUST (2012)
2. Bischof, Z.S., Otto, J.S., Sánchez, M.A., Rula, J.P., Choffnes, D.R., Bustamante, F.E.: Crowdsourcing ISP characterization to the network edge. In: Proc. of W-MUST (2011).
3. Canadi, I., Barford, P., Sommers, J.: Revisiting broadband performance. In: Proc. of IMC (2012)
4. DiCioccio, L., Teixeira, R., May, M., Kreibich, C.: Probe and Pray: Using UPnP for Home Network Measurements. In: Taft, N., Ricciato, F. (eds.) PAM 2012. LNCS, vol. 7192, pp. 96–105. Springer, Heidelberg (2012)
5. DiCioccio, L., Teixeira, R., Rosenberg, C.: Characterizing Home Networks With HomeNet Profiler. Tech. rep., Technicolor, 09, CP-PRL-2011-09-0001 (2011)
6. DiCioccio, L., Teixeira, R., Rosenberg, C.: Measuring and characterizing home networks. In: Proc. of ACM SIGMETRICS (2012)
7. Dischinger, M., Marcon, M., Guha, S., Gummadi, K.P., Mahajan, R., Saroiu, S.: Glasnost: enabling end users to detect traffic differentiation. In: Proc. of USENIX NSDI (2010)
8. Kreibich, C., Weaver, N., Nechaev, B., Paxson, V.: Netalyzr: illuminating the edge network. In: Proc. of IMC (2010)
9. Sánchez, M.A., Otto, J.S., Bischof, Z.S., Choffnes, D.R., Bustamante, F.E., Krishnamurthy, B., Willinger, W.: Dasu: Pushing experiments to the Internet's edge. In: Proc. of USENIX NSDI (2013)
10. Sundaresan, S., de Donato, W., Feamster, N., Teixeira, R., Crawford, S., Pescapè, A.: Broadband Internet performance: a view from the gateway. In: Proc. of ACM SIGCOMM (2011)
11. UPnP Forum. UPnP Device Management - Simplify the Administration of your Devices. Tech. rep., University of Zurich, Department of Informatics (April 2011)

Searching for Spam: Detecting Fraudulent Accounts via Web Search

Marcel Flores and Aleksandar Kuzmanovic

Northwestern University
marcel-flores@u.northwestern.edu, akuzma@cs.northwestern.edu

Abstract. Twitter users are harassed increasingly often by unsolicited messages that waste time and mislead users into clicking nefarious links. While increasingly powerful methods have been designed to detect spam, many depend on complex methods that require training and analyzing message content. While many of these systems are fast, implementing them in real time could present numerous challenges.

Previous work has shown that large portions of spam originate from fraudulent accounts. We therefore propose a system which uses web searches to determine if a given account is fraudulent. The system uses the web searches to measure the online presence of a user and labels accounts with insufficient web presence to likely be fraudulent. Using our system on a collection of actual Twitter messages, we are able to achieve a true positive rate over 74% and a false positive rate below 11%, a detection rate comparable to those achieved by more expensive methods.

Given its ability to operate before an account has produced a single tweet, we propose that our system could be used most effectively by combining it with slower more expensive machine learning methods as a first line of defense, alerting the system of fraudulent accounts before they have an opportunity to inject any spam into the ecosystem.

1 Introduction

As social networks have continued to grow in popularity, so has the problem of spam. The Twitter social network presents a fresh set of challenges to the task of spam detection [1]. The forced brevity of 140 characters has made many of the tools for detecting email spam unusable, as one can no longer depend on legitimate messages being longer [2]. The popularity of URL shorteners further obfuscates messages, making the already difficult task of URL blacklisting even more difficult [1,3]. Social links in the Twitter network are also non-symmetric, complicating detection methods that depend on implicit trust in the network.

While often very effective, current spam detection strategies generally depend on account features that manifest themselves after the account has been active, such as message format and content, as well as position in the social graph. This requirement creates a delay, and even detection methods which are able to train rapidly are unable to stop the first volleys of spam that are injected into the system.

M. Roughan and R. Chang (Eds.) PAM 2013, LNCS 7799, pp. 208–217, 2013.
© Springer-Verlag Berlin Heidelberg 2013

However, the explosive popularity of Online Social Networks (OSNs) has had another effect: legitimate users often participate in multiple, interlinking, online services. Users will often use the same, or similar names, for various accounts across the web. It is therefore not overly difficult to detect the presence of the same user on multiple sites. In contrast, spammers would have difficulty emulating such a dynamic web presence. While creating fraudulent accounts on a single website may often be possible: creating a batch of coordinated accounts across services would require defeating a varied array of spam detection systems. To make matters worse for spammers, if they create an online persona across services which is flagged as spam in one service, it could be easily linked to its other accounts, making it easier to identify as spam in the remaining services.

Therefore, in order to detect fraudulent accounts, one could measure exactly this distributed online presence. Not only is it extremely robust to any sort of escalation by spammers, it can also be performed quickly and cheaply using existing indices of web content. Through nothing more than a web search, one can measure how frequently an account name, or similar identifier, appears on the web, and therefore determine if the account is likely to be legitimate. Since this check requires only that the user have an account, it does not depend on social graph information or content posted by the user, and can therefore be performed before the user has taken any actions in a particular network.

In this paper, we present a spam detection method which uses the results of web searches for accounts to detect the presence of fraudulent accounts in the Twitter social network. First we consider an overview of the current state-of-the-art methods. We then discuss the in-depth design of our system, and some of the challenges of measuring web presence. Next, we describe an analysis on a collection of actual Twitter accounts, and show that we are able to detect 74.23% of the fraudulent accounts. Finally, we discuss how this procedure could be integrated into existing spam detection workflows and be extended beyond the Twitter network.

2 Background

One common form of spam on Twitter is a "mention," an interaction in which a user uses the name of another user in a message, generating a notification for the user whose name was used. Since the user who performs the mention need not be linked to the receiver in any way, these messages may be unsolicited. Often times these mentions will come in response to the use of a keyword for which lurking spam accounts are watching. For example, the use of the word "phone" in the tweet "I recovered my phone!" by user1, received the reply "@user1 Check out great phone cases! http://nefariouslink.info " from a spam bot with no network links to the original poster. While there are other ways for spam URLs and messages to be distributed through Twitter, this method is both the most disruptive and difficult to avoid.

Previous attempts to detect and measure spam in Twitter and other OSNs have considered a number of information sources. Analysis of the URLs posted by spammers has proven effective in certain cases, and has enabled the categorization of spam messages into larger spam campaigns [4,1]. Another method explicitly analyzes the content of posted URLs and aims to determine if the linked pages are spam [5]. While an important part of spam detection, these techniques often perform too slowly to prevent users from being exposed to spam links [1].

Others techniques use both the content of the messages, profile information, and information from the Twitter social graph to try and determine the nature of tweets [6,7,8,9,10,11]. Even more complex methods have further used similar types of information to determine which large scale campaign a spam tweet belongs [2,4,12,3]. These methods are often effective but rely on complex training and analysis.

We propose the use of near-instantly available outside information to make an initial call on the nature of an account. This system is designed to work alongside existing, more computationally heavy systems that may require significant training time. By combining such systems, one could avoid much of the initial exposure to spam, while still accurately eliminating fraudulent accounts.

Outside information from the web has been used previously in determining context of messages on Twitter [13], however it was largely used for the purposes of classification and analysis of actual tweet text, rather than the detection of spam. While past experiments have suggested that most spam originates from compromised accounts [1], more recent studies have found that this may not be the full picture and that fraudulent accounts contribute significantly to spam on Twitter [3]. Our method therefore focuses on the detection of fraudulent accounts created expressly for distributing spam, rather than a per-message analysis. This decision could allow for accounts to be checked even before they are able to send out any malicious messages, rather than attempting to classify messages as they are sent.

3   Design

Our system is designed to work on the account granularity, and therefore analyzes a given account and attempts to determine if the account is fraudulent. We attempt to perform this determination by measuring a user's web presence beyond Twitter.

There are a number of reasons why one might expect that such information could provide a reasonable means by which to differentiate spam from legitimate users. First, creators and users of spam accounts have incentive to create accounts which are not easily linked to other related entities on the web, as they could then easily be flagged as spam and blacklisted. Furthermore, the cost of creating matching fraudulent accounts on different services would be extremely high, as in general each of these services employ their own spam detection algorithms. Legitimate users, on the other hand, experience the exact opposite incentive: linking a Twitter account to other web services (from forum accounts to blogs to businesses), allows users to reach a larger audience.

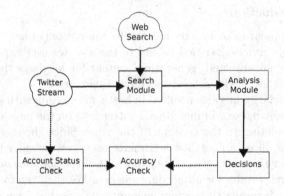

Fig. 1. Spam detection system overview. Dotted lines indicate portions used only in the experiment.

Our system detects these connections, or lack of connections, by use of a web search. Accounts which are easily connected to outside portions of the web are then likely to be legitimate users. We note that this system is not designed to operate on its own as the sole arbiter of spam. Instead, it is designed to act as an additional source of information in a comprehensive spam detection system.

3.1   Methods

We emphasize that our system needs no information from the Twitter network aside from the account's unique username and display name, and can therefore be used on an account as soon as it is created. For our verification in Sect. 4, we only consider accounts which have performed a mention which contains a URL. However this was largely for data collection convenience and is not indicative of any limitation in the system.

Figure 1 provides an overview of the system. First, we feed the input data from Twitter through the search module. This module performs a web search for the username (the unique account name that the user has selected) and the display name (the non-unique name the user has selected for display). We note that Twitter does not require a meaningful display name, and, as a result, many are filled with business names, titles, and nicknames.

After the searches are performed, the result sets are fed into the analysis module. We perform a number of noise-reduction techniques in order to eliminate results that are often returned for any search of a Twitter user, but do not meaningfully distinguish spam and non-spam accounts. We describe these techniques in more detail in Sect. 3.2. Finally, the analysis module examines the remaining results for the account. If there are no results for either the username and the display name, the account is marked as spam. Otherwise, the account is presumed to be legitimate.

3.2   Noise Reduction

The immense popularity of Twitter has resulted in not only many Twitter users, but a number of services designed to add to the Twitter user experience. Many of these services are directed, generating content for all users they find in the network, not just users who actively seek out their service.[1]

Twitter's popularity has also resulted in heavy integration with existing pages. For example, many pages will include a Twitter feed on the page displaying any messages seen relating to the content of the page. Since these services appear in the results for all users, not just legitimate users, we consider them noise. In order to eliminate this noise, we create a blacklist of the domains most commonly returned in search results for all account queries. We then remove the domains on the list from all results the system encounters. In Sect. 4.5 we show that this blacklist can be generated extremely quickly and that a relatively short list is effective in removing noise.

Additionally, it is common that the only result for both a username and a display name is in fact the same page. While this may be the result of a users web activity, we find that these are generally the result of pages which include a Twitter stream that displays both the user's username and display name. Therefore, when a user has a single result for each query which refer to the same page, we remove the matching URLs from both sets.

4   Experiment

4.1   Dataset

Our dataset was collected from the Twitter stream during March 2012. The initial collection contains over 20GB of data collected from a 1% random sample of all Twitter messages. Since this data contain both Twitter control messages and actual user posts, we filter through the set, collecting all messages which contain both a mention (as described in the previous section) and a URL. Since our method relies on the results of a search engine that biases towards results in English, we also eliminate all tweets that are labeled as non-English. Since our analysis is performed on the account level, we remove all messages from accounts that have been seen previously. This filtering leaves us with approximately 110, 000 messages, each corresponding to a unique account. While relatively small, this dataset contains a sufficient number of both fraudulent and legitimate accounts that we are able to observe the effectiveness of the system on real accounts. Both the dataset and the analysis tools have been made available.[2]

4.2   Ground Truth Dataset

In order to measure the performance of our system, we must establish a ground truth of which accounts are spam. Previous work [3] has made use of Twitter's

---

[1] For example: http://klout.com, http://favstar.fm, and
   http://twittercounter.com.
[2] http://eecs.northwestern.edu/~mef294/projects/twitter.html

current mechanisms by checking the accounts at least 2 weeks after the initial collection and recording which accounts have been suspended. We repeat this procedure here. Additionally, if any accounts were deleted between the initial observation and the later check, we remove them from our set, as there is no way to determine the reason or nature of their removal.

After the two week period, we find that 21.25% of accounts have been suspended, and are therefore, for our experiment, considered fraudulent accounts. It is, however, important to recognize that this includes (1) accounts that were originally legitimate, but were compromised, (2) abusive users who are not necessarily spammers, and (3) genuine fraudulent accounts. We explore the effects of these issues in the next section.

In order to understand the number of spam messages Twitter has missed, we perform a manual inspection of 200 randomly sampled un-suspended accounts. We only mark accounts which are clearly fraudulent as spam. In particular, accounts which started legitimate, but appear to have been compromised later are ignored. In our sample, we find that 36 of the accounts are fraudulent, suggesting that 18% of accounts which Twitter has not suspended are fraudulent. Therefore we suspect that at least some of our false positives will result from this error.

4.3   Performance Measurement

In order to properly measure the performance of our system, we compute its true-positive rate (TPR) and false-positive rate (FPR). The TPR is computed as:

$$TPR = \frac{\text{\# of true positives}}{\text{\# of true positives} + \text{\# of false negatives}}.$$

This tells us what fraction of the spam accounts we were able to correctly identify as spam. The FPR is computed as

$$FPR = \frac{\text{\# of false positives}}{\text{\# of false positives} + \text{\# of true negatives}},$$

which tells us the fraction of messages that we incorrectly marked as spam.

As we noted in Sect. 4.2, our FPR may be inflated by the the presence of spam accounts that have not yet been detected by Twitter. On the other hand our TPR may be underestimating our performance for a number of reasons. First, it is possible that accounts which have been suspended by Twitter are not actually spam, but were suspended for other violations. Second, our system only detects whether or not an account is fraudulent. If the account was once legitimate, i.e. became compromised later, a web search, and therefore our system, will likely indicate that the account is legitimate.

4.4   Results

When properly tuned, our system is able to achieve a TPR of 74.23% at a FPR of 10.67%. While the TPR is similar to those seen with other algorithms [6,2,8,10], direct comparison is difficult due to variations in methodologies. In particular, differences in determining a suitable "ground truth" (Twitter suspension information, URL blacklists, and manual verification) and granularity (account and message levels) mean each study is measuring a slightly different value.

In order to understand how greatly our system is affected by the errors in our ground truth set, we manually classify a random sample of 200 accounts which are marked as being false positives. Again, we only classify an account as fraudulent if it is clear that the account has never performed legitimate tweets. We find that 123, or 61%, of the accounts are clearly fraudulent. Of the remaining 77, 15 had begun tweeting spam URLs after long periods of inactivity. This long period of inactivity likely reduces the visible web presence of accounts, causing our system to flag them as spam. We also note that of the further remaining 62 accounts, an additional 18 are non-English, which we have already indicated our system is not designed to handle. If we consider only those accounts which the Twitter ground truth has missed that were clearly fraudulent, we see that our FPR is potentially as low as 4.5% and the TPR is potentially as high as 79.2%.

4.5 Blacklist Tuning

In order to eliminate much of the noise which results from performing a search for a Twitter name, we generate a blacklist of the 10 most frequently occurring domains for each type of query. These domains are then removed from all lists when performing the analysis. Since we know that they will always constitute noise, we always add the various forms of the Twitter domains to the blacklist ("Twitter.com", "Twitter.ru", etc.). Additionally, we perform a reverse DNS on any results which consist of an IP address. If the lookup resolves to an address in the Twitter network, we also add it to the blacklist.

Table 1. A summary of the performance when toggling noise reduction techniques

Method	TPR	FPR
No Blacklist	62.64	2.61
Blacklist on Display Name	67.30	5.53
Blacklist on Username	70.86	8.22
No Blacklist Exceptions	72.92	9.64
Full	74.23	10.67

In order to prevent the blacklist from eliminating valid sites, we manually select 10 sites which are excluded from blacklist generation. These particular sites were selected as they are among those that appear most often and clearly constitute a web presence. These sites consist of other OSNs (Facebook, LinkedIn, MySpace) and sites with OSN-like features (flickr.com, imdb.com, vimeo.com, soundcloud.com, yelp.com, lockerz.com).

We note that the differences in form of the username and display name result in vastly different results. The username results are often filled with Twitter and other social networking services designed to target account holders. Display name results, on the other hand, are often polluted with directory entries designed to find individuals. We therefore generate separate blacklists, one for each type of search. The performance of the system when each of these techniques is deactivated can be seen in Table 1.

When tuning such a parameter, a natural question that arises, is which length will result in the best performance? In order to test this, we perform the analysis with lengths from 0 to 50 with intervals of size 5, comparing the results. A blacklist length of 0 means that no domains were filtered out, 5 means that the top 5 most common results are removed from each analyzed query, and so on. The results of this analysis can be seen in Fig. 2. As expected, increasing the size of the list lowers the threshold for what is considered spam, increasing both TPR and FPR. However, we note that at 10 sites we achieve the best tradeoff.

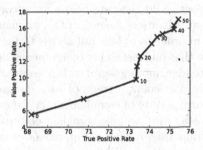

Fig. 2. A blacklist length of 10 seems to provide the best balance between TPR and FPR

Since we would like the list to be generated extremely rapidly so one can obtain meaningful results with minimal delay, we also consider how many sets of results must be considered to produce an effective blacklist. To test this, we generate the blacklist using a random sample of accounts of varying sizes. Figure 3 shows the mean TPR and FPR values for varying sizes of training sets, starting at 5, up to using the entire set of 100, 000. The figure also indicates the standard deviations for each size after 10 iterations. We see that even with a set as small as 500, the quality of the blacklist has already stabilized, as all sets larger than 500 result in similar performance. In an environment such as Twitter, a set of this size could be obtained nearly instantly.

5   Discussion

Given that our method can be applied prior to any activity on the part of the account holder, it would operate best if placed as a first line of defense in

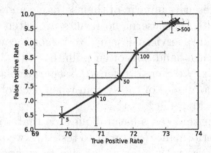

Fig. 3. Both the TPR and FPR stabilize with training sets as small as 500 accounts

spam detection. For example, one could perform our analysis at the time of account creation, using it to inform a more complex system of which accounts are likely fraudulent. Such a system could also be used to place accounts with insufficient web presence on a new-account probation, restricting the amount of spam that such an account could generate before more complex algorithms are able to detect it. Alternatively, users flagged in this manner could be subject to additional verifications in order to obtain full access to their accounts.

Furthermore, we note that our method is by no means limited to Twitter. As it depends only on a broader, more general web presence, the system could be used with any service. In particular, a trend of sites designed to perform single tasks that combine to form a suite of complementary web services (for example Twitter, Tumblr, and Instagram), will likely make web presence easier to detect. In addition, we expect that the growing popularity of cross-logins, which allow users to use the same account to log into multiple sites (popular with Google, Facebook and Twitter accounts), will further aid in detection.

While spammers may attempt to subvert such a system by creating accounts with usernames matching existing accounts on other services, they are still forced to perform a greater amount of manual work for every new account and are potentially limited to a smaller pool of possible accounts.

Additionally, there are natural improvements that could be made to this system to enhance its performance. Rather than considering only the presence of search results to determine if an account is spam, probabilistic methods could be applied. Certain sites that are found to be good indicators could be weighted more heavily, improving the quality of the analysis and further reducing noise.

6   Conclusion

We have presented a system which is able to measure the online presence of a Twitter user by using a web search. By classifying accounts with insufficient presence as spam, we are able to detect 74.67% of fraudulent accounts in a collection of actual Twitter data. Our system is straightforward to implement, and requires no additional content from the suspect accounts, and could therefore be placed as a check at the very beginning of account creation. Furthermore, it has the potential to work extremely well alongside heavier duty algorithms to maximize the amount of spam detected, and minimize spam exposure for legitimate users. Our methods are also generic, and are expected to work equally well beyond Twitter on a number of other web services.

References

1. Grier, C., Thomas, K., Paxson, V., Zhang, M.: @spam: the underground on 140 characters or less. In: Proceedings of the 17th ACM Conference on Computer and Communications Security, CCS 2010, pp. 27–37. ACM, New York (2010)
2. Gao, H., Chen, Y., Lee, K., Palsetia, D., Choudhary, A.: Towards Online Spam Filtering in Social Networks. In: Proceedings of the 19th Annual Network & Distributed System Security Symposium (February 2012)
3. Thomas, K., Grier, C., Song, D., Paxson, V.: Suspended accounts in retrospect: an analysis of twitter spam. In: Proceedings of the 2011 ACM SIGCOMM Conference on Internet Measurement Conference, IMC 2011, pp. 243–258. ACM, New York (2011)
4. Gao, H., Hu, J., Wilson, C., Li, Z., Chen, Y., Zhao, B.: Detecting and characterizing social spam campaigns. In: Proceedings of the 10th Annual Conference on Internet Measurement, IMC 2010, pp. 35–47. ACM, New York (2010)
5. Thomas, K., Grier, C., Ma, J., Vern, P., Song, D.: Design and evaluation of a real-time url spam filtering service. In: 2011 IEEE Symposium on Security and Privacy, SP, pp. 447–462 (May 2011)
6. Benevenuto, F., Magno, G., Rodrigues, T., Almeida, V.: Detecting Spammers on Twitter. In: Collaboration, Electronic Messaging, Anti-Abuse and Spam Conference, CEAS (July 2010)
7. Lee, K., Caverlee, J., Webb, S.: Uncovering social spammers: social honeypots + machine learning. In: Proceedings of the 33rd International ACM SIGIR Conference on Research and Development in Information Retrieval, SIGIR 2010, pp. 435–442. ACM, New York (2010)
8. Song, J., Lee, S., Kim, J.: Spam Filtering in Twitter Using Sender-Receiver Relationship. In: Sommer, R., Balzarotti, D., Maier, G. (eds.) RAID 2011. LNCS, vol. 6961, pp. 301–317. Springer, Heidelberg (2011)
9. Wang, A.: Don't follow me: Spam detection in twitter. In: Proceedings of the 2010 International Conference on Security and Cryptography, SECRYPT, pp. 1–10 (July 2010)
10. Yang, C., Harkreader, R.C., Gu, G.: Die Free or Live Hard? Empirical Evaluation and New Design for Fighting Evolving Twitter Spammers. In: Sommer, R., Balzarotti, D., Maier, G. (eds.) RAID 2011. LNCS, vol. 6961, pp. 318–337. Springer, Heidelberg (2011)
11. Yardi, C., Romero, D., Schoenebeck, G., Boyd, D.: Detecting spam in a twitter network. First Monday 15(1) (2010)
12. Stringhini, G., Kruegel, C., Vigna, G.: Detecting spammers on social networks. In: Proceedings of the 26th Annual Computer Security Applications Conference, ACSAC 2010, pp. 1–9. ACM, New York (2010)
13. Yerva, S., Miklós, Z., Aberer, K.: What have fruits to do with technology?: the case of orange, blackberry and apple. In: Proceedings of the International Conference on Web Intelligence, Mining and Semantics, WIMS 2011, pp. 48:1–48:10. ACM, New York (2011)

Characterization of Blacklists
and Tainted Network Traffic

Jing Zhang[1], Ari Chivukula[1], Michael Bailey[1],
Manish Karir[2], and Mingyan Liu[1]

[1] University of Michigan
Ann Arbor, Michigan, USA
[2] Cyber Security Division, Department of Homeland Security,
Washington DC, USA

Abstract. Threats to the security and availability of the network have
contributed to the use of Real-time Blackhole Lists (RBLs) as an at-
tractive method for implementing dynamic filtering and blocking. While
RBLs have received considerable study, little is known about the impact
of these lists in practice. In this paper, we use nine different RBLs from
three different categories to perform the evaluation of RBL tainted traffic
at a large regional Internet Service Provider.

1   Introduction

A variety of threats, ranging from misconfiguration and mismanagement to
botnets, worms, SPAM, and denial of service attacks, threaten the security and
availability of today's Internet. In response, network operators have sought to
adopt security policies that minimize their impact. Real-time Blackhole Lists
(RBLs) are a form of coarse-grained, reputation-based, dynamic policy enforce-
ment in which real-time feeds of malicious hosts are sent to networks so that
connections to these hosts may be rejected.

Existing work has studied how these lists can be created [14], evaluated
their effectiveness [17,23], and explored the properties of the networks that
make them effective [24,26,22]. In this paper, rather than focusing solely on
the lists themselves, we analyze the *impact* of nine popular blacklists on Merit
Network [8], a large Internet Service Provider (ISP). By examining what network
traffic is tainted by these blacklists, we gain better insight into the utility of these
mechanisms and the nature of malicious traffic on our networks. Our findings
include:

- While stable in size, the RBL populations are highly dynamic, growing
  between 150% to 500% over a one week period.
- Classes of RBLs show significant internal entry overlap, but little similarity
  is seen between classes.
- RBL classes share affinity for specific geographic distributions (e.g., RIPE
  and APNIC dominate SPAM; ARIN and RIPE dominate phishing and malware).

M. Roughan and R. Chang (Eds.) PAM 2013, LNCS 7799, pp. 218–228, 2013.

- A surprisingly high proportion, up to 17%, of the collected network traffic is tainted by at least one of the nine RBLs.
- Our network only saw traffic to a small portion, between 3% and 51%, of IP addresses within the blacklists.
- Heavy hitters account for a significant number of the tainted bytes to the network.

2   Data Collection Methodology

Netflow. We collected records of the traffic at Merit to understand the impact of RBLs. Merit is a large regional ISP, which provides high-performance computer networking and related services to educational, government, healthcare, and nonprofitable organizations located primarily in Michigan. This network experiences a load which varies daily from a low of four Gbps to a high of eight Gbps. Though Merit has over 100 customers, the top five make up more than half of the total traffic, and HTTP accounts for more than half of the traffic volume.

Our traffic data was collected via NetFlow [7] with a sampling ratio of 1:1. The traffic was monitored at all peering edges of the network for a period of one week, starting on June 20, 2012. During this period, we experienced several collection failures, each lasting from one to seven hours, for a total of 17 hours lost. The collected NetFlow represents 118.4TB of traffic with 5.7 billion flows and 175 billion packets.

Table 1. Reputation data sources and types

RBL Type	RBL Name
SPAM	CBL[3], BRBL[2], SpamCop[16], WPBL[13], UCEPROTECT[12]
Phishing/Malware	SURBL[11], PhishTank[9], hpHosts[5]
Active attack/probing behavior	Dshield[4]

Reputation Black Lists. RBLs are lists managed by various organizations that contain IP addresses believed to have originated some malicious behavior. RBLs generally focus on some specific suspicious behavior. Merit collects nine commonly used RBLs on a daily basis, which are typically fetched directly from the publisher via rsync or wget. These lists can be categorized into three types: SPAM, Phishing/Malware, or Active (and prolific) malicious activity (as shown in Table 1).

3   Properties of Reputation Blacklists

Timing. We examined the stability of each RBL with respect to *the daily number of unique IP addresses*. As shown in Figure 1a, the size varied across RBLs with BRBL being much larger than the others, but the size of RBLs

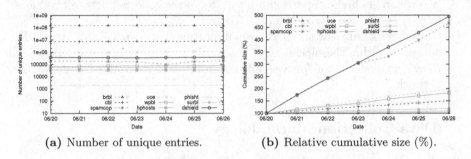

(a) Number of unique entries.   (b) Relative cumulative size (%).

Fig. 1. Daily size and cumulative size of RBLs

was consistent over the week measured. In order to understand the churn of unique IP addresses, we calculated the relative size of cumulative entries in Figure 1b. Spamcop and Dshield updated their entries aggressively, with nearly 500% turnover in one week, while BRBL, hpHosts, and SURBL were relatively static during the week, with less than 110% turnover.

Table 2. Geographic distribution of IPs for each RBL (%)

	Spam					Phishing/Malware			Active
	BRBL	CBL	Spamcop	UCE	WPBL	hpHosts	Phisht	SURBL	Dshield
AFRINIC	3.02	7.70	5.89	6.37	4.19	0.20	0.58	0.04	2.19
APNIC	25.20	47.14	51.94	48.45	51.27	8.45	11.56	5.58	36.19
ARIN	6.23	1.05	2.53	1.84	6.17	53.32	43.93	54.70	13.54
LACNIC	17.11	16.19	12.15	15.89	10.59	1.66	5.32	1.44	8.54
RIPENCC	48.44	27.93	27.50	27.44	27.77	36.37	38.6	38.24	39.53

Regional Characteristics. We mapped the blacklisted IP addresses to their registries by using the IP to ASN mapping services provided by Team Cymru [21]. Table 2 demonstrates that a given class of RBLs has consistent geographical properties. SPAM- and Active-attack-related lists have more entries in the APNIC (Asia/Pacific) and RIPENCC (Europe) regions, while ARIN (North America) and RIPENCC are the most common regions in Phishing/Malware RBLs. Even though monitoring position and listing methodologies are different for each RBL, they share consistent views of the regional distribution of malicious activity.

Overlap. We examined to what extent RBLs overlap with other; we expected that overlap within the same category of RBLs would be significantly larger than the overlap among different classes. Our results in Table 3 match our expectation: BRBL and CBL, the two largest SPAM blacklists, cover about 90% of other SPAM-related lists, and the intersection within hpHosts, PhishTank, and SURBL is also large. Meanwhile, the overlaps between different classes are trivial.

Table 3. The average % (of column) overlap between RBLs (row, column)

	Spam					Phishing/Malware			Active
	BRBL	CBL	Spamcop	UCE	WPBL	hpHosts	Phisht	SURBL	Dshield
BRBL	100.0	75.2	94.6	89.8	93.8	5.3	10.0	30.7	33.2
CBL	3.9	100.0	98.1	91.7	70.2	0.5	0.7	6.2	9.3
Spamcop	0.1	2.3	100.0	12.6	21.5	0.1	0.1	0.8	1.2
UCE	0.6	12.1	69.4	100.0	50.6	0.3	1.5	1.2	4.8
WPBL	0.0	0.7	8.8	3.7	100.0	0.0	0.2	0.9	0.4
hpHosts	0.0	0.0	0.0	0.0	0.0	100.0	33.7	7.3	0.0
Phisht	0.0	0.0	0.0	0.0	0.0	1.8	100.0	1.7	0.0
SURBL	0.0	0.0	0.3	0.1	0.7	11.8	52.8	100.0	0.1
Dshield	0.1	0.4	2.4	1.8	2.2	0.4	0.7	0.3	100.0

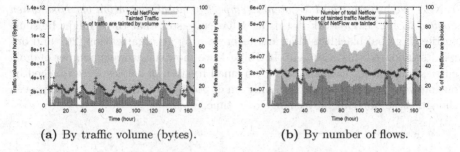

(a) By traffic volume (bytes).   (b) By number of flows.

Fig. 2. Total traffic v.s. tainted traffic

4   Impact of Reputation

One of the key questions we considered in our study was, *what fraction of traffic carries a negative reputation?* In our study, if one or both of the collected NetFlow's source and destination IPs are listed by any RBL, the NetFlow is considered tainted. While we expected that perhaps as much as 10% of network traffic might be potentially malicious [6], we found that tainted traffic accounted for an average of 16.9% of the total traffic volume over the week. When measured by flow count, the proportion is even larger, with 39.9% of the flows being tainted (Figure 2b).

This is, of course, a very liberal approach to tainted traffic analysis: tainting all the traffic of a host by all the entries in all the blacklists. We conjecture that there may be several sources of overestimation: (i) some RBLs are intended to taint only one kind of application traffic instead of an entire host, (ii) the RBLs may contain false positives, (iii) some IP addresses are shared via mechanisms like Network Address Translation (NAT) and therefore some traffic was tainted due to "guilt by association". To provide a tighter lower bound, we applied the RBLs solely to the type of traffic they pertain to (e.g., SPAM blacklists are only applied to SMTP traffic). The results show that 10.5% of total traffic was tainted by this more conservative approach. Further we observed that several list entries were for well known services on the network, such as Amazon Web Services, Facebook, and CDNs. Although previous work has shown that the cloud services have been used for malicious activities [25], we nevertheless conservatively whitelisted these service providers. As a result, the volume of tainted traffic was reduced to 7.5% of total traffic. Therefore, we believe a realistic value for tainted traffic is likely to lie within the range of 7.5% to 17% of the total traffic by bytes.

Table 4. RBL entries touched by our network traffic

	Spam					Phishing/Malware			Active
	BRBL	CBL	Spamcop	UCE	WPBL	hpHosts	Phisht	SURBL	Dshield
Touched entries	4,142,394	577,583	44,383	134,024	16,288	13,989	983	14,043	105,918
% of the list	2.8%	7.7%	29.3%	39.5%	51.2%	25.2%	24.4%	13.9%	22.1%

Next, we investigated *the potential impact of global reputation blacklists when applied locally*. Prior work in this area has suggested that there might be some entries in global blacklists that are never used by an organization [26], and our results validated this argument. In Table 4, we show the average number of daily entries touched for each RBL. Only a small fraction of entries were touched by our network traffic. For our ISP, only small portions of RBLs are relevant, even though these portions may change over time.

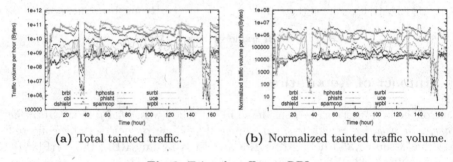

(a) Total tainted traffic.   (b) Normalized tainted traffic volume.

Fig. 3. Tainted traffic per RBL

Finally, we examined *whether lists, or a class of lists, have the greatest impact on our traffic*. The traffic volume tainted by each RBL is shown in Figure 3a. There is a clear variance among tainted traffic volumes, ranging from more than ten GB per hour by Dshield, BRBL, and hpHosts to about tens of MB per hour by Spamcop, PhishTank, and SURBL.

Since the number of entries in each RBL differs, we then normalized the volume of tainted traffic per hour (i.e. $\frac{Volume\ of\ tainted\ traffic\ by\ the\ RBL}{Number\ of\ touched\ entries\ in\ the\ RBL}$) in Figure 3b. Interestingly, we show that each entry in hpHosts, PhishTank, and Dshield taints about one MB of traffic per hour on average; but, the contribution of entries in the SPAM-related RBLs is about two orders of magnitude lower.

5   Impact of Heavy Hitting IPs

In this section, we investigate whether any specific IPs are responsible for skewing the traffic distribution. Toward this end, we divided the traffic into two categories:

those IP addresses belonging to Merit (internal IP addresses) and those not belonging to Merit (external IP addresses).

5.1   External IP Addresses

Of the 11,016,520 unique external IP addresses in the tainted traffic, 99.5% of them had less than 10 MB of tainted traffic each (as shown in Figure 4a). However, the top contributors had more than 100 GB of tainted traffic associated with each of them (Figure 4b). In fact, the top 50 external IP addresses contributed about 40% of total tainted traffic. In the following analysis, we try to define *what these hitters are* and *what comprises their traffic.*

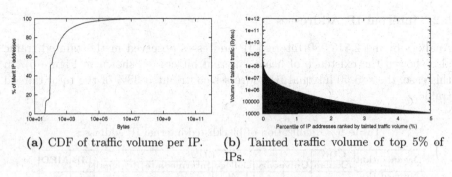

(a) CDF of traffic volume per IP.   (b) Tainted traffic volume of top 5% of IPs.

Fig. 4. Tainted traffic to/from external IP addresses

External Heavy Hitters. Among the top 50 external IP addresses, 39 are listed in at least one RBL. It is surprising to see that 27 of those are hosting service providers or caching servers, including Amazon Web Services hosts (10 IPs listed on hpHosts, Phisht, SURBL, or Dshield), Facebook content distribution network (CDN) servers (six IPs listed on Dshield), Pandora media servers (six IPs listed on Dshield), EDGECAST Network hosts (three IPs listed on hpHosts, Phisht, or Dshield), and BOXNET servers (two IPs listed on BRBL). These hosts are owned by popular service providers and their traffic is dominated by HTTP, as shown in Table 5.

Table 5. Distribution over TCP/UDP ports for top blacklisted external IPs

Ports	80	443	1935	1256	1509	1046	1077	1224	1121	1065
% of volume	60.65	35.31	3.48	1.12	1.06	1.03	0.71	0.66	0.64	0.58

External Heavy Hitters Not on a RBL. The remaining 11 external IP addresses in the top 50 are IP addresses communicating with tainted Merit hosts, who send large volumes of traffic. Of these external destinations, 10 are owned by Netflix and one belongs to Yahoo!. 99% of the tainted traffic within these 11 IP addresses was over HTTP.

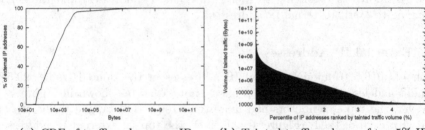

(a) CDF of traffic volume per IP.   (b) Tainted traffic volume of top 5% IPs.

Fig. 5. Tainted traffic to/from internal IP addresses

5.2   Internal IP Addresses

Analysis of the 2,515,080 Internal IP addresses observed in the tainted traffic also showed the existence of heavy internal hitters (as shown in Figure 5). In this case, the top 50 internal IP addresses contributed 38% of the total tainted traffic.

Table 6. Organization of blacklisted internal IP addresses

Organization	CDN	EDU				LIB	MED
	Akamai	University	College	Intermediate	Regional		
Num of IPs	9	6	4	1	1	4	4
Total	9	12				4	4

Internal Heavy Hitters. Our results showed that there are only 35 IP addresses in the top 50 listed by the RBLs, and of the 35 IP addresses, only 29 were resolvable to host names. When categorized by owner (as shown in Table 6), we see that nine of these blacklisted IP addresses are owned by Akamai [1], a provider of content delivery network (CDN) and shared hosting services; others are hosts registered by educational institutions, library network providers, and medical centers. Interestingly, there are two Virtual Private Network servers, a mail server, and one web site server from educational institutions.

Internal Heavy Hitters Not on a RBL. We found the top three internal heavy hitters, which accounted for 12% of total tainted traffic, are not themselves on an RBL, and 81.6% of their traffic is HTTPS traffic. Furthermore, by inspecting the blacklisted hosts they communicated with, we noticed that about 80% of their tainted traffic is to/from Amazon Web Services (AWS) IP addresses that are blacklisted.

5.3   Heavy Hitter Distribution

Heavy hitters constitute a significant portion of tainted traffic. *How are these heavy hitters distributed across RBLs?*

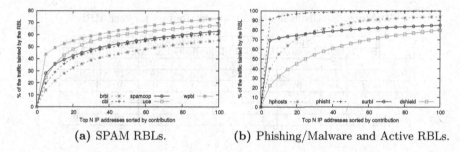

(a) SPAM RBLs.	(b) Phishing/Malware and Active RBLs.

Fig. 6. Cumulative contributions of the top N entries per RBL

To understand the heavy hitters in each RBL, we defined the contribution of $entry_i$ in RBL_j as $\frac{V_{entry_i}}{V_{RBL_j}}$, where V_{entry_i} is the volume of traffic tainted by $entry_i$ and V_{RBL_j} is the total volume of traffic tainted by RBL_j. We then sorted the entries by their contribution in decreasing order for each RBL, and then derived the cumulative contribution of the top N entries (Figure 6). The top entries contribute greatly to the RBLs — the traffic tainted by the top 50 entries accounted for more than half of the total tainted traffic of each. In the case of Phishing/Malware RBLs, the top 50 entries contributed even more (80%) of the tainted traffic (as shown in Figure 6b). Once again, we find a small amount of entries dominating the tainted traffic.

Table 7. Top TCP/UDP ports for traffic tainted by top 50 contributors per RBL

(a) SPAM.

BRBL	CBL	Spamcop	UCE	WPBL
80 (59.62)	80 (34.01)	80 (26.394)	3389 (27.03)	25 (26.71)
443 (22.30)	443 (21.26)	44794 (16.51)	53 (14.16)	80 (23.30)
1935 (2.22)	4444 (11.78)	4025 (16.16)	25345 (12.80)	44794 (19.30)
3578 (1.26)	25 (6.67)	25 (11.14)	80 (12.54)	4025 (18.89)
17391 (1.21)	3389 (4.96)	37101 (7.60)	25 (8.18)	1080 (9.73)

(b) Phishing/Malware.   **(c) Active.**

hpHosts	Phisht	SURBL	Dshield
80 (84.99)	80 (65.05)	443 (52.30)	80 (60.75)
443 (15.00)	443 (32.32)	80 (44.84)	443 (32.26)
1256 (1.95)	49729 (2.96)	25 (1.85)	1935 (3.55)
1121 (1.10)	42652 (1.80)	1288 (1.51)	993 (1.68)
1605 (1.01)	52951 (1.48)	1032 (1.12)	1509 (1.16)

Next, we characterized the tainted traffic by the top 50 contributors for each RBL (Table 7). Though not dominating, SMTP (port 25) traffic occupied a large proportion of the tainted traffic for each of the SPAM related blacklists (except BRBL). This matches our expectation that SPAM related IP addresses send email more aggressively than other hosts. In the other RBLs, we see a higher proportion of Web related traffic. This could be associated with either Phishing and Malware distribution activities or other, potentially benign, traffic from these hosts.

Table 8. Service hosts in top 50 contributors for each RBL

	Spam					Phishing/Malware			Active
	BRBL	CBL	Spamcop	UCE	WPBL	hpHosts	Phisht	SURBL	Dshield
CDN	2	0	0	0	0	35	3	1	26
HOST	0	0	1	0	2	3	19	17	12
TOR	1	11	0	0	0	1	0	0	0
MAIL	0	0	0	3	5	0	1	0	1
VPN	3	0	0	1	0	0	0	0	0
Total	10	13	1	4	7	39	23	18	39

Finally, we looked at the network and domain information of the top contributers (shown in Table 8). We found that 60 of these IP addresses are used by content delivery networks and 51 of them are owned by hosting companies. Four VPN servers are listed in BRBL and UCEProtector, while 11 Tor nodes are shown in CBL. Nine different mail servers (some of them belonging to LinkedIn) are also in the top 50 entries of some RBLs. These entries form a sizable fraction of network traffic. This holds especially true for the Phishing/Malware and Active RBLs, whose tainted traffic included from 29% to 68% of these heavy hitters.

6   Related Work

While there is a great deal of prior work on generating reputation blacklists [15,20,24,26], there are fewer studies which characterize the RBLs themselves or their impact. Prior work has focused on understanding the makeup of RBLs from geographical and topological perspectives [18], as well as the correlation between seven popular RBLs [17]. Other related work has discussed the effectiveness and limitation of blacklists. For example, researchers have shown that blacklists often contain numerous false positives [23] and outdated entries [22]. The study in [19] finds that very few sections of IP space account for the majority of SPAM (meaning that a small, stable RBL would be highly effective at blocking SPAM), and that a small, but increasing, amount of SPAM comes from random and short-lived hijacked prefixes (whose entries in RBLs would quickly become outdated). In [26], the author argues that entries in common blacklists which are never used within an organization should be removed to reduce costs. Our work is complementary to these efforts, as our focus in this study is to gain a better understanding of the key properties of RBLs themselves and their impact on traffic from the perspective of an ISP.

7   Conclusion

In this study, we characterized nine RBLs and their impacts on traffic from a live operational network. The RBLs are highly dynamic, growing between 150% to 500% over a period of one week. While there is a significant overlap among RBLs within the same class, little similarity is seen between classes. We demonstrated that up to 17% of the traffic could be considered tainted, as it flowed to or from addresses on various RBLs. We also show the relative contribution of different entries on a RBL towards this tainted traffic, and we show that heavy hitters dominate both tainted traffic as well as RBLs.

Reputation information is a useful resource for organizations to evaluate and design their security policies. Our work indicates that an organizational view of network threats can differ from the global perspective. Therefore, it is important to consider local information in conjunction with global RBLs in order to build more accurate reputation information.

Dataset Availability. Our RBLs are provided under a licensing agreement that requires they not be publicized or redistributed. NetFlow data represents potentially private information about users of our network. Therefore, we are unable to provide the raw data of RBLs and traffic NetFlow used in our work. An anonymized version of NetFlow traffic annotated with the RBL matches is available through the PREDICT project [10].

Acknowledgments. This work was supported in part by the Department of Homeland Security (DHS) under contract number D08PC75388; the National Science Foundation (NSF) under contract numbers CNS 1111699, CNS 091639, CNS 08311174, and CNS 0751116; and the Department of the Navy under contract number N000.14-09-1-1042.

References

1. Akamai, http://www.akamai.com/
2. Barracuda reputation blocklist, http://www.barracudacentral.org/
3. Cbl: Composite blocking list, http://cbl.abuseat.org/
4. Dshield, http://www.dshield.org/
5. HpHosts for your pretection, http://hosts-file.net/
6. Internet has a garbage problem, researcher says, http://www.pcworld.com/article/144006/article.html
7. Introduction to Cisco IOS NetFlow, http://www.cisco.com/en/US/products/ps6601/prod_white_papers_list.html
8. Merit Network INC, http://www.merit.edu/
9. Phishtank, http://www.phishtank.com/
10. PREDICT: Protected Repository for the Defense of Infrastructure Against Cyber Threats, https://www.predict.org/
11. SURBL: URL Reputation Data, http://www.surbl.org/
12. Uceprotector network, http://www.uceprotect.net/
13. Wpbl: Weighted private block list, http://www.wpbl.info/
14. Antonakakis, M., Perdisci, R., Dagon, D., Lee, W., Feamster, N.: Building a Dynamic Reputation System for DNS. In: USENIX Security Symposium, pp. 273–290 (2010)
15. Esquivel, H., Akella, A., Mori, T.: On the effectiveness of IP reputation for spam filtering. In: Proceedings of COMSNETS 2010, pp. 1–10 (2010)
16. Cisco Systems Inc. SpamCop Blocking List (SCBL), http://www.spamcop.net/

17. Jung, J., Sit, E.: An empirical study of spam traffic and the use of DNS black lists. In: Proceedings of the 4th ACM SIGCOMM Conference on Internet Measurement, pp. 370–375. ACM, New York (2004)
18. Creyts, K., Karir, M., Mentley, N.: Towards network reputation - analyzing the makeup of rbls (June 2011)
19. Ramachandran, A., Feamster, N.: Understanding the network-level behavior of spammers. In: Proceedings of SIGCOMM 2006, pp. 291–302 (2006)
20. Ramachandran, A., Feamster, N., Vempala, S.: Filtering spam with behavioral blacklisting. In: Proceedings of the 14th ACM Conference on Computer and Communications Security (2007)
21. Team Cymru Community Services. IP to ASN Mapping, http://www.team-cymru.org/Services/ip-to-asn.html
22. Shue, C.A., Kalafut, A.J., Gupta, M.: Abnormally malicious autonomous systems and their internet connectivity. IEEE/ACM Trans. Netw. 20(1), 220–230 (2012)
23. Sinha, S., Bailey, M., Jahanian, F.: Shades of Grey: On the Effectiveness of Reputation-based "blacklists". In: Proceedings of MALWARE 2008, pp. 57–64 (October 2008)
24. Venkataraman, S., Sen, S., Spatscheck, O., Haffner, P., Song, D.: Exploiting network structure for proactive spam mitigation. In: Proceedings of 16th USENIX Security Symposium on USENIX Security Symposium. USENIX Association (2007)
25. Xie, Y., Yu, F., Achan, K., Gillum, E., Goldszmidt, M., Wobber, T.: How dynamic are ip addresses? In: Proceedings of SIGCOMM 2007, pp. 301–312 (2007)
26. Zhang, J., Porras, P., Ullrich, J.: Highly Predictive Blacklisting. In: Usenix Security (August 2008)

Characterizing Large-Scale Routing Anomalies: A Case Study of the China Telecom Incident

Rahul Hiran[1], Niklas Carlsson[1], and Phillipa Gill[2],*

[1] Linköping University, Sweden
[2] Citizen Lab, Munk School of Global Affairs
University of Toronto, Canada

Abstract. China Telecom's hijack of approximately 50,000 IP prefixes in April 2010 highlights the potential for traffic interception on the Internet. Indeed, the sensitive nature of the hijacked prefixes, including US government agencies, garnered a great deal of attention and highlights the importance of being able to characterize such incidents after they occur. We use the China Telecom incident as a case study, to understand (1) what can be learned about large-scale routing anomalies using public data sets, and (2) what types of data should be collected to diagnose routing anomalies in the future. We develop a methodology for inferring which prefixes may be impacted by traffic interception using only control-plane data and validate our technique using data-plane traces. The key findings of our study of the China Telecom incident are: (1) The geographic distribution of announced prefixes is similar to the global distribution with a tendency towards prefixes registered in the Asia-Pacific region, (2) there is little evidence for subprefix hijacking which supports the hypothesis that this incident was likely a leak of existing routes, and (3) by preferring customer routes, providers inadvertently enabled interception of their customer's traffic.

Keywords: Measurement, Routing, Security, Border Gateway Protocol.

1 Introduction

On April 8, 2010, AS 23724, an autonomous system (AS) owned by China Telecom, announced approximately 50,000 prefixes registered to other ASes. These prefixes included IPs registered to the US Department of Defense [8], which caught the attention of the US-China Economic and Security Review Commission [5]. Unlike previous routing misconfigurations [6,18], China Telecom's network had the capacity to support the additional traffic attracted [4]. Further, there is ample data-plane evidence suggesting that during the incident, Internet traffic was reaching its correct destination. This unique situation is what led some to suggest this was an attempt to intercept Internet traffic.

While the China Telecom incident has garnered attention in blogs [4,8], news outlets [17], and government reports [5], there has been no academic attempt

---

* Data sets available at: http://www.ida.liu.se/~nikca/papers/pam13.html

M. Roughan and R. Chang (Eds.) PAM 2013, LNCS 7799, pp. 229–238, 2013.

to understand this incident. This dearth of understanding is especially apparent when considering the many questions that remain unanswered about this incident. These include (1) understanding properties of the hijacked prefixes, (2) quantifying the impact of the event in terms of subprefix hijacking, and (3) explaining how interception was possible. We tackle these questions using publicly available control- and data-plane measurements and highlight what types of data would be useful to better understand routing anomalies in the future. We emphasize that while we are able to characterize the incident and show evidence supporting the hypothesis that this incident appears to be an accident, there is currently no way to distinguish between "fat finger" incidents and those that have malicious intent based on empirical data alone.

1.1   Insecurity of the Internet's Routing System

Routing security incidents have happened repeatedly over the past 15 years [6,13, 18]. These incidents involve an AS originating an IP prefix without permission of the autonomous system (AS) to which the prefix is allocated: *hijacking*. Usually when hijacks happen, the misconfigured network either does not have sufficient capacity to handle the traffic [18] or does not have an alternate path to the destination [6]. In these cases, the impact of the incident is immediately felt as a service outage or interruption of connectivity.

More troubling, are cases of traffic *interception*, where traffic is able to flow through the hijacking AS and on to the intended destination. Without continuous monitoring of network delays or AS paths [3], incidents such as these are difficult to detect, thus creating opportunity for the hijacker to monitor or alter intercepted traffic. Traffic interception was demonstrated in 2008 [21] and more recently occurred during the China Telecom incident [8].

Since the China Telecom incident involved interception, measuring its impact is extremely difficult without extensive monitoring infrastructure. We define criteria that allow us to infer potential interceptions using only control-plane data [19]. We use data-plane measurements [15] to validate our criteria and characterize the AS topologies that allowed for inadvertent interception.

1.2   Key Insights

The Geographic Distribution of Announced Prefixes Does Not Support Targeted Hijacking. The distribution of announced prefixes is similar to the geographic distribution of all globally routable prefixes with a tendency towards prefixes in the Asia-Pacific region.

The Prefixes Announced Match Existing Routable Prefixes. We observe that > 99% of the announced prefixes match those existing at the Routeviews monitors. This supports the conclusion that the announced prefixes were a subset of AS 23724's routing table.

Providers Inadvertently Aided in the Interception of Their Customers' Traffic. Many networks that routed traffic from China Telecom to the correct destination did so because the destination was reachable via a customer path which was preferred over the path through China Telecom (a peer).

2   Related Work

While China Telecom incident occurred in April 2010, it received little attention [4, 17] until November 2010 when the US-China Economic and Security Review Commission published their report to congress [5] which included a description of the event. After the release of the report, the incident received attention in news articles and was investigated by some technically-oriented blogs [8,14].

BGPMon, an organization that provides monitoring and analysis of BGP data, performed the first investigation of the China Telecom incident [4]. Using control-plane measurements of BGP messages, they were able to identify anomalous updates as those where the path terminated in "4134 23724 23724." They also study the geographic distribution of the hijacked prefixes and find that the majority of hijacked prefixes belong to organizations in the US and China.

Using both control- and data-plane data, Renesys confirmed the geographic distribution of hijacked prefixes observed by BGPMon [8]. Using traceroute, Renesys was also able to show that network traffic was able to pass into China Telecom's network and back out to the intended destination. Further analysis was performed by Arbor Networks [14] which focused on understanding how much traffic was diverted into China Telecom using traffic flows observed through ASes participating in the ATLAS project [2]. They do not observe a significant increase in traffic entering AS 4134 on the day of the incident.

In contrast to the blog entries, our focus is on analyzing the incident using only publicly available data to understand what can be learned using today's public data and what types of data should be collected in the future.

3   Methodology

To characterize the events that took place on April 8, 2010, we use a combination of publicly available control- and data-plane measurements [7,15,19].

3.1   Control-Plane Measurements

BGP Updates. We use Routeviews monitors as a source of BGP updates from around the time of the attack. We consider updates with the path attribute ending in "4134 23724 23724" as belonging to the incident [4].[1] Table 1 summarizes the updates and prefixes matching this signature from the Routeviews monitors.

Topology Data. We use the Cyclops AS-graph from April 8, 2010 [7] to infer the set of neighbors of China Telecom and their associated business relationships. Knowing the neighbors of China Telecom is particularly important when identifying ASes that potentially forwarded traffic in (and out of) China Telecom during the incident.

---

[1] All but 36 prefixes originated by AS 23724 match this signature.

Table 1. Summary of control-plane updates matching the attack signature

Monitor (Location)	Number of Updates	Number of Unique Prefixes
LINX (London, England)	60,221	11,413
DIXIE (Tokyo, Japan)	80,175	15,773
ISC PAIX (Palo Alto, CA)	123,723	35,957
Route-views2 (Eugene, OR)	216,196	29,998
Route-views4 (Eugene, OR)	49,290	18,624
Equinix (Ashburn, VA)	44,793	13,250
BGPMon list	-	37,213
Total	574,398	43,357

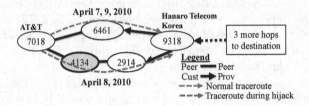

Fig. 1. Interception observed in the traceroute from planet2.pittsburgh.intel-research.net to 125.246.217.1 (DACOM-PUBNETPLUS, KR)

3.2   Data-Plane Measurements

We use data-plane measurements from the iPlane project [15] and extract tracer-outes transiting China Telecom's network on April 8, 2010. We first map each IP in the traceroute to the AS originating the closest covering prefix at the time of the traceroute. If we observe a traceroute AS-path that does not contain China Telecom (AS 4134 or AS 23724) on April 7 or 9, that *does* contain these networks on April 8, we conclude that this traceroute was impacted by the incident. Fur-ther, if we observe a traceroute that was impacted, and the final AS in the path is not AS 4134 or 23724, we conclude that this traceroute was intercepted. Fig-ure 1 shows a traceroute where interception was observed. This traceroute only transits AS 4134 (China Telecom) on April 8 and is able to reach the destination through AS 2914 (NTT) who provides transit for AS 9318 (Hanaro Telecom). In total, we observed 1,575 traceroutes transiting China Telecom on April 8. Of these, 1,124 were impacted by the routing incident and 479 were potentially intercepted, with 357 of these receiving a successful response from the target.

3.3   Limitations

We face limitations in existing data sets as we reuse them for the unintended task of analyzing a large-scale routing anomaly.

Inaccuracies in the AS-Graph. AS-graphs suffer from inaccuracies infer-ring AS-relationships (*e.g.,* because of Internet eXchange Points (IXPs) [1]) and

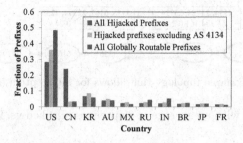

Fig. 2. Top 10 countries impacted by the China Telecom incident

poor visibility into peering links [20]. These inaccuracies impact our analysis of interception which uses the AS-graph to infer China Telecom's existing path to a destination. We discuss this limitation in more detail in Section 5.3.

Inaccurate IP to AS Mappings. We note that our mapping of IP addresses to ASes may be impacted by IXPs or sibling ASes managed by the same institution [16]. Since our primary concern is paths that enter China Telecom *only* on April 8 the impact of siblings (*e.g.*, per-province ASes managed by China Telecom) should be mitigated. This is because paths to China Telecom's siblings would normally transit China Telecom's backbone AS 4134.

4   Impact of the China Telecom Hijack

We now consider the impact of the China Telecom incident in terms of the prefixes that were announced.

4.1   What is the Geographic Distribution of the Announced Prefixes?

Figure 2 shows a breakdown of the prefixes that were hijacked by country, with and without excluding prefixes owned by AS 4134. We see the bulk of prefixes are registered to organizations in US and China, followed by Korea, Australia and Mexico, which is consistent with observations made by BGPMon [4].

Was it Random?. Figure 2 also plots the geographic distribution of all routable prefixes on the Internet. Here we can see a disproportionate number of Chinese prefixes (especially belonging to AS 4134) being hijacked. Additionally, when comparing hijacked prefixes to the global distribution of prefixes there appears to be little evidence for attack. Indeed, the US shows fewer prefixes being hijacked than would be expected based on the global distribution, while countries in the Asia-Pacific region (e.g., China, Korea, Australia) have more hijacked prefixes.

4.2   Which Organizations Were Most Impacted?

Organizations with the most prefixes announced tend to be peers of AS 4134 (table in full version [12]). Indeed, direct neighbors of China Telecom are most

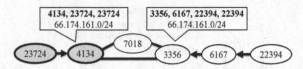

Fig. 3. Example topology that allows for interception of traffic

adversely impacted with an average of 85 prefixes hijacked vs. 9 prefixes hijacked for all impacted ASes.

Critical Networks Were Subject to Hijacking. While they do not make the top five list, China Telecom announced some critical US prefixes. Government agencies such as Department of Defense, United States Patent and Trademark Office, and Department of Transport were impacted.

4.3   Were Any of the Announcements Subprefix Hijacks?

We now consider the length of the prefixes announced by China Telecom relative to existing routes. If the event was simply a leak of routes contained in the routing table, it should be the case that China Telecom's prefixes will be the same length as existing routes. Additionally, prefix length can shed light on the impact of the incident since more specific prefixes are preferred. For each of the six Routeviews monitors (Section 3.1), we use the RIB tables as seen on April 7 to derive the existing prefix lengths. Route aggregation means that the prefix length observed varies between the vantage points.

Subprefix Hijacking Was Extremely Rare. In total, 21% (9,082) of the prefixes were longer than existing prefixes at all six monitors. However, 95% (8,614) of these prefixes belong to China Telecom (table in full version [?]). Most of the observed subprefix hijacking is due to poor visibility of Chinese networks (AS 4134, 4538, and 38283) at the monitors. Excluding these networks, we observe $< 1\%$ (86) prefixes being subprefix hijacked. The lack of subprefix hijacks supports the conclusion that the incident was caused by a routing table leak.

5   The Mechanics of Interception

The fact that traffic was able to flow through China Telecom's network and onto the destination is highly unusual. We now discuss how interception may occur accidentally, based on routing policies employed by networks.

5.1   How Was Interception Possible?

Two key decisions, when combined with inconsistent state within China Telecom's network, allow for traffic to be intercepted. These properties have also been discussed in related work [3]. We illustrate them with an example from the China Telecom incident (Figure 3). This figure was derived using a combination of BGP updates [19] and a traceroute observed during the incident [8].

Table 2. Neighbors that routed the most prefixes to China Telecom

Rank	# of Prefixes	% of Prefixes	Organization
1	32,599	75%	Australian Acad./Res. Net. (AARNet) (AS 7575)
2	19,171	44%	Hurricane Electric (AS 6939)
3	14,101	33%	NTT (AS 2914)
4	14,025	32%	National LambdaRail (AS 11164)
5	13,970	32%	Deutsche Telekom (AS 3320)

Decision 1: AT&T (AS 7018) Chooses to Route to China Telecom. In Figure 3, AT&T (AS 7018) has two available paths to the prefix. However, since the path advertised by China Telecom (AS 4134) is shorter, AT&T (AS 7018) chooses to route to China Telecom.

Decision 2: Level 3 (AS 3356) Chooses *not* to Route to China Telecom. In order for traffic to leave China Telecom's network and flow on to the intended destination, China Telecom requires a neighbor that *does not* choose the path it advertises. In the example above, this occurs when Level 3 (AS 3356) chooses to route through its customer Verizon (AS 6167) instead of through its peer China Telecom (AS 4134). Thus, China Telecom can send traffic towards Level 3 and have it arrive at the intended destination.

We next characterize what causes these decisions to be made using a combination of control- and data-plane data.

5.2   How Many ISPs Chose to Route to China Telecom?

We first consider how many ISPs made **Decision 1**. We observe 44 ASes routing traffic towards China Telecom, with each AS selecting the path through China Telecom for an average of 4,342 prefixes. The distribution of prefixes each AS routes to China Telecom is highly skewed, with some ASes being significantly more impacted than others. The top five ASes are summarized in Table 2, which highlights the role of geography in the hijack, with networks operating in Europe and Asia-Pacific regions being most impacted. Academic networks (AARNet and National LambdaRail) are also heavily impacted.

5.3   Which Prefixes Were Intercepted?

We develop a methodology to locate potentially intercepted prefixes using control-plane data. Control-plane data has the advantage that it may be passively collected in a scalable manner. We validate our technique and further analyze the interception that occurred using data-plane measurements [15] (Section 5.4).

We use the following methodology to locate potentially intercepted prefixes using only control-plane data. First, for each hijacked prefix, we use the Cyclops AS-graph (discussed in Section 3.1) and a standard model of routing policies [9], to compute China Telecom's best path to the prefix.[2] Next, for each of these

---

[2] Since China Telecom does not normally transit traffic for the hijacked prefixes, we were unable to extract the paths normally used by China Telecom from Routeviews.

paths, we check whether the next-hop on China Telecom's best path to the destination was observed routing to China Telecom for the given prefix.

We observe 68% of the hijacked prefixes potentially being intercepted; however, 85% of these prefixes are observed being intercepted via AS 9304, a customer of China Telecom, which may be an artifact of poor visibility of the Routeviews monitors. Excluding paths through AS 9304, we observe a total of 10% (4,430) prefixes potentially being intercepted. We observe direct neighbors of China Telecom such as AT&T, Sprint and Level 3 being most impacted by interception as they still provided China Telecom (a peer) with paths to their prefixes. Additionally, some Department of Defense prefixes may have been intercepted as China Telecom potentially still had a path through Verizon.

Limitations. Our method is limited in two key ways. First, we may not observe all announcements made by China Telecom's neighbors (*i.e.*, we may incorrectly infer that they are *not* routing to China Telecom because their announcement is not seen by the Routeviews monitors). Second, we do not know which neighbor China Telecom would normally use to transit traffic for a given prefix and thus we have to infer it based on topology measurements and a routing policy model.

Validation. Without ground-truth data it is difficult to quantify the inaccuracies of our methodology as we may both over- or under-estimate the potential for interception. We use the data-plane measurements described in Section 3.2 to validate our methodology. Of the 479 traceroutes that were intercepted, 319 (66%) were observed in prefixes detected as intercepted using our criteria. This inaccuracy stems from a lack of control-plane data which leads to the limitations mentioned above. With more complete data, our method could better identify potential interceptions.

5.4   Why Neighboring ASes Did *Not* Route to China Telecom?

We use data-plane measurements to understand why neighboring ASes chose not to route to China Telecom (**Decision 2**). In Figures 3 and 1, the reason that the neighboring AS does not route to China Telecom is because they have a path through a customer to the destination. However, this is only one reason an AS would choose not to route to China Telecom. We consider the cases of interception observed in the iPlane data and determine why the neighboring AS did not route to China Telecom using the Gao-Rexford routing policy model [9].

Table 3 summarizes the reasons neighbors of China Telecom did not route to China Telecom. Here we only consider the 357 traceroutes where interception was observed and a response was received from the target. The majority of neighbors handling intercepted traffic did not choose the China Telecom route because it was longer than their existing route for the prefix in question.

Providers Inadvertently Allowed Interception of Customer Traffic. A significant fraction (39%) of neighbor ASes do not route to China Telecom because they have a path to the destination via a customer, such as AS 3356 in Figure 3. These providers inadvertently aided in the interception of their cus-

Table 3. Why networks chose not to route to China Telecom

Reason	# of traceroutes	% of traceroutes
Had a customer path	139	39%
Had a shorter path	193	54%
Had an equally good path	18	5%
Other	7	2%

tomer's traffic by forwarding China Telecom's traffic to the destination. While providers cannot control the traffic sent to them by neighboring ASes, it may be beneficial to monitor the neighbors sending traffic towards their customers for anomalies, so that customers may be alerted to potential interception events.

We observe seven traceroutes where it is unclear why the China Telecom path was not chosen. These traceroutes involved a provider to China Telecom who chose to route towards other customers likely the result of traffic engineering or static routes being used for the customer ASes.

6   Discussion

Using publicly available data sources we have characterized the China Telecom incident that occurred in April 2010. Our study sheds light on properties of the prefixes announced, and supports the conclusion that the incident was a leak of random prefixes in the routing table, but does not rule out malicious intent.

On Diagnosing Routing Incidents. Our work highlights the challenge of understanding large-scale routing incidents from a purely technical perspective. While empirical analysis can provide evidence to support or refute hypotheses about root cause, it cannot prove the intent behind the incident. However, empirical analysis can provide a starting point for discussions about the incident.

On the Available Data. When the results of analysis can lead to real-world reaction it is important that the data used for analysis is as complete as possible and robustness/limitation of results are clearly stated. These two properties can be achieved by increasing the number of BGP monitors [11] and performing careful analysis of robustness and limitations [10].

Acknowledgments. The authors thank the reviewers and our shepherd Olaf Maennel for constructive suggestions, that helped improve the paper. This work benefited from discussions with Jennifer Rexford and Andy Ogielski. We thank Monia Ghobadi, Sharon Goldberg, and Jennifer Rexford for comments on drafts. We thank Doug Madory for assistance with the analysis in Section 3.2.

References

1. Ager, B., Chatzis, N., Feldmann, A., Sarrar, N., Uhlig, S., Willinger, W.: Anatomy of a large European IXP. In: Proc. of ACM SIGCOMM (2012)
2. ATLAS - Arbor Networks (2012), http://atlas.arbor.net

3. Ballani, H., Francis, P., Zhang, X.: A study of prefix hijacking and interception in the Internet. In: Proc. of ACM SIGCOMM (2007)
4. BGPMon. China telecom hijack (2010), http://bgpmon.net/blog/?p=282
5. Blumenthal, D., Brookes, P., Cleveland, R., Fiedler, J., Mulloy, P., Reinsch, W., Shea, D., Videnieks, P., Wessel, M., Wortzel, L.: Report to Congress of the US-China Economic and Security Review Commission (2010), http://www.uscc.gov/annual_report/2010/annual_report_full_10.pdf
6. Brown, M.: Renesys blog: Pakistan hijacks YouTube, http://www.renesys.com/blog/2008/02/pakistan_hijacks_youtube_1.shtml
7. Chi, Y., Oliveira, R., Zhang, L.: Cyclops: The Internet AS-level observatory. ACM SIGCOMM Computer Communication Review (2008)
8. Cowie, J.: Renesys blog: China's 18-minute mystery, http://www.renesys.com/blog/2010/11/chinas-18-minute-mystery.shtml
9. Gao, L., Rexford, J.: Stable Internet routing without global coordination. Transactions on Networking (2001)
10. Gill, P., Schapira, M., Goldberg, S.: Modeling on quicksand: Dealing with the scarcity of ground truth in interdomain routing data. ACM SIGCOMM Computer Communication Review (2012)
11. Gregori, E., Improta, A., Lenzini, L., Rossi, L., Sani, L.: On the incompleteness of the AS-level graph: a novel methodology for BGP route collector placement. In: ACM Internet Measurement Conference (2012)
12. R. Hiran, N. Carlsson, and P. Gill. Characterizing large-scale routing anomalies: A case study of the China Telecom incident (2012), http://www.ida.liu.se/~nikca/papers/pam13.html
13. Khare, V., Ju, Q., Zhang, B.: Concurrent prefix hijacks: Occurrence and impacts. In: ACM Internet Measurement Conference (2012)
14. Labovitz, C.: China hijacks 15% of Internet traffic (2010), http://ddos.arbornetworks.com/2010/11/china-hijacks-15-of-internet-traffic/
15. Madhyastha, H., Isdal, T., Piatek, M., Dixon, C., Anderson, T., Krishnamurthy, A., Venkataramani, A.: iPlane: An information plane for distributed services. In: Proc. of OSDI (2006)
16. Mao, Z., Rexford, J., Wang, J., Katz, R.H.: Towards an accurate AS-level traceroute tool. In: Proc. of ACM SIGCOMM (2003)
17. McMillan, R.: A Chinese ISP momentarily hijacks the Internet (2010), http://www.nytimes.com/external/idg/2010/04/08/08idg-a-chinese-isp-momentarily-hijacks-the-internet-33717.html
18. Misel, S.: Wow, AS7007! Merit NANOG Archive (1997), http://www.merit.edu/mail.archives/nanog/1997-04/msg00340.html
19. U. of Oregon. Route views project, http://www.routeviews.org/
20. Oliveira, R., Pei, D., Willinger, W., Zhang, B., Zhang, L.: Quantifying the completeness of the observed internet AS-level structure. UCLA Computer Science Department - Techical Report TR-080026-2008 (September 2008)
21. Pilosov, A., Kapela, T.: Stealing the Internet: An Internet-scale man in the middle attack. Presentation at DefCon 16 (2008), http://www.defcon.org/images/defcon-16/dc16-presentations/defcon-16-pilosov-kapela.pdf

PhishLive: A View of Phishing and Malware Attacks from an Edge Router

Lianjie Cao[1], Thibaut Probst[2], and Ramana Kompella[1]

[1] Purdue University, West Lafayette, Indiana, USA
[2] INSA de Toulouse, Toulouse, France

Abstract. Malicious website attacks including phishing, malware, and drive-by downloads have become a huge security threat to today's Internet. Various studies have been focused on approaches to prevent users from being attacked by malicious websites. However, there exist few studies that focus on the prevalence and temporal characteristics of such attack traffic. In this paper, we developed the PhishLive system to study the behavior of malicious website attacks on users and hosts of the campus network of a large University by monitoring the HTTP connections for malicious accesses. During our experiment of one month, we analyzed over 1 billion URLs. Our analysis reveals several interesting findings.

1 Introduction

The rapid development of the Web over the recent few decades has made the Internet a hotbed for a wide range of criminal activities. Numerous types of attacks are hidden behind HTTP connections such as phishing, cross-site scripting, malware, and botnet attacks. The most commonly used solution to defend against such attacks is using blacklisting. A blacklist-based defense system contains a set of URLs that are identified as malicious or suspicious, either through a human-vetting process or other mechanisms. When users are trying to connect to such web pages, the browsers (e.g., Mozilla Firefox) pop out warnings or block the web page directly.

Literature is ripe with several studies that focused on documenting the effectiveness of such browser-based techniques in thwarting malicious website attacks. For example, [1] discusses the effectiveness of passive and active warnings to users. Similarly, [2] studies the efficacy of different anti-phishing tools. There also exist several papers (e.g., [3–6]) proposing different solutions for improving the attack detection and defense using enhanced blacklisting techniques. Other content-based techniques have also been proposed (e.g., [7–12]) for detecting malicious webpages, while [13] combines both URL-based and content-based methods.

Unfortunately, to date, there exists only a few studies that focus on understanding temporal characteristics of phishing or malware accesses in an edge network such as a campus or an enterprise network comprising of a few tens of thousand users. [14] analyzes the malware serving infrastructure of drive-by downloads. The paper indicates that the malware serving networks are composed of tree-like structure and malware are delivered through several redirections. However, they focus only on drive-by downloads ignoring other malicious attacks delivered through webpages and the data set

M. Roughan and R. Chang (Eds.) PAM 2013, LNCS 7799, pp. 239–249, 2013.
© Springer-Verlag Berlin Heidelberg 2013

they use is collected generally not from a specific network. [15] assesses the issue of overt manifestation of three networks consisting of around 30,000 users in total. They study risky behaviors of users including security threats such as scanning, spamming, payload signature and botnet rendezvous. Nevertheless, they only study the probability of triggering malicious activities of users without concluding any possible pattern of vulnerable users and attackers.

There are however several questions that remain to be answered such as whether malicious sites are accessed just once, or a few times, or are repeatedly accessed over time across users, and whether other malicious website attacks are hidden between HTTP redirects. We believe a study to answer such questions is important for many reasons: First, it can help in sizing the resource requirements of security middleboxes that can be deployed to defend against them. Second, the temporal characteristics can help generate insights to inform future defense mechanisms. Thus, in this paper, we focus on studying and understanding the characteristics of HTTP accesses to malicious sites as seen by the edge router of a large campus network comprising upwards of 50,000 users.

A key requirement for our study is the ability to identify whether a given access is to a malicious site or not, for which, we leverage existing blacklisting tools such as the Google Safe Browsing (GSB) [16] back-end server. Thus, we do not invent any new mechanism for detecting malicious website attacks, but instead leverage existing techniques to continuously monitor the network for malicious accesses to phishing/malware websites. Our system called PhishLive monitors the HTTP traffic going through the gateway of the campus network and captures malicious URLs detected by GSB database in HTTP requests and redirect responses in real-time. It analyzes the statistical characteristics of dataset off-line including distribution of attacks over time, geolocation distribution of attacking IP addresses, attacking hostnames clustering and malicious redirect chain analysis.

We deployed PhishLive on a large university gateway for a month during which we captured and analyzed about 1 billion URLs. Some of our key findings are:

- The fraction of URLs that are identified as belonging to phishing/malware sites is relatively small; in our data, it is less than 0.038% of all URLs.
- There is a relatively higher number of malicious URLs accessed during 11:00pm-5:00am compared to other times.
- Most domains (almost 50%) typically existed for less than 1 day. However, close to 10% of the domains were accessed for more than 15 days.
- An extremely small fraction of all HTTP redirection chains contain malicious URLs; in our data less than 2,000 URLs are part of redirection chains out of about 50 million redirection chains.

In the rest of the paper, we give an overview of the PhishLive system in Section 2 and outline our observations from a real deployment of PhishLive in Section 3.

2   System Overview

In this section, we describe the design of the PhishLive system that can continuously monitor HTTP traffic for phishing and malware attacks. We envision PhishLive to be

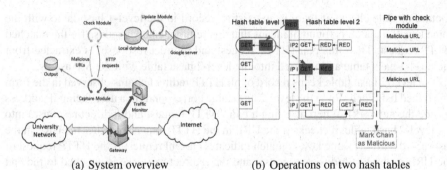

(a) System overview   (b) Operations on two hash tables

Fig. 1. Internals of PhishLive system

deployed at an edge router, such as a campus gateway router, that can track the various HTTP requests issued by a bunch of users. We assume the presence of a standard high-speed capture device (e.g., Endace 10Gbps monitoring card) to collect each packet that is going through the gateway router to the outside world, from which we filter the HTTP traffic (port 80) and extract the URLs from HTTP GET requests. For verifying whether a given URL is malicious or not, each URL is cross checked with the Google Safe Browsing (GSB) database. Since HTTP redirects are also used to hide malicious content [17–19] in some attacks, the system is designed to also track and analyze HTTP redirect chains. We assume access to both directions of traffic for detecting redirects.

The PhishLive system comprises three components: a capture module, a check module and an update module (shown in Figure 1(a)); we describe their details next.

Capture Module. The capture module of our system utilizes the libpcap library to capture the HTTP requests from the hosts inside the university and redirect responses from the external hosts. As of now, the PhishLive system supports up to 5 types of HTTP requests: GET, HEAD, POST, PUT, DELETE, and 4 types of HTTP redirect responses: 301, 302, 303, 307. As of now, we only investigate URL redirection based on HTTP status code; other redirections based on HTML meta tag, Javascript and flash are not studied in this paper. The capture module also uses network libraries and regular expressions to extract the URLs from HTTP requests or the URLs in redirect responses, as well as source/destination IP addresses (SIP, DIP) and source/destination port numbers (SP, DP). For privacy reasons, all user-facing IP addresses are hashed.

As part of our analysis, we also wish to study the role of HTTP redirects in phishing and malware attacks. A redirect chain is a sequence of URLs starting from the first requested URL, ending with the last requested URL, that can be represented as follows: $GET(URL_1) \rightarrow REDIRECT(URL_2) ... \rightarrow GET(URL_n)$, where n is the number of different requested URLs in the chain. Although it appears simple, it is little tricky to track HTTP redirects in an online fashion, since it requires correlation across TCP connections (since each GET request is to a different hostname). Thus, in PhishLive, we build two hash tables (denoted as level-1 hash table and level-2 hash table in Figure 1(b)) to store HTTP redirects. The level-1 hash table holds related information of a HTTP request with a key of $\langle SIP, SP, DIP, DP \rangle$. Because the request and the redirect packet belong to the same TCP session, when a HTTP redirect response is captured, the capture module checks if there is an existing record in the level-1 hash table with the same key. If a match is found, it means that this redirect is the response for the matched HTTP request. Then this pair (HTTP request and redirect response) is extracted from the level-1 hash table and inserted into the level-2 hash table with the SIP as key.

The level-2 hash table keeps record of all HTTP redirect chains observed in the form of a linked list. Each slot in the level-2 hash table corresponds to a user-facing IP address (inside the network). When inserting a pair (HTTP request and redirect response) into the level-2 hash table, it checks if the URL in the HTTP request matches the URL in the last record with the same key. A match indicates current request is the HTTP request of the URL in the last redirect response, and the redirect response is attached to the end of the chain. If not, a new redirect chain is built. Therefore, one slot in the level-2 hash table may contain more than one redirect chain. For instance, slot n in the level-2 hash table includes redirect chains a→b→c and x→y. When a new pair of HTTP redirect y→z is inserted, it searches for the first linked list entry a→b→c and finds that y does not match c. Then it moves to next linked list x→y, which matches and the new pair y→z is attached to the linked list resulting in x→y→z. The operations of the two hash tables are illustrated in Figure 1(b) .

The capture module also receives feedback which includes the malicious URL and the victim's IP address from the check module. It then compares the malicious URL with the records in the level-2 hash table. If the URL is found in the level-2 hash table, it will be marked as malicious and dumped to a file later on. The implementation of the capture module constitutes of three threads: one thread captures and extracts URLs from HTTP packets and feeds them to check module; another thread receives results from check module and scans level-2 hash table for a match; the last thread refreshes the two hash tables periodically to prevent them from growing too large and a fatal memory drop-off in a long-term running.

Check and Update Modules. The check module is based on the PHP API of Google Safe Browsing database provided by Google. The check module maintains a local database of malicious URLs verified by GSB server and interacts with the capture module through two pipes. Once it receives a URL from capture module, it checks the URL against the local database and feeds it back to capture module through a pipe if the URL is identified as malicious. The check module also produces general real-time statistics. The update module updates the local database with Google server periodically to ensure that the content of the local database is up-to-date.

3   Experimental Results

We deployed the PhishLive system at the edge router of a large university network over 30 days from March 19, 2012 to April 18, 2012, during which the system analyzed more than 1 billion HTTP requests (as summarized in Table 1). Out of the 1 billion URLs, only about 0.0381% of all HTTP requests were classified as requests to malicious webpages. We also observed about 50 million HTTP redirect chains out of which only about 7,500 included malicious URLs.

Since PhishLive system only captures the HTTP requests from hosts and HTTP redirect responses from servers and verifies the URL by querying GSB database, the

Table 1. Statistics of the Experiment

Experiment Duration	Mar 19, 2012 - Apr 18, 2012
# of HTTP Requests	1,038,803,540
# of Redirect Chains	50,204,174
# of Malicious URLs	395,671 (0.0381%)
# of Unique Malicious URLs	118,615
# of Malicious Redirect Chains	7,497 (0.0149%)

accuracy of the dataset drawn from the experiment largely depends on the accuracy of the GSB database. Previous studies [13] indicate that GSB database has a false negative rate of less than 10%; so we believe that the results are more or less accurate. However, to improve the credibility of the results, we manually verified a small sample of the URLs. Since there could be many malicious URLs with same hostname, we used a stratified sampling approach to select samples across different hostnames while ensuring larger number of samples for high volume hostnames. Specifically, we assign a weight $\frac{\#\ of\ malicious\ webpages\ of\ the\ cluster}{\#\ of\ malicious\ webpages\ overall}$ for each cluster of URLs that share the same hostname. We chose 400 samples to manually check whether they are malicious. Since total number of hostnames is less than this number, we picked at least one URL from each cluster. The remaining were sampled using the weight calculated above. We found that 93 webpages belonged to a group of fast flux hostnames (discussed in section 3.4), that we are quite certain that they are malicious. Out of the rest, we found that more than 87% of the webpages are actually malicious.

3.1 Temporal Analysis

The PhishLive system computes the number of HTTP requests and number of malicious URLs observed per hour. Host users behave very differently at different times of a day, that could mean different fraction of malicious website accesses depending on the time of day. To investigate this, we focus on the ratio of malicious website visits as a proportion of the total number of HTTP requests (which we call *malicious ratio* in our paper). From the perspective of an IDS, a higher malicious ratio at a certain time means that a HTTP connection observed at this time has higher probability to be malicious website attack.

Figure 2(a) shows the malicious ratio which varies from 0.008% to 0.257% over the one month period. Users usually make more HTTP requests during daytime than night, which could mean more malicious website accesses during daytime than night. However, from Figure 2(b) which displays the average malicious ratio for 24 hours, we observe that the malicious ratio is significantly higher (almost double) from 11 PM to 5 AM compared to daytime. Upon further investigation, we found that the absolute number of attacks is almost the same during daytime and night, with a slight edge during night (average 11,460 during daytime compared with 12,098 during nighttime). We believe the reason for this stems from the fact that these accesses could be automatically initiated by malware already present on infected computers rather than via human accesses. As the study [9] on malware infections indicates, about 58.6% of all

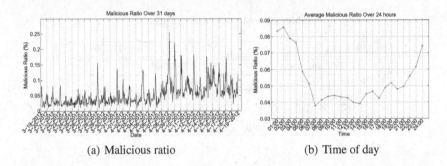

(a) Malicious ratio   (b) Time of day

Fig. 2. Prevalence and location of malicious websites in our dataset. Subplot (a) shows the ratio of malicious URLs to benign over the month. (b) shows per-hour average malicious ratio.

malware make HTTP accesses, which partly explains our observations. In addition, we found a non-negligible numbers of visits to pornographic websites at nights compared to daytime, which are often associated with many types of malware.

3.2   Access Characteristics of Victims

We now analyze the malicious URL access characteristics. Specifically, we focus on the timing of the user accesses to attacker domains (IP addresses) and the relationship between victims (IP addresses) and attacker domains. Figure 3(a) displays the timing characteristics of when the attacker domains have been accessed by users. The y-axis represents distinct hostnames of attackers we observed in our data, while the x-axis is the date, with a resolution of one day. We can see that there are roughly three types of attacker domains. Type I attacker domains are those that users access frequently over a long period of time; such domains are appear as a horizontal line in the figure. Attacker domains of type II are those that may be intermittently accessed by users. They appear as dashed horizontal line in the figure. Type III attackers scatter attacks infrequently, and mostly appear as sparse points in the figure. Figure 3(b) shows the scatter plot between victims and attacker domains. From the figure, we can see that a significant number of victims seem to have contacted a few popular attacker IP addresses. Similarly, vertically, many users seem to have contacted many different attacker IP addresses as well.

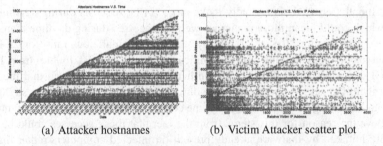

(a) Attacker hostnames   (b) Victim Attacker scatter plot

Fig. 3. Behavior of attacker's hostnames and IP addresses over time

3.3 Persistence of Hostnames

The previous graphs used IP addresses; since a single IP address could host many different hostnames, we now switch to understanding the persistence characteristics of the various hostnames we observed. Since we do not exactly know the lifetime of a hostname, we only focus on duration between the first and last times a URL was observed from a given hostname as an estimate of the lifetime of a given hostname. In Figure 4(a), we plot a histogram of the number of days a particular hostname was observed in our dataset. The x-axis is the number of days an attack hostname was observed, while the y-axis shows the fraction of attacks. Since we have collected only one month's trace, we restrict ourselves to the hostnames collected in the first 15 days, so each hostname has the same chance of appearing in the next 15 days from the first time a hostname appears to eliminate the fringe bias in our data. In Figure 4(a), we found that almost 50% of the attacker hostnames were present for less than 1 day, which confirms the fast-flux like behavior observed in previous studies [20, 21]. But there are a non-trivial number of hostnames that were accessed persistently for a number of days. Close to 10% of the hostnames were accessed for all 15 days; due to lack of data beyond, we cannot conclusively determine how long these campaigns actually persisted.

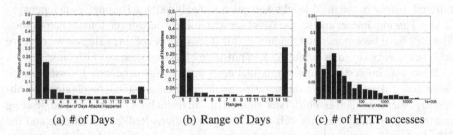

(a) # of Days   (b) Range of Days   (c) # of HTTP accesses

Fig. 4. Temporal characteristics of malicious accesses. Subplot (a) shows distribution of hostnames in terms of number of days a hostname has been accessed. (b) shows the distribution of range, and (c) shows distribution of number of accesses.

A similar behavior can be observed in Figure 4(b), where we plot the range of the days between which we observed a given hostname. While this plot (in Figure 4(b) has similar characteristics as the previous one (Figure 4(a)), the bar for 15 days, which includes all hostnames that were active for greater than or equal to 15 days, is significantly taller (almost 30% compared to only 5%). But, the number of hostnames that were active for only 15 days is small (<10%), leaving a significant number of hostnames (the remaining 20%) active for >15 days.

Finally, we plot the distribution of the number of HTTP accesses to particular hostnames in Figure 4(c). From this figure, we can observe that most hostnames are accessed relatively infrequently. Almost 70% of hostnames were seen only less than 10 times, and 90% were seen less than 100 times in our dataset. A small number of hostnames seem to have been accessed a lot of times, greater than 33,000 times. We manually checked the 43 hostnames that were accessed more than a 1000 times. Those 43 hostnames belong to 27 different websites. Among those websites we found 1 job hunting website, 1 local forum, 2 file sharing websites, 3 porn websites, 3 news websites and the rest of them are general websites with many different types of content.

3.4   Lexical Similarity of Domains

We now study the lexical similarity in attack domains we have observed in our data set. We decompose a malicious URL into three components: hostname, file path and query string, out of which our main interest is just the hostname. We lexically group together hostnames that share some similarity in the form of a tree. All the 395,671 malicious URLs we observed belong to 1686 distinct hostnames, 37 of which are IP addresses that we exclude in the clustering process. We first split each hostname to several tokens which are strings between two dots. For example, we break pann.nate.com into pann, nate and com tokens. Then we start to build the tree in the reverse order, starting from the top level domain name (e.g., com, nate and then pann).

End nodes in this tree are the hostnames we detected in our experiment. Children sharing the same parent node contain the same upper-level domain names. By doing this, we are trying to put different hostnames into clusters indicating the degree of similarity. From the tree, we observed that some prefixes exhibited large subtrees. For example, in our data, we observed PassingGas.net shared by 42 hostnames that differed mainly in the third-level token, such as nealyxadxloa.PassingGas.net, hccayx-adxloa.PassingGas.net and so on. We observe that their third-level domain names look like they have been generated randomly; this discovery is not surprising as we observe such occurrences even in public domain phishing blacklists such as PhishTank.

What was interesting, however, is that each unique hostname was accessed for no more than 2 days by hosts in our network; such information cannot be obtained by observing blacklists such as PhishTank alone. The old hostnames became invalid, leading to a page indicating that this website is using Sitelutions Redirection Engine and the URL is either entered incorrectly or has been removed by itself. Another feature of these hostnames is that they all share the same IP address (located in Herndon, VA) no matter how they change the third level domain name. Obviously, this indicates that the attackers are manipulating the DNS Resource Records dynamically, which is not surprising as attackers often try to evade detection this way [3].

3.5   Redirect Chain Analysis

Researchers in [19] reported that attackers may use long redirect chains to hide malicious content; we therefore study whether redirections are actively used in attacks today. There are many ways to implement HTTP redirections, such as server-side 3XX response, client-side scripting (javascript), META refresh tag and so on. Since, server-side redirection is prominent in both legitimate and spam redirection [22], and since content-based analysis has significant impact on the performance of a real-time system, we choose to only focus on server-side HTTP redirects.

In our dataset, we observed a total of 7,497 redirect chains that contained at least one malicious URL. However, in some of the redirect chains, the original HTTP requests and redirect response belonged to the same hostname. If a redirect chain is created by attackers intentionally, then: (i) the URL in the redirect response typically belongs to

Table 2. Statistics of Effective Malicious Redirect Chain

Type	Number
Total Redirect Chains	50,204,174
Malicious Redirect Chains	7,497
Effective Malicious Chains	1449
Average Number of Redirect	2.221
Number of Chains Longer Than 1	246
Max Number of Redirect	5
Start with Normal Request	988
301 Redirect	231
302 Redirect	1523
303 Redirect	6
307 Redirect	0

a different hostname; (ii) the last redirect is malicious; (iii) the redirect chain usually contains more than one redirect. Therefore, we define a redirect chain to be a *effective malicious redirect chain* if the URLs in the chain belong to at least two different hostnames, and the last redirect is malicious. However, we do not put any restriction on the length of the redirect chain, since it usually does not matter.

For example, the chain consisting of redirecting http://www.dwnews.com/images/ news/blog.gif → http://www.dwnews.com/ is not effective malicious redirect chain since the two URLs belong to the same hostname. However, the chain that involves the following redirection, http://grannymovs.in/ → http://lotaz.in/MyTRAFF/apiLINK da.php → http://servantspywarekeep.info/755063395c4 a385d/ is an effective malicious redirect chain, since the last URL is malicious. We also noticed a special case that the redirect chains caused by the expiration of the hostnames mentioned before. Redirects related to the expiration of those hostnames occurred 2,065 times, which we removed from our set. Among the remaining, we identified 1,449 effective malicious redirect chains, the statistics of whom are summarized in Table 2.

Several conclusions can be derived from our analysis on malicious redirect chains: (1) The number of malicious redirect chains (7497) among all redirects ($\approx$ 50 million) is quite small (<0.0149%). (2) Only a small portion of malicious redirect chains (246 out of 7497) are effective malicious redirect chains and contain more than 1 redirect (about 3.29%) in our experiment. (3) Most of the effective malicious chains (about 988 out of 1449) start from a normal HTTP request and end up with a malicious URL as redirect response.

4   Conclusions

To date, no studies exist on how prevalent phishing/malware attacks are or on the temporal characteristics of malware accesses in edge networks. We designed the Phish-Live system for long-term monitoring of HTTP traffic of a large campus network that enabled us to study various temporal characteristics of phishing/malware attacks.

Using a month-long deployment of the PhishLive system at the university gateway router, we observed many interesting characteristics of phishing attacks. For example, we found that malicious accesses are more common during 11:00-5:00pm than during day times. Similarly, we found that most domains appeared only for one day and redirection was not common among many of the malware URLs we detected.

Acknowledgements. We thank the anonymous reviewers and Changhyun Lee, our shepherd, for their comments that improved the paper significantly. We thank the Purdue University IT staff including Bill Harshbarger and Greg Hedrick for their support in collecting the traces. This work was supported in part by NSF grant 1017915 and a grant from Google.

References

1. Egelman, S., Cranor, L.F., Hong, J.: You've been warned: An empirical study of the effectiveness of web browser phishing warnings. In: CHI, 1065–1074 (April 2008)
2. Zhang, Y., Egelman, S., Cranor, L., Hong, J.: Phinding phish: Evaluating Anti-Phishing tools. In: NDSS (February 2007)
3. Prakash, P., Kumar, M., Kompella, R., Gupta, M.: Phishnet: Predictive blacklisting to detect phishing attacks. In: INFOCOM, pp. 1–5 (March 2010)
4. Ma, J., Saul, L.K., Savage, S., Voelker, G.M.: Beyond blacklists: Learning to detect malicious web sites from suspicious URLs. In: KDD, pp. 1245–1254 (June 2009)
5. Ramachandran, A., Feamster, N., Vempala, S.: Filtering spam with behavioral blacklisting. In: CCS (October 2007)
6. Garera, S., Provos, N., Chew, M., Rubin, A.D.: A framework for detection and measurement of phishing attacks. In: WORM, 1–8 (2007)
7. Zhang, Y., Hong, J.I., Cranor, L.F.: Cantina: A content-based approach to detecting phishing web sites. In: WWW, pp. 639–648 (May 2007)
8. Bayer, U., Habibi, I., Balzarotti, D., Kirda, E., Kruegel, C.: A view on current malware behaviors. In: LEET, pp. 1–11 (April 2009)
9. Rossow, C., Dietrich, C.J., Bos, H., Cavallaro, L., et al.: Sandnet: network traffic analysis of malicious software. In: BADGERS (April 2011)
10. Gu, G., Zhang, J., Wenke, L.: BotSniffer: Detecting botnet command and control channels in network traffic. In: NDSS (February 2008)
11. Perdisci, R., Lee, W., Feamster, N.: Behavioral clustering of http-based malware and signature generation using malicious network traces. In: NSDI (April 2010)
12. Song, C., Zhuge, J., Han, X., Ye, Z.: Preventing drive-by download via inter-module communication monitoring. In: ASIACCS, pp. 124–134 (April 2010)
13. Whittaker, C., Ryner, B., Nazif, M.: Large-scale automatic classification of phishing pages. In: NDSS (February 2010)
14. Provos, N., Mavrommatis, P., Rajab, M.A., Monrose, F.: All your iframes point to us. In: IEEE S&P Conference (Oakland), pp. 1–15 (May 2008)
15. Maier, G., Feldmann, A., Paxson, V., Sommer, R., Vallentin, M.: An Assessment of Overt Malicious Activity Manifest in Residential Networks. In: Holz, T., Bos, H. (eds.) DIMVA 2011. LNCS, vol. 6739, pp. 144–163. Springer, Heidelberg (2011)
16. Google safe browsing API, https://developers.google.com/safe-browsing/

17. Webb, S., Caverlee, J., Pu, C.: Introducing the webb spam corpus: Using email spam to identify web spam automatically. In: CEAS (July 2006)
18. Webb, S., Caverlee, J., Pu, C.: Characterizing web spam using content and http session analysis. In: CEAS (July 2007)
19. Lee, S., Kim, J.: Warningbird: Detecting suspicious URLs in twitter stream. In: NDSS, pp. 1–13 (February 2012)
20. Konte, M., Feamster, N., Jung, J.: Dynamics of Online Scam Hosting Infrastructure. In: Moon, S.B., Teixeira, R., Uhlig, S. (eds.) PAM 2009. LNCS, vol. 5448, pp. 219–228. Springer, Heidelberg (2009)
21. Holz, T., Gorecki, C., Rieck, K., Freiling, F.: Measuring and detecting fast-flux service networks. In: NDSS (February 2008)
22. Bhargrava, K., Brewer, D., Li, K.: A study of URL redirection indicating spam. In: CEAS (July 2009)

Remotely Gauging Upstream Bufferbloat Delays

C. Chirichella[1], D. Rossi[1], C. Testa[1], T. Friedman[2], and Antonio Pescapé[3]

[1] Telecom ParisTech.
first.last@enst.fr
[2] UPMC Sorbonne Universites
timur.friedman@upmc.fr
[3] Univ. Federico II
pescape@unina.it

Abstract. "Bufferbloat" is the growth in buffer size that has led Internet delays to occasionally exceed the light propagation delay from the Earth to the Moon. Manufacturers have built in large buffers to prevent losses on Wi-Fi, cable and ADSL links. But the combination of some links' limited bandwidth with TCP's tendency to saturate that bandwidth results in excessive queuing delays. In response, new congestion control protocols such as BitTorrent's uTP/LEDBAT aim at explicitly limiting the delay that they add over the bottleneck link. This work proposes and validate a methodology to *monitor the upstream queuing delay experienced by remote hosts*, both those using LEDBAT, through LEDBAT's native one-way delay measurements, and those using TCP (via the Timestamp Option).

1 Problem Statement

As a recent *CACM* article points out, "Internet delays now are as common as they are maddening" [3]. Currently, the combination of excessive buffer sizes (aka *bufferbloat*), with TCP's congestion control mechanism (which forces a bottleneck buffer to fill and generate a loss before the sender reduces its rate), queuing delays can potentially reach a few seconds [8]. This is confirmed by recent studies such as [5], showing that most home gateways have a fixed buffer size, irrespective of the uplink capacity. With cable and ADSL modem buffers ranging from, on average, 120 KB to a maximum of 365 KB [5], and common uplink rates of 1 Mbps, worst case queuing delays can range from 1 second on average to a maximum of 3 seconds.

To counter this problem, BitTorrent developers have proposed IETF LEDBAT [9] as a TCP replacement for data transfer. Like TCP, LEDBAT maintains a congestion window – but whereas mainstream TCP variants use loss-based congestion control (growing with ACKs and shrinking with losses), LEDBAT estimates the queuing delay on the bottleneck link and tunes the window size in an effort to achieve a target level of queuing delay (100ms by default). By explicitly capping the queuing delay, LEDBAT aims at protecting VoIP [2] and other interactive traffic (e.g., Web, Gaming) by congestion self-induced by other traffic of the same user.

Although TCP's loss-based congestion control, coupled with large buffers, can clearly cause significant bufferbloat delays, it is unclear how often this happens in practice, and how badly it hurts user performance. Indeed, active approaches such as Netalyzer [8],

M. Roughan and R. Chang (Eds.) PAM 2013, LNCS 7799, pp. 250–252, 2013.

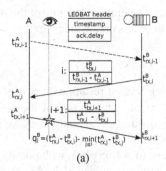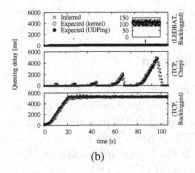

Fig. 1. Bufferbloat measurement methodology: illustration (left) and validation (right)

likely overestimate bufferbloat delay – by purposely filling the pipe, Netalyzer learns the *maximum* bufferbloat delay, but not its *typical* range. To counter this limitation, we design and validate a passive methodology for inferring the queuing delays encountered by remote LEDBAT and TCP hosts.

2 Methodology

We estimate queuing delay by collecting one-way delay (OWD) samples, establishing the minimum as a baseline delay, and then measuring the degree to which a sample differs from the baseline. This is a classic approach used in congestion control to drive congestion window dynamics since the late 1980s [7]. Our innovation is to demonstrate how a passive observer òf LEDBAT or TCP traffic can use this approach to estimate the uplink delays experienced by a remote host.

To infer B queues, in our methodology an observer close to A sniffs the packets and performs the same state updates as does the LEDBAT congestion control protocol running on A. Our methodology is to sniff and inspect LEDBAT and TCP packets, and mimick the way the LEDBAT sender computes queuing delay based on header fields.

Fig. 1(a) illustrates the methodology. On reception of a new packet, the receiver calculates the OWD as the difference between its own local clock and the sender "timestamp" (the latter extracted from packet header[1]), and sends this "ack.delay" value back to the sender (using another header field). At each packet reception, the observer updates the base delay β_{BA} as the minimum over all OWD $B \to A$ samples:

$$\beta_{BA} = \min(\beta_{BA}, t_{\text{rx},i}^A - t_{\text{tx},i}^B), \tag{1}$$

$$q_i^B = (t_{\text{rx},i}^A - t_{\text{tx},i}^B) - \beta_{BA} \tag{2}$$

Then, the queuing delay q_i^B incurred by packet i can be inferred by subtracting β_{BA} from the timestamp difference carried in packet $i+1$.

Omitted here for lack of space but reported in [4], the methodology also applies to TCP traffic provided that the flow has the Timestamps Option [6] enabled. This means

---

[1] In the absence of a finalized LEDBAT standard, our protocol parser is based on BitTorrent's currently implemented BEP-29 definition [1].

the observer must either be one of the hosts, work in cooperation with one of the hosts, or opportunistically measure only those flows that have this option enabled.

3   Validation

We validate our methodology in Fig. 1(b), reporting testbed results with two ground truths: (i) kernel level queue logs (hacking the `sch_print` function of the `netem` emulator) and (ii) UDP ping-like measurements (as queuing occurs only at B, we have $q_i^B = RTT_i - min_{j \leqslant i} RTT_j$).

Host B has an ongoing backlogged LEDBAT flow to A (top plot), with possibly interfering on/off TCP (middle) or backlogged-TCP (bottom) traffic models. As expected, in the LEDBAT case queuing reaches the 100 ms target specified in the draft (top). In the on/off case, queuing can possibly grow very large depending on the amount of cross TCP traffic (middle). Finally, queuing delay attains the maximum value, that Netalyzer [8] would report, under backlogged TCP (bottom). In all cases, we see that our methodology is very reliable agains both ground truths (differences are on the order of 1 packet worth of queuing delay for LEDBAT).

In a typical scenario, however, the observer O will be able to observe *only part* of the traffic generated by the host of interest B (say, the traffic $B \rightarrow A$), but will miss another part (say, $B \rightarrow C$). Omitted here for lack of space but reported in [4], our validation shows the methodology to be accurate even in case the observer O has only a partial view of B traffic: the error in the inferred measure is negligible in cases where a sizable amount of traffic makes it to the observer, but is still robust and reliable even when the observer is able to sniff only very few samples.

Acknowledgement. This work has been carried out at LINCS http://www.lincs. fr and funded by the FP7 mPlane project (grant agreement no. 318627).

References

1. http://bittorrent.org/beps/bep_0029.html
2. ITU Recommendation G.114, One Way Transmission Time.
3. Cerf, V., Jacobson, V., Weaver, N., Gettys, J.: Bufferbloat: what's wrong with the internet? Communications of the ACM 55(2), 40–47 (2012)
4. Chirichella, C., Rossi, D., Testa, C., Friedman, T., Pescape, A.: Passive bufferbloat measurement exploiting transport layer information (2012),
   http://www.enst.fr/ drossi/dataset/
   bufferbloat-methodology/techrep.pdf
5. DiCioccio, L., Teixeira, R., May, M., Kreibich, C.: Probe and Pray: Using UPnP for Home Network Measurements. In: Taft, N., Ricciato, F. (eds.) PAM 2012. LNCS, vol. 7192, pp. 96–105. Springer, Heidelberg (2012)
6. Jacobson, V., et al.: TCP Extensions for High Performance. IETF RFC 1323 (1992)
7. Jain, R.: A delay-based approach for congestion avoidance in interconnected heterogeneous computer networks. ACM SIGCOMM CCR 19(5), 56–71 (1989)
8. Kreibich, C., Weaver, N., Nechaev, B., Paxson, V.: Netalyzr: Illuminating the edge network. In: ACM Internet Measurement Conference, ACM IMC 2010 (2010)
9. Shalunov, S., et al.: Low Extra Delay Background Transport (LEDBAT). IETF draft (2010)

Scaling Out the Performance of Service Monitoring Applications with BlockMon

Davide Simoncelli[1], Maurizio Dusi[2],
Francesco Gringoli[1], and Saverio Niccolini[2,*]

[1] University of Brescia – CNIT, Brescia, Italy
netcelli.tux@gmail.com, francesco.gringoli@ing.unibs.it
[2] NEC Laboratories Europe, Heidelberg, Germany
{maurizio.dusi,saverio.niccolini}@neclab.eu

Abstract. To cope with real-time data analysis as the amount of data being exchanged over the network increases, an idea is to re-design algorithms originally implemented on the monitoring probe to work in a distributed manner over a stream-processing platform. In this paper we show preliminary performance analysis of a Twitter trending algorithm when running over BlockMon, an open-source monitoring platform which we extended to run distributed data-analytics algorithms: we show that it performs up to 23.5x and 34.2x faster on BlockMon than on Storm and Apache S4 respectively, two emerging stream-processing platforms.

1 Introduction

Due to the tremendous growth of data exchanged on the Internet, the traditional (monolytic) approach to data monitoring showed to be inadequate for collecting and processing measurements on the fly and alternative designs based on distributed computing are being explored. While Hadoop and MapReduce [1,2] are well-known frameworks oriented to the off-line (batch) processing of data, brand new frameworks are emerging for the analysis of unbound streams of data, such as Storm and Apache S4.

In this paper we evaluate the performance of **Twitter trending**, an application that monitors and ranks on-the-fly topics discussed by Twitter users over time. We run this application on top of Storm and Apache S4, platforms that have been built around this use case, and on top of BlockMon [3], an open source monitoring platform that we extended to execute distributed applications.

Here follows a quick overview of these three stream-processing systems.

BlockMon is an open-source modular system for *flexible, high-performance traffic monitoring and analysis*, implemented in C++11 under BSD license, being designed to run on a single multi-core machine. We added interfaces for connecting blocks running on different machines, which allow to (de)serialize messages

---

* This work was supported in part by a grant from the European Commission, under the EU FP7 project *DEMONS* (contract-no. 257315).

M. Roughan and R. Chang (Eds.) PAM 2013, LNCS 7799, pp. 253–255, 2013.

inside TCP sessions, so that users can now implement distributed applications for monitoring unbound streams of data on top of it. We release improved Block-Mon to the public [4].

Storm runs on Java Virtual Machine, is written in Clojure and Java and supports multi-language programmability. Data are exchanged in form of *tuples* through ZMQ sockets, which handle local and remote transmission on top of TCP. We used release *v0.8* of the software, available under the EPL license [5].

Apache S4 is written in Java. An external *adapter* converts data into Apache S4 events and injects them into the cluster through the *put* method: elements then exchange events using TCP (or UDP as well). We used version *v0.5* of the software, available under the Open Source Apache 2.0 license [6].

2 Experimental Analysis

We considered a dataset of around 20 million tweets in JSON format: as the performance measures do not depend on actual data, we plan to not disclose the dataset due to privacy concern. Our testbed is composed of 14 commodity machines, each one hosting two AMD Opteron(tm) Processors 246 (single core) and 4GB RAM. A 16-port switch connects the 1GbE interfaces of all machines. We opted for a design with multiple JSON parsers (*Hashtag Finder*), one per each *Tweet Source*, and a single *Hashtag Counter* as reported in Figure 1a.

2.1 Performance Tests

For every experiment, we assigned only one task per machine, and run the controller of the platform under test on a dedicated machine, to avoid the load introduced by the controller to affect our measurements. We also assumed no failure during the experiments.

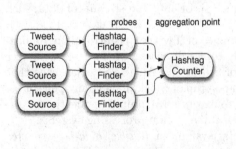

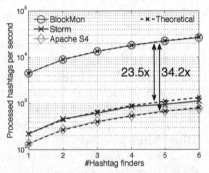

(a) Design: probes parse tweets and send the hashtags to a central counter.

(b) Scalability (y-axis is in log scale).

Fig. 1. Performance of *Twitter trending* when running over the three platforms

Figure 1b reports performance of *Twitter trending* with an increasing number of hashtag finders (HF): on all the platforms, the application scales linearly (dashed line is the theoretical trend). BlockMon outperforms Storm (Apache S4) with a gain in performance of 23.5x (34.2x). The CPU load of the hashtag counter is in the worst case (with six HFs on Storm) below 4% (not shown here), thus suggesting that one is enough to cope with multiple HFs, which account in turn for around 75% of the total CPU resources. We note that in Apache S4 the source is already a limiting factor; a look at the source code shows that sending out an event requires nested copies, thus affecting performance: compared with Storm, the other Java-based platform, the tweet source is 10x slower. As for Storm, the bottleneck is related to the way the platform extracts messages coming from the network and passes them to the HFs, as we verified that the rate of the sources is higher than the one of the HFs, and that *jackson*, the Java-based JSON parser library that we used in Storm, has the same performance of *jsmn*, the one used in BlockMon, when they are used stand-alone. Users should consider this pitfall in applications like *Twitter trending*, where moving data among nodes is crucial.

3 Conclusions

We believe this work can provide developers of monitoring applications with a better insight of the distributed architecture to use, to target on-the-fly data processing. Our preliminary results point out some pitfalls in the existing platforms, and show that BlockMon achieves the best performance.

As future work, we plan to extend the analysis with more applications and use specialized hardware, e.g., equipped with 10Gb/s network cards, to remove the bottleneck represented by the network.

References

1. Apache Hadoop, http://hadoop.apache.org (accessed September 01, 2012)
2. Dean, J., Ghemawat, S.: Mapreduce: simplified data processing on large clusters. Commun. ACM 51(1), 107–113 (2008)
3. di Pietro, A., Huici, F., Bonelli, N., Trammell, B., Kastovsky, P., Groleat, T., Vaton, S., Dusi, M.: Blockmon: Toward high-speed composable network traffic measurement. In: Proceedings of the IEEE Infocom Conference, Mini-conference (2013)
4. BlockMon, http://blockmon.github.com/blockmon (accessed August 30, 2012)
5. Storm, http://storm-project.net (accessed August 30, 2012)
6. Apache S4, http://incubator.apache.org/s4 (accessed August 30, 2012)

Understanding IPv6 Populations in the Wild[*]

Manish Karir[1], Geoff Huston[2], George Michaelson[2], and Michael Bailey[3]

[1] Cyber Security Division, DHS, S&T, Washington DC, USA
[2] Research and Development, APNIC, South Brisbane, Australia
[3] EECS, University of Michigan, Ann Arbor, USA

Abstract. With the global exhaustion of the IPv4 address pool, there has been significant interest in understanding the adoption of IPv6. Previous studies have shown that IPv6 traffic continues to be a very small fraction of the overall total traffic in any network, but its use is gradually increasing. Utilizing a novel display advertising approach to reach behind NAT and other firewall devices, we engage in a seven-month study of IPv6 in which we observe 14M unique IPv6 addresses including native IPv6, teredo, as well as 6to4. We exploit the intrinsic information within IPv6 addresses in order to infer IPv6 properties, such as, coarse grained geographic location, ISPs, the use of native IPv6 versus transition techniques, cone NAT usage, and even network interface manufacturer identifiers. We find that while the number of native IPV6 addresses in the wild is small (1.3%) a large number of IPv6 hosts are IPv6 capable via transition techniques such as teredo and 6to4.

Keywords: IPv6, Transition, Teredo, 6to4, EUI-64.

1 Introduction

Due to the design of native IPv6 as well as the associated transition mechanisms it is possible to infer a significant amount of information from just the address itself by combining it with secondary sources of data. Based on an IPv6 address it is possible to determine which geographic region, and organization it belongs to, whether it was used as a part of a IPv6 transition service, in the case of teredo whether a specific type of NAT was in use, what the public IP address of that NAT was and the port number on the NAT. For 6to4 addresses it is possible easily determine the related IPv4 address for a dual stack host, and in the case of both 6to4 and native IPv6 the 48 bit MAC address of the network interface on end hosts can also be decoded.

There are three primary goals of this study; first to understand the scope and range of IPv6 capabilities that are currently usable; second, to characterize and document the IPv6 capable population of the Internet at this critical moment in the evolution of the Internet; and third to understand regional or technological trends that might be driving IPv6 adoption.

[*] We would like to acknowledge the generous support that has been provided by Google, the Internet Software Consortium and the RIPE NCC.

M. Roughan and R. Chang (Eds.) PAM 2013, LNCS 7799, pp. 256–259, 2013.

1.1   Understanding IPv6 Addressing

An IPv6 address consists of 128bits. There is however sufficient structure in an
IPv6 addresses to help us to understand certain trends in IPv6 adoption and
IPv6 capable host population. Some of these aspects are listed below.

Interface Identifier: The bottom 64 bits of the IPv6 address can be used to
represent an interface identifier. The interface identifier can be derived from a
48-bit IEEE 802 MAC address by mapping the least significant 24 bits into the
least significant 24 bits of a 64 bit identifier. The most significant 24 bits of the
MAC address are then mapped into the most significant 24bits of the identifier
except bit 7 which is set to 1. The middle bits 25 thru 40 of the modified EUI-64
address are then set to 0xFFFE in hexadecimal representation.

Native IPv6: In addition to the information embedded in the fundamental structure of the IPv6 address, there is additional information that can be obtained
about IPv6 global unicast addresses by matching a given IPv6 address with
the IANA allocation of the top level blocks to various regional Internet address
registries.

Teredo: Teredo relies on a set of configuration servers and relays to build IPv6
tunnels between IPv6 capable end hosts and the IPv6 enabled Internet. The
prefix 2001::/32 has been assigned by IANA for Teredo and this distinctive block
that allows such traffic to be easily identified. As part of its operation Teredo
encodes additional information into the IPv6 address. Bits 33-64 specify the
Teredo server being used, bits 65-80 identify whether the end host was behind a
cone NAT, bit 81-96 indicated an obscured port number that was in use by the
end host NAT, and the final 32 bits indicate the external IPv4 address of the
NAT gateway that was used by the end host.

6to4: 6to4 traffic can be easily identified as it uses IP addresses from the
2002::/16 IPv6 address range. The next 32 bits are used to represent the IPv4
address and next 16bits are chosen by the router.

Table 1. IPv6 capability population mix

Address Type	Unique IPv6 Addresses	Percentage
Native	LACNIC.................1.3K APNIC.................41.6K RIPE...................90.9K ARIN...................40.5K AFRINIC...............0.1K TOTAL..............174.4K	1.3
Teredo	11.12M	79.2
6to4	2.75M	19.5
Total IPv6 hosts	14.04M	100%
IPv6 Ready Hosts	1.37M	9.75%
Additional IPv6 Capable Hosts (Literal-only)	3.90M	27.7%

1.2 Experimental Methodology

From January 2012 through July 2012 the Asia Pacific Network Information Centre, (APNIC) ran a unique global experiment to try to understand the adoption and use of IPv6 from the perspective of end hosts. In this experiment, web browsers are used to load a small number images that expose the client's ability to successfully use IPv6. Specifically, the client loads images that are: only accessible using IPv4, accessible over IPv4 or IPv6, only accessible using IPv6, and only accessible using IPv6 but without reliance on the Domain Name System. For this experiment APNIC collaborated with a leading distributor of advertising to develop an advertisement that would be distributed via the global distribution network to various clients based on their advertisement to user matching criteria.

2 Data Analysis and Discussion

Overall Trends: Over the full six months we observed over 14M unique IPv6 addresses at our web servers. Table 1 shows the number of different types of IPv6 addresses that were observed at our severs. Of the 174.4K native IPv6 addresses we observe over 90K from the RIPE region, roughly 40K each from the ARIN and APNIC regions. LACNIC and AFRINIC regions account for very small fraction of the native IPv6 addresses that we were able to observe. These native IPv6 addresses appear to originate from only 1384 unique ASNs. This is close to 23% of the 6K ASNs that are visible in the IPv6 BGP routing table. We notice that RIPE region contains 708 unique AS numbers which reported atleast 1 IPv6 address into our collection system. ARIN has 277 ASNs, APNIC 282, and finally LACNIC and AFRINIC have 109 and 8 ASNs respectively.

6to4 Usage: We observed roughly 2.78M unique IPv6 addresses that were from the 6to4 transition address range. Our analysis indicates that of the 2.78M unique 6to4 addresses 92K could be attributed to the RIPE region, 1.39M to the AP-NIC region, 112K to the ARIN region, 292K to the LACNIC region and 65.4K to the AFRINIC region. We were able to identify 6to4 addresses from a total of 205 unique country codes. Indonesia is by far the largest with over 500K 6to4 addresses (18%) followed by New Zealand (5%), Korea (5%), Brazil (4%), Australia (4%), China (4%) and Taiwan (3%).

Teredo Servers and Cone NATs: There were over 11M IP addresses that were observed to be from the Teredo IP address range. Overall we observed 258 unique Teredo servers from 171 unique ASNs in 39 different countries. However, of the 11M Teredo IP addresses in our data, we observed the vast majority of them to rely on only 4 or 5 key teredo servers. 150 of the 258 unique teredo servers we were able to observe were in the RIPE region 86 in the ARIN region, 19 in APNIC and 3 in the AFRINIC region. Interestingly, we observed no Teredo servers from the LACNIC region. Of the 11M Teredo IP addresses 14.9K had the "cone NAT" flag enabled to indicate that these connection attempts from being originated by hosts behind a cone NAT. Overall we were able to identify 11.48K unique NAT devices from 1037 unique ASNs in 127 different countries.

MAC Addresses: Out of a total of 174K native IP addresses only 13.2K or less than 10% contained this marker. Additionally, out of the 2.78M 6to4 addresses that we were able to observe an EUI-64 tag marker on only 8.94K or less than 0.3% of the addresses.

Conclusions: As the Internet transitions slowly to IPv6, it is important to understand the characteristics of the IPv6 capable population. In this paper we have presented results from a broad experiment that focused on understanding the makeup, distribution and key features of this population. Our current results represent a single sample of the observed IPv6 population in our 7 month time frame. Our goal is to continue to study this data periodically.

On Weather and Internet Traffic Demand

Juan Camilo Cardona[1,3], Rade Stanojevic[2], and Rubén Cuevas[1]

[1] Institute IMDEA Networks
[2] Telefonica Research
[3] UC3M

Abstract. The weather is known to have a major impact on demand of utilities such as electricity or gas. Given that the Internet usage is strongly tied with human activity, one could guess the existence of similar correlation between its traffic demand and weather conditions. In this paper, we empirically quantify such effects. We find that the influence of precipitation depends on both time of the day as well as time of the year, and is maximal in the late afternoon over summer months.

1 Introduction

The analysis and forecasting of the Internet traffic is a well studied topic with a large number of applications [5]. Such studies have used statistical tools to capture the dominant characteristics of the dynamics, without explicitly modeling the dependence with external factors (e.g. social events, weather) that are typically accounted as noise. While it has been known that these factors have a significant impact on the demand of utilities [4] or TV ratings [6], their relationship with the Internet traffic demand is not well understood. In this paper we empirically study the relationship between the Internet traffic demand and one of the factors that plays a significant role in traffic variability: weather.

The interaction between the weather conditions and the traffic demand happens on several timescales. Short term weather events, like precipitations, have a direct effect on the traffic demand. Longer term effects, reflected through seasonal changes in temperature and daylight duration, have a slower influence on the Internet traffic. Here we study the short-term correlations. For the long-term correlation between the traffic and weather and a deeper analysis of the short-term effects we refer the interested reader to our technical report [3].

2 Datasets Description

As indicator of the Internet traffic demand in a particular area we use the traffic data from three Internet eXchange Points (IXP): the Slovak-IX, FICIX and INEX. We obtained 5-minute granular traffic from each IXP by storing and processing their publicly available mrtg images. Our Internet traffic dataset includes 8 months of data from INEX and 18 months of data from Slovak-IX and FICIX. Different from large IXPs [1], the traffic from these IXPs is highly local and thus appropriate for our analysis.

M. Roughan and R. Chang (Eds.) PAM 2013, LNCS 7799, pp. 260–263, 2013.

To obtain weather data, we use the data provided by the Weather Underground, an easily accessible database available at `http://www.wunderground.com/`. The `wunderground.com` publishes a considerable number of weather parameters with a granularity of 30 minutes. For the sake of this paper, we fetched from this website the precipitation data for the cities where each IXP is located over the period that covers our traffic data. '

3 Short Term Correlations

The data described in Section 2 allows us to notice changes that happen on the traffic of the three localities over short-time scales and compare them to the weather conditions. For that purpose we split the time into 2-hour time-slots. We denote by $u(t)$ the total traffic transiting through the IXP. In order to remove the seasonal effects we normalize $u(t)$ with the average traffic over a two week period centered at t:

$$\bar{u}(t) = \frac{u(t)}{average(u(t-84),\ldots,u(t+84))}.$$

Thus the normalized traffic $\bar{u}(t)$ measures the variability of the traffic on the short-term timescale, without the impact of long-term seasonality observable in some regions.

For each 2-hour time-slot t there are 4 or more weather records in our dataset. We set a binary variable $wet(t)$ to be 1 if any of the weather records reports precipitation (e.g. snow, shower, rain, storm) otherwise we set $wet(t) = 0$. This binary variable helps us simplify the exposition of the results. Our goal is to examine whether precipitation impacts the traffic, and quantify its effect. To that end, we split the day in twelve 2-hour intervals, and calculate average normalized traffic with and without precipitation for each of the twelve intervals:

$$A(i) = \frac{\sum\limits_{mod(s,12)=i} \bar{u}(s)wet(s)}{\sum\limits_{mod(s,12)=i} wet(s)} \quad B(i) = \frac{\sum\limits_{mod(s,12)=i} \bar{u}(s)(1-wet(s))}{\sum\limits_{modd(s,12)=i} (1-wet(s))} \quad i = 0..11$$

thus for the twelve time intervals $0h - 2h, 2h - 4h, \ldots, 22h - 24h$, $A(i)$ and $B(i)$ represent the average normalized load in the interval $[2ih, (2i+2)h]$ with and without precipitation, respectively.

In Figure 1 we depict the values of $A(i)$ and $B(i)$ for the three IXPs. To determine whether the difference between $A(i)$ and $B(i)$ is statistically significant to claim that the means of the samples with and without precipitation are different, we use Welch's t-test [8], which is well-suited for this case as the number of samples for each random variable is different and relatively large. Figure 1 also includes the interval outside of which Welch's t-test rejects the null-hypothesis for a significance level of 0.05. Thus from early afternoon to early evening, with 95% of confidence we can affirm for all IXPs that the mean normalized traffic is larger in timeslots with precipitation than in timeslots without precipitation.

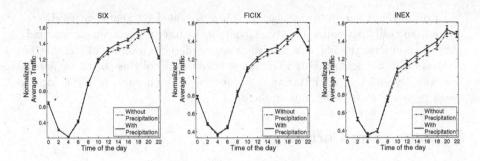

Fig. 1. Normalized daily demand of SIX, FICIX and INEX, with and without precipitation

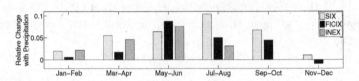

Fig. 2. The relative change with precipitation during the $16h - 18h$ slot over the year

For the other periods of the day, the difference between the means is not statistically significant to support that precipitation impacts the traffic.

Finally, we observe that the impact of precipitation is not uniform across the year. Namely, in Figure 2 we depict the relative increment of precipitation during the $16h - 18h$ interval for the 6 two-month periods and observe that the impact of precipitation is most pronounced in the summer months, while it is insignificant over the winter.

4   Conclusions

In this paper we examined the dependence between the Internet traffic and the weather in short scales. While for other types of utilities the impact of external factors has been studied in depth, our understanding on such relationship in the Internet is very immature. The phenomena observed here is a step towards filling that knowledge gap and affirms our conjecture that measurable external factors are strongly related with the variability of the Internet traffic. Our work complements other studies that analyze the impact of natural events on the Internet [7,2]. We refer the reader to [3] for a more extensive analysis of the impact of weather in Internet traffic over short and long scales.

References

1. Ager, B., et al.: Anatomy of a large european IXP. In: Proc. of ACM SIGCOMM (2012)
2. Bischof, Z.S., Otto, J.S., Bustamante, F.E.: Distributed Systems and Natural Disasters. In: Proc. ACM SWID (2011)
3. Cardona, J.C., Stanojevic, R., Cuevas, R.: On Weather and Internet Traffic Demand. T. Report (September 2012),
   https://svnext.networks.imdea.org/repos/
   WeatherAndInternet/TechReport.pdf
4. Feinberg, E., Genethliou, D.: Load forecasting. Applied Mathematics for Restructured Electric Power Systems (2005)
5. Papagiannaki, K., Taft, N., Zhang, Z.L., Diot, C.: Long-Term Forecasting of Internet Backbone Traffic: Observations and Initial Models. In: Proc. of IEEE INFOCOM (2003)
6. Roe, K., Vandebosch, H.: Weather to view or not: That is the question. European Journal of Communication 11(2), 201–216 (1996)
7. Schulman, A., Spring, N.: Pingin' in the Rain. In: Proc. of ACM IMC 2011 (2011)
8. Welch, B.L.: The generalization of Student's problem when several different population variances are involved. Biometrika 34(1-2), 28–35 (1947), doi:10.1093/biomet/34.1-2.28 MR19277

Spatial and Temporal Locality
of Swarm Dynamics in BitTorrent

Taejoong Chung[1], Jinyoung Han[1], Hojin Lee[1],
Ted "Taekyoung" Kwon[1], Yanghee Choi[1], and Nakjung Choi[2]

[1] School of Computer Science and Engineering, Seoul National University, Korea
[2] Bell-Labs, Alcatel-Lucent, Seoul, Korea

1   Introduction

The locality in BitTorrent refers to how much disparity exists in swarm dynamics from the spatial and temporal perspectives. According to [1], 30% more connections among peers in the same ISP compared to a random graph are observed for more than 45% of peers, which indicates that BitTorrent connections among peers are biased to local peers. [2] found that (1) substantial BitTorrent traffic does not reach higher-tier ISPs, and (2) BitTorrent's temporal usage patterns vary in a diurnal fashion.

While these studies focus on showing how much localized phenomena occur in swarm dynamics, we try to investigate the locality phenomena in BitTorrent from a content perspective (i.e., content categories), which we call *content locality*.

We make the following contributions: (1) We observe that (i) locations of consumers are spatially skewed and (ii) numbers of per-day swarm participants is also temporally skewed, (2) We show that the cultural aspects of content affect how users participate in swarms from a spatial perspective, and (3) We find that the time-sensitivity of content (e.g., TV series) affects temporal locality.

2   Methodology

2.1   Data Collection

We use the same methodology to obtain the BitTorrent user traces as [3]. Our datasets, which have been collected for 33 days for April 6 to May 9, 2011, consist of 27,371 torrents and 2,247,035 peers (unique IP addresses). Using Maxmind, we have identified the user's locale, which maps each IP address (of a peer) to its country or autonomous system (AS). There are 224 countries and 10,529 ASes from the datasets. Throughtout this paper, we investigate the content locality depending on the seven content categories: TV, Porn, E-book, Movie, Music, Application, and Game.

2.2   Locality Metrics

Spatial Locality: We investigate the locality of a swarm by considering the connectivity among peers who actually exchange data among one another.

M. Roughan and R. Chang (Eds.) PAM 2013, LNCS 7799, pp. 264–266, 2013.

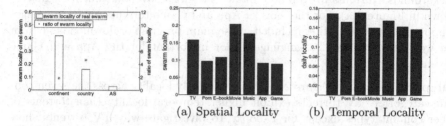

(a) Spatial Locality   (b) Temporal Locality

Fig. 1. Swarm and hypothetical locality

Fig. 2. Spatial and Temporal locality

To this end, we define the swarm locality as the probability that randomly-selected two nodes (in the same swarm) have the same locale:

$$\frac{2}{n(n-1)} \sum_{i=1}^{n-1} \sum_{j=i+1}^{n} \delta\left(L\left(v_i\right), L\left(v_j\right)\right),$$

where $L(v)$ denote the locale (e.g., AS or country) of a peer v, $\delta(i,j)$ is the Kronecker's delta ($\delta(i,j) = 1$ if $i = j$, and $\delta(i,j) = 0$ otherwise).

Temporal Locality: To investigate how swarm dynamics is temporally characterized, we define a metric: *daily locality* which indicates the probability whether two peers in the same swarm download the torrent in the same day.

3   Spatial and Temporal Locality

Existence of Locality: To see whether the spatial and temporal locality exists in a swarm, we first plot the swarm locality of the real swarms, compared with that of hypothetical swarms where peers are uniformly distributed among the observed locales and dates. In Figure 1, we observe that the swarm locality of the real swarms is significantly higher than that of the hypothetical ones. In spatial domain, as the locale is changed from continents to countries and to ASes, the ratio between the swarm locality and the hypothetical one increases from 1.80 times to 4.56 times and to 11.49 times, respectively. Like spatial locality, we find that the daily locality of swarm population is higher (1.46 times) than that of the hypothetical uniform distribution, which indicates that the swarm dynamics in terms of population is temporally skewed.

Spatial Locality: We next plot the average swarm locality for each content category in Figure 2(a). We observe that torrents in Movie and TV categories have the higher swarm locality while the ones in Porn category exhibit the lower swarm locality, even though the three categories are video-centric. We believe that the disparity across the three categories is due to the style of content consumption; movies or video content typically requires the understanding of content by languages and cultures, while porn films typically do not need such backgrounds. Torrents in App and Game categories have low swarm locality as shown in Figure 2(a). For the most of App and Game torrents, multi-language-support packages are either included in the main program or downloadable from the web sites. Hence, the language is not important for the App and Game torrents.

Temporal Locality: Figure 2(b) shows the daily locality across the seven content categories. TV torrents exhibit higher temporal locality than torrents of other content types except for E-book. To investigate why TV torrents show high daily locality, we analyze and find that periodicity for a TV torrent make higher temporal locality (58% of titles of TV torrents follow periodical naming convention (i.e., 'S**E**', where 'S' and 'E' stand for series and episode, respectively.)). Interestingly, E-book torrents also show high temporal locality because the average lifetime of an E-book torrent is around 8∼9 days, which is shorter than that of a torrent in other the categories (around 11∼12 days). The shorter lifetimes of E-book swarms are likely to result in the high temporal locality.

4 Concluding Remarks

We conducted a measurement study to capture and quantify the swarm dynamics in terms of spatial and temporal locality from a content perspective. We found that cultural factors (e.g., language) heavily affect the pattern of swarm dynamics, which results in diverse phenomena in the spatial locality. Also, we observed that the content properties like periodic publication characterize the temporal locality. Our ongoing work includes investigating the content locality from a diverse perspective of content properties (e.g., content types, characteristics of content publishers, or preferences of users) and exploring the possibility to exploit the content locality for efficient content prefetching and caching.

Acknowledgements. This research was supported by the KCC(Korea Communications Commission), Korea,under the R&D program supervised by the KCA(Korea Communications Agency) (KCA-2012-11-911-05-002) and Seoul R&BD Program (WR080951) funded by the Seoul Metropolitan Government.

References

1. Kryczka, et al.: Unrevealing the structure of live bittorrent swarms: Methodology and analysis. In: IEEE P2P (2011)
2. Otto, J.S., et al.: On blind mice and the elephant: understanding the network impact of a large distributed system. In: ACM SIGCOMM (2011)
3. Han, J., et al.: Bundling practice in bittorrent: What, how, and why. In: ACM SIGMETRICS (2012)

What SNMP Data Can Tell
Us about Edge-to-Edge Network Performance

Demetris Antoniades[1], Kejia Hu[2], Alex Sim[2], and Constantine Dovrolis[1]

[1] College of Computing
Georgia Institute of Technology
{danton,constantine}@gatech.edu
[2] Computational Research Division
Lawrence Berkeley National Laboratory
{kjhu,asim}@lbl.gov

With the high speeds of today's networks, monitoring information is most of the time either summarized or sampled. This policy is even more profound in network backbones, where aggregation of data from several sources and in very high speeds is often observed. The Simple Network Management Protocol (SNMP) [5] is widely used to provide aggregated link usage data from network components. These data, even without a great amount of detail, provide a valuable source for network administrators, aiding decisions about network routing, provisioning and configuration. SNMP data are simple to collect and maintain, providing a low disk space for historical network usage log.

On the other end, Netflow data provides detailed information for end-to-end performance. Using Netflow, one can have accurate information about a host pair communication, the amount of data transferred back and forth. The enhanced information given by Netflow requires a computationally expensive procedure for its collection, and raises many privacy concerns that limit the accessibility to the data. To reduce the cost of collecting Netflow data, aggressive sampling (i.e. 1:1000 packets) is often employed, even for relatively low-speed networks [3]. Sampling significantly affects the accuracy of Netflow data and may limit the usage of the data [1]. Netflow records of end-to-end information also include the IP addresses and port numbers used by the participating parties. Such content raises significant user privacy concerns [2,4]. As a result, there is a limitation of Netflow data availability while private content is either censored or completely removed.

In this paper we provide evidence that by using SNMP link counts edge-to-edge (E2E) information about network transfers can be inferred. The motivation for this work came from the need of a statistically significant set of E2E throughput samples, allowing us to perform TCP throughput prediction in a monitored network based on historical measurements [6]. The network wide availability of SNMP data and the limited throughput performance samples from Netflow data motivated us to explore different approaches for increasing our sample data set.

We propose a methodology for inferring network transfers from SNMP traffic utilization time-series data. Our method is the result of two main observations. First, looking at the time series data of a link's usage, we observe events where the usage of the link increases (or decreases) to a different level, deviating from the

M. Roughan and R. Chang (Eds.) PAM 2013, LNCS 7799, pp. 267–269, 2013.

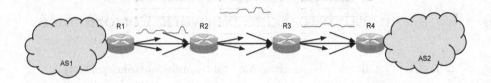

Fig. 1. Simple illustration: network events can be observed from SNMP link utilization data. These events can, also, be tracked down along the network path that they are traversing.

link's normal behavior up to that time point. These events could be considered as starting (or ending) points of high throughput transfers. Second, these events propagate from the input links of a router to the output links of the same router, and from there to the neighboring routers, allowing for the inference of the actual route that the specific event followed.

Figure 1 presents a simple example. In this diagram, $R1$ is the edge router for autonomous system $AS1$ and $R2$ is the edge router for autonomous system $AS2$. Each router has several input and output interfaces, connecting to other routers. The path $R1 - R2 - R3 - R4$ connects the two ASes, carrying all traffic exchanged between them. The graphs plot each link's utilization during the observation period. Each link carries the traffic between a variety of source and destination pairs. Link $R1 - R2$ experiences three different events during the observation period. The first and last events are not visible at link $R2 - R3$. The middle event continues from $R2$ over the link $R2 - R3$ and from there to $R3 - R4$. This event and its transfer route can be attributed to a network transfer initiated at $AS1$ and destined to $AS2$. The magnitude of the deviation on the utilization time series provides the information about the throughput performance this transfer achieved. The time points of the increase and decrease events provide the information regarding the starting and ending times of the transfer.

Based on the two aforementioned observations our inference method involves two stages. In the first stage, we identify events of significant changes of the link's utilization from the 1st-order differentiated time series $V(t)$. The 1st order differentiated time series is a transformation of the utilization time-series $(U(t))$ to the time series of the utilization difference between two consecutive measurements $(V(t) = U(t) - U(t-1))$. Using an outlier detection method, we can detect the events that deviate from the link's utilization during an observation window. After we have identified these events for an input link of a router, we try to find an output link in the same router with an event of a similar magnitude. In case of a match, we follow the output link to the neighboring router and repeat the matching process. Iterating this process allows us to infer the path that the event follows.

The work presented in this paper is, to the best of our knowledge, the first that suggests the possibility of inferring edge-to-edge information from aggregated link utilization measurements. Using our observations we propose a methodology for identifying the increasing and decreasing events in the link's traffic utilization and tracking down the that links these events traverse in the network. Preliminary results, over publicly available SNMP data from ESnet, a large National Research and Educational Network (NREN), suggest that we can identify and track up to 80% of the events that appear in a network link. Furthermore, the magnitude of the identified events does not seem to be limited to the high throughput ones.

Our ongoing work is designed to further evaluate our methodology, comparing the identified transfers with Netflow and traceroute data. Furthermore, we plan to test the performance of our method over a number of different conditions such as (i) commercial networks where the traffic dynamics are very different from the research and educational networks, (ii) the existence of multipath transfers where a transfer may be split over different paths making both the start/end time and route inference more challenging, and (iii) the case of incomplete network data where information for all routers in the path may not be available. Additionally, we plan to test the applicability of the inferred E2E data to a number of applications such as throughput prediction, traffic matrix estimation and anomaly detection.

References

1. Choi, B., Bhattacharyya, S.: On the accuracy and overhead of cisco sampled netflow. In: Proceedings of ACM SIGMETRICS Workshop on Large Scale Network Inference, LSNI (2005)
2. Coull, S., Collins, M., Wright, C., Monrose, F., Reiter, M.: On web browsing privacy in anonymized netflows. In: Proceedings of 16th USENIX Security Symposium on USENIX Security Symposium, p. 23. USENIX Association (2007)
3. Estan, C., Varghese, G.: New directions in traffic measurement and accounting. ACM SIGCOMM Computer Communication Review 32, 323–336 (2002)
4. Foukarakis, M., Antoniades, D., Antonatos, S., Markatos, E.: Flexible and high-performance anonymization of netflow records using anontool. In: Third International Conference on Security and Privacy in Communications Networks and the Workshops, SecureComm 2007, pp. 33–38. IEEE (2007)
5. Harrington, D., Presuhn, R., Wijnen, B.: An architecture for describing simple network management protocol (snmp) management frameworks. Technical report, rfc 3411 (December 2002)
6. He, Q., Dovrolis, C., Ammar, M.: On the predictability of large transfer tcp throughput. ACM SIGCOMM Computer Communication Review 35, 145–156 (2005)

Pathperf: Path Bandwidth Estimation Utilizing Websites

Kun Yu, Congxiao Bao, and Xing Li

Tsinghua University, Beijing, P.R. China

Abstract. Most bandwidth estimation tools require access to both ends of a measured path, which is increasingly difficult considering the constantly expanding size of the Internet. We present Pathperf, a tool for estimating bulk transfer capacity by downloading files from websites at one end of a path. We collect 3.3 million websites in 22,656 ASes and leverage DNS infrastructure to deliver website information. Comparing with Iperf, Pathperf saves more than 50% of the network traffic and its relative error rate is under 10%.

1 Introduction

Bandwidth estimation is essential for network management, negotiations of service level agreement, traffic engineering and protocol design. There are three metrics defining different aspects of bandwidth: capacity, available bandwidth and bulk transfer capacity (referred as BTC hereafter). The differences between these metrics are thoroughly discussed in [1].

Iperf is one of the most successful tools to measure BTC, but it works on both ends of the path so it is not applicable when this requirement is not satisfied. We present Pathperf, a tool working on one end of a path to estimate the BTC of the path (referred as path BTC hereafter). Pathperf locates a website at the other end of the path and chooses an appropriate file to download. Path BTC is derived by dividing the file size by download time. The other end of the path could be anywhere, identified by any globally routable IP address.

2 Design and Implementation of Pathperf

We divide Pathperf into two modules shown in Figure 1. Module 1 collects website information from three different sources and stores the information into a database. The information contains IP address of the website, AS number (abbreviated as ASN hereafter) of the IP address, URL of a web file, file size, and download speed. When there is more than one website available in an AS, module 1 ranks all candidate websites according to download speed and file size; then chooses the best one as vantage website.

Website information comes from Google, FixedOrbit and ODP. After three months of collection, information of 3,536,912 IPv4 websites was collected in 22,656 different ASes; these ASes cover 94% of all IPv4 addresses in BGP RIB. We also tested whether these websites are IPv6 accessible and found 28,552 IPv6 compatible websites scattered in 904 different ASes. All the website information is publicly available at Pathperf homepage [4].

M. Roughan and R. Chang (Eds.) PAM 2013, LNCS 7799, pp. 270–272, 2013.
© Springer-Verlag Berlin Heidelberg 2013

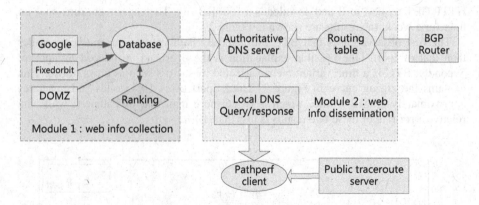

Fig. 1. Modular design of Pathperf

In order to improve scalability, we use aggregation to manage website information. The granularity we choose is AS, that is, we choose the best website in each AS as a vantage website [2]. Using AS as aggregation granularity is fine enough to detect inter-AS bottleneck and coarse enough to keep the number of websites moderate.

Module 2 delivers website information to Pathperf client by DNS [3]. It consists of two parts, BGP RIB from a BGP router and a DNS authoritative server. Pathperf looks up BGP RIB to map IP address to ASN. The DNS server responses queries issued from Pathperf client. Pathperf client takes IP address as input, wraps it into a DNS query and sends it to local DNS server. Local DNS server queries Authoritative server iteratively or recursively and returns the response to Pathperf client. The response contains information about the vantage website in the same AS specified by the IP address. With the information Pathperf can estimate path BTC. Table 1 lists currently available domains and their functions.

Table 1. domains used to query vantage website

Domain	Function
ip2server.sasm4.net	Maps an IPv4 address to website in the same AS
ip2asn.sasm4.net	Maps an IPv4 address to AS number
ip6server.sasm4.net	IPv6 version of ip2server.sasm4.net
ip6asn.sasm4.net	IPv6 version of ip2asn.sasm4.net

3 Experiment Results and Evaluation

We evaluate the accuracy of Pathperf by comparing with Iperf. The experiment uses two servers, called A and B. A attaches to a backbone of an ISP while B resides in Tsinghua campus network. Both servers install Iperf and B uses apache to answer HTTP requests. A runs Iperf in server mode; B acts as Iperf client and sends TCP packets to A. Right after Iperf finishes the estimation, A acts as a web client, sends

HTTP GET request to B and downloads a 1600KB file. The experiment runs once an hour for a week; the results are shown in Figure 2.

The first observation is that BTC estimated by Pathperf is comparatively smaller than that of Iperf. One possible explanation is the overhead introduced by apache. Secondly, BTC is a time variant metric affected by factors such as cross traffic. This explains the zigzag curve in Figure 2. Third, Iperf takes 10 seconds and generates approximately 3.3MB traffic, which is twice more than that of Pathperf; while the relative error rate of these two results is less than 10%.

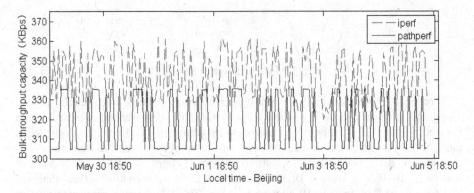

Fig. 2. BTC from Tsinghua campus to CERNET NOC

4   Conclusion

We present Pathperf to estimate BTC from one end of a path by downloading files from vantage website at the other end. We collect 3,558,205 websites in 22,656 ASes then rank them by file size and download speed. Website information is delivered to Pathperf client via DNS protocol that improves the scalability of Pathperf and benefits other network measurement tools such as Abget.

Acknowledgement. The authors would like to thank Hongqiang (Harry) Liu for his advice during the design and implementation of Pathperf.

References

1. Prasad, R., Dovrolis, C., Murray, M., Claffy, K.: Bandwidth estimation: metrics, measurement techniques, and tools. IEEE Network 17(6), 27–35 (2003)
2. Bao, C., Li, X., Jiang, J.: Scalable Application-Specific Measurement Framework for High Performance Network Video. In: Proc. ACM NOSSDAV (2007)
3. Liu, H., Xiong, Y., Bao, C., Li, X., Shen, G., Li, D.: WIND: A Scalable and Lightweight Network Topology Service for Peer-to-Peer Applications. In: Network Operations and Management Symposium, NOMS (2010)
4. Pathperf homepage, http://search.sasm3.net/

The Day after Patch Tuesday:
Effects Observable in IP Darkspace Traffic

Tanja Zseby[1,2], Alistair King[2], Nevil Brownlee[2,3], and KC Claffy[2]

[1] Fraunhofer Institute FOKUS, 10589 Berlin, Germany
[2] CAIDA, UCSD, San Diego, CA 92093, USA
[3] The University of Auckland, Auckland, New Zealand

Abstract. We investigated how Patch Tuesday affects the volume and characteristics of malicious and unwanted traffic as observed by a large IPv4 (/8) darkspace monitor over the first six months of 2012. We did not discover significant changes in overall traffic volume following Patch Tuesday, but we found a significant increase of the number of active hosts sending to our darkspace monitor the day after Patch Tuesday for all six investigated months. Our early results suggest the effects of Patch Tuesday are worth deeper investigation. Detecting time intervals during which new sources become active can help tune sampling methods toward activity periods that likely contain more interesting information (i.e., many new malicious sources) than other time periods.

Microsoft releases accumulated security patches on the second Tuesday of each month, termed "Patch Tuesday" (PT). Attackers can use the released patch information to exploit vulnerabilities on machines that have not yet been patched or to check whether security holes previously exploited are still open. Launching new malware immediately after Patch Tuesday also maximizes the potential lifetime of an exploit before a patch is deployed.

We investigated how Patch Tuesday affects the volume and characteristics of malicious and unwanted traffic as observed by a large IPv4 (/8) darkspace monitor [1] over the first six months of 2012. We used the tools corsaro [5], MATLAB and Wireshark to analyze packet counts, number of unique source addresses, top destination ports and packet content. We used the *IATmon* tool [3] to classify IP source hosts that contributed to observed darkspace traffic into 18 mutually exclusive source types. The classification is based on protocol and temporal patterns across a configured (in our case 1 hour) time interval.

First we analyzed the overall traffic without distinguishing among source types. The overall packet count did not reveal any unusual behavior at all at or around Patch Tuesday. But when we looked at the number of unique source IP addresses we found an interesting pattern that was consistent across all six months, shown in Figure 1. Specifically, immediately at midnight after PT, i.e., the first hour of "Exploit Wednesday" (EW), there was consistently a significant increase in the overall number of active sources, which typically remained elevated above its baseline value for several hours.

M. Roughan and R. Chang (Eds.) PAM 2013, LNCS 7799, pp. 273–275, 2013.

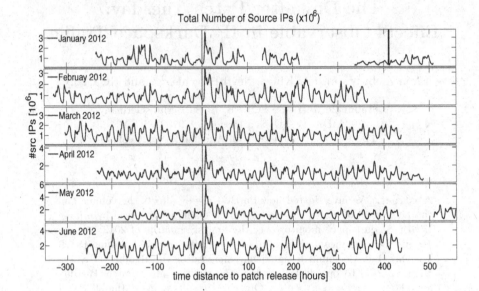

Fig. 1. Total number of unique source IP addresses per hour for 6 months. x-axis shows the time distance (in hours) from the patch release. Each month exhibits a significant increase in the number of unique source IPs shortly after PT. January and March have two other large peaks many days later that are truncated in the graph.

The *IATmon* source type analysis revealed that for all six months, the increase of active sources after Patch Tuesday is mainly caused by sources of the types '1 or 2 packets', i.e. all sources that send fewer than 3 packets, and 'UDP unknown', i.e. UDP sources that send more than 2 packets and target multiple destination addresses and destination ports (see [3]). In some months we also saw a significant increase of other source types on Exploit Wednesday, e.g., UDP probes in February and May, UDP vertical scans in July, UDP horizontal scans in May and μTorrent sources in April. But only the 'UDP unknown' and '1 or 2 packets' sources consistently increased on EW for all six months.

We saw only a few potential Patch Tuesday effects in our analysis of the packet count per source type. We saw an increase in UDP horizontal scans on EW in June and an increase of packets from 'TCP and UDP' sources on EW in July. The packet count for source type '1 or 2 packets' increased in all six months on EW, but just as a direct effect of the increase of the number of sources of this type. The source analysis also showed that 32% (in June) up to 56% (in March) of all darkspace packets originated from sources that performed TCP horizontal scans to port 445, a long-standing behavior that became even more common since the Conficker outbreak [2]. Between 13% (in January) and 42% (in April) of all observed packets were TCP backscatter (TCP-ACK, TCP-RST).

In January 2012 we saw a significant reduction of DNS backscatter traffic directly after PT. A DNS name server sent 4 to 6.5 million DNS backscatter packets per hour throughout the 45 hours before PT in January and suddenly stopped sending within 2 hours after PT. These packets were standard DNS query response packets with a format error, sent in response to a name request for a porn web page. We assume that the queries to the name server were sent with spoofed source addresses, because the response packets have destination addresses in the darkspace. One possible explanation for this sudden drop in backscatter is that a patch was deployed that prevented compromised hosts (in a botnet) from continuing to participate in a DDoS attack against the name server sending us backscatter traffic.

In order to see whether the sources that caused the peaks in the overall source count aimed at specific vulnerabilities, we investigated how many of the sources were targeting specific destination ports. We analyzed the destination ports for all packets from sources of type 'UDP unknown' and from those sources of type '1 or 2 packets' that sent only UDP packets. Since some ports are generally more popular than others, we first calculated, as a baseline, the median number of sources per destination port over the whole month. We then looked at the number of sources per destination port on EW (midnight UTC) and PT (patch release time), and compared it to the median. We saw a broad distribution of destination ports targeted on EW; no ports had an especially high number of sources across all six months. We looked at the payload for some of the UDP packets sent to the top ten ports of the sources that became active every EW in all six months. We did not discover any new or surprising pattern, just more sources sending UDP packets that looked similar to those we see at other times.

Although we have only analyzed a slice of data, our preliminary results indicate that Patch Tuesday effects merit further investigation, ideally on multiple sources of darknet data or in combination with data from networks with active hosts. Longitudinal trends of malicious behavior related to Patch Tuesday may help quantitative assessments of the health of one component of the Internet. Information about source activity patterns can also help to optimize measurement methods, e.g. by tuning sampling techniques toward time periods with high source activities. The data used in this analysis is available at [4].

References

1. UCSD Network Telescope (2010),
   http://www.caida.org/data/passive/network_telescope.xml
2. Aben, E.: Conficker/Conflicker/Downadup as seen from the UCSD Network Telescope. Technical report, CAIDA (February 2009),
   http://www.caida.org/research/security/ms08-067/conficker.xml
3. Brownlee, N.: One-way Traffic Monitoring with iatmon. In: Taft, N., Ricciato, F. (eds.) PAM 2012. LNCS, vol. 7192, pp. 179–188. Springer, Heidelberg (2012)
4. CAIDA. Patch Tuesday Dataset (2012),
   http://www.caida.org/data/passive/telescope-patch-tuesday.xml
5. Alistair King. Corsaro (October 2012),
   http://www.caida.org/tools/measurement/corsaro/

Towards Active Measurements of Edge Network Outages*

Lin Quan, John Heidemann, and Yuri Pradkin

USC/Information Sciences Institute
{linquan,johnh,yuri}@isi.edu

1 Introduction

End-to-end reachability is a fundamental service of the Internet. We study network *outages* caused by natural disasters [2,5], and political upheavals [8].

We propose a new approach to outage detection using active probing. Like prior outage detection methods [3, 4], our method uses ICMP echo requests ("pings") to detect outages, but we probe with greater density and finer granularity, showing pings can detect outages without supplemental probing.

The main contribution of our work is to define how to *interpret pings as outages* (§2): defining an outage as a sharp change in block responsiveness relative to recent behavior. We also provide preliminary analysis of outage rate in the Internet edge. Space constrains this poster abstract to only sketches of our approach; details and validation are in our technical report [6]. Our data is available at no charge, see http://www.isi.edu/ant/traces/internet_outages/.

2 Methodology

Our method for outage detection begins with active probing, followed by outage identification in individual blocks, and correlation into events.

For this paper, we define a network outage as problems in the network core or near the target that prevent reachability from our vantage point. We watch for and manually remove outages local to the monitors. We know that problems often affect only part of the Internet; evaluation of outages from multiple vantage points to distinguish partial and Internet-wide outages is future work.

2.1 Active Probing of Address Blocks

We collect data with active probing, extending our high-performance probing software used to study the Internet address space [1].

---

* This work is based on research sponsored by the U.S. Dept. of Homeland Security, S&T HSARPA, BAA 11-01-RIKA and Air Force Research Laboratory, Info. Dir., agreements FA8750-12-2-0344, and D08PC75599. The U.S. Gov't is authorized to reproduce and distribute reprints notwithstanding any copyright notation thereon. The views herein are those of the authors and do not necessarily represent the official policies or endorsements of the DHS or U.S. Government.

M. Roughan and R. Chang (Eds.) PAM 2013, LNCS 7799, pp. 276–279, 2013.

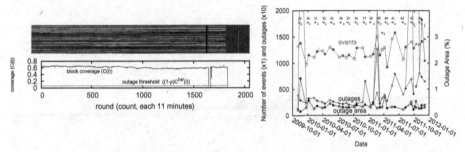

Fig. 1. *Left, top*: responses for one /24 block (green: positive, black: none, blue: not probed). *Left, bottom*: coverage and outage thresholds per round. *Right*: outage events and outage percentage, over 35 2-week surveys.

Reviewing Address Probing: We begin with active probing of addresses in some or all analyzable /24 address blocks in the IPv4 address space. Probes are ICMP echo requests (pings) at 11 minute intervals for one to 14 days. Probes are spread over 11 minutes to minimize impact on the target and effects of burst losses. We classify responses as: non-responses, network or host-specific negative replies, other errors, and positive (*echo reply*). We interpret the first two as an inaccessible network, and the later as a reachable network. We survey all addresses in a random sample of 22k or 41k responding /24 blocks.

Outage-Specific Steps: For outage analysis, we map probe records into *rounds* with index i. Each round is 11 minutes long, with N_r rounds in a dataset; we account for clock drift and duplicate replies. Our whole-Internet outage system probes 20 addresses in all 2.5M measurable /24 blocks for IPv4 [6].

2.2 Probes to Outages

We identify outages by a sharp drop in overall responsiveness of the block, and recovery by an increase. Let $r_j(i)$ represent the state of each address j in a given block at round i, taking 1 for a reply and 0 if down. Fig. 1 (left) shows a graphical representation of $r_j(i)$: each green dot indicates a positive response, while black dots are non-responsive (the blue area on the right is after the survey ends). In this block many addresses are responsive or non-responsive for long periods, as shown by long, horizontal green or black lines.

The *coverage* of a block at round i is defined as: $C(i) = N_s^{-1} \sum_{j=1}^{N_s} r_j(i)$ (where N_s is number targets probed in a block; 256 for experiments and 20 for operation). $C(i)$ is a timeseries of block responsiveness over the observation period. An outage starts when there is a severe drop (90% change or more) of $C(i)$, compared to a running average $\bar{C}$ over the last two rounds. (Exact choice of the threshold is not critical provided it is relatively large [6].) We graph $C(i)$ in Fig. 1 (bottom left), observing that it drops to zero for rounds 1640 to 1654, an outage that shows as a black, vertical band in the top panel. Because we must observe several targets, we exclude blocks that are too sparse. We consider blocks where fewer than 10% of addresses historically respond to be too sparse.

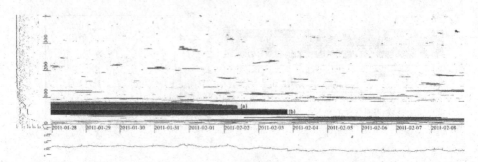

Fig. 2. The 400 largest outages of S_{38c} (see http://www.isi.edu/ant/outage/38c)

The result of this algorithm is a list of outages, represented as binary-valued timeseries $\Omega(i)$, indicating when the block is down ($\Omega(i) = 1$) or up (0). Outages incorporate data measured over the course of a round. Through controlled experiments we verify that we detect all controlled outages that last 1.9 rounds (about 20 minutes), and typically underestimate duration by about 0.5 rounds.

3   Preliminary Analysis

As an example of our outage detection method, Fig. 2 visualizes outages during the Jan. 2011 Egyptian revolution (Survey S_{38c}). This visualization clusters blocks by similarity (as previously described [7]); here we present this data to illustrate outage detection. Fig. 2 shows the 400 blocks with the most outages, with time on the x-axis and each row giving the Ω_j downtime for some /24 block, and colors keyed to country. There are two clusters of blocks that have near-identical outage end times. Cluster (a) covers 19 /24s, corresponding to the Feb. 2011 Egyptian Internet shutdown. Cluster (b) covers 21 /24 blocks for a slightly longer duration, related to flooding in eastern coast of Australia. Our technical report validates these events with external data [6].

This event is one example of the kind of outages we observe. We have been observing from three locations (southern California, Colorado, and Japan) for over two years. Fig. 1 (right) shows data for three years, with different shapes (open, closed, and asterisk) showing different locations. This figure suggests that our results are similar regardless of probing site and date, after we remove outages local to the prober (the dotted lines). Numerically, variation is low: mean outage "area" is 0.33%, standard deviation is only 0.1%. Overall, our data shows the Internet is about 99.7% up, or about 2.5 "nines" of availability.

References

1. Heidemann, J., Pradkin, Y., Govindan, R., Papadopoulos, C., Bartlett, G., Bannister, J.: Census and Survey of the Visible Internet. In: Proc. of ACM IMC (October 2008)

2. International Business Times. Optus, Telstra see service outages after Cyclone Yasi (2011),
   http://hken.ibtimes.com/articles/108249/20110203/
   optus-telstra-see-service-outages-after-cyclone-yasi.htm
3. Katz-Bassett, E., Madhyastha, H.V., John, J.P., Krishnamurthy, A., Wetherall, D., Anderson, T.: Studying black holes in the internet with Hubble. In: NSDI (2008)
4. Madhyastha, H.V., Isdal, T., Piatek, M., Dixon, C., Anderson, T., Krishnamurthy, A., Venkataramani, A.: iPlane: an information plane for distributed services. In: OSDI (2006)
5. Malik, O.: In Japan, many undersea cables are damaged. GigaOM blog (March 14, 2011),
   http://gigaom.com/broadband/
   in-japan-many-under-sea-cables-are-damaged/
6. Quan, L., Heidemann, J., Pradkin, Y.: Detecting internet outages with precise active probing (extended). Technical Report ISI-TR-2012-678, USC/ISI (February 2012)
7. Quan, L., Heidemann, J., Pradkin, Y.: Visualizing sparse internet events: Network outages and route changes. In: ACM Workshop on Internet Visualization (November 2012)
8. Times, N.Y.: Egypt cuts off most internet and cell service,
   http://www.nytimes.com/2011/01/29/technology/internet/29cutoff.html

Author Index